D1731389

The Baker & McKenzie International Arbitration Yearbook 2012-2013

JURIS

Questions About This Publication

For assistance with shipments, billing or other customer service matters,
please call our Customer Services Department at:
1-631-350-2100.

To obtain a copy of this book, call our Sales Department at: 1-631-351-5430
Fax: 1-631-351-5712 or 1-631-351-5430

Toll Free Order Line: 1-800-887-4064 (United States and Canada)

See our web page about this book:
www.arbitrationlaw.com

Printed in the United States of America
ISBN 978-1-937518-20-2

This is the sixth edition of *The Baker & McKenzie International Arbitration Yearbook,* an
annual series established by the Firm in 2007. This collection of articles comprises reports
in key jurisdictions around the globe on arbitration. Leading lawyers of the Firm's
International Arbitration Practice Group, a division of the Firm's Global Dispute Resolution
Practice Group, report on recent developments in national laws relating to arbitration and
address current arbitral trends and tendencies in the jurisdictions in which they practice.

For this 2012-2013 edition, the topic of Section C of each chapter is the grant and
enforcement of interim measures in international arbitration. Each jurisdiction examines
whether arbitral tribunals are authorized to grant interim measures in that jurisdiction, and if
so, the conditions under which those measures are granted and the means by which they are
enforced.

The aim of this *Yearbook* is to highlight the more important recent developments in
international arbitration, without aspiring to be an exhaustive case reporter or a textbook on
arbitration in the broad sense. It is hoped that this volume will prove a useful tool for those
contemplating and using arbitration to resolve international business disputes.

JurisNet, LLC
71 New Street
Huntington, New York 11743 USA
www.arbitrationlaw.com

TABLE OF CONTENTS

Table of Contents

Table of Contents

Table of Contents

Table of Contents

Table of Contents

Table of Contents

Table of Contents

Table of Contents

Table of Contents

Table of Contents

Table of Contents

Table of Contents

Table of Contents

Table of Contents

Table of Contents

Table of Contents

Table of Contents

Table of Contents

Table of Contents

Table of Contents

Table of Contents

Table of Contents

Table of Contents

FOREWORD

On behalf of Baker & McKenzie's International Arbitration Practice Group, it is a great pleasure to present to you the sixth annual edition of our *International Arbitration Yearbook*. Initially published by our European offices in 2007, the *Yearbook* has expanded to include developments in jurisdictions in Asia, Latin America and North America and has become a valuable resource for clients and colleagues in the international business community.

Our 2012-2013 *Yearbook* covers forty (40) jurisdictions and is organized by country. As in past years, the first section (Part A) describes important recent developments and trends in national legislation and practice affecting the conduct of international arbitration. The second section (Part B) refers to noteworthy case law in each country. In a feature that first appeared in the second edition of the book, a third section (Part C) focuses on an important current topic in international arbitration.

This year's topic is the grant and enforcement of interim measures in international arbitration, which we structured into three parts. We first examine tribunal-ordered interim measures, with each jurisdiction describing the types of interim measures that tribunals can order under their arbitration laws, the tests that an applicant must satisfy and whether interim measures are available from tribunals before commencement of arbitral proceedings. We then assess court-ordered interim measures, with each jurisdiction describing whether local courts have concurrent powers to order interim measures, the amount of time the courts ordinarily take to grant a request for interim relief, whether the courts grant anti-suit injunctions and whether they are amenable to granting interim measures in aid of foreign arbitrations. Finally, we survey enforcement of interim measures and ask whether tribunal-ordered interim measures are enforceable in the courts of that jurisdiction, the types of interim measures that are unenforceable and whether local courts apply the same standard to enforce awards for interim measures made within or outside that jurisdiction.

All jurisdictions covered report on some aspect of each section and the Section C discussions and comparative outlook offered by this Yearbook are truly riveting for students of this field. The diversity and breadth of Baker & McKenzie is clearly displayed in these chapters. Overall, this *Yearbook* provides critical commentary about worldwide developments in this fascinating field of law that directly affects the risks and challenges of doing business locally and internationally and managing the disputes that follow.

As with past editions, this *Yearbook* does not aspire to be a guide to arbitration in a general sense; nor is it intended as a comprehensive case reporter. Instead, it is a selection of the most noteworthy developments in the countries on which we comment. We trust that these materials will be helpful to those who contemplate arbitration as a process for resolving disputes in international business transactions, especially with respect to choice of venue. As demonstrated by the *Yearbook*, national courts play a critical role in enforcing arbitration agreements and awards, and supervising the arbitral process generally.

We welcome any comments you may have on the content of this edition and any suggestions about topics you would like to see included in future editions.

This publication would not be possible without the effort and diligence of our colleagues from around the world who drafted the chapters and our regional editors who reviewed their submissions. We take this opportunity to also thank Vivianne Knierim, Michael Atkins and Derek Soller of our New York office for their contributions and assistance in preparing this year's edition.

Nancy M. Thevenin
Executive Editor

012-2013 BAKER & MCKENZIE YEARBOOK EDITORS

Executive Editor

Nancy M. Thevenin is special counsel in the New York office of Baker & McKenzie and the global coordinator of the Firm's International Arbitration Practice Group. She routinely advises on arbitration institutions, mediation, disputes boards and expertise proceedings, *ad hoc* cases and use of pre-arbitral referee procedures. Her experience includes handling international commercial mediation and arbitration under the auspices of the AAA, ICC and ICDR. Ms. Thevenin has handled disputes in various industries, including construction and engineering, financial services, commercial real estate and aviation, often involving issues concerning mergers and acquisition, sales, distribution, licensing, technology transfer and leasing agreements. She currently serves on the executive committees of the International Law Section of the New York State Bar Association and the American Branch of the International Law Association and is a vice-chair of the Arbitration Law Committee of the Inter-American Bar Association. Ms. Thevenin is a Fellow of the Chartered Institute of Arbitrators and an Adjunct Professor of International Commercial Arbitration at St. John's University Law School.

Regional Editors

Asia-Pacific and Africa:

Michael Atkins is an Associate in the New York office of Baker & McKenzie. He is a member of the Litigation Practice group where he assists on a range of complex commercial litigation and arbitration matters.

Laura Zimmerman is an Associate in the Litigation Practice Group of the Firm's New York office. Her practice focuses mainly on international arbitration and commercial litigation matters for foreign and domestic clients, including work on arbitration matters administered by the ICC, ICDR and ICSID.

Europe and Central Asia:

Richard Allen is an Associate and Solicitor Advocate in the London office of Baker & McKenzie and a member of the Firm's Global Dispute Resolution Practice Group. His experience covers a broad spectrum of contentious and non-contentious work, including commercial and competition litigation, international arbitration, public law and regulatory advice. The current focus of his practice is in the fields of aviation law and public international law. He is a member of the Law Society of England & Wales, the LCIA Young International Arbitration Group, the Royal Institute of International Affairs (Chatham House), the International Law Association and the International Legal Network of Avocats Sans Frontières.

Liz Williams is a Senior Professional Support Lawyer in Baker & McKenzie Global Services and is based in the London office. She designs and runs knowhow and training programs for Baker & McKenzie's Global Dispute Resolution Practice Group. She has represented clients, primarily from the insurance and reinsurance industry, in arbitrations under the LCIA, ICC and ARIAS rules and in *ad hoc* arbitrations under the UNCITRAL rules. She is a member of the Law Society of England & Wales and a Fellow of the Higher Education Academy of the United Kingdom. Ms. Williams also serves as chair of the Refugee Law Practice Group in Baker & McKenzie's London office, and is a co-author of Strong & Williams, *Complete Tort Law: Text and Materials* (Oxford University Press.)

Latin America:

Grant Hanessian is a Partner in the New York office of Baker & McKenzie and serves as co-chair of the Firm's International Arbitration Practice Group. He has more than 25 years of experience serving as counsel and arbitrator in disputes concerning contract, energy, construction, commodities, financial services, insurance, intellectual property and other matters. Mr. Hanessian is Vice Chairman of the Arbitration Committee of the U.S. Council for International Business (the U.S. national committee of the ICC), a member of the Commission on Arbitration of the ICC and the ICC Task Force on Arbitration Involving States or State Entities. He is also a founding board member of the New York International Arbitration Center, and a member of the American Society of International Law, American Bar Association, Association of the Bar of the City of New York's International Law Committee, American Arbitration Association's International Advisory Committee and London Court of International Arbitration. He is an editor of *ICDR Awards and Commentaries* (Juris, 2012) and co-editor of the *Gulf War Claims Reporter* (ILI/Kluwer, 1998) and *International Arbitration Checklists* (Juris Pub., 2d ed., 2008).

Jennifer B. Wisnia is the Business Development and Marketing Manager of the Firm's Latin America Dispute Resolution & Litigation Practice Group. Ms. Wisnia was previously an Associate in the Firm's Mergers & Acquisitions group in Santiago, Chile where she assisted with international transactions involving multinational corporations doing business in Latin America. Before her move to Chile, she practiced commercial litigation and bankruptcy in the state and federal courts of New York and New Jersey for six years. Ms. Wisnia graduated from the Boston University School of Law in 2005.

About the Editors

North America:

David Zaslowsky is a Partner in the New York office of Baker & McKenzie and has practiced in the area of international commercial litigation and arbitration for more than 27 years. He has appeared in various federal and state courts (trial and appellate) throughout the country and has participated in arbitrations, both inside and outside the United States, before the AAA, ICC, ICDR, Iran-United States Claims Tribunal, HKIAC and NASD, as well as in *ad hoc* arbitrations. Mr. Zaslowsky currently serves on the ICC Task Force on Decisions as to Costs. He is included in the *Chambers USA Guide* for his expertise in International Arbitration. He is also on the roster of arbitrators for the ICDR and the AAA.

THE BAKER & MCKENZIE INTERNATIONAL ARBITRATION YEARBOOK TOPICS

YEAR	NUMBER OF JURISDICTIONS	TOPICS EXAMINED
2008	28	Independence and Impartiality of Arbitrators
2009	27	Parallel Proceedings Before State Courts and Arbitral Tribunals
2010-2011	35	Insolvency Issues in Arbitration
2011-2012	37	Public Policy in International Arbitration
2012-2013	40	Grant and Enforcement of Interim Measures in International Arbitration

LIST OF ABBREVIATIONS AND ACRONYMS

AAA	American Arbitration Association
BIT	Bilateral Investment Treaty
CIETAC	China International Economic and Trade Arbitration Commission
ECT	Energy Charter Treaty
HKIAC	Hong Kong International Arbitration Centre
JCAA	Japan Commercial Arbitration Association
IBA Rules	International Bar Association Rules on the Taking of Evidence in International Commercial Arbitration
ICC	International Chamber of Commerce
ICC Arbitration Rules or ICC Rules	Rules of Arbitration of the International Chamber of Commerce
ICDR	International Centre for Dispute Resolution (part of the AAA)
ICDR Rules	International Arbitration Rules of the International Centre for Dispute Resolution, 2003
ICSID	International Centre for the Settlement of Investment Disputes
ICSID Convention	Convention on the Settlement of Investment Disputes between States and Nationals of Other States
LCIA	London Court of International Arbitration

LCIA Arbitration Rules or LCIA Rules	Arbitration Rules of the London Court of International Arbitration, 1998
NAFTA	North American Free Trade Agreement
New York Convention	United Nations Convention on the Recognition and Enforcement of Foreign Arbitral Awards, 1958
Panama Convention	Inter-American Convention on International Commercial Arbitration, 1975
SCC	Stockholm Chamber of Commerce
SIAC	Singapore International Arbitration Centre
UNCITRAL	United Nations Commission on International Trade Law
UNCITRAL Model Law	United Nations Commission on International Trade Law Model Law on International Commercial Arbitration, 1985, amended in 2006
UNCITRAL Rules	United Nations Commission on International Trade Law Arbitration Rules, 1976
WIPO	World Intellectual Property Organization
WIPO Rules	World Intellectual Property Organization Arbitration Rules, 1994
ZPO	Zivilprozessordnung [German Code of Civil Procedure]

ARGENTINA

Gonzalo E. Cáceres[1] and Santiago L. Capparelli[2]

A. LEGISLATION, TRENDS AND TENDENCIES

A.1 Legislation

Despite repeated attempts to obtain congressional approval to adopt the UNCITRAL Model Law as the Argentine federal arbitration act, Argentina still lacks of a federal legislation specifically dealing with arbitration. Instead, the country's civil procedure codes contain arbitration regulations. Because Argentina is a federal country, each province has its own code of civil procedure that applies within that province. The National Code of Civil and Commercial Procedure ("CPCCN") applies to the Autonomous City of Buenos Aires (the capital), and in each federal court across the country.[3] Because the provincial codes tend to be consistent with the CPCCN as regards arbitration, this report will only refer to the CPCCN.

---

[1] Gonzalo Enrique Cáceres is a Partner in Baker & McKenzie's Buenos Aires office, and has served as an arbitrator under the rules of the IACA and the ICC. He is a member of the Commercial and International Relationships Committee of the Buenos Aires Bar Association and for several years, served as an associate professor in Commercial Law at the School of Law of the University of Buenos Aires.

[2] Santiago Capparelli is a Partner in Baker & McKenzie's Buenos Aires office. He practices litigation, alternative dispute resolution, international and domestic arbitration and has represented parties in *ad hoc* arbitral proceedings, as well as in proceedings administered by the ICC and local arbitral institutions, such as the General Arbitration Tribunal of the Buenos Aires Stock Exchange, the Arbitral Tribunal of the Buenos Aires Grain Market and the Private Center for Mediation and Arbitration.

[3] Código Procesal Civil y Comercial de la Nación, [National Code of Civil and Commercial Procedure], Law No. 17.454, Sept. 20, 1967, as restated in Decree 1042/1981, Aug. 18, 1981, *et seq.*

This section will discuss the relevant provisions of the CPCCN (A.1.1) and the most relevant international arbitration agreements to which Argentina is a party. These agreements are important because they provide rules in the absence of national legislation. These agreements include the International Commercial Arbitration Act of Mercosur (A.1.2); the Panama Convention (A.1.3); and the New York Convention (A.1.4). Finally, we will provide our comments on the recent legislative developments or related news that occurred on this matter (A.2).

A.1.1 National Code of Civil and Commercial Procedure

Articles 1 and 737 of the CPCCN govern arbitrable issues. Controversies of a monetary nature (Article 1) and which are subject to settlement by the parties (Article 737), are arbitrable. If both of these requisites are met, parties can submit their disputes to international arbitration, provided that the controversy would be "international" (Article 1). However, the law does not provide express guidance for determining when a specific controversy is "international" for purposes of this provision. Nevertheless, there is some consensus that "international" for the purposes of this provision, refers to cases relating to more than one legal system (e.g., parties with different nationalities; parties with addresses in different countries; or different locations of the goods or places where damage has occurred).[4]

Procedure under the CPCCN is obsolete, because it requires establishing a party's consent to arbitration in a document separate from the arbitration agreement itself. This document is

---

[4] Antonio Boggiano, "*Apectos internacionales de las reformas al Código Procesal Civil y Comercial de la Nación (1° parte),*" ED 90-880, *cited by* Julio César Rivera, "*Arbitraje Comercial,*" p. 32.

called a *compromiso*.[5] A party agreeing to arbitration should legalize the *compromiso* before a notary public or the intervening court (Article 739). Unless the parties provide otherwise, evidence is produced in the same manner it would be produced in ordinary court procedures (Article 751). Unless the parties waive their rights to appeal or to file any other post-award remedy, these remedies remain available (Article 758). Thus, when a party wishes to waive the right to appeal an award, the party must provide clear language to this effect in the arbitration agreement or *compromiso*.

Courts in Buenos Aires usually uphold a party's waiver of the right to appeal. However, in *José Cartellone Construcciones Civiles S.A. v. Hidroeléctrica Norpatagónica S.A. o Hidronor*, the National Supreme Court decided that a party's waiver of its right to appeal should be disregarded when public policy considerations so recommend.[6] As the defendant in that case was an Argentine public entity, it is debatable whether the *José Cartellone* doctrine can serve as precedent for future National Supreme Court decisions involving private parties.

Local procedural laws provide that parties cannot waive their right to request an annulment of an award. Parties can file for an annulment only in the following circumstances: (i) when the tribunal issues the award outside the term granted to it; (ii) when it contains issues that the parties did not request, or if it does not provide for the relief that the parties requested; or (iii) when the arbitrators failed to follow the procedures set forth by the parties.

---

5   Similar in nature to the "Terms of Reference" described in Article 23 of the ICC Arbitration Rules.

6   Corte Suprema de Justicia de la Nación [CSJN] [National Supreme Court of Justice], 1/6/2004, *"José Cartellone Construcciones Civiles S.A. v. Hidroeléctrica Norpatagónica S.A. o Hidronor/proceso de conocimiento."*

A.1.2 International Commercial Arbitration Act of Mercosur

Absent any federal arbitration act in force in Argentina, the most important legislation dealing with international arbitration is probably the Mercosur Accord on International Commercial Arbitration (*Acuerdo sobre Arbitraje Comercial Internacional del Mercosur*), issued in Buenos Aires on July 23, 1998 ("Buenos Aires Convention").[7] Argentina, Brazil, Uruguay and Paraguay are parties to this convention.

The Buenos Aires Convention applies to disputes between parties that, at the time of the execution of their agreement: (i) have their domiciles in signatory countries to the convention (Article 3(a)); (ii) have contact with at least one signatory party of the convention; or (iii) have chosen the seat of the arbitration in one signatory party to the convention (Article 3(c)).

Contrary to the CPCCN, the Buenos Aires Convention treatment of international arbitration is in line with most of the relevant international arbitration statutes (e.g., UNCITRAL Model Law). Among the issues contemplated therein, the Buenos Aires Convention explicitly allows—and mandates—a court to assist an international arbitration tribunal in the course of such proceedings (e.g., by issuing interim measures).

One final element to consider regarding this convention is that unless the parties agreed otherwise, each party will be responsible for paying its own attorney's fees and costs. Consequently, if a party applying this convention wants to take a "loser pays all" or "costs follow the event" approach, it must provide specific language to this effect in the relevant arbitration clause or in the *compromiso*.

---

[7]   Incorporated into domestic Argentine law by Law No. 25.223.

A.1.3 Panama Convention

Argentina is also a signatory to the Panama Convention (*Convención Interamericana sobre Arbitraje Comercial Internacional*). Again, given the absence in Argentina of specific legislation dealing with international arbitration, this convention is relevant because it stresses the court's powers (and obligations) to enforce international arbitration clauses, provided that such disputes would be of a commercial nature and that a written arbitration agreement exists. When this arbitrability threshold is met, the convention also mandates that local courts assist international arbitration tribunals.

A.1.4 The New York Convention

Finally, Argentina is a signatory to New York Convention and adopted it in Law No. 23.619. Argentina made two reservations to this convention that affect whether an Argentine court will recognize and enforce a foreign arbitral award: (i) that the award be issued in a country that is a signatory to the convention; and (ii) that the underlying dispute be considered of a commercial nature under Argentine law.

A.2 Draft Legislation

There are currently two draft bills in National Congress providing for specific legislation on arbitration. One of them is under consideration in the House of Representatives[8] and the other one is in the Senate.[9] Hopefully, this signals that arbitration is finally on the political agenda and Argentina could soon have these very important legislations.

---

[8] N° 0003-2012 presented by Congressman Bertol *et al.* contemplating domestic and international arbitration.

[9] N° 2611-S-2011, presented by Senator Negre de Alonso *et al.* contemplating international commercial arbitration.

Argentina is also about to enact a joint Civil and Commercial Code to replace the existing Civil Code and Commercial Code. This legislative development will most likely occur in 2013. The draft Code includes a chapter regulating arbitration agreements (Sections 1649 to 1665); however, the draft chapter has been heavily—and in our view correctly—criticized, as contrary to the predominant trends in arbitration when one considers arbitration from a contractual, rather than jurisdictional, perspective.

B. CASES

B.1 Arbitrability I: Scope of Arbitration Agreement

On March 15, 2012, the National Court of Appeals on Commercial Matters decided an objection to the court's jurisdiction in *Fe S.A. v. Telefónica Móviles Argentina S.A.*[10] In that case, the Court of Appeals confirmed the lower court's decision to admit the defendant's objection to the court's jurisdiction and to refer all claims related to the interpretation or execution of the parties' arbitration agreement to the Buenos Aires Stock Exchange Arbitral Tribunal.

On appeal, the plaintiff had argued, *inter alia*, that (i) the lower court's ruling lacked relevant support, as the court merely agreed with the arguments submitted by the Attorney General; (ii) the language of the arbitration agreement was not clear enough to sustain the court's ruling; and, most significantly, (iii) based on the language of the arbitration agreement, the parties intended to provide for arbitration only for those disputes arising while the

---

[10] Cámara Nacional de Apelaciones de la Capital Federal (CNCom) (National Court of Appeals on Commercial Matters) Section A, 03/15/2012, *Fe S.A. v. Telefónica Móviles Argentina S.A.*

agreement was executed (and not controversies related to its termination).

While confirming the lower court's decision and rejecting the plaintiff's appeal, the Court of Appeals' main argument was that the defendant's alleged violations of the agreement, necessarily related to the analysis of the party's "execution" of such agreement (a matter that was undisputedly within the scope of the arbitration agreement).

Although its approach was correct, the Court of Appeals incidentally noted that arbitral jurisdiction shall be construed *restrictively*. In our view, the court erred in this remark, as there is no provision in Argentine law that would mandate construing arbitration agreements between private parties in such a restricted fashion.

B.2   Arbitrability II: Arbitral Jurisdiction to Decide Constitutional Claims

On March 14, 2012, the Superior Court of Justice of the Province of Córdoba decided *Oliva, Oscar v. Disco S.A.*[11] The case related to the plaintiff's request to have his contractual claim heard in court rather than in arbitration, on the basis that the referenced claim challenged the constitutionality of underlying arbitration legislation and thus exceeded the scope of the arbitrator's jurisdiction. After careful and extensive reasoning, the Superior Court of Córdoba concluded that (a) arbitrators that are required to render an award according to a specific legal framework would inherently have jurisdiction to rule on whether such legal framework was constitutional;

---

[11] Tribunal Superior de Justicia de la Provincia de Córdoba [Sup. Trib. Córdoba] [Superior Court of Justice of the Province of Córdoba] 3/14/2012 *Oliva, Sergio v. Disco SA.*

(b) jurisdictional powers are conferred not only on the court, but on arbitrators as well, as they should be placed on the same footing based on the party's selection; (c) the only restriction on arbitrability would be whether the controversy at hand was subject to resolution[12]; (d) the plaintiff's contention that "public policy" controversies are alien to arbitral jurisdiction was without merit; and (e) arbitration is not intended to rival the judiciary; rather, arbitration constitutes an important tool to complement and assist the judiciary.

In our view, this ruling constitutes a landmark decision about several key aspects of arbitration (scope of arbitrability, arbitrator's ability to resolve constitutional or public policy issues, role of arbitration as a complementary tool to the judiciary), and as such, we can only expect that it will serve for building constructive jurisprudence on those issues.

B.3 Annulment Request Filed against a Jurisdictional Decision

On October 25, 2011, the Federal Court of Appeals in Administrative Matters seated in the city of Buenos Aires, decided *Procuración del Tesoro de la Nación v. Tribunal Arbitral (Arbitraje 12.364/CCI - Exp 111-195270/95).*[13]

In this case, the State Attorney ("*Procuración del Tesoro de la Nación*") filed an annulment request against the jurisdictional award rendered in case "12634/KGA/CCA/JRF *Papel de Tucuman SA (en quiebra) (Argentina) v. Estado Nacional (República Argentina) (Argentina).*"

---

12 Section 602 of the Córdoba Procedural Code.

13 Cámara Nacional de Apelaciones en lo Contencioso Administrativo Federal [CNac. Cont. Adm. Fed.] [Federal Court of Appeals in Administrative Contentious Matters] Section II, 10/25/2011 "Procuración del Tesoro de la Nación c/ Tribunal Arbitral (Arbitraje 12.364 CCI-Exp 111-195270/95)."

In rendering the award, the arbitral tribunal appointed by the ICC rejected Argentina's defenses against the tribunal's jurisdiction. On appeal, Argentina argued that the Court of Appeals had jurisdiction to hear its annulment request, based on Section 760 of the CPCC, which regulates the filing of an annulment request against an arbitration award.

The Court of Appeals rejected Argentina's motion on the basis that the referenced section of the CPCC regulates the requirements and timing to file an annulment request against a "final award," and not other types of awards that might be issued in the course of the arbitral proceedings (like a partial or provisional award on jurisdiction, as was issued here).

Nevertheless, the Court of Appeals noted that it had the power to "re-convert" or "re-shape" the jurisdictional challenge through the appropriate court and procedure, and therefore remanded the case to the lower court for that court to entertain Argentina's request through full evidentiary litigation ("*juicio ordinario*").

In our view, the Court of Appeals approached this matter correctly, clarifying that court intervention or interference with arbitral proceedings shall be made in a **restrictive** manner. However, it is arguable whether the "re-conversion" ordered by the court instructing first instance litigation would have legal support in Argentine law. That is because, in the absence of a legal provision such as Section 16.3 of the UNCITRAL Model Law, the court did not have any existing and binding legislative tool with which to maintain or re-shape the applicant's annulment request.

C. THE GRANT AND ENFORCEMENT OF INTERIM MEASURES IN INTERNATIONAL ARBITRATION

C.1 Tribunal-Ordered Interim Measures

As stressed in A.1 above, Argentina does not yet have a body of law dealing specifically with international arbitration. Hence, the types of interim measures an arbitral tribunal can order in Argentina (seated in any of the Argentine provincial jurisdictions), is governed by the Procedural Codes in force in such jurisdictions.

In the City of Buenos Aires, Section 753 of the CPCC applies. Although this section provides for the general principle that the arbitral tribunals cannot issue interim measures (and that requests for such relief should be made to the judiciary), the National Commercial Court of Appeals did not read that provision as an absolute impediment, but rather, as a general principle that could be set aside by agreement of the parties, either by an express provision in the arbitration clause or by adopting the rules of an arbitral institution that included such power.[14]

As to the type of interim measures that are available in the CPCC, express regulations provide for requesting attachments of goods (*embargo*),[15] seizures (*secuestros*),[16] a judiciary express intervention (*intervención judicial*),[17] a prohibition to dispose of

---

[14] Cámara Nacional de Apelaciones en lo Comercial [CNac. Com.] [National Commercial Court of Appeals] Section B, 11/20/2012 *Soletanche Bachy Arg S.A. c/ Victorio Américo Gualtieri S.A.*

[15] Sections 209 - 220 of the National Procedural Code.

[16] *Id.* at Section 221.

[17] *Id.* at Sections 222 - 227.

registered property (*inhibición general de bienes*),[18] and a prohibition to innovate or contract (*prohibición de innovar o contratar*).[19]

Further, the National Procedural Code does not consider these to be the only types of precautionary relief available, and express regulation exists allowing a party to request different (and specific) interim measures in order to safeguard the rights at stake under the particular circumstances of the litigation.[20]

To obtain any interim measure under local procedural law, the applicant should comply with the following general requirements: (i) provide a preliminary analysis regarding the likelihood of the existence of the rights invoked; (ii) show that delaying the grant of relief would result in irreparable harm (*periculum in mora*); and (iii) provide a safeguard to the court's satisfaction to cover any potential damage caused to the opposing party if the applicant ultimately has no right to relief. The applicant has the burden of proof on these requirements. In addition, requests for interim measures are considered and issued *ex parte*. Such requests are usually analyzed by local courts with caution.

As these measures are protective in nature and the rationale is to safeguard the enforcement of the final ruling, procedural law allows parties to request interim measures not only before the commencement of the dispute on the merits, but also during the course of such dispute until a final decision is rendered.

The procedural rules of the main arbitral institutions in the City of Buenos Aires also contemplate that arbitrators may issue

---

[18]   *Id.* at Sections 228 - 229.

[19]   *Id.* at Sections 230 - 231.

[20]   *Id.* at Sections 232 - 233.

interim measures. In that regard, the rules in force in the General Arbitration Tribunal of the Buenos Aires Stock Exchange expressly allow arbitrators to issue interim measures unless the parties provided otherwise in their arbitration agreement. Requests to enforce interim measures are made to the local courts.[21] Similarly, the *Centro Empresarial de Mediación y Arbitraje* allows for the possibility of interim measures, as this institution has adopted the UNCITRAL Rules as its rules of arbitration;[22] and the same applies to the *"CEMARC."*[23]

All of those arbitration rules acknowledge the judiciary's concurrent jurisdiction to issue interim measures, as none of those rules would deem that applying to the local court for interim measures would constitute a breach of the agreement to arbitrate. Further, none of the rules restrict the court's concurrent jurisdiction, either before or after the arbitral tribunals are constituted.

C.2 Court-Ordered Interim Measures

Argentine courts have granted injunctions both in aid of and against arbitrations.

On October 29, 2002, the National Commercial Court of Appeals decided *S.R., A.A. v. Prime Argentina (Holding)*,[24] in aid of an arbitration pending at the General Arbitration Tribunal of

---

[21]   Section 33 of the procedural rules in force at the General Arbitration Tribunal of the Buenos Aires Stock Exchange.

[22]   Section 26 of the UNCITRAL Rules.

[23]   The institutional body administering arbitration at the Argentine Chamber of Commerce. Section 14 expressly authorizes the tribunal's jurisdiction to issue interim measures.

[24]   Cámara Nacional de Apelaciones de la Capital Federal (CNCom) (National Court of Appeals on Commercial Matters) Section C, 10/29/2002, *S.R., A.A. v. Prime Argentina (Holding)*.

the Buenos Aires Stock Exchange. The scope of the requested interim relief was to freeze certain amounts pertaining to a letter of credit existing between the parties, and to transfer such funds to a bank account subject to the authority and decision of the arbitral tribunal.

It is important to note that, *in dicta*, the court found that it had jurisdiction to issue this type of interim measure, even though the institutional rules to which the parties had submitted provided for arbitrators to also issue such measures. In other words, the court considered that it had concurrent jurisdiction with the arbitral tribunal. It is interesting to note that the court confirmed a liberal reading of Section 753 of the CPCC, whose general principle is that the arbitrators could not issue such measures.

There are also precedents where local courts issued interim measures in aid of international arbitration tribunals.

On September 25, 2009, the National Commercial Court of Appeals decided *Searle Ltd. v. Roemmers S.A.I.C.F.*[25] In that case, the Court of Appeals admitted an interim measure ordered by an international arbitral tribunal and instructed the respondent to refrain from carrying out any commercial activity in Argentina that would involve the manufacturing, commercialization, sale or distribution of a medical component. The order was to remain in place until a final decision was rendered in the arbitration proceedings that the applicant would have to commence before the ICC, on or before 20 days from the date on which the respondent was served with this decision.

---

[25] Cámara Nacional de Apelaciones de la Capital Federal (CNCom) (National Court of Appeals on Commercial Matters) Section D, 09/22/2005, *Searle Ltd v. Roemmers S.A.I.C.F.*

On December 10, 2012, the National Commercial Court of Appeals decided *Peide Industria y Construcciones S.A. v. Mina Pirquitas Inc. Sucursal Argentina,*[26] admitting an interim measure designed to prevent the sale of respondent's registered property during a pending international arbitration proceeding seated in Vancouver, British Columbia, Canada. The Court of Appeals expressly noted in this ruling that it had concurrent jurisdiction to assist an international arbitral tribunal, either with the constitution of such tribunal (if needed), or in matters related to evidence production, or interim measures as in the instant case.

The Court of Appeals' ruling in *Peide* is particularly relevant in light of the lack of a statute dealing with international arbitration, and hence, the absence of an express tool for compelling the judiciary to render the requested assistance. Although one could argue that local courts are currently obliged by law to provide such assistance in light of international arbitration treaties to which Argentina is a party,[27] it is good to see this progressive case law, which in our view should prevail over some decisions to the contrary.[28]

Local courts also issued anti-suit injunctions, and the most publicized decision on this matter probably is *Entidad Nacional*

---

[26] Cámara Nacional de Apelaciones de la Capital Federal (CNCom) (National Court of Appeals on Commercial Matters) Section A, 12/10/2010, *Peide Industrias y Construcciones S.A. v. Mina Pirquitas Inc. Sucursal Argentina.*

[27] The rationale would be that it would make no sense to oblige the judiciary to uphold arbitration clauses and/or arbitration awards, and not to assist the tribunals constituted in accordance with the New York Convention or the Panama Convention, or that are rendering the awards that they nevertheless would be subsequently obliged to execute.

[28] Cámara Nacional de Apelaciones de la Capital Federal (CNCom) (National Court of Appeals on Commercial Matters) Section B, 04/11/2002, *Forever Living Products Argentina SRL et al. v. Beas, Juan et al.*

Yaciretá v. Eriday et al., which was decided by the National First Instance Court on Administrative Matters N° 1, on April 18, 2005. The plaintiff filed this case in order to request that the court: (i) execute the Terms of Reference in accordance with local procedural law; and (ii) request that the members of the arbitral tribunal appointed by the ICC step down from their appointments. While this relief was being considered, the plaintiff requested that the court issue an interim measure ordering the arbitral tribunal not to pursue further actions on this matter.

After being served with the order, the defendant submitted a pleading to the Secretariat of the ICC regarding potential candidates to replace one of the arbitrators that resigned his appointment. The court found that the submission constituted a breach of the court order not to pursue further procedural actions in the arbitral proceedings. Consequently, the court instructed the defendant to notify the ICC that it was to withdraw the potential nomination for replacement, indicating that the defendant's failure to notify the ICC would result in a daily fine until compliance.

It could be reasonably contended that the *Eriday* decision was highly influenced by the particular scenario in which it was issued, and by the fact that the plaintiff seeking the injunctive relief was a public entity. Indeed, other precedents could be cited where commercial courts refused to enforce anti-suit injunctions against an arbitral tribunal in a conflict between private parties, on the basis that the local court did not have jurisdiction to impose any such decision on an arbitral tribunal appointed under the auspices of the ICC.[29]

---

[29] Cámara Nacional de Apelaciones de la Capital Federal (CNCom) (National Court of Appeals on Commercial Matters) Section A, 03/28/2003, *Softron S.A. v. Telecom Argentina Stet France Telecom S.A. et al.*

AUSTRALIA

Leigh Duthie,[1] Alex Wolff[2] and Mia Livingstone[3,4]

A. LEGISLATION, TRENDS AND TENDENCIES

A.1 Legislative Framework

Australia is a signatory to the New York Convention which, together with the UNCITRAL Model Law, forms the basis of Australia's international arbitration framework as implemented by the International Arbitration Act 1974 (Cth) ("IAA"). The IAA also gives effect to the ICSID Convention.

---

[1] Leigh Duthie is a Partner in Baker & McKenzie's Melbourne office, with over 16 years of experience acting for major Australian and international corporations and government agencies in relation to complex claims arising from infrastructure projects, defects in plants, and faults in heavy mining machinery. Leigh's experience includes work in all major Australian courts, as well as expert determination, special referee procedures and domestic and international arbitration.

[2] Alex Wolff is a Partner in Baker & McKenzie's Melbourne office and a highly experienced dispute resolution practitioner who regularly advises domestic and international corporations on complex and sensitive matters requiring strategic negotiation, risk management and resolution. Alex conducts disputes in state and federal superior and appellate courts, international and domestic arbitrations and has experience with specialist tribunals, special references and alternative dispute resolution.

[3] Mia Livingstone is a Senior Associate in Baker & McKenzie's Melbourne office, with over eight years of experience advising clients both in Australia and overseas in respect of dispute resolution and litigation matters across a range of areas including international arbitration, environmental litigation and general commercial disputes. Mia is published in both Australian and international law journals on international arbitration. She is also a member of the Australasian Forum for International Arbitration.

[4] The authors would like to thank Jason Frydman of Baker & McKenzie's Melbourne office and Dominic Delany and Erika Hansen of Baker & McKenzie's Sydney office for their assistance with this chapter.

17

In addition to the IAA, which covers the field for international arbitration, each State and Territory in Australia has its own domestic arbitration legislation. New uniform domestic arbitration legislation is currently being implemented by all States and Territories which, like the IAA, is based on the UNCITRAL Model Law.

A.2   Amendments to Australia's Legislative Framework

As we reported in last year's *Yearbook*, all Australian States and Territories have agreed to the adoption of a new Commercial Arbitration Bill that more closely aligns Australia's domestic arbitration framework with the UNCITRAL Model Law and the IAA. Last year, New South Wales was the first State to enact the new Commercial Arbitration Act, followed by adoption in Victoria and South Australia. As of this year, the new Act is also in force in Tasmania, the Northern Territory and Western Australia. In Queensland, a similar bill was introduced on 30 October 2012 and is expected to be enacted shortly.[5] The Australian Capital Territory has not yet introduced any similar legislation.

A.3   Specialist Arbitration Lists

A new development that seeks to elevate Australia's standing as a viable and attractive forum for international arbitration is the introduction of various Court Lists specializing in arbitration matters.

Specialist Arbitration Lists provide parties to arbitrations seated in Australia with court supervision from Australian judges and

---

[5]   It should be noted that the Commercial Arbitration Bill (Qld), which awaits enactment, is the reintroduction of a bill that previously lapsed on 19 February 2012 with the prorogation of the then State Government.

legal practitioners with experience and expertise in arbitration. As a result, Australia is poised to develop a consistent body of jurisprudence that provides for effective and efficient management and facilitation of arbitrations.

The Federal Court of Australia is the principal jurisdiction to hear and determine matters arising under the IAA. Each State and Territory Registry of the Federal Court is required to have an Arbitration Coordinating Judge who is responsible for international arbitration matters.[6]

Since 1 January 2010, the Supreme Court of Victoria has had an Arbitration List in its Commercial Court jurisdiction under the charge of experienced arbitrator Justice Croft.[7] This List deals with all arbitration proceedings, any applications in arbitration proceedings and any urgent applications with respect to arbitration matters.

In February 2012, the Supreme Court of New South Wales created a Commercial Arbitration List.[8] A proceeding in the List is commenced by summons and the plaintiff must prepare a succinct statement of the issues of fact and issues of law. The parties are encouraged to agree on the best way to proceed to enable the court to perform its supervisory function. In general, substantive interlocutory processes, including pre-trial discovery, are considered to be unnecessary for matters in the List and will only be ordered if necessary for the just and quick disposal of the proceeding.

---

[6] Federal Court of Australia Practice Note ARB 1, 1 August 2011.

[7] Supreme Court of Victoria Practice Note 2 of 2010, 17 December 2009.

[8] New South Wale Supreme Court Practice Note No. SC Eq 9, Commercial Arbitration List, 13 February 2012.

A.4 Australian Arbitral Institutions

There are a number of well-established Australian arbitral institutions that can facilitate an arbitration seated in Australia. The premier institution is the Australian Centre for International Commercial Arbitration ("ACICA"), which has a presence in Sydney, Melbourne and Perth and whose members comprise many of Australia's leading experts in the field of international commercial arbitration. ACICA has its own set of procedural rules, which have recently been amended to enable parties to seek interim measures to assist their arbitration even before proceedings have commenced.[9]

Significantly, under Articles 11(3) and 11(4) of the Model Law, ACICA is the default institution that appoints arbitrators to international arbitrations seated in Australia where the parties have not agreed on an appointment procedure or where the parties' appointment procedure fails.

Other key arbitral institutions in Australia are the Institute of Arbitrators & Mediators Australia ("IAMA") and the ICC through its Australian national committee, ICC Australia. IAMA offers parties its own set of procedural rules and can provide a list of accredited arbitrators in Australia with expertise in different fields to suit the parties' needs. ICC Australia assists Australian parties to arbitrations with help in utilizing the well-known procedural framework of the ICC, including its procedural rules, fast track procedure and expertise rules.

---

[9] *See*, further, Section C1.3 of this chapter.

A.5 Trends

Arbitration in Australia is slowly growing in importance as a practical solution to transnational disputes.[10] In August 2010, Australia opened its first arbitration center in Sydney, the Australian International Disputes Centre ("AIDC"). In 2012, Chief Justice Warren of the Victorian Supreme Court stated that she expected an announcement relating to the construction of a similar center in Victoria to be made "very soon."[11]

In the wake of the opening of the AIDC, several judicial officers within Australia have expressed broad supportive attitudes towards arbitration. In a recent address to the Australian Maritime and Transport Arbitration Commission, Chief Justice Keane of the Federal Court of Australia[12] highlighted the advantages of international arbitration, noting that:

> [T]he perceived advantages of arbitration are well-known. Arbitration enables parties to resolve their disputes while preserving their privacy. . . . There are also perceived advantages in terms of speed and efficiency . . . . And, because arbitration is thought to be quicker and more expert, there is an expectation that it will . . . be cheaper than [court proceedings].[13]

---

[10] *See, e.g.,* discussions of recent developments in A. Monichino & A. Fawke, "International Arbitration in Australia – 2011/2012 in Review," (2012) 23 ADJR 234; A Monichino, "International Arbitration in Australia: The Need to Centralise Judicial Power," (2012) 86 ALJ 118.

[11] A. Boxsell, "AIDC to Set Up Vic Hub," *The Australian Financial Review* (8 June 2012).

[12] Chief Justice Keane has since been appointed to the High Court of Australia from 1 March 2013.

[13] P A Keane, "The Prospects for International Arbitration in Australia: Meeting the Challenge of Regional Forum Competition or Our House Our Rules," address to AMTAC, 25 September 2012; *see also* the decision of Murphy J in *Castel Electronics Pty Ltd. v. TCL Air Conditioner (Zhongshan) Co. Ltd.* [2012] FCA 21.

Exemplifying the increased focus on arbitration in Australia and its attraction for commercial parties, between September 2010 and May 2011, the AIDC heard around 70 cases. This is a relatively strong result in its first year of operation given that about 140 cases are heard annually in Singapore, the current epicenter for arbitration in the Asia Pacific region. [14]

B. CASES

The Australian courts have rendered a number of significant decisions in relation to international arbitration in the last twelve months. Several are summarized below.

B.1 ***Casaceli:* Parties Will Be Compelled to Arbitrate Even if the Arbitration Is to Be Seated Abroad and Includes Claims That Fall under Australia's Mandatory Consumer Laws**

In *Casaceli v. Natuzzi S.p.A.*,[15] Justice Jagot confirmed that where parties to a contract agreed to resolve disputes between them through arbitration, Australian courts are likely to give effect to that intention.

In *Casaceli*, the applicants commenced proceedings in the Federal Court of Australia for damages based upon claims of misrepresentation under the Trade Practices Act 1974 (Cth), now known as the Competition and Consumer Law Act 2010 (Cth) ("Australian Consumer Law"). The respondents sought to stay the proceedings in court and enforce a clause in the parties' agreement to arbitrate all disputes in Italy pursuant to Italian law.

---

[14] "Sydney Arbitration Growing," *The Australian* (31 May 2011), http://www. theaustralian.com.au/business/sydney-arbitration-growing/story-e6frg8zx-122606 5977491, accessed on 19 November 2012.

[15] (2012) 292 ALR 143.

Justice Jagot upheld the parties' arbitration agreement and stayed the proceeding in Australia, finding that: (a) claims for misrepresentation under the now Australian Consumer Law can fall within the scope of an arbitration agreement and did in this case;[16] and (b) there was no evidence to suggest that the arbitral tribunal seated in Italy would not consider claims made under the mandatory consumer laws of Australia in making its determination.

B.2 ***Dampskibsselskabet*: Parties Seeking to Avoid Arbitration Awards Bear the Evidentiary Burden**

In *Dampskibsselskabet Norden A/S v. Beach Building & Civil Group Pty Ltd.*,[17] the Federal Court of Australia considered the enforceability of two arbitration awards made in London pursuant to the Rules of the London Maritime Arbitrators Association.

When the Danish applicant sought to enforce the London arbitral awards in Australia, the Australian respondent resisted. The respondent argued that, although it was correctly named in the arbitration awards, it was mis-described in the arbitration agreement and, as a consequence, the awards were not enforceable. The respondent separately argued that mandatory Australian legislation (Section 11 of the Carriage of Goods by Sea Act (Cth)) prevented the enforcement of the awards.

Justice Foster took an inclusive approach to the question of mis-description. He found that once a valid arbitration award and arbitration agreement is produced, the onus of proof will fall on the party bound by the award to show that it is not the true party

---

[16] Relying on decisions including *Recyclers of Australia, Lighthouse Technologies Australia Pty Ltd. v. Pointsec Mobile Technologies* [2000] 100 FCR 420 at 22; *Francis Marketing Pty Ltd. v. Virgin Atlantic Airway Ltd.* [1996] 39 NSWLR 160 at 166.

[17] (2012) 292 ALR 161.

to the agreement. This element of the decision has been described as giving "full effect" to the New York Convention.[18] However, under mandatory Australian legislation, Justice Foster ultimately held that the arbitration awards were unenforceable.

Last year's *Yearbook* discussed the Victorian Court of Appeal decision in *IMC Aviation Solutions Pty Ltd. v. Altain Khuder LLC.*[19] In that case, the court held that where, on the face of the agreement and award, the person against whom the award was made was not a party to the arbitration agreement, the evidential onus falls on the party seeking to enforce the award to prove on a *prima facie* basis that:

(a) an award has been made by a foreign arbitral tribunal granting relief to the award creditor against the award debtor;

(b) the award was made pursuant to an arbitration agreement; and

(c) the award creditor and the award debtor are parties to the arbitration agreement.

In contrast, the Federal Court's recent decision in *Dampskibsselskabet* adopts a pro-enforcement approach by placing the weight of the evidential onus on the party seeking to set aside the award.[20]

---

[18] A. Monichino and A. Fawke, "International Arbitration in Australia: 2011/2012 In Review," (2012) 23 *Australian Dispute Resolution Journal* 234, 239; *cf IMC Aviation Solutions Pty Ltd. v. Altain Khuder LLC* [2011] 253 FLR 9 at 166, 171-172, 272 (per Hansen JA and Kyrou AJA), which took the opposite approach, as discussed in last year's *Yearbook*.

[19] [2011] 253 FLR 9.

[20] Note that Justice Foster's pro-enforcement approach in *Dampskibsselskabet* was supported by first instance decision of Justice Croft in *Altain Khuder LLC v. IMC Mining & Anor* [2011] 246 FLR 47 and the minority appeal decision of Chief Justice Warren in *IMC Aviation Solutions Pty Ltd. v. Altain Khuder LLC* [2011] 253 FLR 9; note also that Chief Justice Warren has expressed her general support for the

B.3 *Traxys Europe*: Public Policy Cannot Be Used to Escape an Award

In *Traxys Europe SA v. Balaji Coke Industry Pvt Ltd. (No 2),*[21] the Federal Court held that there was no need for an award debtor to be shown to have assets in Australia before an international arbitration award could be enforced.

Traxys Europe concerned a contract for the supply of metallurgical coke. The contract was governed by English law and provided for arbitration in London under the LCIA Rules. A dispute arose and an arbitration award was duly made. The applicant sought to enforce the award in Australia because the respondent appeared to own shares in an Australian company. The respondent resisted enforcement of the award on three bases:

(a) the Federal Court had no power under the IAA to give effect to the award;

(b) unless a party has assets in Australia, the Australian courts cannot enforce an arbitration award there; and

(c) because an injunction had been granted in India preventing the enforcement of the award and the award debtor had no Australian assets, the arbitration award should not be enforced as a matter of public policy.

Justice Foster rejected all three arguments. Notably, in relation to public policy, Justice Foster found that "the pro-enforcement bias of the Convention, as reflected in the IAA, requires that the

---

effectiveness of international arbitration in "Efficient, Effective, Economical? The Victorian Supreme Court's Perspective on Arbitration," Remarks of the Hon Marilyn Warren AC, Chief Justice of the Supreme Court of Victoria, at the International Commercial Arbitration Conference, 4 December 2009.

[21]   [2012] 201 FCR 535.

public policy ground for refusing enforcement not be allowed to be used as an escape route for a defaulting debtor."[22]

B.4 *Castel Electronics v. TCL Air Conditioner*: Breach of Natural Justice Strictly Interpreted in Favor of Enforcing Awards

Castel Electronics Pty Ltd. v. TCL Air Conditioner (Zhonshan) Co. Ltd.[23] involved an agreement between a Chinese company, TCL, and an Australian company, Castel Electronics, which contained an arbitration clause. The parties claimed against each other for breach of the agreement and had their dispute determined by arbitration.

Castel obtained an arbitral award and a costs award in its favor but TCL failed to pay. Castel applied *ex parte* to the Federal Court of Australia seeking enforcement of the awards. TCL opposed the application on the basis that the court did not have jurisdiction under Article 34 of the Model Law. However, the court (in an opinion by Justice Murphy) allowed the application.[24]

TCL also made two additional applications to set aside the awards pursuant to Article 34 of the Model Law. TCL contended that enforcement of the arbitral award would be contrary to public policy due to breaches of the rules of natural justice and that the costs award should not be enforced because it followed the award.

In considering whether the awards should be set aside on grounds of public policy, Justice Murphy provided the following guidance on principles of public policy in Australia:

---

[22]   *Ibid.*, 90.

[23]   *Castel Electronics Pty Ltd. v. TCL Air Conditioner (Zhonshan) Co. Ltd.* [2012] FCA 1214.

[24]   *Id.* at 21.

B. Cases

- Public policy includes procedural questions as well as questions relating to substantive law.

- Because of Section 19(b) of the IAA, any breach of the rules of natural justice in connection with the making of an award means that it is in conflict with or contrary to the public policy of Australia. However, because the powers to set aside an award or to refuse enforcement are discretionary, this does not mean that a minor breach of the rules of natural justice that would not affect the outcome of an arbitration, would cause the award to be set aside or unenforceable.

- In exercising the discretion to set aside an award, relevant considerations include the fact that arbitration is intended to be an efficient, enforceable and timely method of resolving commercial disputes, and that arbitral awards are intended to provide certainty and finality. Accordingly, the discretion to set aside an award for public policy reasons should be exercised sparingly.

- In conducting the review, Justice Murphy found that he should carefully examine the evidence and law to ensure there is in fact no conflict with the rules of natural justice, rather than examine the facts of the case afresh and revisit in full the questions that were before the tribunal.

- Although the decisions of courts in other Convention countries are not binding, it is desirable to take them into account to achieve some uniformity in the meaning of "public policy" amongst convention countries.

- Discretion to set aside or refuse to enforce an award challenged on the ground of public policy should only be exercised where there is offense to fundamental notions of fairness and justice.

Justice Murphy had to determine whether there was rationally probative evidence in support of the three findings TCL complained of and, further, whether the tribunal gave TCL a fair hearing in reaching those findings. Justice Murphy found that there had been no breach of natural justice in connection with the making of the arbitral award, and therefore, there was no compelling reason to set aside or refuse to enforce the awards. Accordingly, the court made orders in the terms of the awards.

TCL filed a notice of appeal on 10 December 2012.

B.5 TCL Air Conditioner (Zhongshan) v. Castel Electronics:[25] Validity of the IAA

In addition to the above proceedings, TCL also brought an application in the High Court of Australia to challenge the validity of the IAA based on two submissions:

1. that the IAA substantially impairs the institutional integrity of the Federal Court by enlisting the Federal Court in an arrangement to facilitate arbitration and then enforce the resulting arbitral awards; and

2. that the IAA impermissibly vests Commonwealth judicial power in arbitral tribunals.

The High Court's judgment was reserved at the time of writing. However, a recent decision in the New South Wales Supreme Court rejected the same arguments raised in relation to the domestic Commercial Arbitration Act 2010 (NSW), which is also based on the Model Law.[26] If the High Court takes guidance from this decision, the validity of the IAA may well be upheld.

---

[25] *TCL Air Conditioner (Zhonshan) Co. Ltd. v. Castel Electronics Pty Ltd.*, High Court of Australia Proceeding No. S178 of 2012.

[26] *Ashjal Pty Ltd. v. Alred Toepfer International (Australia) Pty Ltd.* [2012] NSWSC 1306.

C. THE GRANT AND ENFORCEMENT OF INTERIM MEASURES IN INTERNATIONAL ARBITRATION

C.1 Tribunal-Ordered Interim Measures

Since the incorporation of the Model Law into the IAA in 2006, tribunals in Australia have had wide discretion to grant interim measures. Article 17(2) of the Model Law allows a tribunal to grant any interim measure for the purpose of maintaining or restoring the status quo; preventing harm to the arbitral process itself; providing a means to preserve assets; or preserving evidence that may be relevant.

Since any temporary measure designed to meet one of the above ends is considered an interim measure for the purposes of Article 17(2), a wide range of interim measures are available to Australian tribunals including, but not limited to interlocutory injunctions; security for costs; declarations; freezing orders; and preservation orders.

For interim measures ordered under Article 17(2)(a),(b), or (c), the party requesting the order must satisfy the tribunal that: (a) harm is likely to result if the measure if not granted, that harm is not adequately reparable by damages and that harm substantially outweighs the harm that is likely to be suffered by the party against whom the measure is directed; and (b) there is a reasonable possibility that the requesting party will succeed on the merits of the claim.

For the granting of a preservation order under Article 17(2)(d), the tribunal has discretion to apply the above test to the extent it considers appropriate.

The first limb of the test provides for a high threshold, as the party not only has to demonstrate the probability of harm if the measure is not granted, but also that it "substantially outweighs" any harm that will occur as a result of granting the measure. Conversely, the second limb of the test only requires the applicant to prove that there is a "reasonable possibility" of success on the merits of the claim as a whole. In addition, under Article 17E the tribunal has the power to require the party seeking the interim measure to provide adequate security as a condition for granting the measure. This ensures that the respondent is somewhat protected against suffering harm as a result.

Furthermore, a tribunal also has the power to grant *ex parte* interim measures in the form of a preliminary orders under Article 17B(1). The test for granting preliminary orders is the same as for granting interim measures, with the additional requirement that prior disclosure of the measures to the counterparty would defeat the purpose of the measures. After granting the preliminary order, the party prejudiced by the measure will be given notice of it and then afforded the opportunity to present its case against the granting of the measure.

Australia's premier arbitral institution and sole default appointing authority for the purpose of Articles 11(3) and 11(4) of the Model Law,[27] the ACICA, provides for tribunal ordered interim measures in generally the same way as the Model Law with a few minor differences. The main difference between the Model Law and the ACICA Arbitration Rules 2011 ("ACICA Rules") on interim measures is that under the ACICA Rules *ex parte* orders are not available.

The ACICA Rules have also recently been amended to enable the granting of interim measures before proceedings have commenced. This is important as often initiating an arbitration

---

[27] International Arbitration Regulations 2011 (Cth).

can be timely, necessitating the potential need for an expedient process to preserve assets. Under Schedule 2 of the ACICA Rules, an emergency arbitrator may grant any interim measure they deem appropriate upon any terms they see fit. The ACICA emergency procedure generally mirrors the approach of Article 28 of the ACICA Rules on interim measures.

C.2 Court-Ordered Interim Measures

Article 9 of the Model Law states that it is not incompatible with an arbitration agreement for a party to request interim measures from the court at any stage during or before proceedings. There is also no requirement to request permission from the tribunal prior to the request. Further, Article 17J grants the court the ability to order interim measures in accordance with its own powers and procedures.

In *Electra Air Conditioning BV v. Seeley International Pty Ltd.*,[28] the court found that the presence of an arbitration agreement in a supply contract did not prevent the applicant from seeking an injunction or declaration from the court, and the court did not rule out the possibility that parties may contract out of this right. This case was decided in 2008, when Article 17J was not yet part of the Model Law. Given that Article 17J confirms that "[a] court shall have the same power of issuing an interim measure in relation to arbitration proceedings . . . as it has in relation to proceedings in courts," it is unlikely that parties would now agree to exclude the court's jurisdiction to grant interim measures.

Under Article 17J, Australian courts have the power to issue interim measures with respect to arbitrations taking place outside of Australia. For example, in *Cape Lambert Resources Ltd. v.*

---

[28]   [2008] FCAFC 169.

Mcc Australia Sanjin Mining Pty Ltd.,[29] the Western Australian Supreme Court ordered the third defendant to pay the disputed amount into an escrow account while staying the proceeding and compelling arbitration in Singapore.

While parties have the ability to seek interim measures from arbitrators, often parties to arbitration choose to exercise their rights under Article 9 to request an interim measure from an Australian court and obtain a court-ordered interim measure under Article 17J. One reason for this is that the judicial system for interlocutory relief is quite efficient and expedient in Australia. For example, in *ENRC Marketing AG v. OJSC 'Magnitogorsk Metallurgical Kombinat'*,[30] an *ex parte* freezing order was sought by the applicant on 24 November 2011, and was granted by the court on the following day. It was then further reviewed three days later on 28 November 2011.

A further reason is that, while the cost of seeking an interim measure from the Australian courts is generally higher than seeking measures from an arbitrator, going to the courts removes the risk of non-compliance with a tribunal ordered interim measure. If a measure is granted by an arbitrator but the respondent refuses to accept it, the applicant must then go to the courts to enforce it.[31]

Since the decision of the High Court of Australia in *CSR Ltd. v. Cigna Insurance Australia Ltd.*,[32] Australian courts have had jurisdiction to award anti-suit injunctions to restrain parties from continuing or commencing a proceeding in a foreign court, a

---

[29]   [2012] WASC 228.

[30]   [2011] FCA 1371.

[31]   *Electra Air Conditioning BV v. Seeley International Pty Ltd* [2008] FCAFC 169, para 50.

[32]   [1997] 189 CLR 345.

breach of which constitutes contempt of court. As an anti-suit injunction implicates the doctrine of comity, Australian courts tend to interpret their jurisdiction to award anti-suit injunctions narrowly.

C.3 Enforcement of Interim Measures

Under Article 17H of the Model Law, any interim measure issued by a tribunal is recognized as binding and will be enforced by the court, unless a specific ground for refusal of enforcement applies under Article 17I. Under Article 17I, the grounds for refusing to enforce an interim measure mirror the grounds to refuse enforcement of an arbitral award found in Article 36, which include (a) one of the parties was under an incapacity; (b) the overall agreement is not valid under the substantive law of the contract, or if no substantive law is agreed to, then the law of the country where the award was granted; (c) the respondent was not given proper notice of the appointment of the arbitrator; (d) the measure deals with a dispute not contemplated by the arbitration agreement; (e) the composition of the arbitral tribunal was not in accordance with the agreement of the parties, or in the absence of the agreement, was not in accordance with the law of the country where the arbitration took place; (f) the subject matter of the dispute is not capable of settlement by arbitration in Australia; and (g) the recognition and enforcement of the measure would be contrary to the public policy of Australia.

Under section 19 of the IAA, examples of when interim measures will be against the public policy of Australia include (a) when the granting of the measure was induced by fraud or corruption; or (b) when there is a breach of the rules of natural justice occasioned in connection with the granting of the interim measure.

Finally, under Article 17H(1), Australian courts not only have jurisdiction to enforce an award for interim measures made within Australia, but they can also enforce measures made by a tribunal outside of Australia. This is important as it removes the unsettled issue of whether interim measures are awards or orders under the New York Convention and whether or not they are enforceable.

AUSTRIA

Alexander Petsche[1] and Heidrun E. Preidt[2]

A. LEGISLATION, TRENDS AND TENDENCIES

There were no legislative changes to the Austrian Arbitration Law in 2012.

The Advisory Board of the Vienna International Arbitral Center ("VIAC") has established a committee for the revision of VIAC's Rules of Arbitration and Conciliation (the "Vienna Rules"), which had several meetings in 2012 involving many users and representatives of other arbitration institutions. The new Vienna Rules have not yet been finally approved by the Board of VIAC. However, the main changes will relate to third-party intervention and fast-track arbitration. VIAC's Board has also decided not to follow all international arbitration trends, but to keep the Vienna Rules simple by applying a pragmatic approach, reflecting the wishes of the users of VIAC.

---

[1]   Alexander Petsche heads the Litigation and Arbitration Practice Group at Baker & McKenzie in Vienna. He advises clients in connection with the assertion of their claims before state courts and arbitral tribunals, particularly in matters related to construction and infrastructure projects, damage claims, distribution law and corporate disputes, as well as in investment arbitrations. Mr. Petsche also advises clients on the implementation of compliance systems, especially in the field of anti-corruption, and has significant experience serving as an arbitrator and an accredited business mediator.

[2]   Heidrun E. Preidt is an Associate at Baker & McKenzie's office in Vienna. She acts as counsel in state court litigation and international commercial as well as investment arbitration proceedings.

B. CASES

B.1 Lack of Oral Hearing Does Not Constitute a Violation of the Right to Be Heard

On 18 April 2012, the Austrian Supreme Court ("OGH") dealt with a claim to refuse the enforcement of a foreign arbitral award according to Article V(1)(b) of the New York Convention.[3] The party against whom the arbitral award was to be enforced alleged that its right to be heard had been violated, as an expert's opinion was only presented in writing but never discussed during an oral hearing. In particular, the party alleged that the arbitral tribunal had ignored the written questions that it had submitted to the expert because they were of a legal nature, and had based the arbitral award on facts and evidence on which the parties were not able to comment, in an alleged breach of Article V(1)(b) of the New York Convention.

In its findings, the OGH relied on prior case law dealing with the violation of the right to be heard. According to this reasoning, Article V(1)(b) of the New York Convention is only violated if a party against which the foreign award is invoked was not given proper notice of the arbitration proceedings or had otherwise not been able to exercise its rights to raise its claim or defense. In the present case it was undisputed that the parties had the right to submit written questions to the expert. The OGH found that the unexplained failure to deal with these questions did not fall within the scope of Article V(1)(b) of the New York Convention, as the parties were not hindered in exercising their rights to submit their claim or defense. The OGH granted the enforcement of the foreign arbitral award.

---

[3]   OGH, 18 April 2012, 3Ob 38/12b.

B. Cases

B.2 The Parties and Not the Arbitral Institution Are Liable for Payment of the Arbitrators' Fees

On 18 September 2012, the OGH dealt with a claim filed against the VIAC.[4] The claimant, who was an arbitrator in a proceeding administered by the VIAC, not only claimed fees, but also compensation for damages resulting out of purported violations of the VIAC Secretary General's duties (the arbitrator mainly argued that the amount in dispute had not been fixed correctly and that therefore the deposit for the arbitrator's fees was too low). The OGH had to consider whether there was a contract between the institution and the arbitrator in order to determine whether it was the VIAC's liability to pay the arbitrator's fees and/or the compensation claimed. To resolve this question, the OGH differentiated between non-institutional ("ad-hoc") and institutional arbitral tribunals. It found that regarding non-institutional arbitral tribunals, it was undisputed that the arbitrator's contract was at least tacitly concluded between the arbitrators and the parties of the arbitration proceedings. Consequently, the parties were obliged to pay the arbitrators' fees. In institutional arbitral proceedings, however, the institutions were chosen by the parties and provided a range of administrative services to the parties of the arbitral proceedings. Thus, the contract existed between the parties and the institution. The OGH noted that it was disputed in legal doctrine between whom the contract with the arbitrators was concluded in institutional arbitral proceedings. The OGH referred to two views, the first holding that the arbitrator's contract was always concluded with the parties themselves (even if the tribunal's chairman was nominated by the institution), while the other suggested that the contract between the parties and the institution might also contain the duty to implement the entire proceedings,

---

4   OGH, 18 September 2012, 4Ob 30/12h.

including the contract with the arbitrators. Following the latter view, the arbitrators would act on behalf of the institution, which would then be required to pay their fees.

Since all these legal relationships were subject to the parties' agreement, the OGH emphasized the significance of the applicable arbitration rules in institutional proceedings. Considering the relevant provisions of the Vienna Rules, the OGH held that the arbitrators would, unless agreed otherwise, enter into the contractual relationship with the parties and not with the VIAC. In its reasoning, the OGH found that the arbitrator's contract was generally concluded between the parties and the arbitrators, a rule which equally applied to non-institutional as well as institutional tribunals. Consequently, only the parties could be held liable to pay the fees of the arbitrators and any compensation resulting out of a breach of their contract.

B.3 Claim for Annulment of a Shareholders' Resolution Is Arbitrable Even if the Award Might Have an Effect on Third Parties

On 19 April 2012, the OGH had to consider whether the annulment of a shareholders' resolution was arbitrable if the outcome might have an effect on the relationship with third parties (non-shareholders of the relevant company) who were not granted the right to be heard in the arbitral proceedings.[5] The OGH found that the fact that an arbitral award could have an effect on third parties did not grant those third parties the right to be heard either before an ordinary court or before that arbitral tribunal.

---

[5]   OGH, 19 April 2012, 6Ob 42/12p.

The OGH found that the law had not changed after the revision of the Austrian Arbitration Act in 2006 (SchiedsRÄG). Thus, claims for the annulment of shareholders' resolutions (Section 41 *et seq.* of the Limited Liability Company Act ("GmbHG")) were effectively arbitrable, as such claims could also be subject to a settlement agreement. The OGH dismissed the argument of the third party (the appellant) that it should have had the right to be heard as a prerequisite for the objective arbitrability of the annulment claim. The OGH found that the appellant did not have a right to be heard given that it was not a shareholder of the company and thus was entitled neither to participate at the shareholders' meeting nor to vote on the resolution concerning the approval of the contract between the company and itself. The court found that as the third party was not entitled to be involved in the decision on the approval of its contract, it would be incomprehensible that it should be involved in the procedure of annulling the relevant shareholders' resolution.

C. THE GRANT AND ENFORCEMENT OF INTERIM MEASURES IN INTERNATIONAL ARBITRATION

C.1 Tribunal-Ordered Interim Measures

Section 593(1) of the Austrian Code of Civil Procedure ("ACCP") entitles arbitrators to grant "interim or protective measures," but does not specify the type and scope of such measures. The language of this provision leaves it to the discretion of the arbitral tribunal to grant any form of interim measure it considers necessary in order to secure the party's rights and/or to preserve the *status quo* of a dispute. Such measures could be issued to secure the enforcement of the arbitral award (e.g., a freezing order or an order to deposit the disputed object) or to temporarily regulate legal relationships (e.g., a temporary revocation of a power of attorney). As the tribunal may, according to Section 593(1) ACCP, issue interim measures "in respect of the subject-matter of the dispute," it is disputed whether security for costs might also be subject to an interim measure of protection.[6]

The parties can agree to deprive the arbitral tribunal of the power to order interim measures and leave the power to grant such measures exclusively to the state courts. The parties can also limit the arbitral tribunal's power to granting only certain types of interim measures.

An arbitral tribunal may only order interim measures for protection upon the request of a party and after having heard the opposing party. An arbitral tribunal is strictly prohibited from issuing *ex parte* measures. The measure has to be directed against one of the parties to the arbitration proceedings, thus, measures against third parties are inadmissible.

According to Section 593(1) ACCP, the arbitral tribunal may order interim measures if it considers it necessary in respect of the subject matter of the dispute because (i) otherwise the enforcement of the claim would be frustrated or considerably impeded; or, (ii) a danger of irreparable damage exists. The requesting party has to demonstrate *prima facie* that it would suffer irreparable harm if the protective measures were not granted. No particular standard of proof is specified.[7] However, the parties are free to agree on a strict standard of proof.

---

[6] *Platte* states that security for costs can only be ordered as an interim measure, if the parties have agreed to authorize the tribunal to do so: *Platte* in Riegler, Petsche *et al.*, *Arbitration Law of Austria: Practice and Procedure* (2007), p. 321; *Reiner* states that the arbitral tribunal may also order security for costs: Reiner, *The New Austrian Arbitration Law – Arbitration Act 2006* (2006), § 593 note 101.

[7] *Zeiler*, in *Liebscher et al*, Schiedsverfahrensrecht, Vol. I, p 578; *Schwarz/Konrad*, p. 564; *Riegler et al.*, p. 322.

It lies within the arbitral tribunal's discretion whether to grant the requested interim measure. The arbitral tribunal is entitled under Section 593(1) ACCP (last sentence) to request any party to provide appropriate security to compensate the opposing party in case any damage results from the grant of the interim measure. The law is silent as to the type of security that should be provided.

The Vienna Rules do not offer a pre-arbitral or emergency arbitrator procedure. The VIAC Board, while adopting the 2013 Vienna Rules after consultation with its users, found it unnecessary to provide an emergency arbitrator. Any request for interim measures for protection prior to the constitution of the arbitral tribunal has to be sought from local courts.[8]

C.2 Court-Ordered Interim Measures

There are no specific provisions under Austrian law concerning the relationship between state courts and arbitral tribunals regarding the competence to grant interim measures. In effect, Austrian law establishes a parallel competence of state courts and arbitral tribunals. Once the arbitral tribunal is constituted and the arbitral proceeding is commenced, the parties are free to choose whether to seek interim measures for protection from the relevant arbitral tribunal or from state courts. They are entitled to request interim measures from state courts at any stage of the arbitral proceeding. The parties could even apply simultaneously to state courts and to the arbitral tribunal, which might have the advantage of securing a fast decision. However, such parallel applications would not only be costly, but the decisions of the court and the tribunal could be contradictory. In that case, only the court's decision could be enforced. While the parties may

---

[8]   *Schwarz/Konrad*, p. 546f.

agree to exclude the arbitral tribunal's competence to order interim measures, the parties are not entitled to waive their access to state courts.

The time required to obtain an interim measure from a state court depends on the type of interim measure sought, the particular circumstances of the case and the judge in charge. If a party seeks, e.g., an order to freeze a bank account, this might be obtained within a few days.

Austrian law does not recognize the concept of anti-suit injunctions. Furthermore, it is highly unlikely that an Austrian court would recognize an anti-suit injunction issued by a foreign court or arbitral tribunal.

When Austrian courts are not the supervisory courts, they are only competent to grant interim measures in cases for which their obligatory competence is established under Section 387 (2) of the Enforcement Act ("EO"). This requires that the interim measure be requested before commencement of the arbitral proceeding or after its termination and that the opponent of the measure has its seat in Austria. Thus, in most international arbitration cases, the Austrian courts will not be entitled to grant interim measures.[9] However, according to Section 577(2) ACCP, state courts are obliged to enforce interim or protective measures even if the seat of arbitration lies outside the jurisdiction of Austrian courts or the seat of arbitration has not yet been determined.

C.3   Enforcement of Interim Measures

The form of interim measures is governed by Section 593(2) ACCP. Interim measures are considered neither as orders nor as

---

[9]   *Zeiler*, Einstweilige Maßnahmen, in *Liebscher* et.al, Schiedsverfahrensrecht, Vol. I (2011), para 7/23.

awards, but as a legal type *sui generis*. Nonetheless, Section 593(2) ACCP provides that certain requirements as to the form and content of awards on the merits are applicable to interim measures as well (Sections 606(2), (3),(5) and (6) ACCP). In particular, they have to be made in writing and have to be reasoned. Further, they need to be signed either by the sole arbitrator or the chairman of an arbitral tribunal and have to be delivered to each party and indicate the place of issuance.

Section 593 ACCP governs the enforcement of interim measures and sets forth a statutory regime that obliges state courts to enforce interim measures granted by an arbitral tribunal in domestic and international proceedings, unless there are grounds for refusal of enforcement, as long as they comply with the formal and substantive legal requirements.

When enforcing an interim measure, the court may hear the opposing party before granting the enforcement order. If for any reason the opposing party was not heard in the process where the interim measure was granted, it would be entitled to object against the enforcement order based on Section 397 EO.

According to Section 593(3) ACCP, the tribunal may also order types of interim measures unknown under Austrian law. If an Austrian court is required to enforce such types of interim measures it may, upon request and after hearing the opposing party, enforce whichever interim measure under Austrian law comes closest to the measure ordered by the arbitral tribunal. However, Austrian courts are entitled to refuse the enforcement of interim measures if (i) the seat of arbitration is in Austria and the measure suffers from a defect which would constitute a reason to set aside the award; (ii) the seat of arbitration is outside of Austria and the measure suffers from a defect that would constitute a cause to refuse the enforcement of the arbitral award; (iii) the enforcement of the measure would be incompatible with a measure ordered by an Austrian state court prior to this measure or by a foreign court which has to be recognized; or (iv) such measure of protection is unknown under Austrian law and no appropriate measure under Austrian law was applied for (Section 593(4) No 1 – 4 ACCP).

AZERBAIJAN

Gunduz Karimov[1] and Jamil Alizada[2]

A. LEGISLATION, TRENDS AND TENDENCIES

A.1 General

The governing arbitration statute in Azerbaijan is the Law of the Republic of Azerbaijan *On International Commercial Arbitration* (the "Arbitration Law"), dated 1 November 18, 1999. Azerbaijan is also a party to the New York Convention, the Washington Convention and the European Convention.

Additionally, the Civil Procedure Code of the Republic of Azerbaijan (the "Civil Procedure Code"), effective 1 September 2001, contains provisions on the enforcement and recognition of foreign arbitral awards.

A.2 Types of Arbitration

Azerbaijani law distinguishes international arbitration from domestic arbitration and currently recognizes international arbitration only as a dispute resolution mechanism between foreign and Azerbaijani companies.

---

[1] Gunduz Karimov is the Managing Partner of the Baku Office of Baker & McKenzie specializing in dispute resolution, intellectual property and compliance matters. Mr. Karimov graduated from Baku State University and received his LL.M. from Indiana University in Bloomington. As a member of Azerbaijan Bar Association and a registered trademark attorney, Mr. Karimov is also Vice-Dean of the School of Law of Baku State University.

[2] Jamil Alizada is an Associate in the Baku Office of Baker & McKenzie specializing in corporate, intellectual property and employment matters. He graduated from Moscow State Institute of International Relations (MGIMO) and Maastricht University with degrees in Intellectual Property Law and Knowledge Management. Mr. Alizada joined Baker & McKenzie in September 2011.

Section 1(1)(3) of the Arbitration Law permits international commercial arbitration where:

- the parties to an arbitration agreement have, at the time of the conclusion of that agreement, their places of business in different states;

- one of the following is outside the state in which parties have their places of business:

  o the seat or legal place of arbitration as specified in the arbitration agreement; or

  o any place where a substantial part of the obligations of the commercial relationship is or were to be performed or the place with which the subject matter of the dispute is most closely connected; or

- the parties have expressly agreed that the subject matter of the arbitration agreement relates to more than one country.

As stated above, the Arbitration Law governs only international arbitration. The Civil Procedure Code permits parties to settle disputes through *ad hoc* arbitration with the consent of the parties. It does not, however, provide for any mechanism or procedure for such arbitration. To date, there has been no domestic arbitration between local entities.

A.3 Regulation of International Arbitration

The Arbitration Law applies only if the place of arbitration is Azerbaijan. Parties may appoint independent arbitrators of any nationality. The arbitral proceedings may be conducted in any language chosen by the parties. The procedural law and all matters pertaining to the dispute (except for those matters that must be exclusively resolved under Azerbaijani law, as indicated in Section A.4 below) may be determined by the parties, and, in general, the parties may stipulate other terms of the arbitration.

The Supreme Court of the Republic of Azerbaijan (the "Supreme Court") is the authority that controls and supports international arbitration proceedings in Azerbaijan. The Supreme Court has the right to (i) appoint arbitrators if the parties have not agreed on them; (ii) consider the parties' objections with respect to the arbitrators; (iii) annul an arbitrator's mandate for reasons provided in the Arbitration Law; (iv) assist an arbitral tribunal in the collection of evidence; and (v) annul an arbitral award.

The Supreme Court can annul an arbitral award issued in Azerbaijan where one of the parties demonstrates that:

- one of the parties to the arbitration agreement did not have the legal capacity to enter into the agreement to arbitrate, or the agreement is otherwise invalid under applicable law;

- one of the parties was not notified of the appointment of the arbitrators or the date of the arbitration hearing, or could not provide its arguments for other reasons;

- the arbitral award concerns a dispute or issues not regulated by the arbitration agreement; or

- the structure and procedure of the arbitral tribunal does not comply with the arbitration agreement, or in the absence of such agreement, with the Arbitration Law.

If the Supreme Court determines that the dispute is not subject to arbitration under Azerbaijani law or that the arbitral award is contrary to the sovereignty and laws of the Republic of Azerbaijan, it has the right to annul the award.

A.4 Protection of Foreign Investment

Under the Law of the Republic of Azerbaijan *On Protection of Foreign Investment*, dated 15 January 1992 (the "Investment Protection Law"), foreign investment is defined as investment of any property or proprietary right, including intellectual property rights, for the purposes of realizing profit from the investment. Generally, Azerbaijani law recognizes the right of foreign investors to arbitrate with state agencies both locally and internationally. Disputes between foreign investors and state agencies may be resolved by arbitration if the parties have agreed to arbitration or if so provided under an international treaty to which Azerbaijan is a signatory.

Whether Azerbaijani legal entities with foreign investment may choose arbitration outside Azerbaijan is unclear. Theoretically, international arbitration is possible between a wholly foreign-owned company incorporated in Azerbaijan and a local entity with a local investment. Under Article 42 of the Law of the Republic of Azerbaijan *On Foreign Investments* of 1992 (the "Foreign Investment Law"), any dispute between foreign-owned companies and local entities may be resolved either by a court, or by domestic or international arbitration if there is an arbitration agreement between the parties. The Foreign Investment Law also provides that disputes between foreign investors and Azerbaijani state bodies or legal entities concerning the amount of damages may be adjudicated by an arbitral tribunal if the parties have agreed to arbitration. While the language of Article 42 is vague, the Civil Procedure Code does not specifically grant Azerbaijani legal entities the right to arbitrate. Accordingly, absent guidance from the Supreme Court, it is unclear whether two Azerbaijani legal entities (one with local investment and the other with foreign investment) can choose international arbitration.

In addition, Azerbaijani courts have exclusive jurisdiction to hear certain types of disputes. Pursuant to the Civil Procedure Code, the exclusive jurisdiction of Azerbaijani courts extends to:

(a) disputes relating to property rights over immovable property, including claims in respect of a lease or pledge of the property, if the property is located in Azerbaijan;

(b) disputes relating to the invalidation of decisions, recognition of validity or invalidity, or dissolution of a legal entity whose legal address is in the Republic of Azerbaijan;

(c) disputes relating to claims in respect of the recognition of the validity of patents, trademarks or other rights, if registration or application for registration of these rights has taken place in the Republic of Azerbaijan;

(d) judgments or orders on compulsory enforcement measures requested and to be enforced in the Republic of Azerbaijan;

(e) disputes relating to claims against carriers arising out of transportation contracts;

(f) disputes relating to the termination of marriage between citizens of the Republic of Azerbaijan and foreigners or stateless persons, if both spouses reside in Azerbaijan.

A.5 Public Policy Considerations

The concept of public policy is expressed in different forms and in various laws regulating the rules of private international law. Thus, the Civil Procedure Code provides that international letters of requests (or rogatory letters) issued by foreign courts should not be executed if such execution is contrary to the sovereignty of the Republic of Azerbaijan and the general principles of law. The Civil Procedure Code further provides that the recognition and enforcement of decisions of foreign courts and arbitral tribunals is possible if they are not contrary to the legislation of the Republic of Azerbaijan and legal order and are mutually guaranteed. The compulsory enforcement of decisions can be waived on similar grounds.

Article 4 of the Law of the Republic of Azerbaijan On Private International Law, dated 6 June 2000, provides that foreign legal provisions are not applied in the Republic of Azerbaijan if they contradict the Constitution and any regulations adopted through a referendum.

Under Article 34 of the Arbitration Law, an arbitral decision can be annulled by the Supreme Court if it determines that the decision is contrary to the Constitution of the Republic of Azerbaijan.

Finally, under Article 157 of the Family Code of the Republic of Azerbaijan, dated 28 December 1999, the provisions of foreign family law are not applied if such application would contradict the fundamental principles of legal order of the Republic of Azerbaijan. In this event, Azerbaijani law would be applied.

However, although the laws provide a theoretical basis for public policy arguments, to date we are unaware of any disputes considered in Azerbaijan where a party invoked public policy considerations.

A.6 The International Commercial Arbitration Court

The International Commercial Arbitration Court ("ICAC") is a local institution established on 11 November 2003 to resolve international commercial disputes in Azerbaijan. It was founded by a non-governmental organization of the same name funded through various grants. The ICAC has its own official regulations, arbitrators and schedule of fees.

Pursuant to its charter, the ICAC considers commercial disputes within 120 days. The charter provides for three grounds on which a dispute may be brought before an ICAC arbitral tribunal:

* an independent arbitration agreement;
* an arbitral clause;
* an arbitral note.

The registration fee, which is paid at the time of filing the statement of claim, is USD 300 and is not refundable. The arbitration fee must be paid in advance. It must be paid in the national currency (AZN) if the claim amount is expressed in AZN. If the claim amount is expressed in any foreign currency, the arbitration fee should be paid in U.S. dollars. The ICAC also provides special rules governing the reduction of the arbitration fee, its apportionment, extra expenses, and the payment procedure.

Arbitration proceedings are generally held in Baku, the capital of Azerbaijan. The parties can, however, agree to hold the hearing at any place within the country. In this case, payment of any additional expenses incurred as a result of holding the arbitration outside the Baku is borne by the disputing parties. The parties also have the opportunity to select any arbitrator, which creates the opportunity of having a professional person skilled in dispute resolution. Further, although arbitration proceedings are normally conducted in the Azerbaijani language, the parties may also choose to have their hearing conducted in another language.

Recognition and enforcement of ICAC arbitral awards is regulated primarily by the New York Convention. Azerbaijan ratified the New York Convention on 9 November 1999. Azerbaijan is also a party to a number of bilateral and multilateral international treaties that ensure the recognition and enforcement of ICAC arbitral awards in most countries of the world.

B. CASES

B.1 General

Arbitration practice in Azerbaijan is generally limited to obtaining recognition by the Supreme Court of foreign arbitral awards. The Supreme Court may refuse to recognize a foreign arbitral award on the grounds listed in section A.3 above. Additionally, recognition of a foreign arbitral award may be rejected if (i) the award has not entered into force with respect to the parties or was annulled by a court or arbitral tribunal in another country, or (ii) the enforcement of the award contradicts the sovereignty and laws of Azerbaijan.

B.2 Recognition of Cases in 2012

In 2012, the Supreme Court recognized the case between Belshina OJSC and Azershina (in Azerbaijani—Azərşina) CJSC, considered by the Mogilev Economic Court in the Republic of Belarus, which was submitted to the Supreme Court in 2011, but was initially not duly translated and therefore returned to the Ministry of Justice.

The Supreme Court also recognized the following cases in 2012:

- The case between Baki-Alnas Servis LLC and Shelfgaztehnologiya LLC, a company established under the laws of the Republic of Azerbaijan, relating to Shelfgaztehnologiya LLC's failure to pay for the purchase of pumping installations for oil production, considered by the International Commercial Arbitration Court for the Russian Chamber of Commerce in the Russian Federation; and

- The case between Baumatex LLC and Dayaq-T LTD, a company established under the laws of the Republic of Azerbaijan, relating to the failure of Dayaq-T LTD to pay for the purchase of construction-site equipment, considered by the Economic Court of Rovno Region.

The consideration of cases between (i) Qapali Sehmdar Yol Inshasi Shirketi (*Qapalı Səhmdar Yol İnşası Şirkəti*) and El.Se.Ni. LLC and (ii) Golgun Kollektiv Shirketi (*Gölgün Kollektiv Şirkəti*) and Mahmud Keleshi and Ozdoganlar Inshaat-NeqliyyatSenaye Ticaret Limited Shirketi (*Özdoğanlar İnşaat-Nəqliyyət Sənayə Ticarət Limited Şirkəti*) was adjourned to 2013.

C. THE GRANT AND ENFORCEMENT OF INTERIM MEASURES IN INTERNATIONAL ARBITRATION

C.1 Tribunal-Ordered Interim Measures

Article 17 of the Arbitration Law allows the grant and enforcement of interim measures by an arbitral tribunal only in cases where the place of arbitration is Azerbaijan.

Whether a disputing party may submit a request for interim measures from an arbitral tribunal, located outside Azerbaijan, is unclear. While this is theoretically possible, the Azerbaijani law does not specifically grant the disputing parties such rights. Absent guidance from the Supreme Court, it is unclear whether a disputing party may apply for interim measures from an arbitral tribunal located outside Azerbaijan, and thereafter enforce the interim measures in Azerbaijan.

C.2 Court-Ordered Interim Measures

The grant and enforcement of court-ordered interim measures is allowed under Azerbaijani law. Article 9 of the Arbitration Law provides that a party can file a request to a local court to take interim measures before the commencement of or during arbitration proceedings. Under Article 9, such filing does not contradict an agreement to arbitrate. This implies that if any of the parties submits a request to an Azerbaijani court for interim measures, e.g., an injunction, that party will not be deemed to have waived its right to arbitrate. The Arbitration Law was drafted based on the UNCITRAL Model Law, and Article 9 of the Arbitration Law closely corresponds to Article 9 of the Model Law.

The current court practice, supported by the position of the Supreme Court, interprets Article 9 of the Arbitration Law as allowing parties to apply for interim measures before the arbitration proceedings have commenced in earnest, but after the request for arbitration has been filed and registered with the arbitral tribunal.

The Civil Procedure Code further regulates the procedure for the grant of interim measures. While the relevant provisions of the Civil Procedure Code govern the case where a party seeking injunctive relief files the underlying claim in an Azerbaijani court, the same rules also apply to international arbitrations.

To secure claims and maintain the status quo pending the results of a full evidentiary hearing, Azerbaijani courts are empowered to issue:

• temporary restraining orders prohibiting a defendant or third party from engaging in activities disputed by the claimant;

• writs of attachment or garnishment; and

• stays of execution.

To secure a claimant's position, an Azerbaijani court may issue a writ of attachment directing the seizure of specific assets. For attachment purposes, property is classified into the following priority groups:

- assets not directly involved in the defendant's manufacturing activities—such as securities, bank accounts and motor vehicles;

- manufactured products and raw materials not directly used in the defendant's manufacturing activities;

- immovable property, equipment, machinery, other means of production and raw materials directly involved, and used, in the defendant's manufacturing activities; and

- assets disposed of by the defendant and held by third parties.

Although not clearly stated in the law, it appears that the assets of one priority group may be attached only to the extent that all the assets of the higher priority group(s) are not sufficient to satisfy the claim. Likewise, a claimant may seek the attachment of the defendant's assets which have a value in excess of the amount of its claim only if other assets sufficient to satisfy the claim are not available.

Under Article 158.2 of the Civil Procedure Code, the courts are also empowered to issue other interim measures and may take several security measures simultaneously.

It is noteworthy that although the law generally provides for the possibility to request interim measures from a local court, obtaining an injunction from a local court may take considerable efforts in practice.

C.3 Enforcement of Interim Measures

Under the Civil Procedure Code, once an application for interim relief is filed, an Azerbaijani court is required to conduct a hearing on the application that same day. In practice, however, the enforcement of interim injunctions takes up to one week. Although a court may conduct the hearing on an *ex parte* basis, i.e., without notice to the other party, that party must be notified immediately of the outcome of the hearing. Preliminary injunctions, temporary restraining orders and writs of attachments are immediately appealable by the party against whom such relief has been obtained.

The court which provided prejudgment relief may, at its own discretion, re-examine and reverse its decision. An appeal of the reversed decision, however, does not stay the effectiveness of the reversed decision.

Article 164 of the Civil Procedure Code provides the possibility for a party damaged by an order granting interim relief to recover damages from the claimant if the claimant does not ultimately prevail on its underlying claim.

BELARUS

Alexander Korobeinikov[1]

A. LEGISLATION, TRENDS AND TENDENCIES

A.1 Domestic Legislation

The Belarusian law *On the International Arbitration Court*[2] (the "International Arbitration Law") was enacted on 9 July 1999. The Law is based on the UNCITRAL Model Law and, since 1999, no amendments have been made to it. The International Arbitration Law regulates arbitration proceedings in commercial disputes between both local and foreign entities, as well as the status of international arbitration courts. Under the general rules provided in Article 4 of the International Arbitration Law, all commercial disputes may be resolved by arbitration unless other legislation provides to the contrary. There is, however, no specific list of non-arbitrable disputes in the International Arbitration Law, although such information can be found from a review of other legislation.

There are now two international arbitration courts in Belarus: the International Arbitration Court at the Belarusian Chamber of Commerce and Industry; and the Chamber of Arbitrators at the Belarusian Union of Lawyers. In addition, in 2009, a law *On Commodity Exchanges*[3] provided arbitration as a means of resolving disputes arising from stock-exchange transactions. As

---

[1]   Alexander Korobeinikov is a Senior Associate in Baker & McKenzie's Almaty office and a member of the Firm's International Arbitration Practice Group.

[2]   The Law of the Republic of Belarus *On the International Arbitration Court* No. 279-Z dated 9 July 1999 (as amended).

[3]   The Law of the Republic of Belarus *On Commodity Exchanges* No 10-Z dated 5 January 2009.

a result, the Belarusian stock exchange established an arbitration commission, which acts under rules approved by the stock exchange.

In 2011, the Belarusian Parliament adopted a new law *On Domestic Arbitration Courts*[4] (the "Domestic Arbitration Law"), which regulates domestic arbitrations and came into force in January 2012. While the main provisions of the Domestic Arbitration Law are based on UNCITRAL Model Law principles, as well as principles arising from the existing International Arbitration Law, there are some significant innovations. The key points are:

(i) the new law contains rules regarding the establishment and registration of domestic arbitration institutions and their arbitrators, as well as *ad hoc* arbitrators. Any violation of these rules will lead to the invalidation of an award;

(ii) an arbitration agreement that does not contain either the name of an arbitration institution or the procedure for composing an *ad hoc* arbitral tribunal will be considered null and void. Therefore it seems likely that the Belarusian courts will take a very conservative approach when examining the validity of an arbitration agreement;

(iii) State authorities cannot be a party to an arbitration agreement;

(iv) the new law also places restrictions on the types of disputes that can be arbitrated. In particular, an institutional arbitration court cannot review disputes with its "founder" - it is unclear what this means. Furthermore, disputes affecting the rights and obligations of third parties (who are not party to the arbitration clause) cannot be determined by arbitration;

---

[4]   The Law of the Republic of Belarus *On Domestic Arbitration Courts* No 301-Z dated 18 July 2011.

(v) finally, the law allows state courts to set aside an arbitral award if facts which would have been important for a proper review of the case, come to light that were, at the time, unknown to the arbitral tribunal and one of the parties. Although such a provision is unusual in arbitration legislation, it may have been adopted under the influence of the state courts who enjoy the same power under Belarusian procedural legislation.

At present, many of the provisions contained in the Domestic Arbitration Law are generally unclear, and their application will need to be clarified by the courts as cases come before them.

Since 2011, with assistance from the state authorities, state commercial courts and the Belarusian Union of Lawyers, domestic arbitration courts have been established in each region (*oblast*) of Belarus and in Minsk.

In addition to these arbitration institutions, in 2012 the Belarusian Union of Lawyers established the Sport Arbitration Court. As stated in its statutory documents, the Sport Arbitration Court specializes in disputes between sportsmen, coaches, sport federations and the National Olympic Committee.

Together with the laws identified above, arbitration in Belarus is also regulated by the relevant provisions of the Commercial Procedural Code and the Civil Procedural Code. The Civil Procedural Code contains rules regarding the arbitration procedure and the enforcement of domestic and foreign arbitration awards relating to non-commercial disputes. The Commercial Procedural Code sets out the rules applicable to the enforcement of both domestic and foreign arbitral awards for commercial disputes, as well as the procedures for court-appointed mediation. In October 2011, the Plenum of the Supreme Economic Court adopted the resolution *On Certain Issues Relating to Reviewing Disputes with Foreign Persons by*

Economic Courts[5] (the "Resolution"), which provides guidance for economic courts considering the validity and enforceability of arbitration agreements. The Resolution also imposes on the court an obligation to disclose to a respondent the right to file an objection against the court's jurisdiction if there is an arbitration agreement between the parties. The Resolution highlights the increasingly pro-arbitration stance of the Belarusian economic courts.

A.2 International Treaties

Belarus is party to a number of international and regional treaties relating to arbitration proceedings, including the New York Convention and the European Convention, as well as several CIS treaties.[6]

It should also be noted that, although certain investment treaties that have been ratified by Belarus refer to the ICSID, it is unclear whether Belarus is bound by the ICSID Convention[7] because Belarus has not formally ratified the ICSID Convention.

A.3 Trends and Tendencies

Over the past few years, arbitration and mediation have become increasingly popular as alternative methods of resolving commercial disputes. Additionally, state authorities are promoting arbitration and court-appointed meditation to reduce the amount of claims filed with the state courts.

---

[5] The Resolution of the Plenum of the Supreme Economic Court of the Republic of Belarus *On Certain Issues on Reviewing Disputes with Foreign Persons by Economic Courts* No. 30 dated 31 October 2011.

[6] Although Belarus was member of the Soviet Union until 1991, it has maintained the right to be party to international treaties since the 1940s.

[7] The Convention on the Settlement of Investment Disputes between States and Nationals of Other States, which came into force on 14 October 1966.

In 2011, approximately 50% of commercial disputes initiated in the Belarusian courts were resolved by court-appointed mediation. Furthermore, in the first half of 2011, all 16 claims relating to the enforcement of foreign arbitral awards filed with the economic courts were granted.

The process of court-appointed mediation is established by the Commercial Procedure Code and is used as a means of resolving commercial disputes once legal proceedings have been initiated before the state court. Mediation may be ordered by the judge upon the request of one of the parties, or by the court's own initiative at any stage of the proceedings, including the appellate and enforcement stages.

The mediator must have the required qualifications and can either be selected from the relevant court's staff or from the list of mediators approved by the Supreme Commercial Court. In the event that mediation is successful, the parties must conclude a settlement agreement, which must be approved by the court.

B. CASES

While court decisions relating to the enforcement or setting aside of arbitral awards are generally in line with international practice, the Belarusian courts have comparatively limited experience in dealing with arbitration-related cases. Therefore, from time to time, their decisions are controversial.

A summary of a controversial case where a Belarusian court deemed an arbitration clause providing for disputes to be resolved by arbitration or by the state court to be ineffective is set out below:

In 2005, a foreign company (the "claimant") and a Belarusian company (the "respondent") executed a contract that contained the following arbitration clause:

> disputes will be referred for final settlement to the International Arbitration Court of the Belarusian Chamber of Industry and Commerce or the Supreme Commercial Court of the Republic of Belarus.

The claimant filed a claim against the respondent with the Minsk City Economic Court. However, the respondent asked the court to dismiss the claim on the basis that the contract contained an arbitration clause. The claimant objected, arguing that the jurisdiction clause did not confirm the parties' intention to solve disputes by arbitration only. The court of first instance dismissed the claim and referred the parties to arbitration. However, the Court of Appeal and the Supreme Commercial Court, acting as the cassation court, set aside the decision of the trial court and agreed with the position of the claimant.

It should be noted that the Supreme Commercial Court during review of another case in 2008, found that there were no issues with enforceability of optional arbitration clauses under Belarusian legislation.

C. THE GRANT AND ENFORCEMENT OF INTERIM MEASURES IN INTERNATIONAL ARBITRATION

Under Belarusian legislation, provisions relating to interim measures are established in both the Domestic Arbitration Law and the International Arbitration Law.

Under the Domestic Arbitration Law, the arbitral tribunal does not have a right to issue interim measures for securing the claim and so parties must seek assistance of the state court.

Under the general provisions of the International Arbitration Law, an arbitral tribunal may issue orders granting interim measures upon request by one of the parties or on its own initiative; however, the order cannot be enforced via the state courts. In order to obtain assistance from the state court, a party (or the tribunal) needs to file a separate motion with the state court. The parties have the right to seek an interim order from the court regardless of the tribunal's decision on this issue.

Therefore, in practice, the right of an arbitral tribunal to grant interim measures is of limited benefit unless a party voluntarily complies with the order or it can be enforced in another jurisdiction.

Despite these provisions having been in existence since 1999, at the time of writing, neither legislation nor court practice has provided a clear procedure concerning interim measures in international arbitration. Consequently, the application of these provisions remains uncertain and open to interpretation by court practice.

BELGIUM

Koen De Winter[1] and Michaël De Vroey[2]

A. LEGISLATION, TRENDS AND TENDENCIES

There have been no legislative changes in the arbitration law of Belgium since the overview provided in the 2011-2012 edition of the *Baker & McKenzie International Arbitration Yearbook*.

B. CASES

B.1 State Courts Competent Notwithstanding Valid Arbitration Clause

Pursuant to Article 2(1) of the New York Convention[3] "[e]ach Contracting State shall recognize an agreement in writing under which the parties undertake to submit to arbitration all or any differences which have arisen or which may arise between them in respect of a defined legal relationship, whether contractual or not, concerning a subject matter capable of settlement by arbitration."

Article 2(3) of the New York Convention further stipulates that "[t]he court of a Contracting State, when seized of an action in a matter in respect of which the parties have made an agreement

---

[1]   Koen De Winter is a Partner in Baker & McKenzie's Antwerp office and heads the office's Dispute Resolution Practice Group. During his 30-year professional career he has gained extensive experience in domestic and international litigation and arbitration on a large variety of commercial matters.

[2]   Michaël De Vroey is an Associate in Baker & McKenzie's Antwerp office and a member of the Firm's Global Dispute Resolution Practice Group, as well as a member of the Intellectual Property Practice Group.

[3]   Belgium has ratified the New York Convention by an Act of 5 June 1975.

within the meaning of this article, shall, at the request of one of the parties, refer the parties to arbitration, unless it finds that the said agreement is null and void, inoperative or incapable of being performed."

By a judgment of 5 April 2012 in *United Antwerp Maritime Agencies (UNAMAR) NV v. Navigation Maritime Bulgare*,[4] the Supreme Court (Hof van Cassatie/Cour de Cassation) held that the above provisions of the New York Convention do not preclude a Belgian court before which an action is brought in relation to a contract governed by a foreign law chosen by the parties, from denying the application of an arbitration clause, even if such clause is valid under the chosen foreign law. The Supreme Court clarified, however, that the refusal to apply a valid arbitration clause is only possible on the basis of a rule of the *lex fori* which considers that the subject of the dispute is not capable of settlement by arbitration.

In *United Antwerp*, the action was initially brought before the commercial court in Antwerp which had to rule on the alleged unlawful termination of a commercial agency agreement between a principal based in Bulgaria and a commercial agent headquartered in Belgium. The agency agreement contained a choice for Bulgarian law and the parties agreed to submit any dispute to the Arbitration Court at the Bulgarian Chamber of Commerce and Industry in Sofia.

Notwithstanding this choice of law and the parties' agreement to submit their dispute to arbitration, the commercial agent decided to initiate proceedings in Belgium on the basis of Belgian law, in particular the Act of 13 April 1995 on commercial agency agreements (transposing EU Directive 86/653 of 18 December 1986 on the coordination of the laws of the Member States

---

[4]   Supreme Court 5 April 2012, *TBH* 2012, vol. 9, 937.

relating to self-employed commercial agents), thereby claiming an indemnity in lieu of notice, a goodwill indemnity and additional compensation for dismissal of staff. The Act of 13 April 1995 on commercial agency agreements contains mandatory law provisions that cannot be derogated from by agreement regarding the termination of agency agreements and the calculation of the goodwill indemnity and can be invoked before any Belgian court by a commercial agent with headquarters in Belgium.

Pursuant to Articles 3 and 7(2) of the Rome Convention,[5] mandatory rules of the *lex fori* shall remain applicable, irrespective of the law chosen by the parties. To establish the competence of the Belgian courts in *United Antwerp*, the Supreme Court thought it necessary to obtain further guidance on the application of these provisions and referred the following question for a preliminary ruling to the Court of Justice of the European Union:

> Having regard, not least, to the classification under Belgian law of the provisions at issue in this case (Articles 18, 20 and 21 of the Belgian Law of 13 April 1995 relating to commercial agency contracts) as special mandatory rules of law within the terms of Article 7(2) of the Rome Convention, must Articles 3 and 7(2) of the Rome Convention, read, as appropriate, in conjunction with Council Directive 86/653/EEC of 18 December 1986 on the coordination of the laws of the Member States relating to self-employed commercial agents, be interpreted as meaning that special mandatory rules of law of the forum that offer wider protection than the minimum laid down by Directive 86/653/EEC may be applied to the contract, even if it

---

[5] Convention on the law applicable to contractual obligations opened for signature in Rome on 19 June 1980.

appears that the law applicable to the contract is the law of another Member State of the European Union in which the minimum protection provided by Directive 86/653/EEC has also been implemented?[6]

B.2 State Courts Competent to Order Interim or Conservatory Measures

Article 10 of the Belgian Conflict of Laws Code 2004[7] ("CLC") provides that, in urgent cases, Belgian courts have jurisdiction to order interim or conservatory measures concerning persons or assets located in Belgium at the time of filing the application, even if they have no jurisdiction to decide on the merits of the case. By analogy with Article 31 Brussels I Regulation,[8] Article 10 of the CLC provides an autonomous jurisdictional basis that is applicable regardless of the nature or purpose of the main proceedings. The subject of the dispute in the preliminary proceedings is then decisive for determining the courts' international jurisdiction under Article 10 of the CLC.

By a judgment of 6 August 2012, the President of the Commercial Court of Kortrijk[9] held that the scope of Article 10 of the CLC is not affected by an arbitration clause. According to the President of the Commercial Court, neither the fact that the parties had agreed by contract to submit their claim to

---

[6] Reference for a preliminary ruling from the Hof van Cassatie van België (Belgium) lodged on 20 April 2012 — *United Antwerp Maritime Agencies (UNAMAR) NV v. Navigation Maritime Bulgare* (Case C-184/12), Official Journal of the European Union of 7.7.2012, C-200/6.

[7] *Wet van 16 juli 2004 houdende het Wetboek van internationaal privaatrecht / Loi du 16 juillet 2004 portant le Code de droit international privé*

[8] Regulation (EC) No 44/2001 of 22 December 2000 on jurisdiction and the recognition and enforcement of judgments in civil and commercial matters.

[9] Pres. Comm. Court Kortrijk 6 August 2012, vol. 3, 46.

arbitration, nor the fact that allegedly a much faster result would be obtainable by means of an arbitration under the terms of Hamburger Waren-Verein, would prevent the President from ordering the requested interim or conservatory measures when urgency is being invoked and proved by the claimant in the framework of summary proceedings.

The President granted the claimant's interlocutory application for a court-appointed expert, arguing that the appointment of an expert is a provisional and protective measure, even though it contributes to the provision of evidence. The President's view is in line with established case-law in this respect (see below under Section C.2).

C. THE GRANT AND ENFORCEMENT OF INTERIM MEASURES IN INTERNATIONAL ARBITRATION

C.1 Tribunal-Ordered Interim Measures

Arbitrators have the power, upon request of a party, to order interim or conservatory measures, with the exception of attachment orders (Article 1696, al. 1 of the Code of Civil Procedure, "CCP"), which remain within the exclusive competence of local courts.

This provision, however, does not preclude a party from also bringing an action before a local court for conservatory or interim measures, provided that the parties did not waive this right, e.g., in an arbitral agreement (Article 1679, al. 2 of the CCP). An application to a local court for conservatory or interim measures is indeed not incompatible with an arbitral agreement and shall not imply a waiver of said agreement (see below under Section C.2).

However, where parties have waived the right to bring an action before a local court for conservatory or interim measures, they will only be able to apply to the arbitral tribunal for any interim or conservatory measures they may require, on the basis of Article 1696, al. 1 of the CCP.

If a party were to choose not to voluntarily comply with the arbitral tribunal's interim or conservatory measure, it is obvious that this could potentially result in delay of enforcement of such measures because in such cases, the party seeking enforcement would have to apply for the *exequatur* (i.e., a formal authorization of enforcement) of the arbitrator's order by a local court, which can take time.

An order from an arbitrator for interim or conservatory measures is enforceable under the same conditions as a final arbitral award. In order to be enforceable, an arbitral award must be granted *exequatur* by the President at the seat of the arbitration, following an *ex parte* request. The party seeking enforcement will need to submit the original arbitral award and the original arbitral agreement, or certified copies thereof, as well as sworn translations in the language of the relevant region (depending on the circumstances, French, Flemish or German) if they are in a language other than that used in the courts of that region.

The President will grant the *exequatur* when the arbitral award is no longer open for appeal before the arbitrators or if the arbitrators have made an order granting provisional enforcement notwithstanding an appeal. The President's order granting the *exequatur* is enforceable notwithstanding the existence of any appeal. In that case, the President's order must be served on the party against whom enforcement is sought. The latter has one month from the date of such service to oppose the order. The opposition is then examined by the court of first instance, whose judgment can be appealed by the losing party to the court of appeal.

If, on the other hand, the request is dismissed, the party seeking enforcement may (within one month of the notification of the dismissal of the request) lodge an appeal against the decision before the court of appeal. The party against whom enforcement is sought receives notification of the appeal and the proceedings thereafter continue *inter partes*. The President will dismiss the request if the award or its enforcement is contrary to public policy or if the dispute was not capable of settlement by arbitration.

With respect to foreign arbitral awards, it is important to emphasize that Belgium has ratified the New York Convention (and the 1961 European Convention).[10] For awards originating from countries that have not ratified the New York Convention, the enforcement procedure is set out in Articles 1719–1723 of the CCP, and those provisions are to a large extent similar to those applicable to the enforcement of domestic awards. A party seeking enforcement of a foreign award may always base its request on these provisions (in accordance with Article VII of the New York Convention), even if the latter would apply, if it considers these rules more favorable than those contained in the New York Convention.

C.2 Court-Ordered Interim Measures

The principle that an application to a local court for conservatory or interim measures is not incompatible with an arbitral agreement and shall not imply a waiver of that agreement has been confirmed on numerous occasions, including by the Court

---

[10] European Convention on International Commercial Arbitration of 1961.

of Appeal of Liège in a judgment of 12 June 1985,[11] the President of the Commercial Court of Hasselt in summary proceedings in a judgment of 15 February 1999[12] and the President of the Commercial Court of Namur in summary proceedings in a judgment of 16 July 2007.[13]

In a judgment of 6 September 2004, the Commercial Court of Kortrijk considered the appointment of an expert as a precautionary measure, thus allowing for an application to a local court, notwithstanding the existence of an arbitral agreement, since it involved only an inquiry and not a decision regarding the merits of the case.[14] Indeed, according to the President of the Commercial Court of Liège in a judgment of 15 June 1978, appointing an expert does not prejudice the merits of the case, since the arbitrator retains the ability to assess all elements described by the expert.[15]

In a judgment of 30 April 1993, the President of the Commercial Court of Brussels further held that the local court must also be allowed to intervene even after the arbitral tribunal has been constituted. Nevertheless, the court in summary proceedings may not prejudice the principal claim, and although its powers may be legitimate given urgent necessity, it must confine itself to taking conservatory and/or provisional measures without intervening in the course of the arbitration proceedings.[16]

---

[11] Liège Court of Appeal, 12 June 1985, *Ann. dr. Liège* 1990, 233.

[12] Pres. Comm. Court Hasselt, 15 February 1999, *TBH* 1999, 872.

[13] Pres. Comm. Court Namur, 16 July 2007, *JLMB* 2007, vol. 36, 1515.

[14] Comm. Court Kortrijk, 6 September 2004, *TGR-TWVR* 2004, vol. 4, 302.

[15] Pres. Comm. Court Liège, 15 June 1978, *JL* 1979, 52.

[16] Pres. Comm. Court Brussels, 30 April 1993, *JLMB* 1994, 240.

By a judgment of 11 February 1994, the Court of Appeal of Liège decided that a local court had jurisdiction to grant an injunction in relation to an act contrary to honest commercial practices, notwithstanding an arbitral agreement, finding that an injunction concerned a measure of public order that a court should be allowed to impose regardless of an arbitral agreement.[17]

Moreover, it is important to bear in mind that provisional measures must not lead to an improvement in the contractual position of the party requesting such measures, and the provisional measures should be based on a new fact that did not already exist at the time of executing the disputed agreement. Although urgency is not a requirement, it is an established principle that the new facts must be such that provisional measures are necessary without awaiting the final verdict. Finally, the provisional measures should be proportionate to the *prima facie* rights invoked by the party requesting the measures.

---

[17] Liège Court of Appeal 11 February, 1994, *Ing.-Cons.* 1994, 169.

BRAZIL

Joaquim de Paiva Muniz,[1] Luis Alberto Salton Peretti,[2] and
Leonardo Mäder Furtado[3]

A.   LEGISLATION, TRENDS AND TENDENCIES

A.1   Commission to Review Brazilian Arbitration Act

The Brazilian Senate recently created a commission to evaluate
the need to change the Brazilian Arbitration Act and to draft, if
necessary, a law on mediation. The drafting commission, created
on November 22, 2012,[4] is composed of thirteen individuals,
including arbitration practitioners and scholars. The commission's
work is expected to start in early 2013 and will take about six
months.

---

[1]   Joaquim T. de Paiva Muniz is a Partner in Baker & McKenzie's Rio de Janeiro
office and a professor of Business Law and Arbitration, teaching graduate courses
at Fundação Getúlio Vargas (FGV). Mr. Muniz is Chairman of the Arbitration
Commission of the Rio de Janeiro Bar (OAB/RJ) and coordinator to the
arbitration courses of the Rio de Janeiro Bar, including a *lato sensu* graduate
course, Chairman of the Rio de Janeiro section of the Brazilian Institute of
Corporate Law (IBRADEMP) and author of many articles on international
arbitration and Brazilian corporate law, including co-author of *Arbitration Law of
Brazil: Practice and Procedure* (Juris Publishing 2006) and *Arbitragem
Internacional e Doméstica* (Forense 2009).

[2]   Luis Alberto Salton Peretti is an Associate in the São Paulo office and his practice
includes commercial arbitration and litigation.

[3]   Leonardo Mäder Furtado is an Associate in the São Paulo office and his practice
includes commercial arbitration and litigation.

[4]   As reported in the Brazilian Senate's webpage: http://www.senado.gov.br
/atividade/comissoes/comissao.asp?origem=SF&com=1632

A.2 Brazil Ratified the CISG

On October 28, 2012, the Brazilian House of Representatives passed a decree[5] ratifying the United Nations Convention on Contracts for the International Sale of Goods ("CISG"). The CISG is a model legislation drafted under the auspices of the United Nations that establishes a uniform set of rules to govern the international sale of goods and is in force in 78 different countries. In order to become effective in Brazil, the CISG only has to be promulgated by the President of the Republic.

B. CASES

B.1 Anti-Arbitration Injunction in Connection With an Arbitration Agreement Deemed Null and Void

Energia Sustentável do Brasil S/A et al. v. Sul América Cia Nacional de Seguros S/A et al.[6]

This case arises from two all-risk insurance policies that cover the works of the Jirau hydroelectric power plant in the Amazon rainforest, which is conducted by a joint venture of electric power companies and construction firms: Energia Sustentável do Brasil S/A, Construções e Comércio Camargo Corrêa S/A e Enesa Engenharia S/A. The insurance policies included both a clause foreseeing the exclusive jurisdiction of Brazilian judicial courts to resolve any disputes <u>and</u> an arbitration provision referring to the Insurance and Reinsurance Arbitration Society ("ARIAS") in London.

---

[5] Legislative Decree 538 of October 18, 2012.

[6] São Paulo Court of Appeals, Sixth Chamber of Private Law. Interlocutory Appeal Number 0304979-49.2011.8.26.0000, judged on April 19, 2012.

B. Cases

When a dispute arose, the insurance companies, Sul América Companhia Nacional de Seguros S/A, Mapfre Seguros S/A, Allianz Seguros S/A e Companhia de Seguros Aliança do Brasil S/A, Itaú-Unibanco Seguros Corporativos S/A e Zurich Brasil Seguros S/A, brought arbitration before the ARIAS, while the joint venture filed a lawsuit before the Brazilian courts requesting an anti-arbitration injunction to suspend the arbitral proceedings.

The first level court denied the anti-arbitration injunction and the joint venture appealed to the São Paulo State Court of Appeals.

The joint venture claimed that the insurance policies were a standard "take it or leave it" agreement (*contrato de adesão*) and that, according to the Brazilian Arbitration Act, reference to arbitration is only deemed enforceable in these types of contracts "if the adhering party initiates arbitral proceedings or if it expressly agrees to arbitration by means of an attached written document, or if it signs or initials the corresponding contractual clause, inserted in boldface type."[7]

The Court of Appeals of São Paulo decided that the insurance policies were really standard agreements and that the formalities to enforce the policies' arbitration clauses were not met. The Court of Appeals held that the dispute should be resolved before the Brazilian courts and set an elevated daily fine in case of the parties' noncompliance.

In summary, the decision purports to "curb the Kompetenz-Kompetenz principle" and thus rekindles the debate over anti-suit injunctions in Brazil, an issue that remained dormant after a couple of unfortunate early cases.[8] Yet, from these early cases

---

[7] Article 4(2) of the Brazilian Arbitration Act.

[8] Such as *Companhia Paranaense de Energia Elétrica – COPEL v. UEG Araucária Ltda.* (Third Section of the Public Treasury of Curitiba. Docket 24334/0000. Decision rendered on 3 June 2003) and *AES Uruguaiana Empreendimentos Ltda. v. Companhia Estadual de Energia Elétrica CEEE* (STJ, Second Chamber, REsp

77

until this decision, the trend was to deny anti-suit injunctions. Although this is an isolated precedent, there may be a judicial tendency developing to disregard the "Kompetenz-Kompetenz" principle whenever the invalidity or unenforceability of the arbitration clause may be inferred *prima facie*.

B.2 State Courts Are Competent to Grant Interim Measures before the Commencement of Arbitration

Itarumã Participações S/A v. Participações em Complexos Bioenergéticos S/A - PCBIOS[9]

In a special appeal, the Third Chamber of the Brazilian Superior Court of Justice ("STJ"), Brazil's highest court for non-constitutional matters, confirmed that courts are competent to render interim measures before the commencement of arbitration, and that, after the commencement of arbitration, the arbitrators are competent to uphold or to overturn the interim measures previously rendered by the courts.

In this case, one of the parties to a partnership agreement alleged a breach thereof and requested an interim order from the Rio de Janeiro State Court. The lower court denied the request, holding that it was the arbitrator's province to render such an order. The party appealed, the Rio de Janeiro Court of Appeals upheld the lower court decision and the claimant filed a special appeal. The STJ then ruled that, once the arbitration panel had been constituted and the Terms of Reference had been signed, only the arbitrators could issue an interim order in the case. The only

---

n° 612.439 – RS (2003/0212460-3). Reporter: Minister João Otávio de Noronha. judged on 25 October 2005. STJ, Second Chamber, REsp 606.345/RS, Reporter Justice João Otávio de Noronha, judged on 17 May 2007.)

[9] STJ, 3rd Chamber. Special Appeal Number 1.297.974 - RJ (2011/0240991-9), judged on June 12, 2012.

exception would be in case of urgency, when the arbitrators are not able to issue the order promptly, but even then, the arbitrators could later review the court's decision.

B.3 The Application of the *Jura Novit Curia* Principle to Arbitration

Matlinpatterson Global Opportunities Partners II L. P and Matlinpatterson Global Opportunities Partners (Cayman) II L. P v. VRG Linhas Aéreas S/A[10]

In this lawsuit to set aside an arbitral award, the São Paulo State Court of Appeals acknowledged the application in arbitration of the principle of *jura novit curia*, that is to say, that the judge/arbitrator may decide the case based on a legal argument that was not raised by the parties. In this lawsuit, among several grounds to set aside the arbitral award, the claimant argued that the arbitrators violated the due process of law and the principle of adversary proceeding because they based their judgment (i.e., their *ratio decidendi*) on a legal ground not discussed by the parties during the arbitral proceeding.

The Court of Appeals held, however, that arbitrators are not bound solely by the legal arguments that the parties raised. The arbitration panel is only restricted by the factual allegations— as goes the Roman Law maxim, *"da mihi factum, dabo tibi ius,"* i.e., "give the judges the facts and they shall give you the law."

---

[10] São Paulo Court of Appeals. Second Chamber of Corporate Law. Appeal Number 0214068-16.2010.8.26.0100, judged on October 16, 2012.

B.4 Disputes Deriving from Consumer Relations Are Not Arbitrable

CZ6 Empreendimentos Comerciais Ltda et al. v. Davidson Roberto de Faria Meira Júnior[11]

The Third Chamber of the STJ ruled that arbitration clauses providing for mandatory arbitration in contracts involving consumer relationships are non-enforceable, unless the consumer brings the arbitration or otherwise confirms the commitment to arbitrate once the dispute arises.

The Brazilian Consumer Protection Code provides that mandatory arbitration clauses are null and void in consumer relations.[12] The Brazilian Arbitration Act, which was enacted later, provides that, in standard contracts (*contratos de adesão*), the effectiveness of the arbitration agreement depends on the adhering party taking the initiative to commence arbitration or if the clause is in an attached document or in bold, with a signature or endorsement made especially for this clause.[13] There was a fierce debate as to whether the Brazilian Arbitration Act derogated from the Brazilian Consumer Protection Code as regards standard arbitration clauses in agreement with consumers.

The STJ rendered this relevant, while non-binding, precedent, holding that the Brazilian Consumer Protection Code applies to arbitration clauses in consumer agreements. Accordingly, an arbitration clause cannot bind the consumer, even if it is in bold

---

[11] STJ, 3rd Chamber, Special Appeal Number 1.169.841 - RJ (2009/0239399-0), judged on November 6, 2012.

[12] Article 51(7) of the Brazilian Consumer Protection Code.

[13] Article 4(2) of the Brazilian Arbitration Act.

or subject to a specific signature, unless the consumer decides to commence the arbitration proceeding.

B.5 Awards Set Aside at the Seat of the Arbitration Are Not Enforceable in Brazil

EDF Internacional S/A vs. Endessa Latinoamérica S/A and YPF S/A[14]

The Brazilian Attorney General issued an opinion in *EDF v. Endessa* finding that arbitral awards that are annulled by a court located in the seat of arbitration may not be recognized in Brazil.

According to the Article V(e) of the New York Convention,[15] which Brazil ratified,[16] a country may refuse enforcement of a foreign arbitral award where that award has been set aside or suspended in the country where it was issued.

The possibility of enforcing a foreign arbitral award annulled at the seat is a heated topic of discussion in international arbitration. Notwithstanding the wording of Article V(e) of the New York Convention,), there are precedents in France[17] and the

---

[14] STJ. Special Court. Contested Foreign Judgment number 5782/AR. Legal opinion filed by the Public Prosecutor's Office (Ministério Público Federal) on November 26, 2012.

[15] Article V (1) (e) of the NYC: "1. Recognition and enforcement of the award may be refused, at the request of the party against whom it is invoked, only if that party furnishes to the competent authority where the recognition and enforcement is sought, proof that: (...) (e) The award has not yet become binding on the parties, or has been set aside or suspended by a competent authority of the country in which, or under the law of which, that award was made."

[16] Legislative Decree 4311 of July 23, 2002.

[17] See *Omnium de Traitement et de Valorisation - OTV v. Hilmarton.* France No. 24, Omnium de Traitement et de Valorisation - OTV v. Hilmarton, Cour d'Appel [Court of Appeal], Versailles, 315; 316, 29 June 1995 in Albert Jan van den Berg (ed), *Yearbook Commercial Arbitration* 1996 - Volume XXI, Volume XXI

United States[18] that recognize arbitral awards set aside at the seat. Those decisions were based on Article VII of the New York Convention,[19] that is construed as a "most-favorable-right provision" allowing the party that seeks enforcement to benefit from domestic legislation if it is more favorable than the New York Convention.

In this on-going case, EDF seeks to enforce in Brazil an award against Endessa and YPF that the Argentine courts set aside. EDF argues that since Article V(1)(e) of the New York Convention provides that an annulled decision "may" not be recognized, the Brazilian court has discretion to grant or to deny the *exequatur*. A final decision has not yet been rendered, but the Brazilian Public Prosecutor's office filed a legal opinion strongly rejecting EDF's arguments and concluding that the annulled award shall not be recognized in Brazil. The enforcement proceeding will likely continue to judgment, but it is unknown when a final decision will be rendered.

(Kluwer Law International 1996) pp. 524 - 531 and *PT Putrabali Adyamulia v. Rena Holding*. France No. 42, PT Putrabali Adyamulia (Indonesia) v. Rena Holding, et al., Cour de Cassation [Supreme Court], First Civil Chamber, Not Indicated, 29 June 2007 in Albert Jan van den Berg (ed), *Yearbook Commercial Arbitration* 2007 - Volume XXXII, Volume XXXII (Kluwer Law International 2007) pp. 299 - 302.

[18] *Chromalloy Aeroservices Inc. v. the Arab Republic of Egypt*. US No. 230, Chromalloy Aeroservices Inc. v. The Arab Republic of Egypt, United States District Court, District of Columbia, Civil No. 94-2339 (JLG), 31 July 1996 in Albert Jan van den Berg (ed), *Yearbook Commercial Arbitration* 1997 - Volume XXII, Volume XXII (Kluwer Law International 1997) pp. 1001 - 1012.

[19] Article VII of the NYC: "The provisions of the present Convention shall not affect the validity of multilateral or bilateral agreements concerning the recognition and enforcement of arbitral awards entered into by the Contracting States nor deprive any interested party of any right he may have to avail himself of an arbitral award in the manner and to the extent allowed by the law or the treaties of the country where such award is sought to be relied upon."

C. THE GRANT AND ENFORCEMENT OF INTERIM MEASURES IN INTERNATIONAL ARBITRATION

C.1 Tribunal-Ordered Interim Measures

In Brazil, the arbitration panel may render in principle any interim measure related to the arbitration proceeding, as long as such measure deals with arbitrable issues, i.e., patrimonial rights over which the parties may dispose.[20] Such measures typically include affirmative or restraining orders compelling the practice or the avoidance of certain acts on the pains of a daily fine (*astreintes*).

The party seeking the measure must present compelling evidence of (i) a plausible likelihood of prevailing on the merits of the dispute (*fumus boni iuris*), and (ii) a risk that its rights may be lost or severely affected if the measure is not granted (*periculum in mora*).

Even though the largest Brazilian domestic chambers have not yet contemplated emergency arbitrators or similar arrangements in their rules, this possibility is admissible under Brazilian law as long as the emergency arbitrator procedure may be considered as part of an arbitration as defined by Brazilian law. However, parties may also resort to courts for urgent matters.

---

[20] Article 1 of the Brazilian Arbitration Act: "Persons capable of contracting may settle through arbitration disputes related to patrimonial rights over which they may dispose."

C.2 Court-Ordered Interim Measures

Before the arbitration panel is vested in the office,[21] the parties may seek emergency measures before judicial courts, in light of two principles: (i) the constitutional principle of free access to the courts,[22] according to which there shall always be a court available to protect a right; and (ii) the general principle of law *quando est periculum in mora incompetentia non attenditur*, i.e., when damages are imminent, the parties are not strictly bound to the originally competent forum.

After the institution of the arbitration, in principle, the arbitration panel has exclusive jurisdiction to issue emergency measures, as well as to decide whether to maintain or to quash an interim measure that a court may have issued beforehand.[23] Nevertheless, the arbitration agreement may contemplate that arbitrators shall not be empowered to render interim measures, which may only be issued by courts. In addition, the STJ recently stated in an *obiter dictum* that the courts may render interim measures even after the institution of arbitration in the event that the arbitrators cannot timely consider the matter, as mentioned in Section A.1 above.

---

[21] Article 19 of the Brazilian Arbitration Act: "An arbitral procedure is commenced when the appointment is accepted by the sole arbitrator or by the arbitrators, if several."

[22] Brazilian Constitution, Article 5, item XXXV: "All persons are equal before the law, without any distinction whatsoever, Brazilians and foreigners residing in the country being ensured of inviolability of the right to life, to liberty, to equality, to security and to property, on the following terms: (...) XXXV - the law shall not exclude any injury or threat to a right from the consideration of the Judicial Power."

[23] *See* Section B.2 above: *Itarumã Participações S/A v. Participações em Complexos Bioenergéticos S/A - PCBIOS.* STJ, 3rd Chamber. Special Appeal Number 1.297.974 - RJ (2011/0240991-9), judged on June 12, 2012.

In case an interim order is granted, the party must file the main lawsuit within 30 days, or the interim order will lose its effects.[24] When appropriate, the filing of a request of arbitration is deemed as the filing of a main lawsuit on the matter. The arbitration panel does not have the right to enforce its interim orders, which courts shall enforce.

The necessary time for obtaining an emergency measure from a court depends heavily on the court's perception of the *periculum in mora* involved. In urgent matters, the judge may render *ex parte* injunctions (also called *inaudita altera parte* injunctions), in which case it may be issued within a couple of days. The judge may also decide to notify the party to whom the injunction order is directed and grant them a five-day period to answer.[25] In that case, the judge will only decide the matter after the answer is received or the period expires. Brazilian courts may also intervene to disfavor arbitration proceedings. Brazilian judges have been reluctant to grant injunctions to suspend arbitration proceedings. However, the São Paulo State Court of Appeals recently rendered the decision reported in Section B.1 that revives this debate.

C.3 Enforcement of Interim Measures

In Brazil, the same court that renders the interim measure may directly execute upon it. Arbitrators, on the other hand, do not have imperium powers allowing them to compel enforcement of their decisions.

---

[24] Article 808(1) of the Brazilian Code of Civil Procedure: "The effectiveness of interim measure ceases: I - if the party does not file the main suit within the term specified in Art. 806."

[25] Article 802 of the Brazilian Code of Civil Procedure: "The respondent shall be notified, whatsoever the interim procedure, to answer the request for interim measure, within 5 days, indicating the evidence to be produced."

As regards arbitrations seated in Brazil, if an arbitration panel renders an interim measure in the form of a procedural order and there is no voluntary compliance, the arbitration panel must communicate with the court that may then be able to order performance, per Article 22(4) of the Brazilian Arbitration Act,[26] which allows for direct cooperation between state courts and arbitration panels. However, the Brazilian Arbitration Act is unclear as to how the arbitration panel shall interact with the courts in this case, since there is no legal provision detailing the procedure to follow for the arbitration panel to obtain direct court assistance for the enforcement of procedural orders and there are no relevant judicial precedents on the matter.

The situation is clearer in the framework of the Mercosur, whose member states executed on 1998 the Mercosur Agreement on International Arbitration, providing a mechanism for the enforcement of interim measures rendered by arbitral panels seated in the Mercosur member states. The agreement refers to another regional instrument, the Mercosul Interim Measures Protocol of 1996, and provides for the exchange of requests between the central authorities of each member state and the enforcement of such measures.

Outside the realm of the Mercosur, the situation is undefined, as neither the New York Convention nor the Brazilian regulations have been construed to support the enforcement of interim measures rendered by foreign arbitration panels.

First, it is conceivable that arbitration panels may render interim measures under the form of partial awards, but since such measures are not final decisions, or decisions that finally settle

---

[26] Article 22(4) of the Brazilian Arbitration Act: "With the exception of the provisions of Paragraph 2, if coercive or injunctive orders become necessary, the arbitrators may request them from the State Court originally competent to decide the case."

the dispute, it is probable that interim measures presented as partial awards would not be considered enforceable under the New York Convention in Brazil.

Second, the regulation that allows for the recognition of foreign court decisions in Brazil, STJ Resolution 9 of 2005, refers only to final court decisions (*sentenças*),[27] and does not expressly contemplate interim or provisional measures, or procedural orders. This question is being examined by the commission preparing a new Brazilian civil procedure code that may provide for recognition and enforcement of foreign interim measures.

It is also noteworthy that the STJ may—in urgent cases—render interim measures during the proceeding for the recognition and enforcement of foreign arbitral awards. The STJ recently recognized that the effects of a foreign judgment may be anticipated in an interim measure if the party justifies the requirements of *fumus boni juris* and *periculum in mora*, which were deemed absent in that occasion.

There are no express limits to the Brazilian courts' powers to render interim measures, and scholarly comment and case law, such as in the precedent reported in Section B.2 above, extend such powers to arbitrators. Still, interim measures are conceived under Brazilian law as instrumental decisions aimed at preserving the rights involved in a main lawsuit; they are also provisional[28] and may be revoked at any time.[29] Therefore,

---

[27] Resolution 9 of 2005 of the STJ: "The foreign court decision will not be effective in Brazil without prior approval by the STJ or its President. § 1° The non-judicial proceedings that would qualify, under Brazilian law, as a final court judgment [sentence] are eligible for homologation."

[28] Interim measures are rendered for a limited period of time and their effectiveness is dependent upon the efficacy of the main lawsuit.

[29] Article 807 of the Brazilian Civil Procedure Code provides that the judge can at any time modify or revoke an interim measure.

Brazilian judges and arbitrators are likely to refuse enforcement of interim measures that anticipate the full outcome of the main lawsuit, thereby exceeding their precautionary purpose, in a stance that is generally confirmed by arbitral case law.[30]

---

[30] Ali Yesilirmak, *Provisional Measures in International Commercial Arbitration* (Kluwer Law International 2005), p. 183.

CANADA

Matthew J. Latella[1] and Christina I. Doria[2]

A. LEGISLATION, TRENDS AND TENDENCIES

A.1 Legislation

International arbitration in Canada is primarily a matter of provincial jurisdiction. Each province and territory has enacted legislation adopting the UNCITRAL Model Law, sometimes with slight variations, as the basic law for international arbitration. The federal Parliament has also adopted a commercial arbitration code based on the Model Law, which is applicable when the federal government or one of its agencies is a party to an arbitration agreement, or where a matter involves an area of exclusive federal jurisdiction. In 2011, the Uniform Law Conference of Canada Project appointed a working group to formulate recommendations to update Canada's laws relating to international commercial arbitration in accordance with the 2006 Model Law. It is expected that recommendations to update Canada's international commercial arbitration statutes will be available for adoption by the Conference and enactment by the federal and provincial governments in 2013.

Each Canadian jurisdiction has also, either directly or indirectly, adopted the New York Convention.

---

[1]   Matthew Latella is a Partner in Baker & McKenzie's Toronto office, and the head of the office's International Arbitration Practice Group.

[2]   Christina Doria is an Associate in Baker & McKenzie's Toronto office, and practices in the area of international arbitration as a member of the Firm's Global Dispute Resolution Practice Group.

A.2 Trends and Tendencies

Canada is a jurisdiction that is supportive of international arbitration. In the international field, arbitration has gained momentum and support in Canada. This past year has been marked by increased awareness of international arbitration, the promotion and utilization of arbitration for international commercial matters, and the promotion of Canada as an ideal place to arbitrate international commercial disputes.

In general, Canadian courts apply the Model Law and the general principles of arbitration in favor of holding parties to the bargains they have made by enforcing arbitration agreements and referring parties to arbitration. Where an arbitration agreement exists between parties, and it is arguable the arbitration agreement is valid and covers the dispute, the courts will stay the judicial proceedings in favor of arbitration.

Courts may also be called upon to address the narrow issue of interim relief. Although arbitrators are given broad powers to grant interim relief, courts, consistent with the Model Law, may make interim orders for the detention, preservation and inspection of property, and for injunctions. The granting and enforcement of interim measures in international arbitration is dealt with in further detail in section C of this chapter.

Unlike domestic arbitration awards in Canada, which may be appealed, with leave, on a question of law, international arbitral awards are final and cannot be appealed. The powers of the court are limited to a judicial review of whether the tribunal lacked jurisdiction or exceeded its jurisdiction in making an award, or where there was a lack of proper conduct and procedure during the arbitration, consistent with the New York Convention.

B.   CASES

B.1   *Momentous.ca Corp. v. Canadian American Association of Professional Baseball Ltd.*

In *Momentous.ca Corp. v. Canadian American Association of Professional Baseball Ltd.*,[3] the Supreme Court of Canada considered whether a party waived its right to rely on arbitration and forum selection clauses by filing a statement of defense on the merits in an Ontario Superior Court. The court ruled that there had been no waiver, and stated that "when another forum— an arbitration panel, a tribunal or another court—has the exclusive jurisdiction to deal with the claim, [an Ontario court] will not take jurisdiction, based upon agreement or statute."

The dispute before the court arose from a series of contracts regarding the operation of Rapidz Baseball—a professional baseball team in the Can-Am Baseball League. Pursuant to the League's by-laws, Rapidz Baseball applied for voluntary withdrawal from the League, but the League's Board of Directors rejected the team's application. The team and its related companies sued the League, both in contract and tort. In turn, the League filed a statement of defense on the merits that specifically pleaded a foreign forum selection clause. Subsequently, the League relied on the choice of forum and arbitration clauses in agreements signed by both parties to bring a motion to stay or dismiss the action on the ground that Ontario courts have no jurisdiction.

Notwithstanding the fact that the League had filed a statement of defense on the merits, the Supreme Court held that the forum selection clause precluded the jurisdiction of the Ontario Superior Court. In lending primacy to the forum selection clause,

---

[3]   2012 SCC 9.

the court emphasized that order and fairness are better achieved in this case when parties are held to their bargains. Of note, the Supreme Court specified that a statement of defense that pleads a foreign forum selection clause does not amount to consent that an Ontario court assume jurisdiction so as to preclude consideration on the merits of whether to enforce the clause. As such, in the absence of legislation providing otherwise, the forum agreed to by the parties will not be displaced unless there is "strong cause." Evident from this decision is that the delivery of a statement of defense does not, by itself, constitute "strong cause."

B.2 *Telestat Canada v. Juch-Tech Inc.*

In *Telestat Canada v. Juch-Tech Inc.*,[4] the Ontario Superior Court dealt with whether the recognition and enforcement of a costs award should be refused on the basis that the tribunal acted outside its jurisdiction.

Telestat had obtained an UNCITRAL arbitration award against Juch-Tech Inc. ("JTI") and sought to recognize and enforce the award in Ontario. JTI resisted enforcement on the basis that the costs award dealt with a matter beyond the scope of the arbitration (Article 36(1)(a)(iii) of the Model Law). The arbitration clause specifically provided that "each party shall bear its own expenses (including attorney's fees) and shall pay an equal share of the arbitration fees and the expenses of the arbitrators." However, the tribunal found that, at the hearing and through their legal memoranda, each party had expressly requested the panel to make an award to the prevailing party with respect to fees. As such, the tribunal awarded costs for attorney fees and arbitrator expenses to Telestat, the successful party.

---

[4]   2012 ONSC 2785.

Before the superior court, JTI argued that the tribunal acted outside the scope of its jurisdiction. Telestat argued that JTI had waived its right to split costs equally, pursuant to Article 4 of the Model Law. The court, applying a standard of review of correctness,[5] found that JTI in its pleadings, had requested costs relating to a very specific penalty provision of the contract relating to an early termination charge. It noted that the tribunal found that the early termination charge provision was not payable and instead awarded liquidated damages for breach of contract. The court held that JTI did not waive its right to make an objection on costs relating to the arbitration dispute (breach of contract) based on its pleading and its general conduct. Further, the court noted that there was no specific written agreement to amend the arbitration clause with respect to costs. The court held that "[t]he arbitrators cannot give what the arbitration clause does not permit or provides for otherwise." This case serves as a reminder for counsel to carefully consider the arbitration agreement and any restrictions on the arbitrator's jurisdiction therein. This case has not been appealed.

B.3 *Nearctic Nickel Mines v. Canadian Royalties Inc.*

In *Nearctic Nickel Mines Inc. v. Canadian Royalties Inc.*,[6] the Québec Court of Appeal upheld a decision of the Québec Superior Court to homologate (i.e., confirm) an arbitration award, dismissing arguments that the arbitrator acted outside his jurisdiction by ordering specific performance and by "rewording" the contract.

---

[5] The court of appeal applied the decision of *Mexico v. Cargill* 2011 ONCA 622, which held that the standard of review for arbitral awards is one of "correctness." The *Mexico* case was reported in the *Baker & McKenzie International Arbitration Yearbook 2011-2012*, and leave to appeal to the Supreme Court of Canada has since been refused, see 2012 CanLII 25159 (SCC).

[6] 2012 QCCA 385 (CanLII).

In Québec, a civil law jurisdiction, arbitration is governed by the Code of Civil Procedure, under which an award can only be put into compulsory execution once it has been homologated (Article 946). The grounds for refusing homologation of an arbitral award (Article 946.4) mirror the grounds to refuse recognition and enforcement of an award under the New York Convention (Article V) and the Model Law (Article 36(1)).

The court of appeal in *Nearctic Nickel Mines* dealt with the issue of whether an arbitrator acting under an arbitration agreement has the authority to order injunctive relief or specific performance. Further, the court dealt with an arbitrator's authority to interpret a contract under Québec law.

The contract at issue concerned a joint venture and option arrangement between two mining companies in Northern Québec. There was a dispute as to whether an adequate "Bankable Feasibility Study" had been completed, which was a condition precedent to transfer a further 10% interest in the subject property. After 25 days of hearing, the arbitrator found that the condition precedent had been met and that the claimant was entitled to specific performance of the transfer obligation. Accordingly, the arbitrator's award required the respondent to implement the transfer.

Following a two-week motion hearing, the claimant successfully homologated the award before the superior court. The respondent obtained leave to appeal that decision, to determine whether the arbitrator exceeded his jurisdiction by rendering conclusions of an injunctive nature, and regarding whether the arbitrator "rewrote" the contract and/or ignored certain provisions.

The court of appeal noted that, in Québec, unlike common law jurisdictions in Canada, the remedy of specific performance is not an exceptional remedy. Rather, ordering specific performance of obligations has become the general rule in Québec, while pecuniary damages are the exception.

The court of appeal relied on the *Desputeaux c. Éditions Chouette Inc.*[7] decision of the Supreme Court of Canada, stating that: "the analysis of the powers granted to an arbitrator under an arbitration agreement should also be made through a generous and liberal vision which is more in line with the modern interpretation of conventional arbitration as proposed by the Supreme Court of Canada."

By analogy to international arbitrations, the court noted that, under the Code of Civil Procedure, the adoption of the Model Law specifically allowed for injunctive measures and suggested that, accordingly, domestic arbitrations should not follow different rules. This is an example of how harmonized international arbitration laws (e.g., the Model Law) continue to shape both domestic and international arbitration law in Canada.

On the issue of specific performance, the court held that the arbitrator had jurisdiction to order specific performance, which, in this case, was tantamount to an action to convey title. In any event, the court concluded that the orders made by the arbitrator were not in the nature of an injunction.

With respect to the issue of whether the arbitrator "rewrote" the contract, the court held that "[a]ll arbitrators ... are bound to give meaning to the parties' agreement in accordance with its terms. If need be, they are empowered to determine the true intentions of the parties in order to complete such terms." However, an arbitrator is not without limits, as s/he "cannot pretend to determine the true intentions of the parties while, as a matter of fact, modifying their rights by adding to or removing from the agreement obligations which are the result of the meeting of the

---

[7]   2003 SCC 17.

parties' minds." In the latter case, an arbitrator would be acting in excess of his/her jurisdiction. However, in *Nearctic Mines,* the court found that the arbitrator did not exceed his jurisdiction, but "interpreted the agreement while searching, albeit generously, for the true intentions of the parties," This was held to amount to interpreting, not rewriting, the contract.

C. THE GRANT AND ENFORCEMENT OF INTERIM MEASURES IN INTERNATIONAL ARBITRATION

C.1 Tribunal-Ordered Interim Measures

In Canada, a tribunal has the power to make orders for interim injunctions, the preservation or sale of assets, and, in an appropriate case, to appoint a receiver as part of the powers given to the tribunal by agreement of the parties.

The test that an applicant must satisfy in order for the tribunal to order interim measures will depend on the procedural rules adopted by the tribunal. While the tribunal is bound by the law of the place of the arbitration for the substance of the dispute, the tribunal may craft its own rules for both evidence and procedure in the arbitration, which includes the test for an interim measure. Therefore, the test to be applied will depend on the relevant Rules. By way of example, the 2010 UNCITRAL Rules set out the following test for an interim measure of protection:

Article 26(3) The party requesting an interim measure under paragraphs 2(a) to (c) shall satisfy the arbitral tribunal that:

(a) Harm not adequately reparable by an award of damages is likely to result if the measure is not ordered, and such harm substantially outweighs the harm that is likely to result to the party against whom the measure is directed if the measure is granted; and

(b) There is a reasonable possibility that the requesting party will succeed on the merits of the claim. The determination on this possibility shall not affect the discretion of the arbitral tribunal in making any subsequent determination.

In Canada, the core of the test of whether to grant an interim measure is determined by the applicant's evidence that there is a necessity and urgency to protect its rights which, absent protective measures, could be lost definitively.

Emergency interim measures are also available in Canada. This extends to arbitration rules of local institutions, like the ADR Chambers Arbitration Rules, which provide optional rules for emergency measures of protection from the tribunal, which are available before the commencement of arbitral proceedings.

C.2 Court-Ordered Interim Measures

The courts in Canada have concurrent powers to order interim measures. The various provincial international commercial arbitration Acts provide that a party may seek assistance from the local court if interim measures of protection are required. Under the Model Law, which has been adopted by Canada's provinces, once an arbitration has commenced, a party should first go to the arbitral tribunal to seek interim relief and only thereafter seek relief from the courts. However, where there are third parties involved who are not part of the arbitration, it may be necessary to go to court before going to the tribunal.

In a straightforward case, assuming no scheduling issues that could delay a hearing, it should not take longer than a few weeks from the time court materials are prepared to obtain an interim measure in a Canadian court. In emergency situations, relief can be obtained within a truncated timeline (as soon as a judge can be located following the completion of materials).

Courts in Canada have the power to grant an anti-suit injunction, but will only entertain such an application where a serious injustice will occur because of the failure of a foreign court to decline jurisdiction applying the *forum non conveniens* test.

A provincial court also has the jurisdiction to grant interim measures in aid of foreign arbitration, however, such orders are rare.

C.3   Enforcement of Interim Measures

Although the tribunal has the power to make interim orders or directions, there is no provision for enforcement of such orders or directions. While awards are enforceable under the Model Law or New York Convention, a procedural order or direction is not an "award" under the Model Law. The province of Ontario included a provision in its International Commercial Arbitration Act that stipulates that an order of an arbitral tribunal under Article 17 of the Model Law for an interim measure of protection and the provision of security in connection with it, is subject to the provisions of the Model Law as if it were an award. The result of this modification is that the enforcement provisions of the Model Law gives Ontario courts the power to enforce interim measures granted by an arbitral tribunal as it would an award. It is an open question as to whether the New York Convention applies to interim measures of protection.

A court could theoretically refuse to enforce certain types of interim orders, based on public policy reasons, or simply because it finds that it lacks the jurisdiction to do so under either the Model Law or New York Convention.

With respect to appeals of interim measures, it should be noted that, in Ontario, interlocutory orders are typically excluded from the court's jurisdiction to set aside arbitral awards. The Ontario

Court of Appeal has held that a significant feature of the modern approach limiting access to the courts to review decisions of arbitrators is that there are no appeals from procedural or interlocutory orders.

CHILE

Antonio Ortúzar, Sr.,[1] Rodrigo Díaz de Valdés[2] and
Francisco Grob[3]

A.   LEGISLATION, TRENDS AND TENDENCIES

A.1   Legislative Framework

Arbitration in Chile is primarily governed by the Organic Code
of Courts ("OCC"), the Code of Civil Procedure ("CCP") and
Law 19.971 on International Commercial Arbitration (the "ICA
Law").[4] Chile is also a signatory to the New York Convention,
the Panama Convention and the ICSID Convention.
Additionally, most of the free trade agreements, as well as the
bilateral investment treaties ("BITs"), that Chile has entered into
provide for specific arbitration mechanisms to settle disputes
arising from their application.

---

[1]   Antonio Ortuzar, Sr. is Of Counsel in the Santiago office of Baker & McKenzie
and the chairman of its Dispute Resolution Practice Group. His areas of expertise
include litigation, domestic and international arbitration, antitrust, torts, product
liability, bankruptcy and insolvency. He is a listed arbitrator with the Arbitration
and Mediation Centre of the Santiago Chamber of Commerce.

[2]   Rodrigo Díaz de Valdés is a Partner in the Santiago office of Baker & McKenzie
and a member of the Dispute Resolution and Antitrust Practice Groups. He is
widely experienced in civil, commercial and constitutional litigation as well as in
arbitration. He also serves as arbitrator at the Center of Arbitration and the
Chamber of Commerce of Santiago.

[3]   Francisco Grob Duhalde is an Associate in the Santiago office of Baker &
McKenzie and member of the Dispute Resolution Practice Group as well as the
International Arbitration Group. He focuses his practice domestic and
international litigation and arbitration.

[4]   The ICA Law is entirely based on the UNCITRAL Model Law.

A.2 Enforcement of Foreign Arbitral Awards

For a foreign arbitral award to be recognized and enforced in Chile, it must be subject to an *exequatur* procedure as set forth by Article 246 of the CCP. This procedure is heard by the Supreme Court which, without re-examining the merits of the case, will generally grant the *exequatur,* provided that the arbitral award is "authentic" and "effective" and complies with the requirements set forth in Articles 35 and 36 of the ICA Law, as well as the requirements set forth in the New York Convention (and, when applicable, the Panama Convention).

To this effect, once the foreign arbitral award has been duly legalized by the Chilean consulate abroad and translated into Spanish, it shall be submitted to the Supreme Court along with a petition requesting that the *exequatur* be granted. If the Supreme Court concludes that the above legal requirements have been complied with, it will grant the *exequatur*, ordering the enforcement of the award in Chile.

A.3 Trends and Tendencies

There was no significant legislative change in arbitration law in Chile during 2012.

B. CASES

This year, two cases relating to the application of the ICA Law were reported. The first concerns a complaint appeal (*recurso de queja*) to challenge an arbitral award, and the second relates to an application for an interim measure in the context of an international arbitration. Both cases are discussed below.

B. Cases

B.1 Application for the Complaint Appeal in an International Arbitration

In *Inversiones Santa Florencia S.A. v. Guerrero del Rio* (Ct. App. Santiago, docket No. 4902-2012) one of the parties to an international arbitration agreement filed a complaint appeal against an arbitration award. The Santiago Court of Appeals, however, dismissed the appeal, holding that such a remedy was inconsistent with the ICA Law that only provides for the setting aside recourse set forth in Article 34. Consulting Articles 545, 548 and 549 of the OCC that regulate the "complaint appeal," the court concluded that the complaint could not proceed because the arbitral award could yet be set aside by the recourse contemplated in Article 34 of the ICA Law.

B.2 Application for Interim Measures in an International Arbitration

In *Constructora Hochtief-Tecsa S.A. v. Hidroelectrica La Confluencia S.A.* (19th Civil Court of Santiago) the 19th Civil Court of Santiago granted a prejudicial interim measure in favor of Constructora Hochtief-Tecsa S.A. ("CHT") that enjoined Hidroelectrica La Confluencia S.A ("HLC") from concluding certain legal acts and contracts regarding a specific bank guarantee issued in HLC's favor. In other words, HLC was barred from enforcing the bank guarantee.

In 2007, CHT and HLC agreed that the CHT would construct a hydroelectric power station for HLC. To assure its performance, CHT provided a set of bank guarantees in the form of bonds issued in HLC's favor. HLC was meant to cancel the various bank guarantees as the different stages of the construction process were completed. The agreement also stipulated that any relevant issue in the interpretation or execution of the contract would be resolved by arbitration under the ICC Arbitration Rules.

During the second stage of the constructing process, HLC required CHT to provide new bank guarantees. According to the applicant, HLC threatened that if CHT refused to comply with its demands, HLC would call on all of the bank guarantees, even if they were constituted to assure future stages of the construction process.

For this reason, CHT filed an application with the 19th Civil Court of Santiago requesting that the court prohibit HLC from concluding any legal acts and contracts concerning the bank guarantees—a type of interim measure specifically provided for under Chilean law. CHT argued that its petition fulfilled all of the requirements for a prejudicial interim measure (see point C.1), and that HLC's demands were arbitrary and abusive. CHT also advised the court that it would request that the ICC constitute an arbitral tribunal in accordance with clause 23.4 of the parties' agreement.

The court granted CHT's petition.

C. THE GRANT AND ENFORCEMENT OF INTERIM MEASURES IN INTERNATIONAL ARBITRATION

C.1 Tribunal-Ordered Interim Measures

Pursuant to ICA Law, Article 17, "[u]nless otherwise agreed by the parties, the arbitral tribunal may, at the request of a party, order any party to take such interim measure of protection as the arbitral tribunal may consider necessary in respect of the subject-matter of the dispute. The arbitral tribunal may require any party to provide appropriate security in connection with such measure."

Based on this provision, there is no doubt that an arbitral tribunal seated in Chile[5] is empowered to order interim measures. Article 17, however, does not specify what types of interim measures the tribunal may order, nor does it specify the requirements for granting such measures.[6]

- Given the above gap in the ICA Law, it has been held that *lex fori* shall apply to regulate the application of interim measures. However, it has been suggested that such a solution could hardly be reconciled with the uniformity that the UNCITRAL Model Law—upon which the ICA Law is entirely based—seeks to promote. Therefore, other commentators prefer to deal with this gap through the application of general criteria that the international arbitration practice has developed when granting interim measures. This criteria generally requires the applicant to submit evidence showing a presumption of sufficient legal basis (*fumus boni juris*) and to show that there is a danger that the time lag between adjudication on the merits and the issuance of the final award may cause irreparable damage to the applicant (*periculum in mora*).

- Likewise, it is also stated that arbitral tribunals should be considered empowered to order a party to: (i) maintain or restore the status quo pending determination of the dispute; (ii) take action that would prevent harm, or refrain from taking action that is likely to cause harm; or (iii) provide a means of preserving assets out of which a subsequent award may be enforced.

---

[5] *See* Article 1 of the ICA Law.

[6] These questions are easily answered in domestic arbitrations, because the OCC provides that domestic arbitrators are invested with almost the same jurisdictional powers as courts. Therefore, they can order interim measures provided that they comply with the requirements of the CCP.

It is worth noting that, unlike other arbitral institutions, the International Arbitration Rules of the Santiago Arbitration and Mediation Center of the Santiago Chamber of Commerce, which is the main local arbitral institution in Chile, do not allow for interim measure petitions before commencement of arbitral proceedings (e.g., emergency arbitrators). In such cases, the applicant must apply for interim measure to the correspondent court if interim relief is necessary.

C.2 Court-Ordered Interim Measures

Generally speaking, Chilean courts have concurrent powers to order interim measures once arbitral proceedings have commenced. This is expressly recognized in the ICA Law, Article 9 providing that, "[i]t is not incompatible with an arbitration agreement for a party to request, before or during arbitral proceedings, from a court an interim measure of protection and for a court to grant such measure."

Notably, this provision applies whether the tribunal is located within or outside of Chile.[7] Thus, courts can issue an interim measure in aid of a foreign arbitration as well.

Depending on a various number of factors, courts in Chile generally take between one to four weeks to rule on an application for interim measures.

Interim measures are mainly regulated in the CCP.[8] Even though Chilean law regulates specific types of interim measures, that list is not exhaustive, and Article 298 of the CCP enables a tribunal to issue interim measures not specifically enumerated under the

---

[7]   *See* Article 1 of the ICA Law.

[8]   *See* CCP, Art. 290 to 302.

statute, provided that they meet the general requirements established for granting such relief.

Pursuant to Chilean law, the general requirements to obtain an interim measure are the following: (i) party's request; (ii) risk of a frustrated award due to the delay of the final decision and; (iii) submission of evidence that make plausible the right invoked at trial.

Nevertheless, if the interim measure is requested before the proceedings begin, it is necessary, in addition to the requirements listed in the previous paragraph to: (i) submit a guarantee to answer for the potential damages that such a measure may cause the defendant, and (ii) the petitioner shall also set out the action that he or she will later file. According to Chilean law, the proceedings are deemed to start when the defendant is served with the lawsuit.

It should be noted that if necessary, such measures may be enforced even before the defendant has been notified. In such cases, however, the petitioner must generally file its lawsuit within five days, as counted from the notice of the measure, which must occur no later than five days after the measure is granted. Otherwise, the measure will cease to be in effect and the petitioner will be liable for the defendant's damages caused as a consequence of the intended measure. Upon the petitioner's request, however, the court is authorized to grant additional time to serve the defendant notice of the interim measure.

C.3   Enforcement of Interim Measures

Arbitral awards and court judgments in Chile are enforced in accordance with the "incidental procedure" (*procedimiento incidental*) or the "executive procedure" (*procedimiento ejecutivo*) regulated in the CCP.[9] Interim measures, however, are regulated differently. Generally, interim measures are enforced simply by requesting that the court issue a constraint measure in case of non-compliance.[10]

Chilean courts typically enforce any interim measure that an arbitral tribunal sitting in Chile has ordered, provided that the general or specific requirements of the issued interim measure are met (see point C.1).

The situation is different, however, when it comes to arbitral tribunals sitting in a foreign jurisdiction. Indeed, the Chilean Supreme Court has refused to grant the *exequatur* to interim measures ordered by foreign arbitral tribunals.[11] In doing so, the Supreme Court has argued that relevant regulations that provide for the recognition of foreign judgments or arbitral awards do not apply to interim measures that foreign courts or arbitrators issue, but solely to the so-called final judgments or awards (*sentencias o laudos definitivos*) or interlocutory judgments (*interlocutorias*) as defined under Chilean law.[12] The Supreme Court's position is that enforcing such measures could result in prior judgment of the merits of the arbitration.

This decision, however, does not preclude the ability to obtain and enforce an interim measure in Chile when arbitrating abroad. On the contrary, it is entirely possible provided that the interested party requests the issuance of the interim measure from the appropriate Chilean court if the measure is intended to be enforced within Chile. To date, there have been at least three

---

[9] *See* CCP, Articles 434 and following.

[10] *See* CCP, Article 635.

[11] *Western Technology Services International Inc. v. Cauchos Industriales S.A.* (Supreme Court. 2010).

[12] *See* CCP Art. 158.

cases in which the Chilean courts have granted interim measures upon the request of an interested party involved in an arbitration proceeding abroad.[13]

---

[13] *See* the case reported in B.2. above and the decisions of the 28th Civil Court of Santiago, Docket No.: C-5243-2005 (May 26, 2005), and 26th Civil Court of Santiago, Docket No.: C-24011-2009 (August 24, 2009).

CHINA

James Kwan,[1] Peng Shen[2] and Sarah Zhu[3]

A.   LEGISLATION, TRENDS AND TENDENCIES

A.1   Revision of the CIETAC Arbitration Rules

CIETAC's recent revision of its 2005 Arbitration Rules ("2005 Rules") came into force on 1 May 2012 ("2012 Rules").

The 2012 Rules bring CIETAC procedures closer to international best practice. The new rules aim to address the increasing complexity of contemporary arbitration proceedings, to provide greater autonomy to parties, and to codify and clarify CIETAC's existing practice. The key amendments are discussed below.

---

[1]   James Kwan is a Partner in the Dispute Resolution Group of Baker & McKenzie in Hong Kong, where he leads the arbitration practice. He specializes in infrastructure, engineering, and energy disputes and has a range of international experience, having represented clients in arbitrations in Hong Kong, Asia, the Middle East, and Europe under the major institutional rules. He is recognized in legal directories as "best known for his tremendous skill in energy, infrastructure and construction disputes" (Chambers Global 2011), "'extremely good, quality lawyer,' 'high profile,' and 'a very fine practitioner'" (Who's Who Legal UAE 2008), and "singled out for his expertise in arbitration," "genuine arbitration specialist . . . he has a fine reputation" (Asia Pacific Legal 500 2012 edition).

[2]   Shen Peng is a Consultant in the Dispute Resolution Group of Baker & McKenzie in Beijing. He represents international and domestic clients in domestic and international disputes in China. Prior to working in private practice, Shen Peng was a judge of the Beijing People's Court.

[3]   Sarah Zhu is an International Associate in the Dispute Resolution Group of Baker & McKenzie in Shanghai. Her practice focuses on arbitration and litigation for clients in the automobile, pharmaceutical and insurance sectors.

A.1.1 Interim measures may be granted by the arbitral tribunal in certain circumstances[4]

In China, arbitrators have no power to grant any interim measures to preserve property and evidence. Such power rests with the People's Courts.

Under the PRC Arbitration Law and the PRC Civil Procedure Law, the power to grant conservatory measures (including orders for the preservation of property or the protection of evidence) is reserved for the competent Chinese court. However, where a procedural law other than PRC law applies in a CIETAC arbitration (for example, where the parties agree to a seat outside Mainland China), the 2012 Rules expressly provide that the arbitral tribunal has the power to grant interim measures—in the form of a procedural order or an interlocutory award—in accordance with the applicable law. In such circumstances, the scope of "interim measures" will depend on the types of interim measures available under the law of the seat.

A.1.2 Expert witnesses required to give oral evidence if called[5]

Under the 2005 Rules, expert witnesses can decide whether to attend a hearing in arbitral proceedings in order to give oral evidence. This limits the opportunity to cross-examine experts on their reports. The 2012 Rules provide that it is now mandatory for experts to give oral evidence if called to do so by the tribunal. However, this requirement is limited to experts and does not extend to factual witnesses.

---

4   Article 21(2) of the CIETAC Arbitration Rules.

5   *Id.* at Article 42(3).

A.1.3 Consolidation of related arbitration proceedings[6]

The 2012 Rules provide a mechanism for parallel proceedings to be consolidated into a single arbitration (for example, arbitrations involving multiple parties under a suite of related contracts). In determining whether a consolidation application is allowed, CIETAC has wide discretion to take into consideration "any factors it considers relevant." A non-exhaustive list of factors includes: (i) whether all of the claims are made under the same arbitration agreement; (ii) whether the arbitrations are between the same parties; and (iii) whether one or more arbitrators have been nominated or appointed in the arbitrations.

A.1.4 Seat of arbitration[7]

Under the 2005 Rules, where parties have not agreed on the seat of arbitration it is deemed to be the city where CIETAC (or any of its sub-commissions) is located. The 2012 Rules provide that CIETAC can determine the seat of arbitration to be a place other than "the domicile of CIETAC or its sub-commission," taking into account the circumstances of the case. This provision, for the first time, allows the seat to be a city outside Mainland China, although only where the dispute is "foreign-related." A dispute may be "foreign-related" where: (i) at least one of the parties is "foreign"; (ii) the subject matter of the contract is or will be wholly or partly outside Mainland China; or (iii) there are other legally relevant facts "as to occurrence, modification or termination of civil rights and obligations" which occurred outside Mainland China. This is a significant change, at least on paper, given that the seat determines both the governing law of the arbitration and the courts that retain supervisory jurisdiction over the proceedings. Users of CIETAC arbitration will watch

---

6   *Id.* at Article 17.

7   *Id.* at Article 34(2).

with interest to see whether —and how—these rules are invoked in practice.

A.1.5 Use of other arbitration rules in CIETAC-administered arbitrations[8]

Under the 2012 Rules, CIETAC will administer proceedings commenced under the rules of other arbitral institutions, as well as *ad hoc* arbitrations. This conflicts with rules of other arbitration institutions such as the ICC, which explicitly provides that only the ICC Court is authorized to administer ICC arbitration proceedings. Therefore, despite this provision, it is advisable to avoid drafting arbitration clauses that purport to permit one arbitral institution to administer proceedings brought under the rules of another institution. In addition to the obvious uncertainty it may bring to the conduct of the proceedings, it may also expose the award to challenge at the setting aside and enforcement stages.

A.1.6 Default language no longer Chinese[9]

Chinese is no longer the default language of the arbitration if parties have not expressly agreed on language. The 2012 Rules allow CIETAC to choose "any other language . . . having regard to the circumstances of the case." This is useful in cases where the majority of relevant documents are not in Chinese.

A.1.7 Administration by CIETAC Beijing where the clause is ambiguous[10]

If a clause does not validly specify administration by CIETAC Beijing or a different CIETAC sub-commission, CIETAC

---

8 *Id.* at Article 4(3).

9 *Id.* at Article 71(1).

10 *Id.* at Article 2(6).

Beijing will administer the arbitration. Previously, in such circumstances, the party that filed the arbitration was entitled to propose CIETAC Beijing or a sub-commission to administer the arbitration. The other party could agree or disagree, a system that often resulted in unnecessary delay.

A.1.8 Multi-party appointment of arbitrators[11]

Where there are multiple parties on either the claimant side or the respondent side, if the multi-party side fails to jointly nominate an arbitrator, CIETAC will now appoint all members of the tribunal and designate the presiding arbitrator. Previously, CIETAC would appoint only the arbitrator for the side that failed to do so. This brings CIETAC into line with other institutions, including the ICC and SIAC. The aim is to avoid a situation where one side has been able to choose its own arbitrator, whilst the other side has had its arbitrator imposed on it by CIETAC, and the respondent subsequently relies on this to bring a challenge based on unfair treatment.

A.1.9 Mediation in CIETAC arbitrations[12]

With the parties' agreement, CIETAC can now conduct mediation during the arbitration process if the parties do not wish to involve the tribunal. This gives parties maximum flexibility to adopt a mediation process with which they are comfortable, with a view to achieving a mutually agreeable settlement wherever possible. However, the 2012 Rules provide no information on who conducts the mediation, i.e., the administrative staff of CIETAC or professional mediators engaged externally by CIETAC, so it remains to be seen how this will operate in practice.

---

[11] *Id.* at Article 27(3).

[12] *Id.* at Article 45.

A.1.10 New criteria for selection of arbitrators[13]

The 2012 Rules allows the Chairman of CIETAC to consider the nationalities of the parties when appointing an arbitrator in the absence of party agreement. The 2012 Rules do not, however, require that the presiding or sole arbitrator be of a nationality other than the nationality of the parties. Parties should therefore make express provision in their arbitration clauses if they want the arbitrators to be of a different nationality than the parties.

A.2 Disputes among CIETAC Branches

A.2.1 Disputes between CIETAC Beijing and CIETAC Shanghai

On 1 August 2012, CIETAC issued the "China International Economic and Trade Arbitration Commission Announcement on the Administration of Cases Agreed to Be Arbitrated by CIETAC Shanghai Sub-Commission and CIETAC South China Sub-Commission" ("Announcement").

The Announcement stated that as of 1 August 2012, CIETAC's authorization to CIETAC South China Sub-Commission ("CIETAC Shenzhen") and CIETAC Shanghai Sub-Commission ("CIETAC Shanghai") for accepting and administering arbitration cases would be suspended.

The Announcement further provides that to safeguard parties' arbitration rights, parties who had agreed to arbitrate their disputes by CIETAC Shanghai or CIETAC Shenzhen had to seek prior authorization from CIETAC's headquarters in Beijing ("CIETAC Beijing"). Upon acceptance of the case, CIETAC Beijing would administer the case and select Shanghai or Shenzhen for those cases previously agreed to be arbitrated by

---

[13]   *Id.* at Article 28.

CIETAC Shanghai or CIETAC Shenzhen respectively, unless the parties agree otherwise.

CIETAC Shenzhen and CIETAC Shanghai have refused to adopt the 2012 Rules. CIETAC Shanghai published its own arbitration rules ("Shanghai Rules") based on the 2005 Rules and announced on 4 August 2012 that it was an independent arbitration commission named "CIETAC Shanghai Commission." CIETAC Shenzhen has also decided to retain the 2005 Rules.[14]

On 4 August 2012, CIETAC Shanghai and CIETAC Shenzhen jointly issued an announcement stating that CIETAC Beijing's 1 August Announcement was not binding and would not impact their operations or any entities who wished to proceed to arbitrate before them.

Other sub-commissions include CIETAC Southwest Sub-Commission ("CIETAC Chongqing") and CIETAC Tianjin Sub-Commission ("CIETAC Tianjin"). On 9 September 2011, CIETAC announced the change of name of CIETAC Tianjin. This clarified the uncertainty over whether CIETAC Tianjin was an arbitration center or a sub-commission. Such announcement stated that "CIETAC Tianjin International Economic and Financial Arbitration Center has launched its new name 'China International Economic and Trade Arbitration Commission Tianjin Sub-Commission,' to be used concurrently with the original name."

In response to direct enquiries, CIETAC Tianjin and CIETAC Chongqing have confirmed that they will adopt the new 2012 Rules when administering cases.

The conflict between CIETAC's central body and its Shanghai and Shenzhen sub-commissions has important implications for

---

[14] *See* section A.2.2 below for further development in respect of CIETAC Shenzhen.

future disputes and the enforcement of arbitral awards rendered from clauses that specify the CIETAC Shanghai and Shenzhen Sub-Commissions.

A.3 South China International Economic and Trade Arbitration Commission Arbitration Rules

The CIETAC South China Sub-Commission (i.e., CIETAC Shenzhen) was renamed the South China International Economic and Trade Arbitration Commission from 22 October 2012. It is concurrently using the name of "Shenzhen Court of International Arbitration" (i.e., the SCIA).

The South China International Economic and Trade Arbitration Commission Arbitration Rules were recently approved by the Council of Shenzhen Court of International Arbitration ("SCIA"). The new Arbitration Rules apply to cases accepted by SCIA from 1 December 2012. The Rules provide for arbitration by the South China International Economic and Trade Arbitration Commission, the Shenzhen Court of International Arbitration, the China International Economic and Trade Arbitration Commission South China Sub-commission or the China International Economic and Trade Arbitration Commission Shenzhen Sub-commission, or where the name of the arbitration institution in the arbitration agreement can be inferred as the SCIA.

A.4 Amendments to PRC Civil Procedure Law

On 31 August 2012, the Standing Committee of the National People's Congress passed an amendment to the Civil Procedure Law following a third deliberation of the bill. The amendments took effect from 1 January 2013, and aim to further streamline the way in which civil disputes are handled.

A.4.1 Pre-filing evidence preservation[15]

A party will be able to seek an order to preserve evidence within 30 days before filing the litigation or arbitration application.

A.4.2 Expanded interim injunctive mechanism[16]

Injunctive relief will be available for all types of civil cases. A party will be entitled to obtain a court order requesting the opposing party to cease or undertake certain acts on the basis that the party's interest is likely to be damaged by the other party, or that the other party's acts may cause difficulties in enforcing the judgment.

A.4.3 Updated evidence rules[17]

Electronic evidence is now admissible in civil litigation. Previously, court practice varied in different regions. Some courts were reluctant to admit electronic evidence, such as emails and instant messages. Now the law is clear—courts are required to admit electronic evidence in determining cases.

In addition, the amendment emphasizes that a party has an obligation to produce evidence upon the court's request. Otherwise, the party may face an oral reprimand by the judge, an adverse inference being drawn, a monetary fine or an order to bear the cost due to delay.

A.4.4 Retrial right granted to the third party[18]

A non-party to proceedings whose interests are prejudiced will be able to pursue certain remedies. A third party will now be able

---

[15] Article 81 of PRC Civil Procedure Law.

[16] *Id.* at Article 100.

[17] *Id.* at Chapter 6.

[18] *Id.* at Article 56.

to initiate a separate action to challenge a court's judgment within six months of notice that its rights have been prejudiced.

A.4.5 Means for Advanced Service[19]

Courts are now permitted to serve documents (except judgments, orders and mediation letters) to parties by way of facsimile, email or other electronic means, provided that the parties agree to such service.

A.4.6 Public Interest Actions[20]

The amendment provides that "the institutions and relevant groups stipulated by law" are permitted to initiate action in cases where the social public interest is injured, such as in environmental pollution and consumer rights matters.

A.4.7 Malicious Actions[21]

The amendment provides that the court should dismiss an action where it finds that the parties maliciously colluded to achieve an illegal purpose and endangered the rights and interests of others. Sanctions for such parties include fines, imprisonment and criminal liabilities.

B. CASES

There are limited sources of reported case law in China, partly because the legal system does not rely on precedent to the same extent as common law jurisdictions.

---

[19] *Id.* at Section 2, Chapter 7.

[20] *Id.* at Article 55.

[21] *Id.* at Articles 112 and 113.

From this limited pool of reported cases, there were no significant cases during the past year.

C. THE GRANT AND ENFORCEMENT OF INTERIM MEASURES IN INTERNATIONAL ARBITRATION

The new Amendment of PRC Civil Procedure Law ("2012 Amendment") will impact the availability and enforcement of interim measures in arbitration. The 2012 Amendments came into effect on 1 January 2013.

C.1 Tribunal-Ordered Interim Measures

A party may apply for preservation of property if an award will become impossible or difficult to implement due to an act of the other party or another cause.

Under circumstances where evidence may be lost or destroyed, or difficult to obtain afterwards, a party may apply for preservation of evidence.

A party seeking preservation of property or evidence must apply to the arbitration commission administering the dispute (e.g., CIETAC). The arbitration commission then forwards the party's application to a People's Court in accordance with the relevant provisions of the Civil Procedure Law and the Arbitration Law.[22]

PRC Arbitration Law and Civil Procedure Law do not address the issue of whether the parties can make an *ex parte* application for interim measures. In practice, it is generally understood and accepted that a party can file its application for interim measures directly with the arbitration commission without notifying the other side.

---

[22] *Id.* at Article 272; *see also* Articles 28, 46 and 68 of the Arbitration Law.

The types of interim measures available include sealing (using the court's official seal to seize an asset, for example, ordering the *in situ* seizure of a bulky asset that cannot be transported easily); distraining (arrangement by which the court transports the asset under preservation to another location); and freezing (subjecting the respondent's bank accounts to preservation). PRC Arbitration Law does not require the applicant to show there is a reasonable possibility that the requesting party will succeed on the merits of the claim.

As explained in Section A.1.1. above, under the 2012 CIETAC Arbitration Rules, the arbitral tribunal may, in certain circumstances, order any interim measure it deems necessary or proper in accordance with the applicable law, and may require the requesting party to provide appropriate security in connection with the measure. The order of an interim measure by the arbitral tribunal may take the form of a procedural order or an interlocutory award.

C.2 Court-Ordered Interim Measures

Unless the place of arbitration is outside Mainland China, there is no issue of the courts and tribunals having concurrent powers. As discussed previously, a party seeking preservation of property or evidence must make an application to the arbitration commission administering the dispute, which in turn forwards the application to a People's Court.

PRC courts require the applicant to deposit a sum equivalent to the value of the property or evidence to be preserved, so that if the application turns out to be wrong, the deposit may be used to compensate the respondent for its losses. Once the deposit is paid, the court would normally proceed with the relevant application.

An anti-suit injunction is not available. It should be noted that if a Chinese court has decided to exercise jurisdiction on a matter, and yet the same matter is entertained by a foreign court or a foreign arbitration tribunal, then any judgment or award resulting from that foreign litigation/arbitration is unlikely to be recognized and enforced in China.

A Chinese court cannot grant an order for interim measures in aid of a foreign arbitration.

C.2.1 Interim measures before commencement of arbitration

Prior to the 2012 Amendment, the courts were not allowed to issue an order for interim measures before the commencement of an arbitration. Pursuant to Article 101 of the 2012 Amendment, a party in urgent need of asset preservation may now apply directly to a competent court for asset preservation measures before the initiation of arbitration. The remedies available are the same as those available during the course of arbitration.

This change improves the process by which asset preservation had to be sought under the former Civil Procedure Law. Under the former law, a party had to wait until after the arbitration had commenced before submitting an application for preservation measures to the arbitration commission, which would then forward the application to the court for an order.

In practice, this two-step "relay" process is unnecessarily complex and can even frustrate the applicant's purpose. This is because, if the process is not carefully managed, there can be a considerable time gap between the filing of the application to the arbitration commission and the passing of the application for asset preservation to the competent court—during which time the party against whom the order is sought often becomes alerted and is able to hide the assets.

The changes brought about by Article 101 of the 2012 Amendment will greatly increase the speed by which an order for preservation of asset can be obtained. The court will need to make an order within 48 hours of acceptance of an application for relief and preservation measures will be implemented immediately. The applicant will need to provide security to the court at the time of the application, and this is consistent with the practice in domestic litigation.

C.3   Enforcement of Interim Measures

Based on the 2012 Amendment, there is no limitation on the scope of interim measures that the courts can enforce. All types of interim measures are enforceable.

Traditionally, the docketing division of the court is generally in charge of enforcing all effective interim orders and awards. Recently, courts in developed areas have started to set up a special department called a Juridical Enforcement Office to deal with all enforcement matters, including enforcement of interim measures.

It should be noted that a Chinese court will not enforce an interim measures award/order made by an arbitral tribunal outside of Mainland China under the current legal regime.

COLOMBIA

Claudia Benavides[1]

A.   LEGISLATION, TRENDS AND TENDENCIES

A.1   Overview on the Arbitral Legal Framework

Arbitration is a lawful practice for dispute resolution in Colombia. Private individuals may be vested by the parties to a controversy with the power to act as arbitrators according to the Colombian Political Constitution[2] and are entitled to exercise jurisdictional functions according to the Statutory Law on the Administration of Justice.[3]

A.1.1   Arbitration legislation before 2012

Prior to 2012, Colombian arbitration regulations differentiated between domestic and international arbitration.[4] The five articles

---

[1]   Claudia Benavides heads the Litigation and Arbitration practice in the Bogotá office of Baker & McKenzie. She has extensive experience in transnational litigation, acting for national and foreign corporations in disputes involving complex contractual and non-contractual claims. Claudia has represented clients before courts and arbitral tribunals in different types of commercial disputes, as well as in controversies involving distributorship agreements, unfair competition, insurance and real estate, amongst others. She is currently a listed, authorized secretary for the arbitral tribunals of the Center of Arbitration of the Chamber of Commerce of Bogotá.

[2]   Article 116 of the Colombian Political Constitution: "Private individuals may be temporally vested with the function of administering justice as members of the jury in criminal cases, mediators or arbitrators empowered by the parties to render decisions according to the law or in equity, in accordance with the terms provided by the law."

[3]   Law 270 of 1996 as amended by Law 1285 of 2009.

[4]   Decree 1818 of 1998 compiled provisions that ruled domestic and international arbitration separately. Law 315 of 1996 specifically governed international arbitration.

contained in Law 315 of 1996 that used to govern international arbitration, although partially based on the UNCITRAL Model Law, were very sparse. Colombian legislation was silent on several crucial issues within the specific context of international arbitration such as, the possibility, nature and extent of the support of local courts with respect to interim measures and actions to set aside awards. Law 315 of 1996 did not specify the procedure to be followed for the recognition and enforcement of awards, or the specifics of an arbitral proceeding.

As a result, arbitrators had to rely on domestic procedural rules to fill in the gaps. International arbitration was thus, mainly regulated through the case law of the Colombian Supreme Court of Justice ("SCJ") and the Constitutional Court ("CC"). This created uncertainty about the final and binding effects of arbitral awards.

Attempts were made to amend the arbitration legislation to set clear arbitration dispute resolution rules in consideration of this legal uncertainty and the friendly arbitration environment fostered in Colombia. Finally, on July 12, 2012, a new unified Arbitration Statute (the "Statute") was adopted through Law 1563 of 2012.

A.1.2 The genesis of the new statute on domestic and international arbitration

Two sub-committees of arbitration experts, one for domestic and the other for international arbitration, were created to draft the new Statute. The Statute had three purposes: to improve efficiency in the judicial system, attract investment through the arbitration regime, and make Colombia an attractive seat for international arbitration.

The drafters took into account applicable CC arbitration case law and adopted the 2006 UNCITRAL Model Law for international arbitration. The legislator conducted a comparative research on foreign international arbitration legislations[5] in order to incorporate arbitration-friendly provisions.

The Statute was designed to maintain a dualist regime. It governs any arbitration proceeding, domestic or international. With this, Colombia positioned itself as an attractive seat for international arbitration.

After an intense job of socialization by the Colombian Government and four debates, the bill was approved by Congress on June 14, 2012, approved by the President on July 12, 2012 and inserted into the Official Journal on the same date.

A.1.3 General arbitration legal framework under the new Statute

The Statute sets forth different provisions for domestic and international arbitration. The domestic arbitration rules are close to the Colombian procedural regime, while the international arbitration rules are based on the UNCITRAL Model Law. This means that international arbitration rules rest on autonomy of the parties and limit the local courts' power to intervene in international arbitration matters.

There is confidence in the new regime for two reasons: (i) the SCJ took a friendly stance on recognition and enforcement of arbitral awards in its July 27, 2011 ruling;[6] (ii) the adoption of the 2006 UNCITRAL Model Law encourages Colombian courts to interpret the Statute's section on international arbitration, taking into account its international character as well as the necessity to promote uniformity in its application.

---

[5] Informe de Ponencia para Primer Debate del Proyecto de Ley 176 de 2011 Cámara - 018 de 2011 Senado.

[6] This ruling follows the provisions of the New York Convention.

Parties may agree to *ad hoc* or institutional arbitration.[7] The arbitral decision may be legal or *ex aequo et bono*.[8] Arbitral proceedings follow basic principles such as *Kompetenz-Kompetenz*[9] and autonomy of the agreement. The arbitration clause and the submission agreement are accepted.[10] The tribunal has the power to adopt interim measures.[11] The action to set aside an award is an available recourse against it.[12]

Private individuals and public entities are free to enter into domestic and international arbitration agreements to resolve their disputes, with the exception of certain restrictions depending on the arbitration subject matter. Interestingly, under the Statute, state entities that are parties to an international arbitration agreement may not resort to their domestic law to challenge their capacity to be a party to an arbitral proceeding or the arbitrability of a certain controversy.[13]

A.1.4 Arbitration practice in Colombia

Colombia has a strong arbitral tradition. Both private and public sectors use it as a mechanism to settle their disputes. Before the reform, Colombia was already highly ranked within Latin American countries in terms of strength of laws governing international arbitration.[14] Parties more frequently turn to the use

---

[7] Articles 53 to 57 and 63 of Law 1563 of 2012.

[8] *See id.* at Articles 1 and 101.

[9] *See id.* at Articles 20 and 79.

[10] *Id.* at Articles 3,4,5 and 69.

[11] *See id.* at Articles 32 and 80 to 90.

[12] *See id.* at Articles 40 to 43 and 107 to 110.

[13] *Id.* at Article 62.

[14] *See* World Bank Group (2012), *Investing across borders: indicators of Foreign Direct Investment Regulation*, available at: http://iab.worldbank.org/Data/ Explore%20Economies/Colombia#/Arbitrating-disputes.

of institutional arbitration whereas *ad hoc* arbitration has been almost nonexistent.

A.2 International Arbitration Specifics

The previous, undefined regime was replaced with a detailed, organized and modern system. According to Article 62 of the new Statute, arbitration is considered to be international when:

(a) The parties to an arbitration agreement are, at the time of the conclusion of that agreement, domiciled in different states, or

(b) The place where a substantial part of the obligations are to be performed, or the place with the closest connection to the dispute subject matter, is situated outside the State where the parties are domiciled, or

(c) The dispute to be decided in arbitration affects the interests of international trade.

Following CC case law, the Statute does not allow a dispute to be characterized as international solely based on the parties' will.

The Statute establishes principles that reinforce the ease of the process and judicial assistance. Its four main innovations include: (1) the local court assistance in arbitral proceedings, (2) the ability of the tribunal to issue interim measures, (3) the regulation of the action to set aside an award, and (4) the new procedure for enforcement and recognition of awards. With these features, parties who select Colombia as their seat of arbitration are ensured to find an arbitration regime that emphasizes flexibility and party autonomy, strengthens legal certainty, aims for faster and easier arbitral proceedings, and seeks efficacy through the assistance of local courts.

A.2.1 Assistance by local courts to arbitral tribunals

The new Statute regulates the assistance local courts provide to arbitral proceedings. Civil or administrative judges are to assist arbitral tribunals in: (i) the appointment of arbitrators (Articles 73 and 74), the procedure to challenge the confirmation of the tribunal (Article 76) and termination of the arbitrator's assignment (Article 77); (ii) the ordering of interim measures (Articles 71 and 88); (iii) the gathering of evidence (Article 100); and (iv) the enforcement of the award (Article 116). In addition, if a state entity is a party to the dispute, the SCJ and the State Council ("SC"), will assist in the recognition of the award (Article 111) and the annulment proceeding (Article 109).

A.2.2 Express entitlement for arbitral tribunal to order interim measures

The new Statute allows local courts to order and execute interim measures as explained further in Section C below.

A.2.3 Action to set aside an award

The sole recourse allowed against an arbitral award issued by an international arbitration tribunal seated in Colombia is an action to set aside the award.[15] The action to set aside an award shall not be based on the merits of the award and a ruling of its annulment may not be appealed. [16] The grounds to file an action to set aside an award are essentially the same as those contained in the 2006 UNCITRAL Model Law and thus, an arbitral award may be set aside if the applicant proves that: (i) a party to the arbitration agreement was under some incapacity; or the arbitration agreement is not valid under the law the parties

---

[15]   Article 107 of Law 1563 of 2012.

[16]   *Id.* at Articles 108(1) and 109(5).

subjected it or under the law of Colombia; or (ii) the applicant was not given proper notice of the arbitrator's appointment or of the arbitral proceedings, or was otherwise unable to present his case; or (iii) the award deals with a dispute not contemplated by or not falling within the terms of the submission to arbitration, or contains decisions on matters beyond the scope of the submission to arbitration, provided that, if the decisions on matters submitted to arbitration can be separated from those not so submitted, only that part of the award which contains decisions on matters not submitted to arbitration may be set aside; or (iv) the composition of the arbitral tribunal or the arbitral procedure was not in accordance with the agreement of the parties, unless such agreement was in conflict with a provision of the Statute from which the parties cannot derogate, or, failing such agreement, was not in accordance with the Statute. According to the new Statute an award may also not be set aside if the court finds that: (i) the subject-matter of the dispute cannot be settled by arbitration under the law of Colombia; or (ii) the award is in conflict with the Colombia's international public policy.[17]

The recourse must be brought to the competent judicial authority within a month following service of the award.[18] Nevertheless, a party may waive the action to set aside an award as long as both parties to the arbitration agreement are not domiciled or do not reside in Colombia.[19]

The Statute provides that an action to set aside an award issued by an international arbitral tribunal seated in Colombia is the only recourse against such award. The Statute uses the wording

---

[17]   *Id.* at Article 108(2).

[18]   *Id.* at Article 109(1).

[19]   *Id.* at Article 107.

"*la anulación como único recurso judicial contra un laudo arbitral*" as a means to demonstrate an underlying interest in preventing a party from questioning a decision taken by an arbitral tribunal by recurring to the constitutional action for the protection of fundamental rights (*acción de tutela*). Furthermore, Law 1563 of 2012 expressly establishes that no recourse or action[20] may be filed against the ruling deciding an action to set aside an award.

A.2.4 Recognition and enforcement of arbitral awards

Colombia is a party to the New York Convention, which the Statute closely follows as well as the UNCITRAL Model Law regarding the recognition of awards. It maintains the difference between arbitral awards granted by tribunals seated within and outside Colombian territory. Any award granted in Colombian territory is treated as a national award[21] and is enforceable without a recognition procedure. Recognition is required prior to the enforcement of awards granted outside Colombia. However, the new Statute simplified the procedure. *Exequatur,* as regulated by the Colombian Code of Civil Procedure, is now irrelevant to international arbitration. Parties need only submit an application to the SCJ or SC[22] with the original or copy of the award for its recognition. Not only is the procedure simpler, but it is also much faster. Article 115 requires the court to decide whether or not to recognize the award within 30 working days after the reception of the complete application, including the time given to the other parties to oppose recognition.

---

[20] *Cf.* Articles 79 and 109(5).

[21] *Id.* at Article 111(3).

[22] Article 30 of the General Code of Procedure.

A.2.5 Additional arbitration-friendly innovations

Proceedings under the Statute are more flexible. For example, electronic notifications are now permitted.[23] It amplifies party autonomy with respect to the appointment of arbitrators. Foreigners are allowed to participate as arbitrators, with no restriction other than those the parties impose.[24] Articles 73 (2) and (3) of Law 1563 of 2012 provide that it is not necessary to qualify as a lawyer in the seat of arbitration to be appointed an arbitrator. Parties are thus entitled to choose any person that is best suited to decide the issues at stake in the dispute. Finally, when parties have not agreed to the procedural rules, arbitrators are not compelled to refer to the domestic procedural norms and may determine the applicable procedure.[25]

A.3 Trends and Tendencies

There is no doubt that Colombia is positioning itself as an interesting seat for international arbitration through the Statute's recent enactment. It is yet to be seen how the Statute will evolve, particularly how the Colombian courts will apply its international arbitration provisions.

Colombia has signed free trade agreements with other countries and regional organizations. It is likely that this trend will continue, as indicated by several pending negotiations with foreign countries.[26] All of these free trade agreements include provisions for dispute settlement that diminish risks for investment and potential disputes. Colombia is seen as a reliable

---

[23] Article 65(b) of Law 1563 of 2012.

[24] *Id.* at Article 73(1).

[25] *Id.* at Article 92.

[26] E.g., European Union and Peru (signed in June 2012) and South Korea (signed in June 2012)

country for foreign investment as it has not been subjected to any expropriation or nationalization disputes for over twenty years.[27]

B. CASES

Since the Statute was recently enacted and just entered into force in October 2012, there are no cases that specifically refers to its new provisions yet. It is relevant to mention, however, a few cases that were decided over the past few years that may be useful for interpreting the new Statute, especially since most of them influenced the new regulations.

Regarding the distinction between domestic and international public policy, the Statute refers to international public policy and no longer to just public policy. This new set of rules refer to Colombia's international public policy in three instances: (i) as a reason to deny an interim measure,[28] (ii) as a reason to annul an award,[29] and (iii) to deny the recognition or the enforcement of an award.[30] Such provisions are consistent with an SCJ ruling of July 2011,[31] upheld by another SCJ ruling of December 2011,[32] that acknowledged the distinction and established that it is international public policy and not domestic public policy that

---

[27] London: The UK wakes up to Colombia's potential, Global Arbitration Review, 2 Aug. 2012: 7-5.

[28] Article 89 b)-ii of Law 1563 of 2012.

[29] *Id.* at Article 108 2. b).

[30] *Id.* at Article 112 b)-ii.

[31] Colombian Supreme Court of Justice, *Petrotesting Colombia S.A. and Southeast Investment Corporation,* 27 July 2011, file 2007-01956.

[32] Colombian Supreme Court of Justice, *Drummond Ltd. – Ferrovias en Liquidación and FENOCO,* 19 December 2011, file 2008-01760.

must be considered when deciding to recognize or enforce a foreign award.

The Statute puts aside Colombian Code of Civil Procedure Article 114 regarding the recognition and enforcement of awards. The Statute's provisions mirror the SJC's July 2011 ruling holding that only those standards established in the New York Convention apply to the recognition and enforcement of foreign awards, i.e., the Colombian Code of Civil Procedure is inapplicable.

A very recent SCJ ruling decided an action for the protection of constitutional rights (*acción de tutela*), specifically for the protection of procedural due process, against an award issued by an international arbitration tribunal seated in Bogotá, Colombia.[33] The SCJ denied the protection the plaintiff requested and found that the award did not violate the constitutional right of procedural due process. Furthermore, the plaintiff had previously filed before the Higher Court of Bogotá an action to set aside the award that was also dismissed. Thus, the award issued by the international arbitration tribunal seated in Bogotá remained untouched, thereby fostering an arbitration-friendly environment in Colombia. It is noteworthy that the SCJ issued its ruling just a few days before the new Statute came into force.

It is still to be seen how Article 109 of the Statute that forbids "actions or recourses" against the court's rulings that decide annulment actions and Article 107 that provides for annulment actions as the only judicial recourse against an award, will be interpreted.

---

[33] Colombian Supreme Court of Justice, *Scrolling S.A. v. Arbitral Tribunal and Higher Court of Bogotá*, 27 September 2012, file 2012-02014-00.

C. THE GRANT AND ENFORCEMENT OF INTERIM MEASURES IN INTERNATIONAL ARBITRATION

C.1 Tribunal-Ordered Interim Measures

The Arbitration Statute vests the arbitral tribunal with the ability to issue interim measures, i.e., an order requiring another party to do or to refrain from doing determined actions while the arbitration is pending, adopting almost integrally Chapter IV A of the 2006 UNCITRAL Model Law.[34] In providing a prolix set of provisions,[35] the Statute broadened the type of interim measures available in the context of international arbitration in Colombia, further protecting parties' rights.

Now, the tribunal may grant interim measures at the request of one of the parties,[36] providing that the petitioner proves to the tribunal the relevance, appropriateness, effectiveness and

---

[34] Article 80 of the Statute establishes the type of interim measures that a tribunal may order in the context of international arbitration, following the 2006 UNCITRAL Model Law:

An interim measure is any temporary measure, whether in the form of an award or in another form, by which, at any time prior to the issuance of the award by which the dispute is finally decided, the arbitral tribunal orders a party to:

(a) Maintain or restore the status quo pending determination of the dispute;

(b) Take action that would prevent, or refrain from taking action that is likely to cause, current or imminent harm or prejudice to the arbitral process itself;

(c) Provide a means of preserving assets out of which a subsequent award may be satisfied; or

(d) Preserve evidence that may be relevant and material to the resolution of the dispute.

[35] Articles 80 to 90 of Law 1563 of 2012.

[36] *Id.* at Article 80.

reasonableness of such measures.[37] The tribunal may also order *ex parte* preliminary orders that are governed pursuant to the 2006 UNCITRAL Model Law.[38] Interim measures from the tribunal are not available before the commencement of arbitral proceedings (e.g., emergency arbitrators) under the arbitration rules of local arbitral institutions.

C.2 Court-Ordered Interim Measures

Colombian local courts do have concurrent powers to order interim measures.[39] Furthermore, once arbitral proceedings have commenced, the parties do not need to apply to the tribunal for those measures before they do so with the local court.

As the Statute has been in force for a very short period of time, it is too soon to tell how long it will take to obtain an interim measure related to international arbitration from a Colombian court. Beyond the context of international arbitration, it usually takes an average of two to six weeks to obtain an interim measure from a Colombian court.

Pursuant to the new Statute, Colombian courts are empowered to grant interim measures in aid of a foreign arbitration (i.e., outside the jurisdiction of the supervisory court).

---

[37] Id. at Article 81.

[38] The Statute follows Article 17B of the 2006 UNCITRAL Model Law:

(1) Unless otherwise agreed by the parties, a party may, without notice to any other party, make a request for an interim measure together with an application for a preliminary order directing a party not to frustrate the purpose of the interim measure requested. (2) The arbitral tribunal may grant a preliminary order provided it considers that prior disclosure of the request for the interim measure to the party against whom it is directed risks frustrating the purpose of the measure."

[39] Articles 71 and 90 of Law 1563 of 2012.

C.3 Enforcement of Interim Measures

Under the new Statute, interim measures are binding and no recognition procedure is required.[40] The seat of the arbitral tribunal that orders the interim measure is irrelevant when requesting its enforcement before Colombian courts.[41] Tribunal interim orders are enforceable by Colombian courts in the same way as a Colombian court judgment. This is the case whether the tribunal is seated in Colombia or abroad.

Article 89 of the Statute sets forth the exceptional cases when a court may deny the enforcement of an interim measure in the context of international arbitration. Although not identical, the Statute basically follows the UNCITRAL Model Law in this respect. At the request of the party against whom the interim measure is invoked, the court may deny enforcement if it is satisfied about the incapacity of a party to the arbitration agreement; invalidity of the arbitration agreement; insufficient notice given of the commencement of the arbitral proceeding; the award deals with a dispute not contemplated by or not falling within the terms of the submission to arbitration, or it contains decisions on matters beyond the scope of the submission to arbitration; the composition of the arbitral tribunal or the arbitral procedure was not in accordance with the agreement of the parties, or failing such agreement, was not in accordance with the law of the country where the arbitration took place; the arbitral tribunal's decision with respect to the provision of security in connection with the interim measure issued by the arbitral tribunal has not been complied with; or the interim measure has been terminated or suspended by the arbitral tribunal, or where so empowered, by the court of the state in

---

[40]   *Id.* at Article 88.1.

[41]   *Id.*

which the arbitration takes place or under the law of which that interim measure was granted. Enforcement could also be denied by a local court if the court finds that the subject-matter of the dispute is not capable of settlement by arbitration under the laws of Colombia; or the recognition or enforcement of the interim measure would be contrary to the international public policy of Colombia. National courts are only authorized to assess the existence of one of those exceptions but are not to consider the merits of the measure itself.

Finally, any party can go before the courts, before or during the arbitration, to petition interim measures. These may be granted under the seat's procedural law and taking into account the specific features of international arbitration.[42] This does not imply a renouncement of arbitration.

---

[42] *Id.* at Article 90.

CZECH REPUBLIC

Martin Hrodek[1] and Jan Zrcek[2]

A. LEGISLATION, TRENDS AND TENDENCIES

A.1 Recent Developments in Legislation

Both international and domestic arbitration seated in the Czech Republic are governed by Act No. 216/1994 Coll., on Arbitration Proceedings and Enforcement of Arbitration Awards, as amended (the "Arbitration Act"). The Arbitration Act is based on the UNCITRAL Model Law and entered into force in 1995. Pursuant to Section 30 of the Arbitration Act, the Czech Rules of Civil Procedure (Act No. 99/1963 Coll.) are to be used as a subsidiary law.

In the 2011-2012 *Yearbook*, we noted that the Arbitration Act was subject to an extensive amendment focusing on disputes arising from consumer contracts. There have not been any further changes in the Arbitration Act since this amendment. However, in connection with the recodification of Czech civil law, which is expected on 1 January 2014, a part of the Arbitration Act dealing with international matters will be replaced by a new Act on International Private Law.[3] Therefore, we expect that a comprehensive report on the new Act on International Private Law will follow in the 2013-2014 *Yearbook*.

---

[1] Martin Hrodek heads the Dispute Resolution Practice Group in the Firm's Prague office. He specializes in litigation and arbitration matters, particularly those related to mergers and acquisitions. He also advises industry clients on a wide range of commercial matters, including private equity, divestitures and private competition claims, among others.

[2] Jan Zrcek is an Associate in the Dispute Resolution Practice Group in the Firm's Prague office.

[3] Act No. 91/2012 Coll., which will become effective on 1 January 2014.

A.2 Trends

Arbitration continues to be popular among Czech companies, including in matters without any international element. This has arisen because Czech courts are still deemed to be quite slow at handling commercial disputes, although they have improved substantially in recent times. For their domestic disputes, companies tend to use the Arbitration Court of the Czech Economic Chamber and the Czech Agrarian Chamber (which handles approximately 3,000 disputes annually), as well as arbitration under the ICC Rules, mostly for more complex disputes.

B. CASES

B.1 Courts Cannot Review Merits of Awards in Proceedings to Enforce Foreign Arbitral Awards

A rule that courts cannot review the merits of an arbitration award unless the parties have otherwise agreed has already been established in the decision-making practices of the Czech Supreme Court in proceedings to set aside an award. Last year, the Supreme Court issued a decision[4] in which it explicitly ruled that the merits of the case also cannot be reviewed in proceedings to enforce arbitral awards.

The case concerned enforcement of an award rendered in an international dispute handled by the LCIA, in which the claimant was unsuccessful and the sole arbitrator imposed a duty on the claimant to pay the costs of the arbitration. The claimant argued against the enforcement of the award in the Czech Republic on many grounds, among which were failure to meet formal

---

[4]   Decision No. 20 Cdo 2214/2009, dated 20 December 2011.

requirements, non-conformity with Czech public policy and insufficient reasoning.

After being unsuccessful in the first- and second-instance courts, the claimant filed an extraordinary appeal to the Supreme Court. The Supreme Court dealt with the alleged lack of formal requirements by stating that although the form of the award may not comply with Czech laws, these were not applicable as the New York Convention has priority over Czech law in international enforcement of arbitration awards.

Concerning non-conformity with Czech public policy, the claimant argued that the sole arbitrator failed to understand or purposefully misinterpreted the basic principles of Czech law when deciding on the costs of the proceedings. Therefore, the sole arbitrator's decision deprived the claimant of its right to a fair trial. The Supreme Court dismissed this argument by stating that the claimant, in fact, merely objected to the merits of the award and did not dispute the correctness of the procedure which preceded the award. The Supreme Court, therefore, did not find any relevance in the claimant's reference to Czech public policy issues.

The claimant also argued that the award could not be enforced because it could not be considered as final, since the sole arbitrator failed to sufficiently state the reasons for his decision. The claimant emphasized that the award did not comply with Article 32 of the UNCITRAL Arbitration Rules, which governed the arbitration proceedings in question. The claimant further supported this argument by showing that it had requested an interpretation of the award pursuant to Article 35 of the UNCITRAL Arbitration Rules, and this request was denied. The Supreme Court ruled that: "If the obligated party questions the content (or extent) of reasoning of an arbitration award and then even in a reply that it receives to a request for interpretation of the award, the obligated party is in fact arguing an incorrectness of the merits of the award. The court enforcing the award is, however, not allowed to review the correctness of the merits of the enforced decision and is bound by its content under Section 159a of the Czech Rules of Civil Procedure." Based on this conclusion, the Supreme Court denied that there were grounds for review of the reasoning or interpretation of the award.

By this decision, the Supreme Court has established a strong precedent, which will be used in interpretations of the New York Convention in the Czech Republic. Furthermore, the ruling that the reasoning or interpretation of an award is a part of its merits should also be followed by Czech courts in similar cases.

B.2 New Grounds for Setting Aside an Award Can Be Asserted until First Oral Hearing in the Set Aside Proceedings

Pursuant to Section 32(1) of the Arbitration Act, a party can file an action to set aside an arbitration award within three months from delivery of the award to that party. However, it was previously unclear whether within this three-month period for filing the action the claimant also had to assert all the grounds that it intended to rely on for setting aside the award.

This uncertainty has been resolved by the Czech Supreme Court in one of its recent decisions.[5] The Supreme Court has ruled that the party requesting that the award be set aside can raise additional grounds for setting aside the award at any time during the proceedings, subject to certain limitations included in the Czech Rules of Civil Procedure.

The Czech Rules of Civil Procedure generally prevent parties from raising new arguments only after the oral hearing is held.

---

5   Decision No. 23 Cdo 3728/2011, dated 9 May 2012.

Consequently, the deadline for raising grounds for setting aside an award is effectively the first oral hearing in proceedings to set aside the award.

B.3 Matters within the Scope of an Arbitration Agreement Can Be Assessed by Courts as Preliminary Issues in Other Claims

Under Section 2(4) of the Arbitration Act, any disputes arising out of or in connection with an arbitration agreement or an agreement that includes an arbitration clause are generally arbitrable, unless the parties agree otherwise. In one of its recent decisions,[6] the Czech Supreme Court has provided guidance as to the scope of disputes that are deemed to be "in connection with" an agreement containing an arbitration clause.

In this case, one party attempted to withdraw from a purchase contract and claimed the ownership title to assets transferred under that contract. The purchase price under the contract was set off against receivables arising out of a tax advisory contract. The other party challenged the validity of the withdrawal from the contract, and the dispute was referred to a court. As the tax advisory contract contained an arbitration clause, one of the parties objected that the court did not have jurisdiction.

The Supreme Court stated that there was insufficient connection between the tax advisory contract and the purchase contract at hand; therefore, withdrawal from the purchase contract was not within the scope of the arbitration clause contained in the tax advisory contract. According to the Supreme Court, payment of the purchase price by means of a set-off against receivables arising from the tax advisory contract was only a preliminary issue for assessing the alleged withdrawal from the purchase contract, and this preliminary issue did not constitute a sufficient

---

[6]   Decision No. 32 Cdo 3163/2011, dated 9 February 2012.

connection within the meaning of Section 2(4) of the Arbitration Act. The Supreme Court also noted that the courts should apply Section 135(2) of the Czech Rules of Civil Procedure, which allows a court to decide on preliminary issues despite other bodies (such as an arbitral tribunal) being competent to decide these issues; however, if there is a prior decision of a competent body on a preliminary issue, the court's decision on the consequent issue should be based on such prior decision.

This decision makes it clear that the courts have jurisdiction to assess preliminary issues that are within the scope of arbitration agreements and may rely on their assessment in deciding on the merits. However, if preliminary issues have been resolved by a competent arbitrator or arbitration tribunal in advance, the court's decision on the merits should be based on the assessment of preliminary issues in the arbitration.

B.4 Arbitration Clause in a Lease Not Affected by Transfer of Title or Termination of the Lease

In another recent decision,[7] the Czech Supreme Court dealt with an arbitration clause contained in a lease agreement. The first question submitted to the Supreme Court was whether the arbitration clause terminated upon termination of the lease agreement, and in particular, whether the arbitration clause extended to a dispute concerning the vacation of leased property following termination of the lease agreement. The second question was whether the arbitration clause was binding on a new owner of the leased property who was not a party to the lease agreement containing the arbitration clause.

The Supreme Court ruled that a dispute arising in connection with an agreement that contains an arbitration clause is arbitrable

---

7   Decision No. 22 Cdo 1643/2012, dated 23 July 2012.

even after the agreement is terminated, pursuant to Section 2(4) of the Arbitration Act, if there is a connection between the agreement and the dispute, and provided that termination of the agreement does not make the dispute irrelevant. In the case at hand, the Supreme Court considered the vacation of leased property sufficiently connected with the lease agreement that contained the arbitration clause.

Regarding the second question, the Supreme Court stated that pursuant to Section 680(2) of the Czech Civil Code,[8] upon transfer of an ownership title to a leased property, the transferee assumes the legal position of the transferor with regard to the leased property. According to the Supreme Court, this includes the transferor's position under an arbitration clause contained in the lease agreement.

B.4.1 Award May Impose a Duty That Is Not in Line With a Court-Ordered Interim Measure

One of the grounds for setting aside an arbitration award is that the award imposes a duty that is prohibited or impossible under Czech law.[9] The Czech Supreme Court recently provided an interesting interpretation of this provision.[10]

The case concerned an award that imposed a duty on one party to hand over certain shares to the other party. However, the party holding the shares was also bound by an interim measure ordered by a Czech court that prohibited any transfers of these shares. As further described in Section C below, an act or step of a party violating a duty imposed by an interim measure is null and void

---

[8] Act No. 40/1964 Coll., as amended.

[9] Section 31 f) of the Arbitration Act.

[10] Decision No. 29 Cdo 5146/2009, dated 21 June 2012.

ex lege.[11] Relying on this rule, the obligated party applied to set aside the award, since it allegedly imposed a duty that was prohibited or impossible under Czech law.

The Supreme Court dismissed the motion, finding that the interim measure was merely a prohibition imposed on a party to take certain steps or perform certain acts. However, an arbitration award was not an act of a party, and therefore, the interim measure did not affect the validity and permissibility of the duty imposed by the respective award.

C. THE GRANT AND ENFORCEMENT OF INTERIM MEASURES IN INTERNATIONAL ARBITRATION

C.1 Tribunal-Ordered Interim Measures

Czech law does not provide for enforcing any interim measures ordered by sole arbitrators and/or tribunals. The reason for this is that only an "arbitration award" (as opposed to interim measures or orders) can be enforced under Czech law.[12] Similarly, only foreign "awards" and not "orders" or other measures are recognized and enforced in the Czech Republic under Article III of the New York Convention.

In theory, foreign interim measures in the form of a regular award should be enforceable in the Czech Republic under Article III of the New York Convention. However, we are not aware of any arbitration rules or cases where interim measures have been ordered in the form of a regular award. Consequently, although domestic and foreign arbitrators and tribunals are not prevented from ordering any types of interim measures under Czech law,

---

[11] Section 76e(1) of the Czech Rules of Civil Procedure.

[12] Section 28(2) of the Arbitration Act.

parties who seek an interim measure that is enforceable in the Czech Republic are in practice restricted to interim measures ordered by competent Czech courts and/or foreign courts, provided that interim measures of the foreign courts in question are enforceable in the Czech Republic (for example, under Council Regulation (EC) No 44/2001).

C.2 Court-Ordered Interim Measures

Czech courts have concurrent powers to order interim measures and applicants are not required to first apply to a sole arbitrator or tribunal. Under Czech law, parties to a dispute may apply to the courts for interim measures for the purposes of arbitration proceedings concerning a certain principal claim of the applicant. Courts will issue an interim measure if the applicant proves that it is necessary:

(a) to temporarily establish, modify or terminate a certain legal relationship of a party to the proceedings[13] and/or, if it is reasonably required, a third party;[14]

(b) to ensure that a final award on the principal claim will be effectively enforced;[15] and/or

(c) to secure certain evidence.[16]

In addition, the applicant must demonstrate (i.e., to a lower standard of proof) the principal claim that is to be protected by the requested interim measure.[17]

---

[13]   Section 74(1) of the Czech Rules of Civil Procedure.

[14]   *Id.* at Section 76(2).

[15]   *Id.* at Section 74(1).

[16]   *Id.* at Section 78 *et seq.*

The applicant is also required to pay a deposit against potential damage caused by the interim measure amounting to CZK 50,000 (approximately EUR 2,000) in commercial and CZK 10,000 (approximately EUR 400) in non-commercial matters. This amount must be deposited with the court on the day the application is submitted, at the latest.[18] The court may also request that an applicant pay an additional deposit if the interim measure is issued and effective and if a party affected by such measure reasonably invites the court to do so.[19] Applicants in certain non-commercial matters (custody, household violence, labor and alimony matters, etc.) are exempted from paying any deposits.[20]

A decision on the application for an interim measure should be issued within seven days from its submission (in custody matters, within one day, and in domestic violence matters, within two days).[21]

There is no oral hearing or examination of witnesses before the decision on the application is issued.[22] Consequently, the decision is based only on the application and documentary evidence attached to it.

---

[17] *Drápal, L., Bureš, J. a kol.*Občanský soudní řád I, II Komentář, C. H. Beck, 2009, p. 423 *et seq.*

[18] Section 75b(1) of the Czech Rules of Civil Procedure.

[19] *Ibid* and Section 76g of the Czech Rules of Civil Procedure.

[20] *Id.* at Section 75b(3).

[21] *Id.* at Section 75c(2).

[22] *Id.* at Section 75c(3).

There are no limitations on an interim measure's subject matter. However, typically, an interim measure can impose the following duties on the parties:[23]

(a) to deposit specific amounts or things with the court;

(b) not to exercise, transfer or otherwise dispose of specific rights or things;

(c) to refrain from taking specific steps or actions; or

(d) to carry out specific steps or actions and/or allow a third party to take specific steps or actions.

However, an applicant should avoid seeking an interim measure the effect of which would be equivalent to achieving the applicant's principal claim in the arbitration proceedings, since such applications exceed the purpose of interim measures and should therefore be dismissed.[24]

A decision issuing an interim measure becomes enforceable upon its announcement (i.e., delivery) to the party on which it imposes a duty.[25] Any steps or actions that violate such a decision are null and void *ex lege*.[26] If the interim measure prevents a party from transferring or otherwise disposing of certain Czech real property, no such disposals can be effectively made, since these cannot be registered in the Czech Real Estate Register, and therefore, cannot become effective.[27]

---

[23]   *Id.* at Section 76(1).

[24]   *Drápal, L., Bureš, J. a kol.*Občanský soudní řád I, II Komentář, C. H. Beck, 2009 p. 424.

[25]   Section 76d of the Czech Rules of Civil Procedure.

[26]   *Id.* at Section 76f(1).

[27]   *Id.* at Section 76f(2).

Effects of an interim measure terminate when the first of the events specified below occurs:[28]

(a) the applicant fails to initiate proceedings concerning its principal claim within a certain statutory period or within a period determined in the decision whereby an interim measure is issued;

(b) the applicant's principal claim is finally dismissed;

(c) a decision granting the applicant's principal claim is enforceable for more than 15 days; or

(d) a period specified in the decision whereby an interim measure is issued expires.

In addition, an interim measure can be terminated if the grounds for such measure cease to exist or if the additional deposit against potential damage is not paid in time.[29]

If an interim measure is terminated and the applicant's principal claim is not awarded or voluntarily complied with, the applicant is obligated to compensate the parties affected by such measure for any damage, unless the damage would have occurred regardless of the measure.[30]

A party that is required to comply with a duty under the decision on an interim measure can file an appeal against the decision and submit new evidence. The appellate court may then revoke the decision on the interim measure and dismiss the application, or may confirm the decision. However, there are no statutory periods within which the appellate court must decide on the appeal. The appellate court may also (but is not obligated to)

---

[28]   *Id.* at Section 77(1).

[29]   *Id.* at Section 77(2).

[30]   *Id.* at Section 77a(1).

hold an oral hearing on the appeal. In practice, appeals are most frequently dealt with within several weeks or a few months without any oral hearing.

Czech procedural rules governing court-ordered interim measures are independent of any arbitration agreements and/or rules. Therefore, an applicant may request that a competent Czech court order an interim measure at any time during the course of arbitration proceedings or prior to commencing such proceedings, subject to adhering to the general requirements on such application as summarized above.

The competent court is established under the same rules that would be applied to establish a competent court to decide the underlying dispute if there was no arbitration agreement.[31] It should be noted, however, pursuant to these competence rules, Czech courts are competent if, amongst other reasons, one of the parties has assets located in the Czech Republic.[32] Therefore, non-Czech parties to a foreign arbitration (i.e., one outside the supervisory jurisdiction of Czech courts) can seek interim measures from Czech courts.

In practice, we have also experienced that Czech courts have granted interim measures in aid of a foreign arbitration.

C.3   Enforcement of Interim Measures

As stated in C.1 above, Czech law principally does not provide for enforcing any interim measures ordered in domestic or foreign arbitration proceedings.

On the other hand, as explained in C.2 above, at any stage of arbitration proceedings—or before commencing arbitration

---

[31]   Section 43 of the Arbitration Act.

[32]   Section 86(2) of the Czech Rules of Civil Procedure.

proceedings—a party may apply for an interim measure with the Czech courts. These measures are also available to parties of a foreign arbitration, if there are respective assets located in the Czech Republic. A party may also apply for an interim measure with a competent foreign court and such interim measure may also be enforceable in the Czech Republic.

There are also practical benefits of applying for interim measures with Czech courts if these measures are to be enforced in the Czech Republic: an applicant does not need to arrange for translations of the enforced decision, and more importantly, interim measures ordered by Czech courts should reflect Czech law requirements on enforceable decisions, thus avoiding cross-border enforcement differences and corresponding difficulties.

FRANCE

Jean-Dominique Touraille,[1] Eric Borysewicz[2] and
Karim Boulmelh[3]

A.   LEGISLATION, TRENDS AND TENDENCIES

International arbitration in France is governed by the Decree of
13 January 2011 that came into force on 1 May 2011 ("the
Decree"), which introduced Articles 1504 to 1527 into the
French Code of Civil Procedure.[4] No legislative changes were
made to these provisions in 2012.

---

[1]   Jean-Dominique Touraille is a Partner in Baker & McKenzie's Paris office and
leads the office's Litigation & Arbitration Practice Group. He regularly delivers
presentations on various subjects related to his area of practice, which includes
distribution, product liability and post-acquisition disputes. He is actively
involved in cases relating to ICC arbitration and in enforcement measures in the
French legal system.

[2]   Eric Borysewicz is a Partner in Baker & McKenzie's Paris office and a member of
the Litigation and Arbitration Practice Group in Paris. He represents clients in
international arbitrations under ICC rules and other arbitration institutions. He
focuses his practice on risk management issues, advising clients on major
litigations involving industrial and infrastructure project. He also assists clients in
drafting and negotiating complex industrial and infrastructure project agreements,
as well as in renegotiating existing agreements following an unforeseen change in
circumstances.

[3]   Karim Boulmelh is a Senior Associate in Baker & McKenzie's Paris office and a
member of the Litigation and Arbitration Practice Group in Paris. He intervenes in
lawsuits related to commercial law and industrial risks before judicial courts and
arbitral panels, whether under major arbitration institutions and rules (ICC,
UNCITRAL, AAA, ICSID, OHADA) or under *ad hoc* arbitral tribunals. He
handles litigation matters related to telecommunication services, energy and
industrial gases, engineering and construction, aircraft and satellite industries.

[4]   Further comments on the decree of 13 January 2011 can be found in the 2010-
2011 issue of the *Baker & McKenzie International Arbitration Yearbook*.

French law on international arbitration further to the Decree of 13 January 2011, is generally regarded as an extremely "arbitration friendly" set of rules that has significantly enhanced the accessibility of French arbitration law for foreign parties to international transactions. More than ever, arbitration is regarded in France as the natural dispute resolution mechanism in international transactions.

This year, Paris has also maintained its position as one of the most prominent arbitration places as the ICC has been very much in the spotlight. First, the presentation of the new ICC Arbitration Rules that entered into force on 1 January 2012, gave rise to numerous conferences and events in Paris. Secondly, the ICC has confirmed that while it would move from its current premises it would remain based in Paris.

In addition, French courts have continued to favor solutions that uphold the enforceability of arbitration agreements and international arbitration awards as further described below.

B. CASES

B.1 Enforcement of an Arbitral Award during an Action to Set Aside the Award or during Appeal Proceedings against the Recognition and Enforcement Order

One of the most important changes resulting from the enactment of the Decree is the introduction of Article 1526 into the Code of Civil Procedure. This Article provides that an action to set aside an award or an appeal against a recognition and enforcement order (*ordonnance d'exequatur*) does not suspend the enforcement of an international award. This rule is the exact opposite of the previous rule before the new Decree came into force on 1 May 2011.[5]

Article 1526 of the Code of Civil Procedure provides that the President of the Court of Appeal[6] can suspend the enforcement of an international award or subject it to conditions only "when such enforcement would seriously infringe on the rights of one of the parties." In two recent decisions, the Paris Court of Appeal has applied this provision and provided some guidance for its interpretation.

In the first case,[7] a company was applying before the President of the Court of Appeal to stay enforcement of an award until the court's decision on the pending action to set aside the award on the grounds that the financial situation of the party seeking enforcement of the award casted doubt on its ability to pay back the amount of the award should the court eventually set the award aside. The President of the Court of Appeal rejected the application, as it was not established that the immediate enforcement of the award would "seriously infringe on the rights of a party." As this was the first time that the President of the Court of Appeal had ruled on the application of the new Article 1526, the President stressed that, under the new rule, the general principle is the immediate enforceability of an international

---

[5] Former Article 1506 of the Code of Civil Procedure provided that enforcement of an international award was suspended for the period of time during which an appeal against the recognition and enforcement order or an action for setting aside an international award was open, as well as for the entire duration of such proceedings.

[6] Or the judge in charge of the proceedings (*Conseiller de la Mise en Etat*) if an appeal against the recognition and enforcement order or an action to set aside the award has already been introduced and a judge in charge of the proceedings has been appointed.

[7] Paris Court of Appeal, 18 October 2011, No 11/14286, *SAS Mambo Commodities v. Société Compagnie Malienne Pour le Développement Des Textiles.*

award notwithstanding any appeal against the recognition and enforcement order or an action to set aside the award. He also stressed that any suspension of enforcement must therefore remain exceptional and that the test for enforcement that would "seriously infringe on the rights of a party" as set forth in Article 1526, is even more severe than the test of enforcement that would "induce excessively harsh consequences," which is the standard test for suspension of enforcement where a court or a domestic arbitral tribunal has ordered provisional enforcement of a judgment or of an award.

The President of the Court of Appeal specified that it is not sufficient to establish the existence of a risk that the party seeking enforcement would not be in a position to reimburse the amount of the award, should said award be set aside, nor that the enforcement of the award would put the party seeking suspension of the award in a difficult financial situation.

In the second case,[8] the party seeking to suspend enforcement of the award argued that should the award be enforced, this would cause it to become insolvent and to file bankruptcy, which would deprive it of its right to effectively challenge the award. The President rejected the argument on the grounds that, even if the party was to become insolvent and file bankruptcy, this would not prevent it from pursuing the action to set aside the award through the receiver. The applicant also argued that the award should be set aside as a violation of international public order and of Article 6-1 of the European Convention on Human Rights. Again, the argument was rejected on the grounds that the applicant was in effect objecting to the findings of the arbitrators on the merits rather than to the way the arbitrators had carried out the arbitral proceedings.

---

[8] Paris Court of Appeal, 13 July 2012, No 12/11616, *CIEC Engineering v. Carlson SNC.*

These decisions clearly show that, under the new French arbitration statute, it is only under very exceptional circumstances that a party will be in a position to obtain an order suspending the enforcement of an international arbitral award pending the outcome of an action to set aside the award.

B.2 Scope of the Arbitration Clause

French courts continue to promote a broad interpretation of the enforceability of arbitration clauses, both as regards the parties involved and the subject-matters that are covered by the clause.

In a first case,[9] a company had introduced an action before the Paris District Court on a number of grounds including counterfeiting, breach of long lasting commercial relationship without due notice period, unfair competition, unfair hiring away of its employees, and payment of invoices. While it was not disputed that the issue of counterfeiting remained under the exclusive jurisdiction of the state court (Article L331-1 of the Code of Intellectual Property), the defending party objected to the jurisdiction of state courts for all the other issues as the contract contained an arbitration clause. The claimant maintained that the arbitration clause would not cover any matter of a non-contractual nature such as unfair competition, breach of long lasting commercial relationship without due notice period, or unfair hiring away of employees.

The Paris Court ruled that on all these issues, it was for the arbitral tribunal to decide on its own jurisdiction under the "competence competence principle." The court specified that an arbitration clause that applies to "all disputes arising out of or in connection with the present contract" could not be regarded

---

[9] Paris Court of Appeal, 14 March 2012, No 11/12354, *SA Conforama France v. SPA Group SOFA.*

prima facie as excluding noncontractual issues, provided those issues bear some relationship with the contract, e.g., the conditions surrounding the termination of the contract.

In a second case, a French company had contracted with a Greek company for the distribution of its products in Greece. The contract contained an arbitration clause. A second Greek company, linked to the first one both as regards its share capital and its management, also distributed the products of the French company in Greece through separate orders. Following the termination of the contract, an arbitration was initiated by the two Greek companies against the French one, and an award was rendered that provided for damages to be paid by the French company to both Greek companies. The respondent challenged the award on the grounds that no arbitration agreement existed as far as the second Greek company was concerned. The *Cour de Cassation* rejected the respondent's appeal on the grounds that the second Greek company had effectively been substituted for the first one in the performance of the contract and that "the jurisdictional effect of the arbitration clause in an international contract must extend to all parties that directly took part in the performance of the contract."

The interesting feature in both these decisions is the generality of the terms used by French courts in order to expand the effectiveness of the arbitration clause to cover a vast series of situations.

C. THE GRANT AND ENFORCEMENT OF INTERIM MEASURES IN INTERNATIONAL ARBITRATION

C.1 Tribunal-Ordered Interim Measures

For a long time, the French legal corpus did not include any legal basis for arbitral tribunals to order interim measures. The majority of scholars were of the opinion that arbitral tribunals could not grant or order interim measures of any kind as they lack coercive powers necessary for such measures contrary to judicial courts. French courts, however, began in the early 1980s to admit that arbitral tribunals may grant or order interim measures.[10]

France has codified this liberal approach adopted by the courts on interim measures - though with some restrictions - in the new decree on arbitration law entered into force in France on 1 May 2011. Under the new Article 1468 of the French Code of Civil Procedure, an arbitral tribunal may order upon the parties any provisional or conservatory measures it deems appropriate.

Hence, arbitral tribunals with their seats in France or acting under French procedural law have very wide powers—almost similar to those of a state court—to grant or order any kind of interim measures of whatever nature they may be: injunction to take an action or refrain from taking an action, preservation of evidence or assets, putting in place escrows or ordering a security from a party, ordering status quo or suspension of a particular action pending a ruling on the merits, etc. Arbitral tribunals are entitled to attach penalties to such orders. There are only two types of interim measures which remain under the exclusive jurisdiction of the courts: conservatory attachments of movable properties and judicial securities.

Pursuant to Article 1468 of the French Code of Civil Procedure, an arbitral tribunal may order any interim measure "it deems appropriate." The only test is therefore for an applicant to demonstrate the appropriateness of the requested measure in light of the circumstances of the dispute. This is an important

---

[10] E.g., Rennes, 26 October 1984, *Rev.arb.* 1985. 439; Paris, 7 October 2004, *Rev. arb.* 2005. 737.

feature compared to the conditions set forth by French law for provisional or conservatory measures that can be ordered by state courts where, depending on the nature of the matter, the applicant may have to demonstrate existence of an emergency; existence of an obligation that is not seriously disputable; existence of an imminent risk of damage and/or a manifestly illegal nuisance; or absence of existing proceedings on the merits of the dispute.

Therefore, arbitral tribunals benefit from very wide powers to order interim measures. This strong role is consistent with the French tradition that tends to favor a secure recourse to international arbitration and efficiency of arbitration proceedings. Recourse to French state courts has been limited to situations where the arbitral tribunal has not yet been constituted and the arbitral proceedings not yet commenced. However, even this last role of French courts is tapering off as arbitral institutions put in place procedures to respond to the parties' needs for urgent interim measures.

Since 1 January 2012, the ICC has introduced new Rules that now offer the possibility for a party to apply for urgent interim or conservatory measures prior to the constitution of the arbitral tribunal. Article 29 of the ICC Rules has instituted an emergency arbitrator who may intervene and order urgent interim measures as long as the file has not yet been transmitted to the arbitral tribunal by the ICC Secretariat. After that date, the arbitral tribunal has sole jurisdiction to decide on interim measures. It is also worth noting that while the arbitral tribunal is not bound by the emergency arbitrator's order, reallocation of costs by the arbitral tribunal in its final award is evaluated in light of compliance or non-compliance by the parties with the order. This provides a clear incentive for the parties to comply.

Recourse to the emergency arbitrator is available only for arbitration agreements entered into after 1 January 2012. The parties remain free to exclude such recourse in their arbitration agreement or choose to refer to the ICC pre-arbitral referee instead. However, the pre-arbitral referee rules require that the parties have specifically agreed on this procedure, while a mere reference to the ICC Rules in arbitration agreements drafted after 1 January 2012 is now sufficient to request an interim measure from the emergency arbitrator.

The possibility of obtaining interim measures under the arbitration rules chosen by the parties is an increasing trend that is followed by other arbitral institutions: for instance, the International Arbitration Chamber of Paris has introduced a provision in its arbitration rules for a fast-track procedure to constitute a three-member arbitral tribunal to rule on interim measures requested by a party on an emergency basis. The members of this emergency arbitral tribunal cannot later be appointed in a subsequent arbitral tribunal seized of the merits of the dispute.[11]

In the absence of an arbitral mechanism for interim measures prior to commencement of the arbitration proceedings, the parties of course still have the possibility to seek assistance from the French courts.

C.2 Court-Ordered Interim Measures

Under French law, the existence of an arbitration agreement does not prevent a party from seeking a provisional or conservatory measure from the state courts[12] provided that (i) the arbitral

---

[11]   Article 53 of the Arbitration Rules of the International Chamber of Arbitration of Paris, in force as of 1 September 2011.

[12]   This well-settled courts practice has been codified in 2011 in a new Article 1449 of the French Code of Civil Procedure.

tribunal is not yet constituted and that (ii) the existence of an emergency is demonstrated.[13] This policy clearly aims at avoiding any concurrent powers between a state court and an arbitral tribunal.[14] Once the arbitral tribunal is constituted, the state court must decline jurisdiction.[15]

The request for interim measures is generally filed before the *juge des référés*, who has jurisdiction to rule on provisional or conservatory measures through summary proceedings. The *juge des référés* may rule within a few days in cases of particular emergency or within a period of time of about one month after the request has been filed in all other cases.

Anti-suit injunctions are not part of the French legal tradition. We are not aware of any instance where a French court has been requested to issue an anti-suit injunction. In France, the issue has been whether or not a foreign anti-suit injunction issued in support of an arbitration agreement may be recognized and enforced within the French territory. At European level, the European Court of Justice ruled in February 2009, in *West Tankers,* that an anti-suit injunction rendered by an English court preventing a party from commencing a judicial procedure in Italy because of the existence of an arbitration agreement was contrary to Council Regulation 44/2001 and the underlying principle of trust that the EU Member States accord to one another's legal systems and judicial institutions.

---

[13] The condition of urgency is however not requested for expertise measure grounded on Article 145 of the French Code of Civile Procedure which aims at obtaining or preserving evidence before any trial on the merits has commenced.

[14] Court of Appeal of Reims, 3 July 2012, ruling that the court has jurisdiction and may order an interim measure once the arbitral tribunal has rendered its award and does not exist anymore.

[15] Except for conservatory attachments of movable properties and judicial securities, which can only be granted by a judicial court.

However, a few months later, in October 2009, the French *Cour de cassation* ruled that an anti-suit injunction issued by a US court preventing a French distributor from commencing proceedings before a French court did not contravene international public order and thus could be recognized and enforced in France. In doing so, the *Cour de cassation* determined that (i) the anti-suit injunction did not fall within the application of an international convention or European law, and that (ii) the purpose of the anti-suit injunction was to enforce a choice of forum clause agreed upon between the parties by which exclusive jurisdiction was given to US courts. Thus, the French supreme court clearly distinguished between anti-suit injunctions issued by a non-European court, which may be recognized and enforced in France, and anti-suit injunctions rendered by a European court, which would most probably be refused recognition by virtue of EU rules as interpreted by the European Court of Justice. One has to note, however, that the matter is not well settled and yet to be confirmed, particularly with respect to arbitration agreements.

Article 1449 of the French Code of Civil Procedure, which allows court-ordered interim measures, does not distinguish between "national" and "foreign" arbitration. Therefore, a court may grant an interim measures in aid of a foreign arbitration provided that the arbitral tribunal is not yet constituted.

C.3 Enforcement of Interim Measures

Under French law, a mere interim order issued by an arbitral tribunal cannot be enforced. Therefore, to be enforceable within the French territory (i.e., receive the required *exequatur*), interim measures ordered by an arbitral tribunal must be in a form of an award.[16] Any type of interim measures ordered by way of an

---

[16]   Court of Appeal of Paris, 7 October 2004, *SARL Carlyle*.

award, irrespective of whether the award has been made within the French territory or abroad, may be enforced provided they do not manifestly contravene public policy. The only exceptions relate to conservatory attachments of movable properties and judicial securities, which are expressly excluded by Article 1449 of the French Code of Civil Procedure from the measures that can be ordered by an arbitral tribunal. Therefore, under current French case law, a party requesting an interim measure from an arbitral tribunal must take particular care to ensure that the measure is ordered by way of an award rather than a mere procedural order.

GERMANY

Ragnar Harbst,[1] Heiko Plassmeier[2] and Jürgen Mark[3]

A. LEGISLATION, TRENDS AND TENDENCIES

A.1 New Act on the Promotion of Mediation and Other Procedures of Alternative Dispute Resolution Comes into Force

The new German Act on the Promotion of Mediation and other Procedures of Alternative Dispute Resolution ("Mediation Act") came into force on 26 July 2012.

The Mediation Act goes back to the European Directive 2008/52/EC on certain aspects of mediation in civil and commercial matters dated 21 May 2008. EU member states were obligated to transpose the directive into national laws by 21 May 2011. Due to lengthy consultation procedures with various interest groups, the draft act could only be presented to the German National Assembly ("Bundestag") on 1 April 2011. After further detailed discussions in the Bundestag's legal

---

[1] Ragnar Harbst is a Partner in Baker & McKenzie's Frankfurt office. He has acted in numerous international arbitration proceedings, both as party representative and as arbitrator. His practice focus is on construction and infrastructure related disputes. Mr. Harbst is also qualified as a Solicitor in England and Wales.

[2] Heiko Plassmeier is a Counsel in Baker & McKenzie's Düsseldorf office. He advises and represents clients from various industries, including the energy and automotive sectors, in domestic and international litigation and arbitration cases and has been acting as an arbitrator. Besides his dispute resolution practice, he also handles insolvency matters.

[3] Jürgen Mark is a Partner in Baker & McKenzie's Düsseldorf office. He practices in the areas of litigation and domestic and international arbitration. Mr. Mark has also acted as arbitrator in ad-hoc, ICC and DIS arbitration proceedings relating to corporate and post M&A disputes, major construction projects, product distribution and product liability.

committee, the Mediation Act came into force on 26 July 2012. Despite this timeline, the legislative content of the Mediation Act's eight sections is limited. The act basically records what can be called best practice in mediation proceedings. After a broad definition of "mediation" in Section 1, Section 2 sets out the basic principles that the mediator is chosen by the parties, that the mediator may also conduct separate talks with the parties, and that any participant may terminate the mediation at any time. Section 3 sets out the mediator's obligation to inform the parties of any circumstances that may prevent him or her from acting as a mediator (conflict of interest). Section 4 concerns the mediator's obligation of confidentiality towards the parties; Sections 5 and 6 establish the official title of "certified mediator," a title that may only be used by individuals who have undertaken the prescribed training. This title, however, is not required in order to act as a mediator. Details of the training to be performed in order to be called "certified mediator" have yet to be determined by way of a regulation. Sections 7 and 8 do not concern the mediation proceedings themselves, but rather the monitoring of mediation by the state in order to evaluate the need for further legislative measures and/or financial aid for mediation proceedings.

Two noteworthy innovations concern the relation between mediation and court proceedings. First, the new Section 253(3)(1) of the German Code of Civil Procedure ("ZPO") provides that a statement of claim in state court proceedings should include a statement as to whether the parties attempted to settle the dispute by way of mediation or other forms of dispute resolution before commencing proceedings. The introduction of this provision has been criticized because of potential conflicts with the concept of confidentiality (Section 4 Mediation Act). It is not uncommon in mediation agreements that parties agree to keep even the fact that mediation took place confidential.

Statutes should therefore not require parties, not even by way of a soft obligation ("should") to disclose such information. Second, the German federal states are authorized to introduce provisions to reduce or dispense with court fees if the parties settle a dispute by way of mediation. As a condition precedent, however, such reductions of court fees shall only be possible if the statement of claim indicates that the parties will, or intend to, carry out a mediation, or if the (successful) mediation was carried out upon suggestion of the court. The rationale is to give a monetary incentive to the parties to settle and thus to reduce the case load of state courts. It remains to be seen whether the federal states make use of this authorization.

All in all, the operative content of the act is limited. Mediation as such has traditionally been a procedure devised as a counter-model to adjudication by state authorities. As such, it was traditionally "state free" and only governed by private agreement; this will remain unchanged under the Mediation Act. As a positive side effect, the Act and the significant echo that it found in press coverage may help to remind potential users of the opportunities and benefits afforded by mediation. At present, mediation is rarely used for commercial disputes in Germany.

A.2 Changes within the German Institution of Arbitration

On 20 April 2012, the General Assembly of the German Institution of Arbitration ("DIS") elected its new Board of Directors. Prof. Dr. Karl-Heinz Böckstiegel, (Chairman of the DIS from 1996 to 2012) did not run for reelection. Prof. Dr. Klaus Peter Berger, Deputy Chairman since 2008, was elected as the new Chairman.

Further, in October 2012, Dr. Francesca Mazza joined the DIS as incoming Secretary General. The current Secretary General, Jens Bredow, will retire from his position at the end of 2013.

Francesca Mazza joined the DIS from the ICC International Court of Arbitration in Paris, where she recently supervised the rules revision process and was responsible for co-drafting the new 2012 ICC Rules of Arbitration.

B. CASES

B.1 An Arbitral Tribunal May Be Composed of More Than Three Arbitrators

In a recent decision[4], the Court of Appeal Koblenz rejected the application of the claimant in arbitration proceedings with three respondents to appoint one arbitrator between them, rather than one each.

The dispute related to the liquidation of a partnership of lawyers. The applicant had withdrawn from the partnership in 2006. In 2009, he refuted the settlement agreement which he had concluded with his former partners for fraudulent misrepresentation. He initiated arbitration proceedings against the three former partners and requested the payment of damages. After each of his former partners had nominated an arbitrator in accordance with the wording of the arbitration clause, the applicant asked the Court of Appeal Koblenz to appoint only one arbitrator for all three respondents. He argued that otherwise, the respondents would have a stronger influence on the composition of the arbitral tribunal than he had.

---

[4] Court of Appeal Koblenz, order of 17 July 2012, file no. 2 Sch 2/12. Most decisions cited in this chapter can be found in the database on the website of the German Institution of Arbitration ("DIS") (www.dis-arb.de) (often with an English summary). Where applicable, it is noted if a decision was also published in a law journal.

This application was dismissed. The Court of Appeal pointed out that the parties are free to determine the number of arbitrators and that the number of arbitrators shall only be three if the parties did not agree otherwise, Section 1034(1) ZPO. As the partnership agreement had provided for the right of every partner to nominate an arbitrator, the Court of Appeal held that this clear provision had to be observed. In particular, the court found that the arbitration clause did not grant a preponderant right to the respondents with regard to the composition of the arbitral tribunal which could place the claimant at a disadvantage in the arbitration proceedings (Section 1034(2) ZPO).

B.2 Breach of *Ne Ultra Petita* Rule Is Contrary to Public Policy and Justifies the Setting Aside of an Award[5]

According to Section 1059(2)(2)(b) ZPO, an arbitral award can be set aside if its enforcement leads to a result that is not in line with public policy. Not every mandatory provision of German substantive or procedural law is part of public policy, but only those rules that protect fundamental values, which constitute the basis for the proper functioning of public and economic life or which protect the most basic notions and principles of German law.[6] A mere misinterpretation or a mere breach of mandatory German law will not suffice. Enforcement is therefore only refused for breach of public policy in exceptional cases.

In a decision rendered in June 2011, the Court of Appeal Cologne may have applied a lower standard. In the case at hand, the court had to decide about the enforceability of an arbitral

---

[5] Court of Appeal Cologne, judgment of 28 June 2011, file no. 19 Sch 11/10; SchiedsVZ, 2012, 161.

[6] For details, see *Baker & McKenzie International Arbitration Yearbook* 2011/2012, page 214 *et seq*; Arbitration in Germany, 2007, Section 1059, note 78 *et seq*.

award in a dispute between the partners of a bidding consortium for the building of a magnetic levitation train between two Chinese cities. Both the claimants and the respondents had been partners to this bidding consortium which had been created in 1998 to participate in the bidding procedure. After the tender had been officially closed for political reasons—the Chinese authorities had decided not to build the magnetic levitation train line—the respondents were excluded from the bidding consortium.

A few months later, a Chinese delegation came to Germany and visited the test track for the magnetic levitation train. In 2001, a Chinese entity concluded a know-how transfer agreement with another consortium regarding the construction and operation of a hybrid travel track carrier system. The partners in this new consortium were the respondents.

After the claimant had learned about the agreement between the second consortium and the Chinese partner, it initiated arbitration proceedings against the respondents based on the arbitration agreement in the contract for the creation of the bidding consortium, alleging that the bidding consortium had developed the travel track carrier, that this technical development had been disclosed to the second consortium and that this disclosure constituted a breach of the consortium agreement. The claimant asked the arbitral tribunal in the separate arbitrations to order each respondent to disclose to the first consortium which types of business transactions they had carried out as a partner of the second consortium and which revenues had accrued or will accrue in the future as a result of these transactions. The separate arbitration proceedings were later consolidated upon the application of the claimant.

The arbitral tribunal ordered the respondents, as jointly and severally liable debtors, to disclose which types of business transactions they had carried out in their role as partners of the second consortium and which revenues had accrued or will accrue for these transactions.

The Court of Appeal Cologne held the arbitral award to be unenforceable because it violated German procedural public policy by ordering the respondents to do more than the claimant had asked for. This is a surprising result, given the high hurdle which needs to be overcome for an arbitral award to violate public policy. The court admitted in the judgment that it was not necessary for the claimant expressly to ask the arbitral tribunal to hold the respondents jointly and severely liable but that it was possible for the tribunal to interpret the new application of the claimant in the consolidated arbitration proceedings to mean that the respondents were to be held jointly and severally liable. Nevertheless, the court found that with its interpretation, the arbitral tribunal had breached the *ne ultra petita* rule. A convincing reason was not given for this decision. It may well be that in the case at hand, the tribunal's interpretation was not considered by the court to be obvious. A more reasonable interpretation might have been to view the consolidated application as a request for the disclosure of information about the individual contributions of each of the respondents to the new consortium and not about their joint contributions. Nevertheless, the tribunal's interpretation was possible and the court's judgment therefore constituted a *revision au fond*.

The court argued that in case of a joint and several liability of the respondents for the information requested, each respondent could provide this information and thereby release the other respondents from their own liability. This would be to the disadvantage of the claimant. As it was the claimant who had requested the enforcement of the award and apparently did not feel to be put in a disadvantage by the award, this argument is not convincing. On the contrary, the fact that the claimant was seeking the enforcement of the award showed that the tribunal had correctly interpreted the claimant's consolidated application. In any event, the interpretation of the tribunal breached neither the fundamental values which constitute the basis for the proper functioning of public and economic life in Germany, nor the most basic notions and principles of German law.

B.3 Interpretation of "Arbitration Agreement"[7]

In a recent decision, the Court of Appeal Munich had to decide whether a contract for the delivery of seeds contained a valid arbitration clause. In the written contract in dispute, the parties had agreed that the respondent had to deliver seeds to the applicant and the applicant had to cultivate and deliver spelt to the respondent. The contract provided for the application of the uniform provisions of German Corn Trade and in case of a dispute for the "arbitration tribunal of the buyer."

After the applicant failed to deliver crop in 2011, the respondent filed for arbitration with the Bavarian Commodity Exchange in Munich, Bavaria, the German federal state in which the buyer had its seat. The applicant asked the Court of Appeal Munich to declare that the arbitral proceedings initiated by the respondent were inadmissible due to the non-existence of an arbitration agreement. The Court of Appeal Munich found this application to be without merit. It referred to the uniform conditions of the German Corn Trade which provide in Section 1 that all disputes relating to corn trade contracts will be settled by arbitration without recourse to the ordinary courts of law through an arbitral tribunal established by one of the German Commodity Exchanges. As the buyer was a Bavarian company, the

---

[7]   Court of Appeal Munich, order of 29 March 2012, file no. 34 Sch 12/11; SchiedsVZ, 2012, 159.

arbitration court of the Bavarian Commodity Exchange in Munich had jurisdiction. The Court of Appeal expressly stated that the arbitration agreement was transparent. The reference to the uniform conditions of the German Corn Trade and to the arbitration tribunal of the buyer made it easy for the parties to determine which tribunal had competence to decide a dispute.

B.4 An Arbitral Tribunal That Determines the Amount in Dispute for Purposes of a Cost Decision Does Not Inadmissibly Act as a Judge in Its Own Affairs[8]

It is a fundamental principle of German procedural law that a person must not act as a judge in his or her own affairs; this principle also applies to arbitration proceedings.[9] It was a topic of some debate whether arbitrators get in conflict with this basic principle when determining the amount in dispute in arbitral proceedings for the purposes of a cost decision. According to Section 1057 ZPO, the arbitral tribunal shall decide on the allocation of the costs between the parties. In German arbitration proceedings, it is not uncommon that the fees of the arbitrators are proportionate to the amount in dispute (e.g., using the Attorneys' Remuneration Act ("RVG") as a benchmark, or in arbitrations according to the DIS Rules). For such cases, is has been argued that an arbitral tribunal fixing the amount in dispute for purposes of a cost decision also acts as a judge in its own affairs, as the amount in dispute indirectly determines the amount of the arbitrator's fees. Arguably, this could render the cost decision, or possibly the entire arbitral award, challengeable.

---

[8] Federal Supreme Court, Order of March 28, 2012, file no. III ZB 63/10, SchiedsVZ 2012, 154.

[9] Cf. the cases reported in the *Baker & McKenzie International Arbitration Yearbook* 2007, p. 55 *et seq.*

The Federal Supreme Court has now clarified that an arbitral tribunal fixing the amount in dispute for the purposes of a cost decision does not violate the rule against acting as a judge in its own affairs. In the instant case, the applicant had commenced arbitral proceedings, but then withdrawn its request for arbitration before a hearing took place. The arbitral tribunal rendered a cost decision and also fixed the amount in dispute at € 30 million. In a separate cost decision, the arbitral tribunal then ordered the applicant to compensate the responding parties for the advances on costs they had made. The applicant challenged the arbitral awards (on the merits and on costs) arguing, *inter alia*, that the arbitral tribunal had acted as a judge in its own affairs by determining the amount in dispute.

The Federal Supreme Court rejected this argument. In doing so, the court drew a distinction between the relationship between the two parties on the one hand and the relationship between the parties and the arbitrators (as well as the parties and their attorneys) on the other hand. The arbitral tribunal's determination of the amount in dispute will only be binding between the parties and cannot be challenged. However, with regard to the fee claims of the arbitrators, and also the fee claims of the parties' legal representatives, the determination of the amount in dispute is not binding. Accordingly, the parties cannot challenge the arbitral award arguing that an arbitral tribunal violated the rule against acting as judges in their own affairs when rendering the cost decision; however, the parties can commence legal proceedings against the arbitrators in order to challenge the determination of the amount in dispute for purposes of the arbitrator's fee claims. To the same extent, the parties could commence proceedings against their attorneys (or vice-versa) in case the attorney's fees were also determined based on the amount in dispute. If the court does not uphold the arbitrators' determination of the amount in dispute, this decision is only relevant for the relationship between the respective party and the arbitrators with regard to the fees payable; between the parties, the rendered award and/or cost award is not affected by such decision.

B.5 Attorneys' Time Charges Recognized as Recoverable Costs

In litigation before German state courts, the attorneys' fees that the prevailing party can recover are capped by the amount of fees derived from the statutory fee schedule that is part of the RVG. Under the RVG, fees are calculated in "fee units" that accrue at successive stages in the proceedings. The amount of the individual fees depends on the amount at issue in the particular case. Agreements between client and attorney on remuneration based on a time charge instead of the statutory fee scheme have to be concluded in writing (Section 3a(1) RVG). For clients who pay their attorneys by the time they spend on their case, the restriction of the amount of fees recoverable from the opposing party frequently[10] means that they cannot recover the entire fee paid, even if they prevail in full.

As between attorney and client, the same statutory provisions apply to arbitration (Section 36(1) RVG). Traditionally, the German view was that the above restriction on the amount of fees recoverable in court proceedings also applies in arbitration. However, as *Bredow/Mulder*[11] pointed out in 2007, there are no statutory rules on reimbursement of costs in arbitration; the determination of costs to be reimbursed is rather in the tribunal's

---

[10] Exceptions can apply in comparatively straightforward cases with very high amounts at issue. However, Section 22 para. 2 RVG provides for a fee cap at € 30 m. For amounts at issue that exceed this threshold, German attorneys are thus not entitled to increased fees under the statutory scheme.

[11] In: *Böckstiegel/Kröll/Nacimiento*, Arbitration in Germany, Section 35 DIS Rules, note 15.

discretion. In both international arbitrations with a German seat and domestic cases, tribunals have in the past occasionally awarded costs based on a time charge. This trend has been increasing lately, but it was not clear whether in cases where enforcement of the award is required, German state courts would be prepared to assist by declaring enforceable an award that grants reimbursement of time-based costs that exceed the statutory German fees.

In two orders rendered on 11 April and 23 July 2012, the Court of Appeal Munich now seized the opportunity to clarify that such awards can be declared enforceable. The first of these cases[12] concerned an application for recognition of a Swiss award on costs rendered in proceedings between two German companies under the DIS Rules. The tribunal had awarded the claimant a reimbursement of time charges in a total amount of approx. € 326,000. The respondent requested the court to deny recognition of the award insofar as it exceeded the statutory fee amount of approx. € 119,000. However, the respondent did not attack the award "head-on" by claiming that it constitutes a breach of public policy within the meaning of Section 1061(1) ZPO in conjunction with Art. V (2) (b) of the New York Convention. Instead, it sought to rely on alleged breaches of due process, among others by claiming that the tribunal should have required the claimant to disclose the details of the time charges, i.e., to show which amount had been invoiced for the individual pieces of the claimant's attorneys' work.

The court of appeal noted that because of the prohibition of a *révision au fond*, it was unable to re-open the case on the merits. It found that if a tribunal is satisfied with a lower measure of substantiation, its decision may be wrong, but that it does not amount to a breach of due process if only the factual basis for the

---

[12]   File No. 34 Sch 21/11, SchiedsVZ 2012, 156.

decision was known to both parties. The court also held that the tribunal's finding that lawyers' fees exceeding the statutory amount could be considered "costs incurred by the parties ... which were necessary for the proper pursuit of their claim or defense" within the meaning of Section 35.1 of the DIS Rules was well-reasoned and not open to objections.

The subject matter of the other decision[13] on the same issue was an ICC award in a German arbitration between a German claimant and an Austrian respondent, in which the respondent had prevailed almost entirely. Among other things, the tribunal had granted the respondent reimbursement of its Austrian lawyers' time charges in an amount of € 61,525, while—based on the German claimant's application for recovery of costs—its lawyers' fees had only been considered in the statutory amount of € 9,010. The Court of Appeal Munich granted the respondent's application for a declaration of enforceability of the award. With respect to the recoverable lawyers' fees, it held that Article 31(1) of the ICC Rules (1998 version) provided the sole basis for the tribunal's decision and that recourse to German statutory provisions was not warranted. The tribunal had to determine the "reasonable legal and other costs incurred by the parties for the arbitration" within the meaning of Article 31(1) of the ICC Rules in its sole discretion. In doing so, it was free to assume that reimbursement of costs on a time charge basis was reasonable for both parties. The court of appeal expressly recognized that billing by the time spent is customary in international proceedings of a certain magnitude and complexity.

---

[13] File No. 34 Sch 19/11, SchiedsVZ 2012, 282.

B.6 **Non-compliance with an Agreed Procedure for the Taking of Evidence Justifies Vacation of an Award**[14]

According to Section 1059(2)(1)(d) ZPO, an arbitral award can be set aside if the arbitral procedure was not in accordance with an admissible agreement between the parties and if this presumably affected the award. The Court of Appeal Frankfurt/Main had to decide whether the fact that an arbitral tribunal had not complied with an agreement between the parties as to the taking of evidence rendered an award challengeable. The arbitration at issue concerned a sale and purchase agreement for the transfer of company shares. After the SPA was signed, the buyer did not perform the transaction because the seller had allegedly violated an "ordinary course of business" clause in the SPA. The seller then commenced arbitration proceedings and pursued damage claims for non-performance of the SPA. One of the main issues in dispute was the purchase price that would have been payable if the transaction had been completed. The claimant based its calculation of the purchase price and the damages mainly on the opinion of a party-appointed expert. In a procedural order, the tribunal had determined that any party expert opinion had to indicate all documents considered and reviewed by the expert, and that such documents had to be submitted together with the expert opinion. The procedural order stated in its introduction that the order recorded the agreements between the parties with regard to the written submission in the proceedings. When the claimant produced its expert opinion, it did not submit all documents considered by the expert to the record. Upon request of the respondent, some more, but not all

---

[14] Court of Appeal Frankfurt am Main, order of 17 February 2011, file no. 26 Sch 13/10. In November 2012, the Federal Supreme Court decided not to accept the decision for appeal, file number III ZR 3/11; the decision is therefore final and binding).

documents, were produced. Eventually, the tribunal appointed a neutral expert who rendered an expert opinion in which he took into account the expert opinion by the claimant's party-appointed expert. Notwithstanding the respondent's further requests for production of documents, the tribunal finally considered the opinion of the independent expert to be a reliable source on which the award could be based, even without further document production. Eventually, the arbitral tribunal ordered the respondent to pay damages in an amount of € 210,658,362.

The respondent challenged the award, arguing, among other things, that the tribunal had failed to comply with an admissible agreement of the parties with regard to the procedure according to Section 1059 (20(1)(d) ZPO. It argued that the tribunal was obliged to order the claimant to produce all documents considered and reviewed by the party-appointed expert. In a decision that surprised many arbitration practitioners, the Court of Appeal Frankfurt/Main set the arbitral award aside. The court held that the arbitral tribunal had no discretion to refuse the respondent's request for production of all documents mentioned in the claimant's party expert opinion. It held that the parties had reached an agreement, which was then recorded in the aforementioned procedural order. Whereas an arbitral tribunal was usually free to determine the procedure of the arbitration, such discretion was by law subject to agreements between the parties.

The decision is certainly in line with the provisions of the German ZPO. However, it leaves the reader with the uneasy feeling that the decision, to a large extent, was influenced by the phraseology in the introduction of the procedural order. Had the procedural order not referred to an agreement between the parties, but rather determined the same procedure from the tribunal's perspective, the award may have been upheld.

B.7 Termination of an Arbitration Agreement because of Allegations of Procedural Misconduct and Fraud[15]

The Court of Appeal Munich had to deal with the question of whether an arbitration agreement can be terminated for cause if a party to the arbitration breaches its procedural obligations. It is accepted under German law that an arbitration agreement is subject to substantive private law; according to Section 314 of the German Civil Code ("BGB"), an agreement can be terminated without notice if the terminating party cannot reasonably be expected to continue the contractual relationship. It is generally accepted that this provision also applies to arbitration agreements. There is, however, a scarcity of authorities as to when such termination may be justified. In the case at hand, the claimant first initiated arbitration proceedings, but then attempted to terminate the arbitration agreement at a later point in time. Among other things, the claimant based its termination on the allegation that the respondent intentionally made wrongful statements that were tantamount to procedural fraud. The claimant further alleged that the respondent had forged documents and intentionally delayed the resolution of the dispute.

The court dismissed the application, holding that a termination of the arbitration agreement was not justified. The decision is interesting not so much for the findings on the specific grounds of termination alleged by the claimant, but rather for the general guidance that the court gave concerning the termination of arbitration agreements. It held that only a severe breach of the obligation to further the proceedings or the contractual duty of loyalty can justify a termination. It must be restricted, the court

---

[15] Court of Appeal Munich, order of 29 February 2012, file no. 34 SchH 6/11, SchiedsVZ 2012, 96.

ruled, so that parties cannot try to sabotage arbitration proceedings by alleging procedural misconduct on which they then base a termination. Even the severe allegation that a party intentionally made wrongful statements does not justify a termination. Otherwise, such allegations would have to be tested in state court proceedings and would therefore lead to parallel proceedings before state courts and arbitral tribunals.

As a matter of principle, German law accepts that state courts and arbitral tribunals are on an equal footing when it comes to the adjudication of disputes; just as a state court would have to deal with allegations of procedural misconduct, fraud and violations of the duty to make true statements, such allegations must be dealt with by the arbitral tribunal when it comes to arbitration. A termination was therefore only held to be justified if circumstances occur under which effective legal protection can no longer be expected so that the arbitration agreement has become incapable of being performed. Unless and until there is clear evidence that no effective legal protection is granted, even severe conflicts have to be resolved in arbitral proceedings. The decision is a sensible and welcome rejection of attempts to sabotage arbitration proceedings by way of unilaterally terminating the arbitration agreement.

B.8 Preclusion of Reliance on Reasons to Vacate after Failure to Challenge in the Country of Origin

As reported in last year's edition,[16] the question of whether a party is barred from raising defenses against an arbitral award in *exequatur* proceedings that could have been argued in challenge proceedings in the award's country of origin is subject to

---

[16] *Baker & McKenzie International Arbitration Yearbook 2011 – 2012*, p. 201 *et seq.*

considerable debate. Under the former German arbitration law (in effect until 31 December 1997), the Federal Supreme Court had held in favor of such preclusion.[17] However, under the current Section 1061(1) ZPO that refers to the New York Convention and other treaties on recognition of foreign awards, the Federal Supreme Court allowed at least a defense relating to jurisdiction of the arbitral tribunal where proceedings for vacation of the award had not been initiated in the country of origin.[18]

In a decision of 4 January 2012,[19] the Court of Appeal Karlsruhe had to revisit the issue of preclusion of non-jurisdiction related defenses against recognition of a foreign award. In the underlying arbitration proceedings that had their seat in the US, an ICC tribunal had, among other things, ordered the insolvent German respondent to pay to the claimant an amount of approx. USD 2.3 million out of the respondent's insolvency estate.[20] The claimant brought an application to the Court of Appeal Karlsruhe for recognition of the award. In its defense, the respondent sought to rely on a host of alleged breaches of international public policy, including the submission that one of the arbitrators had fallen asleep during the hearings. However, the respondent had failed to raise these issues in a motion to vacate which under

---

[17]   Federal Supreme Court, decision of 26 June 1969, file no. VII ZR 32/67, BGHZ 52, 184, 188; BGH NJW 1984, 2763, 2764.

[18]   Federal Supreme Court, decision of 16 December 2010, file no. III ZB 100/09; SchiedsVZ 2011, 105.

[19]   File No. 9 Sch 02/09, SchiedsVZ 2012, 101.

[20]   As explained in the *Baker & McKenzie International Arbitration Yearbooks* 2009 (p. 161 *et seq.*) and 2010 – 2011 (p. 263), the Federal Supreme Court had held in a decision of 29 January 2009 (file no. III ZB 88/07, SchiedsVZ 2009, 176) that it does not *per se* amount to a breach of public policy if an award includes an order against the insolvent party to effect payment. Instead, the operating provisions of the award could be construed in such way as to amount to a mere acknowledgement of the claims awarded in the insolvency table.

Section 12 of the US Federal Arbitration Act it would have had to file within three months after delivery of the award.

The court of appeal restated its previous jurisprudence[21] to the effect that Section 1061(1) ZPO had not changed the legal framework, at least where non-jurisdictional issues are at stake. It held that all grounds to deny recognition—including those based on alleged breaches of public policy—that could have been raised in proceedings to vacate the award in the US were precluded. The court acknowledged that it is subject to dispute whether its previous line of authority continues to apply after the reform of German arbitration law in 1998, since Article V of the New York Convention does not speak to a preclusion of grounds to deny recognition.[22] However, it found that the New York Convention does not prevent a restrictive application of the grounds to deny recognition and that the reasons that justified preclusion before the law reform still applied. Where enforcement of a foreign award in Germany is an option, a party who fails to apply for vacation of the award in its country of origin does so at its peril.

---

[21] Decision of March 27, 2006, file no. 9 Sch 2/05, SchiedsVZ 2006, 335; decision of July 3, 2006, file no. 9 Sch 1/06, SchiedsVZ 2006, 281 with affirmative note *Gruber*, SchiedsVZ 2006, 283; decision of 14 September 2007, file no. 9 Sch 2/07, SchiedsVZ 2008, 47.

[22] In favor of a continued application among others Court of Appeal Stuttgart, decisions of 14 October 2003, file nos. 1 Sch 16/02 and 1 Sch 6/03, available in the database on the DIS website; Court of Appeal Hamm, decision of 27 September 2005, file no. 29 Sch 1/05, SchiedsVZ 2006, 106; Münchener Kommentar-ZPO-*Münch*, 3rd ed., Section 1061, note 12; Münchener Kommentar-ZPO-*Adolphsen*, 3rd ed., Section 1061, Appendix 1, Art. V New York Convention, note 11 *et seq.*; Musielak-*Voit*, ZPO, 1st ed. Section 1061, note 20; against a continued application among others Bavarian Higher Court of Appeal, decision of March 16, 2000, file no. 4Z Sch 50/99, NJW-RR 2001, 431; *Mallmann*, SchiedsVZ 2004, 152, 157; *Schwab/Walter*, Schiedsgerichtsbarkeit, 7th ed. 2005, Chapter 30, note 19; Stein/Jonas-*Schlosser*, ZPO, 22nd ed., Appendix to Section 1061, note 76.

B.9 No Recognition of Awards Vacated in Their Country of Origin

In a decision of 30 July 2012,[23] the Court of Appeal Munich reconfirmed[24] that a foreign award that was vacated in its country of origin cannot be recognized and declared enforceable in Germany. The decision is notable because it also constitutes one of the few instances in which German courts considered provisions of foreign law under the heading of "public policy."[25]

The parties in the underlying proceedings had concluded a distributorship agreement under Ukrainian law in which a German manufacturer of agricultural machines (respondent) granted a Ukrainian company (claimant) an exclusive right to distribute its products in Ukraine. The respondent undertook to pay a contractual penalty for each case of direct sales of the contractual products in the territory in circumvention of the claimant's exclusive distribution right. The claimant later alleged that ten such direct sales had occurred during the term of the contract and brought arbitration proceedings before the International Commercial Arbitration Court at the Ukrainian Chamber of Commerce and Industry ("ICAC at the UCCI"), for payment of the contractual penalty; the arbitration clause in the distributorship agreement provided for disputes to be settled by "an arbitral award in accordance with the arbitration rules of the Ukrainian chamber of trade and industry".

---

[23] File No. 34 Sch 18/10, SchiedsVZ 2012, 339.

[24] Cf. the decision of the Court of Appeal Dresden, file no. 11 Sch 18/07 reported in the *Baker & McKenzie International Arbitration Yearbook* 2007, p. 57 *et seq.*; this decision was confirmed by the Federal Supreme Court in file no. III ZB 14/07, SchiedsVZ 2008, 195.

[25] Cf. *Baker & McKenzie International Arbitration Yearbook 2011 – 2012*, p. 218.

The arbitral tribunal issued an award in which it ordered the respondent to pay € 355,600 to the claimant. Upon the respondent's application, the District Court Kiev vacated the award, holding that the distributorship agreement violated Ukrainian law: The contractual penalty clause was held to breach Art. 12 of the Ukrainian Act for Protection of the Rights of Buyers of Agricultural Machines in that it obstructed the buyers' choice of sellers of the respondent's machines and thus effectively required the respondent to violate Ukrainian law. This in turn was held to amount to a breach of Ukrainian public policy. In addition, the District Court Kiev held that the tribunal did not have jurisdiction, since the parties had only agreed on jurisdiction of "an arbitral tribunal" without specifying the competence of an ICAC tribunal. After the first instance decision to vacate the award, the claimant brought no less than three appeals. However, the decision was upheld by all higher Ukrainian courts involved.

The claimant then pursued a different route by bringing an application to the Court of Appeal Munich to recognize the award and declare it enforceable in Germany. This application was denied for two reasons, either of which would have sufficed:

- The award had been vacated in its country of origin. Under Article V (1)(e) of the New York Convention in conjunction with Art. IX of the European Convention on International Commercial Arbitration of 1961,[26] it could thus not be declared enforceable. The court of appeal emphasized that the *exequatur* court has to follow the decision of a foreign state court to vacate an arbitration award if this decision was (1) rendered by the competent court in the award's country of origin and (2) based on one of the grounds in Article IX of the European Convention. In the present case, jurisdiction of the

---

[26] This Convention applies as between Germany and Ukraine, among others.

Ukrainian courts was undisputed, and the award had been vacated based on the reason mentioned in Article IX (1)(d) of the European Convention.[27] The court of appeal expressly noted that the *exequatur* court must not review the merits of the decision to vacate.[28]

- The award was held to breach German public policy, which caused the court of appeal to deny recognition under Article V(2)(b) of the New York Convention. In the court's view, the contractual penalty clause was designed to force the respondent to deny direct offers from Ukrainian customers to purchase its products even though under Article 12 of the Ukrainian Act for Protection of the Rights of Buyers of Agricultural Machines, the respondent ought to have entered into such direct contracts. The decision emphasizes that it is the function of public policy to safeguard that a state's commercial law provision are not being circumvented "via the detour of arbitration."[29]

---

[27] "The setting aside in a Contracting State of an arbitral award covered by this Convention shall only constitute a ground for the refusal of recognition or enforcement in another Contracting State where such setting aside took place in a State in which, or under the law of which, the award has been made and for one of the following reasons:

(…)

(d) the composition of the arbitral authority or the arbitral procedure was not in accordance with the agreement of the parties (…)."

[28] In a domestic case, a German court would in all likelihood not have doubted the jurisdiction of a tribunal under the rules of the ICAC at the UCCI based on an arbitration clause that calls for arbitration "in accordance with the arbitration rules of the Ukrainian chamber of trade and industry."

[29] Stein/Jonas-Schlosser, ZPO, 22nd ed., Appendix to Section 1061, note 135.

C. THE GRANT AND ENFORCEMENT OF INTERIM MEASURES IN INTERNATIONAL ARBITRATION

Express provisions that confer upon arbitral tribunals the power to grant interim measures were only introduced into German law by virtue of the reform of 1998. The core provision is modeled after Article 17 of the UNCITRAL Model Law in its original shape of 1985, while most of the amendments to the Model Law of 2006 were not expressly adopted. Since the 1998 reform, the competence of state courts and arbitral tribunals to grant interim measure in cases that are governed by arbitration agreements have been existing in parallel. Jurisdiction of the former is governed by Section 1033 ZPO[30] and is mandatory,[31] while jurisdiction of the latter follows from Section 1041 ZPO and can be derogated.[32]

Since the express statutory power of arbitral tribunals to grant interim measures is a relative novelty of German arbitration law and since this power is not very frequently used in practice, this

---

[30] Section 1033 ZPO restates Art. 9 of the UNCITRAL Model Law almost verbatim, except that it contains an additional qualification to the extent that interim measures granted under this provision must relate "to the subject matter of the arbitration". However, this qualification is of no practical significance, since state courts are also empowered to grant interim relief in matters unrelated to an arbitration, cf. Böckstiegel/Kröll/Nacimiento-*Kreindler/Schäfer*, Arbitration in Germany, Section 1033, note 6.

[31] Court of Appeal Munich, decision of 26 October 2000, file no. U (K) 3208/00, NJW-RR 2001, 711; Münchener Kommentar-ZPO-*Münch*, 3rd ed., Section 1033, note 18. Others (Zöller-*Geimer*, ZPO, 29th ed., Section 1033, note 6; *Schütze*, IPRax 2006, 442) argue that the parties may opt out of the state courts' jurisdiction. In any event, this jurisdiction must be expressly derogated.

[32] Under Section 1041 para. 1 sentence 1 ZPO (which is equivalent to Art. 17 (1) UNCITRAL Model Law), the tribunal may only grant interim measures "unless otherwise agreed by the parties".

area of law is still largely marked by an absence of court decisions and thus by a degree of uncertainty.

C.1 Tribunal-Ordered Interim Measures

An arbitral tribunal can issue the same measures as a state court, (see section C2 below), but is not limited to "German style" measures.[33] However, the scope of matters in which an arbitral tribunal can grant interim measures is limited to issues "relating to the subject matter of the dispute" (Section 1041(1) sentence 1 ZPO). This principle shows the major prerequisites (and disadvantages) of tribunal-ordered interim measures: to apply for protection with the tribunal,

- the arbitration agreement must be *prima facie* valid;[34]
- arbitration proceedings must have been initiated;
- the tribunal must have been fully constituted (German arbitration law does not recognize and institutional rules such as the DIS Rules[35] do not provide for an "emergency arbitrator");
- the requested measure must be related to the dispute before this tribunal.

---

[33] *Hobeck/Weyhreter*, SchiedsVZ 2005, 238, 239, Zöller-*Geimer*, ZPO, 29th ed., Section 1041, notes 1, 8 and *Gottwald/Adolphsen,* DStR 1998, 1017, 1020 point out that a tribunal in an arbitration with its seat in Germany can also issue measures that are not as such recognized in German procedural law, such as "freezing orders". However, such measures may be subject to variation by the state court when leave to enforcement is required, Böckstiegel/Kröll/Nacimiento-*Kreindler/Schäfer*, Arbitration in Germany, Section 1041, note 22.

[34] Böckstiegel/Kröll/Nacimiento-*Kreindler/Schäfer*, Arbitration in Germany, Section 1041, note 8; Stein/Jonas-*Schlosser*, ZPO, 22nd ed., Section 1041, note 1.

[35] The only exception applies in sports arbitration, where Section 20.2 of the DIS-Sportschiedsgerichtsordnung ("DIS-SportSchO") allows interim measures before constitution of the tribunal.

C. The Grant and Enforcement of Interim Measures in International Arbitration

Due to these shortcomings—plus the fact that if enforcement is required, a state court must in any event be involved—it is still the natural choice of parties in arbitration seeking interim relief to apply directly to a court instead of the tribunal.[36]

The procedure to be applied up until the decision to grant or reject an application for interim relief does not differ significantly between courts and tribunals. However, the relative novelty of the express power of arbitrators to grant interim measures and the sparseness of court decisions in this area give rise to uncertainty:

- While a court is compelled to grant interim measures if the respective preconditions for the relief sought are met,[37] tribunals may in their discretion decide not to grant such measures.[38] This is taken to follow from the wording of Section 1041(1) sentence 1 ZPO which provides that "the arbitral tribunal *may* order ... provisional measures or measures serving to provide security as it deems fit."

- The tribunal may not accept an affidavit as a means of *prima facie* evidence; this power is only vested in the state courts.[39]

---

[36] *Hobeck/Weyhreter*, SchiedsVZ 2005, 238, 239.

[37] Böckstiegel/Kröll/Nacimiento-*Kreindler/Schäfer*, Arbitration in Germany, Section 1033, note 13.

[38] Prevailing opinion, Münchener Kommentar-ZPO-*Münch*, 3rd ed., Section 1041, note 14, 22; Stein/Jonas-*Schlosser*, ZPO, 22nd ed., Section 1041, note 2, 11; *Gottwald/Adolphsen,* DStR 1998, 1017, 1020; Böckstiegel/Kröll/Nacimiento-*Kreindler/Schäfer*, Arbitration in Germany, Section 1041, note 10. *Lachmann*, Handbuch der Schiedsgerichtspraxis, 3rd ed., note 2901, takes a different view, pointing out that tribunals have to apply the law unless empowered to act as *amiable compositeur*.

[39] Musielak-*Voit*, ZPO, 9th ed., Section 1041, note 3, Stein/Jonas-*Schlosser*, ZPO, 22nd ed., Section 1041, note 11; Münchener Kommentar-ZPO-*Münch*, 3rd ed., Section 1041, note 24; Böckstiegel/Kröll/Nacimiento-*Kreindler/Schäfer*, Arbitration in Germany, Section 1041, note 17.

However, the tribunal may request assistance from the court under Section 1050 ZPO in taking affidavits.[40]

- It is subject to dispute among commentators whether a tribunal may issue interim measures *ex parte*.[41] In any event, the opposing party must be given an *ex post* chance to be heard.[42]

- While a presiding judge in a state court may decide on an application for interim relief without consulting his colleagues, the position is not so clear with respect to the chairman of an arbitral tribunal: this power clearly exists only if the parties have agreed that the chairman may issue interim measures alone.[43] However, it is disputed whether the co-arbitrators may convey this power to the chairman under Section 1052 para. 3 ZPO.[44] [45]

---

[40] Stein/Jonas-*Schlosser*, *ibid.*

[41] Musielak-*Voit*, ZPO, 9th ed., Section 1041, note 3; Stein/Jonas-*Schlosser*, ZPO, 22nd ed., Section 1041, note 11; *Lachmann*, Handbuch der Schiedsgerichtspraxis, 3rd ed., note Rn. 2907; *Schwab/Walter*, Schiedsgerichtsbarkeit, 7th ed. 2005, Chapter 17a, note 20; *Westpfahl/Busse*, SchiedsVZ 2006, 21, 27 and others argue in favor of this power, while Münchener Kommentar-ZPO-*Münch*, 3rd ed., Section 1041, note 25 and Thomas/Putzo-*Reichold*, ZPO, 33rd ed.; Section 1041, note 2 and others require a prior waiver of a hearing from both parties.

[42] Stein/Jonas-*Schlosser*, ZPO, 22nd ed., Section 1041, notes 11, 13; Böckstiegel/ Kröll/Nacimiento-*Kreindler/Schäfer*, Arbitration in Germany, Section 1041, note 19; *Westpfahl/Busse*, *ibid.*

[43] Musielak-*Voit*, ZPO, 9th ed., Section 1041, note 3, Stein/Jonas-*Schlosser*, ZPO, 22nd ed., Section 1041, note 12.

[44] Section 1052(3) ZPO provides that the chairman "may decide on individual procedural issues alone if the parties to the dispute or the other members of the arbitral tribunal have authorized him to do so".

[45] Stein/Jonas-*Schlosser*, ZPO, 22nd ed., Section 1041, note 12 and *Schwab/Walter*, Schiedsgerichtsbarkeit, 7th ed. 2005, Chapter 17a, note 17 argue in favor of this power, while Musielak-*Voit*, ZPO, 9th ed., Section 1041, note 3, opposes this view, pointing out that interim measures exceed the scope of "individual procedural issues" within the meaning of Section 1052(3) ZPO.

C.2 Court-Ordered Interim Measures

There are two types of interim measures that a state court can issue:

- an interim injunction (*"einstweilige Verfügung"*) to enforce or prevent a certain action until the parties' rights have been finally determined; and

- an attachment order (*"Arrest"*) to prevent the removal or dissipation of assets if there is evidence of an intention to remove or conceal those assets.

Proceedings for both forms of preliminary relief essentially follow the same rules, and the requirements that an applicant must satisfy to obtain either form of interim measure are also identical: the applicant must submit *prima facie* evidence that it has a valid claim against the respondent (*"Arrestanspruch"* or *"Verfügungsanspruch"*) and that there are urgent reasons (*"Arrestgrund"* or *"Verfügungsgrund"*)[46] for granting interim relief, i.e., that enforcement of its claim would be jeopardized without such protection.[47] In proceedings for interim measures

---

[46] Section 917(2) ZPO exempts the applicant from the need to establish prima facie evidence for "urgent reasons" to grant an attachment order in cases where a judgment would have to be enforced abroad and reciprocity is not granted in relation to the respective country. Where enforcement would have to take place in a country that is not a member of the EEA or the Lugano Convention, this fact alone justifies an attachment order from a German court concerning assets situated within its jurisdiction.

[47] By way of example: in an application for an attachment order, the applicant must set forth in detail that the respondent is removing or dissipating property in a way that jeopardizes future enforcement of a "judgment" (Section 917(1) ZPO). It is not a requirement that a "judgment" within this meaning already exists at the time of the application or that the respondent *intends* to frustrate future enforcement; the applicant only has to show that the respondent's conduct actually endangers such enforcement.

before state courts, affidavits are a permissible—and frequently used—means to establish the facts of the case.

In very urgent cases, the presiding judge in a district court chamber may decide on an application for interim measures alone instead of the full panel of three judges. If an applicant brings a convincing application that is supported by all the required evidence and impresses upon the court the urgency of the measure requested, German courts can order interim measures within a matter of hours.

The decision may in appropriate cases (i.e., where the purpose of the measure would be jeopardized if the respondent was heard before the measure is granted) be made *ex parte*. The respondent may object to the interim measure after it has been granted and request a hearing, following which the order may be changed or lifted.

If an interim measure is granted, the applicant must execute[48] the order within one month, failing which it may be lifted. If the interim order is executed, but subsequently lifted, or if the main proceedings show that the applicant does not have a valid claim, the applicant is liable for the respondent's damage caused and costs incurred as a result of the interim measure.[49]

To the extent a German court has jurisdiction, it can grant interim relief in any matter regardless of whether it relates to a case that is pending or intended to be brought before the court in

---

[48] "Execution" (*"Vollziehung"*) in this sense is not necessarily tantamount to "enforcement." With respect to an interim cease and desist order, it is for instance sufficient for the applicant to serve the order upon the respondent through a court bailiff within one month.

[49] Section 945 ZPO for proceedings before state courts, Section 1041 ZPO for interim measures granted by arbitral tribunals.

question. However, there are types of interim measures a German court will not normally order or not order at all:

- Interim measures are conservatory by definition; they must—subject to very few exceptions – not foreclose the outcome of the main proceedings. Actual performance of one party's obligations at issue can therefore only in very rare cases be ordered by way of interim measures.[50]

- It can be assumed with a high degree of certainty that a German court would neither issue an anti-suit injunction nor recognize or serve a foreign anti-suit injunction. There appears to be only one published German decision on the issue that dates back to 1996. In this case, the Court of Appeal Düsseldorf[51] denied the application of a UK party for service in Germany of an anti-suit injunction that the English High Court had issued. The injunction restrained the defendant, a German citizen, from continuing court proceedings in Germany in a matter that was allegedly subject to arbitration under the LCIA Rules. The Court of Appeal Düsseldorf held that service of the anti-suit injunction was capable of infringing the sovereignty of the German courts and thus refused service under Art. 13 of the Hague Service Convention.[52] German courts were to determine without the interference of foreign courts whether they had to decline jurisdiction in favor of a foreign court or arbitral tribunal. This

---

[50] For an example of one of these rare cases, cf. the decision of the Court of Appeal Frankfurt/Main on 5 April 2001, file no. 24 Sch 1/01, NJW-RR 2001, 1078 regarding the right of an athlete barred for doping to compete in a major championship.

[51] Decision of 10 January 1996, file no. 3 VA 11/95, EuZW 1996, 351 with affirmative note *Mansel*, EuZW 1996, 335 (= IPRax 1997, 260 = ZIP 1996, 294).

[52] Convention on the Service Abroad of Judicial and Extrajudicial Documents in Civil or Commercial Matters of 15 November 1965.

was held to apply regardless of the fact that the anti-suit injunction was not addressed to the German judiciary, but to a party to litigation in Germany. It was taken to amount to an indirect obstruction of German proceedings to subject a party to liability for contempt of court if such party were to continue its case in a German court.

This judgment can still be taken as accurately reflecting the current state of German law, particularly after the judgment in the *West Tankers* case[53] in which the European Court of Justice held that it is incompatible with the Brussels Regulation "for a court of a Member State to make an order to restrain a person from commencing or continuing proceedings before the courts of another Member State on the ground that such proceedings would be contrary to an arbitration agreement."

In cases that are subject to an arbitration agreement, the powers of courts and tribunals to issue interim measures exist in parallel. Throughout the course of arbitral proceedings, the parties are free in their choice to apply for protection to either of these bodies,[54] and if a party fails in one forum, it can still have a second attempt in the other.

German courts do also grant interim measures in aid of foreign arbitrations. Section 1025(2) ZPO[55] provides that Section 1033 ZPO (i.e., the basis for jurisdiction to grant interim measures in support of arbitrations) also applies "where the venue of the arbitration proceedings is located abroad". Where jurisdiction of

---

[53] Decision of February 10, 2009, *Allianz SpA and Generali Assicurazioni Generali SpA v. West Tankers Inc.*, Case C-185/07.

[54] The only exception is that where a tribunal has granted an interim measure and the applicant has asked the court to declare it enforceable, the court must not comply with this request if the applicant has also brought an application for the same measure before the court (Section 1041(2) sentence 1 ZPO).

[55] Equivalent to Art. 1 (2) UNCITRAL Model Law.

a German court can be established under German procedural law but for an agreement to arbitrate, the fact that the parties agreed on arbitration outside Germany should thus not be taken as derogating this jurisdiction.[56] However, the Court of Appeal Nuremberg in one unfortunate decision[57] held otherwise: in this case, arbitration proceedings were pending between the parties to a supply contract (a German and an Algerian company) at the agreed seat in Geneva. Even though the tribunal had already been constituted, the German party brought an application for an injunction before the District Court Regensburg to restrain its Algerian counterpart from demanding payment under a bank guarantee that was also the subject matter of the arbitration. The district court denied the application for lack of jurisdiction, and the court of appeal upheld this decision. It held that the arbitration agreement was clear evidence that the parties had ousted jurisdiction of all state courts—including jurisdiction for applications for interim measures—except for the "neutral" courts in Switzerland. This decision was unanimously criticized in academic literature,[58] and it was not followed in practice so it is likely to remain an outlier. The Court of Appeal Nuremberg appears to have overlooked Section 1025(2) ZPO.[59]

---

[56] Münchener Kommentar-ZPO-*Münch*, 3rd ed., Section 1033, note 20; Böckstiegel/ Kröll/Nacimiento-*Kreindler/Schäfer*, Arbitration in Germany, Section 1033, note 23; Court of Appeal Cologne, decision of 12 April 2002, file no. 6 U 142/01 (available in the database on the DIS website).

[57] Decision of 30 November 2004, file no. 12 U 2881/04, SchiedsVZ 2005, 50.

[58] *Geimer*, SchiedsVZ 2005, 52; *Kröll*, SchiedsVZ 2005, 139 (143); *Schütze*, IPRax 2006, 442; Böckstiegel/Kröll/Nacimiento-*Kreindler/Schäfer*, *ibid.*

[59] *Kröll, ibid.*

C.3 Enforcement of Interim Measures

Since arbitral tribunals lack the power to enforce their own orders, enforcement of any interim measure granted under Section 1041(1) ZPO requires permission from a state court (Section 1041(2) ZPO).

An interim measure issued in arbitral proceedings with a German seat can be declared enforceable either by the court of appeal expressly designated in the arbitration agreement or by the court of appeal that has jurisdiction over the district in which the seat is located (Section 1062(1)(3) ZPO).

For leave to enforce an interim measure ordered in proceedings abroad, Section 1062(2) ZPO provides for jurisdiction of the court of appeal competent for the district (i) in which the respondent has its registered seat or habitual residence; (ii) in which assets of the respondent are located; or (iii) in which the subject matter claimed in the arbitration or affected by the measure is located; or for default jurisdiction of the *Kammergericht* (Court of Appeal Berlin). However, it is subject to debate whether interim measures from foreign tribunals can be enforced in Germany at all. While the prevailing opinion[60] supports the view that they can, others[61] argue that a foreign interim measure cannot be enforced in Germany either under Section 1041 or under Section 1061 ZPO. The latter view is difficult to sustain given the existence of Section 1062(2) ZPO.

---

[60] Stein/Jonas-*Schlosser*, ZPO, 22nd ed., Section 1041, note 20; Münchener Kommentar-ZPO-*Münch*, 3rd ed., Section 1041, note 29; *Schwab/Walter*, Schiedsgerichtsbarkeit, 7th ed. 2005, Chapter 30, note 12; Böckstiegel/Kröll/Nacimiento-*Kreindler/Schäfer*, Arbitration in Germany, Section 1041, note 27

[61] Musielak-*Voit*, ZPO, 9th ed., Section 1041, note 6; *Gottwald/Adolphsen*, DStR 1998, 1017, 1020.

C. The Grant and Enforcement of Interim Measures in International Arbitration

The decision of the state court to grant or refuse leave to enforce interim measures is discretionary. Section 1041(2) ZPO thus allows the court to review the validity of the underlying arbitration agreement and to deny enforcement of excessive interim measures.[62] Also in this respect, a *révision au fond* is not permissible, but the court may deny leave to enforce if the measure in question violates German public policy.[63] The court may modify the terms of an interim measure granted by the tribunal if this is required for enforcement (Section 1041(2) sentence 2 ZPO).

While German state courts can thus in principle be expected to grant support for interim measures ordered by a domestic or a foreign tribunal, this does not extend to tribunal-ordered anti-suit injunctions[64] for the same reasons as explained above.

Another class of interim measures, for which the support of German state courts in granting leave of enforcement is doubtful, are tribunal-ordered measures that were granted *ex parte*:

- With respect to interim measures ordered by a German tribunal, those who argue that arbitrators are in any event not entitled to issue *ex parte* measures[65] also deny the power of the state courts to grant leave to enforce such measures. However, the prevailing opinion[66] is that tribunals may grant

---

[62]   Zöller-*Geimer*, ZPO, 29th ed., Section 1041, note 3; Stein/Jonas-*Schlosser*, ZPO, 22nd ed., Section 1041, note 14; Böckstiegel/Kröll/Nacimiento-*Kreindler/ Schäfer*, Arbitration in Germany, Section 1041, notes 31 *et seq.*

[63]   Böckstiegel/Kröll/Nacimiento-*Kreindler/Schäfer*, Arbitration in Germany, Section 1041, note 33.

[64]   Musielak-*Voit*, ZPO, 9th ed., Section 1041, note 4 with reference to the reasoning of the ECJ in the "West Tankers" case.

[65]   Münchener Kommentar-ZPO-*Münch*, 3rd ed., Section 1041, note 25; Thomas/ Putzo-*Reichold*, ZPO, 33rd ed.; Section 1041, note 2.

[66]   Cf. footnote 41.

ex parte measures. The advocates of this view are also compelled to allow their enforcement.

- Even though the requirements for a declaration of enforceability under Section 1059 ZPO and under the New York Convention are the same for domestic and foreign awards, it is even more doubtful whether foreign *ex-parte* orders can be enforced in Germany. The objections under the New York Convention are that the party against whom the interim measure is invoked was unable to present its case before the measure was granted (Art. V(1) (b)) and that the interim measure does not finally resolve a point in dispute and is thus not "binding" (Article V(1)(e)).[67]

Where the circumstances of a case require an *ex parte* application for interim measures to take effect in Germany, the requesting party is thus well advised to apply to a state court and not to the arbitral tribunal.

---

[67] *Hobeck/Weyhreter*, SchiedsVZ 2005, 238, 240; Musielak-*Voit*, ZPO, 9th ed., Section 1061, note 3; for a comparative overview, cf. Wolf-*Borris/Hennecke*, New York Convention, 2012, Art. V, note 372 *et seq.*

HONG KONG

James Kwan[1] and Jasmine Chan[2]

A. LEGISLATION, TRENDS AND TENDENCIES

A.1 Proposed Changes to the HKIAC Administered Arbitration Rules

The revised version of the Hong Kong International Arbitration Centre ("HKIAC") Administered Arbitration Rules ("Revised Rules") is expected to come into force in early 2013. Modifications reflect the latest trends in international commercial arbitration. Key changes under the draft Revised Rules include joinder of parties, consolidation of arbitrations, fees of arbitral tribunal, interim measures of protection and emergency arbitrators.

A.1.1 Joinder of additional parties[3]

An arbitral tribunal is given the power to allow additional parties to be joined to an existing arbitration provided that there are one

---

[1] James Kwan is a Partner in the Dispute Resolution Group of Baker & McKenzie in Hong Kong, where he leads the arbitration practice. He specializes in infrastructure, engineering, and energy disputes and has a range of international experience, having represented clients in arbitrations in Hong Kong, Asia, the Middle East, and Europe under the major institutional rules. He is recognized in legal directories as *"best known for his tremendous skill in energy, infrastructure and construction disputes"* (Chambers Global 2011), *"extremely good, quality lawyer,' 'high profile,' and 'a very fine practitioner'"* (Who's Who Legal UAE 2008), and *"singled out for his expertise in arbitration," "genuine arbitration specialist . . . he has a fine reputation"* (Asia Pacific Legal 500 2012 edition).

[2] Jasmine Chan is an Associate in the Dispute Resolution Group of Baker & McKenzie in Hong Kong. Her practice focuses on international arbitration and commercial litigation.

[3] Articles 8.3 and 26, Revised Rules.

or more valid arbitration agreements under the Revised Rules that bind all parties. However, the HKIAC has *prima facie* power to join additional parties if a request for joinder of such parties is submitted before the arbitral tribunal is constituted. The tribunal can then hear and decide any objection to jurisdiction after it has been constituted. Where a joinder request is submitted after the constitution of the arbitral tribunal, the tribunal will determine the request. If an additional party is joined before the tribunal is constituted, all parties will be deemed to have waived their right to designate an arbitrator and the HKIAC may revoke any existing appointment. In such circumstances, the HKIAC will appoint all arbitrators. The termination of any existing arbitrator's appointment is without prejudice to (a) the validity of any act done by that arbitrator before his appointment was terminated; and (b) the arbitrator's entitlement to be paid his fees and expenses.

A.1.2 Consolidation of arbitrations[4]

HKIAC will have power to consolidate two or more HKIAC arbitrations into the arbitration that commenced first. Where the HKIAC, having considered the circumstances of the case, decides to consolidate an arbitration with other arbitrations, the parties to all such arbitrations will be deemed to have waived their right to designate an arbitrator and the HKIAC may revoke any existing appointment. In the circumstances, the HKIAC will appoint the arbitral tribunal in respect of the consolidated proceedings. The termination of any arbitrator's appointment following the HKIAC's decision to consolidate is without prejudice to (a) the validity of any act done by that arbitrator or by the court in support of the relevant arbitration before the arbitrator's appointment was terminated; (b) the arbitrator's

---

[4]   Articles 8.4 and 27, Revised Rules.

entitlement to be paid his fees and expenses; and (c) the date on which any claim or defense was raised for the purposes of applying any limitation bar. The parties waive any objection, on the basis of the HKIAC's decision to consolidate, to the validity and enforcement of any award made by the arbitral tribunal in the consolidated proceedings.

A.1.3 Fees of arbitral tribunal[5]

An arbitral tribunal's fees will be calculated, at the option of the parties, in accordance with either the HKIAC's schedule of fees based on the sum in dispute (Schedule 2), or the schedule based on agreed hourly rates (Schedule 3) subject to a cap at HK$6,500, with the latter option as the default position. Each schedule contains standard terms of appointment, which are subject to any variation agreed by all parties or made by the HKIAC. The HKIAC will confirm the designation of any arbitrator on the terms of the applicable schedule. Each schedule is also supplemented by a practice note providing further guidance regarding arbitrators' fees and expenses.

A.1.4 Interim measures of protection[6]

The provisions regarding interim measures have been expanded to cover, in particular, the meaning and the purposes of an interim measure, and factors to be taken into account when deciding whether to grant such interim measure. Arbitral tribunals have also been given an express power to order security for costs. The expanded provisions are in line with the Arbitration Ordinance (as amended in 2011) and the UNCITRAL Model Law (as amended in 2006).

---

[5] Articles 9.2 and 10, Schedules 2 and 3, Revised Rules.

[6] Article 23, Revised Rules.

A.1.5 Emergency arbitrators[7]

The Revised Rules will contain new provisions to introduce a procedure for appointing an emergency arbitrator to deal with applications for urgent relief before the constitution of an arbitral tribunal. An emergency arbitrator will normally be appointed within two days following the HKIAC's acceptance of an application for the appointment of such arbitrator. A decision on the application will normally be made within 15 days from the date on which the emergency arbitrator received the file from the HKIAC. The procedure also contains other provisions including those relating to an emergency arbitrator's power to conduct proceedings, the effect of his decision, the ability to act as an arbitrator in subsequent proceedings and the availability of judicial remedies, in addition to any urgent relief sought from the emergency arbitrator.

A.2 Latest Developments in Hong Kong Arbitration

A.2.1 Establishment of CIETAC Hong Kong Arbitration Centre

On 24 September 2012, the China International Economic and Trade Arbitration Commission ("CIETAC") opened an arbitration center in Hong Kong. This is the first arbitration center set up by CIETAC outside Mainland China.

The establishment of the CIETAC Hong Kong Arbitration Centre, together with the existing arbitral institutions in Hong Kong, including the HKIAC and the International Chamber of Commerce ("ICC") International Court of Arbitration (Asia Office), provides options for parties in their choice of institution

---

[7]   Article 23.2 and Schedule 4, Revised Rules.

and enhances Hong Kong's position as a leading center for international arbitration.

CIETAC disputes seated in Hong Kong will be governed by the Hong Kong Arbitration Ordinance. An award issued by the CIETAC Hong Kong Arbitration Centre will be treated and enforced as a Hong Kong award.

A.2.2 Launch of HKIAC's new premises

In October 2012, the HKIAC officially launched its brand-new expanded premises at its existing address. The new premises contain seven large hearing rooms and numerous meeting and breakout rooms, which double the HKIAC's former capacity.

A.2.3 Enforceability of Hong Kong arbitral awards in India clarified

Under the India Arbitration and Conciliation Act 1996, an Indian court is permitted to recognize and enforce a foreign arbitral award only if it is made in a country which has been notified by the Indian Government in its Official Gazette as a territory to which the New York Convention applies. On 19 March 2012, the Indian Government formally declared that the People's Republic of China (including Hong Kong and Macau) is a territory to which the New York Convention applies for the purpose of enforcement of arbitral awards in India. The enforcement of an award made in China, Hong Kong or Macau on or after 19 March 2012 in India should no longer be a concern.

B. CASES

B.1 Court of Appeal Refused to Set Aside ICC Award

Pacific China Holdings Ltd (In Liquidation) v. Grand Pacific Holdings Ltd.[8]

As reported in the 2011-2012 International Arbitration Yearbook, this case is a rare example of the Hong Kong courts setting aside an arbitral award. The Court of First Instance's decision to set aside has since been overturned by the Court of Appeal.

In 2006, Grand Pacific Holdings Ltd ("Grand Pacific") commenced an ICC arbitration in Hong Kong against Pacific China Holdings Ltd ("Pacific China") in relation to a loan agreement worth USD40 million. On 24 August 2009, an award was made in favor of Grand Pacific.

B.1.1 Court of First Instance decision

Pacific China applied to set aside the award in the Court of First Instance for serious procedural irregularity pursuant to Article 34(2) of the UNCITRAL Model Law. Three distinct issues were considered by the Court of First Instance to determine a violation of Article 34(2) of the UNCITRAL Model Law and thus, set aside the award:

i. Pre-hearing submissions on Taiwanese law

Both parties agreed on a procedural timetable whereby both.had to file their pre-hearing submissions simultaneously. Because Pacific China amended its pleadings the day before the filing date, the tribunal gave Grand Pacific ten days to file

---

[8]   [2012] 4 HKLRD 1.

supplemental submissions dealing with the latest amendments. Pacific China argued that this was unfair since it had already set down its "best case" in full and could not further develop the same. The proceedings were also no longer in accordance with the agreed timetable.

The Court of First Instance found that this resulted in Grand Pacific having advance notice of Pacific China's best case before filing its submissions. Pacific China was also unable to present its case. There were breaches of Article 34(2)(a)(ii) and (iv) of the UNCITRAL Model Law.

ii. Additional legal authorities

The tribunal had indicated that both parties agreed that no new Taiwanese legal authorities could be adduced without leave, and such introduction would not be granted unless the new authorities were "sensational." Pacific China subsequently made an application for leave to rely on additional authorities, which the tribunal refused. Because the Tribunal refused to receive or consider the additional authorities, it had no basis to determine whether such authorities were "sensational."

The Court of First Instance found that by refusing to admit additional authorities, the tribunal prevented Pacific China from presenting its case and thus, it violated Article 34(2)(a)(ii) of the UNCITRAL Model Law.

iii. Post-hearing submissions on Hong Kong Law

While Grand Pacific objected to Pacific China's raising issues relating to Hong Kong law, it nonetheless responded substantively to Pacific China's submissions on the issue. The tribunal subsequently wrote to both parties as regards the Hong Kong law issue to which Grand Pacific made further substantive submissions by citing two new cases. Pacific China sought leave to respond to the new material adduced by Grand Pacific, but the tribunal refused and informed the parties that it had sufficient material to decide the issue. In deciding the Hong Kong law issue, the tribunal relied upon the new cases referred to by Grand Pacific.

In this regard, the Court of First Instance found that Pacific China was denied the right to present its case, thus establishing a violation of Article 34(2)(a)(ii) of the UNICTRAL Model Law.

The Court of First Instance concluded that once a violation of Article 34(2) is found, it has the discretion to set aside the arbitral award. If the court finds that the result of the arbitration may have been different had the violation not occurred, it must exercise its discretion to set aside the award. Therefore, the court's residual discretion of refusing to set aside the award, despite the establishment of the requisite grounds, is narrowly construed.

Nonetheless, the Court of First Instance was unable to conclude that even if the violations of Article 34(2) had not occurred, the result could not have been different. The award was therefore set aside.

Grand Pacific appealed to the Court of Appeal.

B.1.2 Court of Appeal decision

On 9 May 2012, the Court of Appeal overturned the Court of First Instance's decision and reinstated the award.

The Court of Appeal stated at the outset that it was concerned with "the structural integrity of the arbitration proceedings." The remedy of setting aside is not an appeal, and the court will not consider the substantive merits of the dispute or the correctness of the award, whether concerning errors of fact or law.

B. Cases

For each of the three issues, the Court of Appeal found that there was no violation of Article 34(2)(a)(ii) or (iv) of the UNCITRAL Model Law:

i. Pre-hearing submissions on Taiwanese Law

The Court of Appeal held that the tribunal was entitled to use procedures that were appropriate to the case. The tribunal clearly took the view that Grand Pacific was prejudiced by the late submission of Pacific China's amendment. The lower court should not have questioned the merits of the tribunal's decision to grant leave for Pacific China to amend and the terms on which such leave was granted.

ii. Additional legal authorities

The Court of Appeal held that the lower court was not entitled to interfere with a case management decision which was within the tribunal's decision to make.

iii. Post-hearing submissions on Hong Kong Law

The Court of Appeal considered that the tribunal was entitled to take the view that the Hong Kong law issue was raised at a late stage of the proceedings and that Pacific China already had two opportunities to make submissions on the Hong Kong law issue, and that submissions should end with Grand Pacific's submissions. The Court of Appeal disagreed with the lower court's view that the result might have been different if Pacific China had been given leave to respond.

Obiter

Since the Court of Appeal was not satisfied that there was a violation of Article 34(2)(a)(ii) or (iv), it was not necessary for the court to resolve whether the court had the discretion to refuse to set aside the award in the event of any violation. The Court of Appeal briefly stated the following in its obiter dictum:

- The court may refuse to set aside an award notwithstanding a violation if it is satisfied that the outcome could not have been different. If the violation had no effect on the outcome of the arbitration, that is a good basis for exercising one's discretion against setting aside.

- Only a sufficiently serious error could be regarded as a violation of Article 34(2)(a)(ii). An error would only be sufficiently serious if it has undermined due process. A party who has had a reasonable opportunity to present its case would rarely be able to establish that he has been denied due process.

- The court's exercise of its discretion will depend on its view on the seriousness of the breach. Some breaches may be so egregious that an award would be set aside although the result could not be different.

- The burden of proof to show that he has been prejudiced is on the applicant.

Overall, the Court of Appeal judgment confirms Hong Kong's pro-enforcement approach. Although it remains to be answered what amounts to serious or egregious violations justifying an award to be set aside, this case illustrates that the Hong Kong court will be reluctant to interfere with arbitral awards except in rare circumstances.

B.2 Derivative Action Based on Enforcement Order Dismissed

Xiamen Xinjingdi Group Limited v. Eton Properties Limited & Others[9]

In this case, the Plaintiff ("P") sought to bring a common law derivative action based on an order made by the Hong Kong

---

[9] Unreported, HCCL13/2011.

court for the enforcement of a CIETAC award. Such attempt was unsuccessful.

There were a total of 11 defendants in this action. The first and second Defendants ("D1" and "D2") were companies in the Eton Group. The third to fifth Defendants ("D3" to "D5") were related corporate entities. The sixth to eleventh Defendants ("D6" to "D11") were individuals related to D1 and D2.

In July 2003, P entered into a contract (the "Agreement") with D1 and D2 for the development of a piece of land in Xiamen, China. The land was owned by the fourth Defendant ("D4"), whose entire shareholding was held by D1 and D2. It was anticipated that the Agreement would be completed in three steps.

First, D1 and D2 would give up their possession of the land in return for P paying RMB120 million. Second, P would construct apartments on the land. Third, once the apartments were completed, D1 and D2 would transfer their shareholding in D4 to P.

D1 and D2 subsequently reneged on the Agreement. The land was not delivered to P. In fact, D5 (which was wholly owned by D4) developed the land and sold the apartments built. P commenced CIETAC arbitration in Beijing against D1 and D2 for breach of Agreement. An award was made ordering specific performance of the Agreement by D1 and D2.

Unbeknownst to the tribunal, the Eton Group had restructured. D1 and D2 had already transferred their shareholding in D4 to D3. Therefore, even though a Hong Kong court allowed enforcement of the award, the award was of no practical value to P since the restructuring in the Eton Group prevented the transfer of shareholdings in D4 to P.

P brought proceedings in the Hong Kong court against D1 to D11. The action consisted of two elements:

(i) Common law derivation action against D1 and D2. P sought to use the enforcement order to seek damages/equitable compensation in lieu of specific performance of the Agreement as ordered in the award; and

(ii) Original action against all the defendants. P alleged that restructuring of the Eton Group was a conspiracy to injure P and to avoid the Agreement.

All claims were dismissed. In respect of the derivative action, the Court of First Instance held that P was, in effect, attempting to "recharacterize" the specific performance remedy granted by the CIETAC tribunal with a new claim for damages/equitable compensation.

The court highlighted the following principles:

- The court's role in enforcing an award is purely mechanistic. The enforcing court shall not question the substantive merits of the case.

- The court should not rule on an issue that was not ruled upon or contemplated by the arbitral tribunal.

- The claim for damages in lieu of specific performance was beyond the scope of the award and was never contemplated by the tribunal. It was not a remedy which the tribunal had ruled on, nor had it been asked to rule on.

- The court had no jurisdiction to usurp the arbitral tribunal and impose a new remedy under "the guise of enforcement".

The judgment confirms the principle that the procedure for enforcing foreign arbitral awards is mechanistic. It also highlights the importance of seeking appropriate remedies in the course of the arbitration, rather than seeking to rectify any omissions at the enforcement stage.

B.3 Application to Set Aside Enforcement Order on Public Policy Ground Dismissed

Granton Natural Resources Co Limited v Armco Metals International Limited[10]

In 2010, Granton Natural Resources Co Limited ("Granton") and Armco Metals International Limited ("Armco") entered into a contract whereby Granton would purchase iron ores from Armco for onward sale to Poly Resources (Asia) Limited ("Poly"). Poly alleged that the iron ores were of sub-standard quality. As a result, Poly resold the iron ores to China National Minerals Co Ltd ("China National") at a discount and suffered loss.

Poly commenced a CIETAC arbitration against Granton for breach of contract ("Poly Arbitration") and was awarded damages in the sum of US$585,860, plus legal costs and arbitration fees. Granton in turn commenced a CIETAC arbitration against Armco seeking to recover the damages paid to Poly. In January 2012, CIETAC gave an award in favor of Granton against Armco.

In February 2012, the Hong Kong court issued an order granting leave to Granton to enforce the award. Armco applied to set aside the court's order on the ground that it would be contrary to public policy to enforce the award. Armco relied on two arguments:

(i) apparent bias of Mr. Wang, one of the arbitrators in the Poly Arbitration — Armco's complaint of bias was that Mr. Wang was the senior legal consultant of Minmetals Development Company Limited ("Minmetals") and Minmetals was and still is one of the two shareholders of China National, the ultimate buyer of the iron ores. Armco argued that Granton

---

[10] Unreported, HCCT5/2012.

sought and obtained an award to "mirror" the award in the Poly Arbitration, which was implicated by Mr. Wang's conduct; and

(ii) the possibility that the Entry-Exit Inspection and Quarantine Certificate ("CIQ Certificate") required under the contract was implicated by corruption — Armco argued that the head of the state authority issuing CIQ Certificates had been sentenced to life imprisonment in April 2012 for corruption. This implicated the genuineness of the CIQ Certificate which was the only evidence to prove the iron ores were sub-standard.

Notably, shortly before the hearing of Armco's set aside application in the Hong Kong court, the Beijing court had already dismissed Armco's appeal to set aside the award.

The Hong Kong court dismissed both arguments because there was no factual basis in support. There was no evidence that Mr. Wang was an employee of Minmetals at the time of the Poly Arbitration. There was also no evidence of any corrupt activity connected with the issue of the CIQ Certificate. Such issue was not raised in Armco's application to set aside in the Beijing court.

Although Armco's application was dismissed due to the weaknesses in the factual evidence, the court did examine the law on public policy and confirmed the following:

• The primary supervisory function in respect of arbitrations rests with the court of supervisory jurisdiction, i.e., the Mainland courts in respect of Mainland awards, as distinct from the enforcement court, i.e., the Hong Kong courts.

• In view of the principles of finality and comity, the expression "contrary to public policy" has to be given a narrow construction. The discretion to refuse enforcement will not be exercised unless the enforcement would violate the most basic notions of morality and justice in Hong Kong.

- It is not enough for the party seeking to resist enforcement to show violation of some conceptions of morality and justice which are being enjoyed in Hong Kong. The violation has to go to the root of the fundamental conceptions of morality and justice, and has to go beyond the minimum which is sufficient to set aside a domestic judgment or award.

- Apparent bias could justify refusal to enforce an award, but it would require a much stronger case to justify refusal based on apparent than on actual bias. The test for apparent bias is whether an objective fair-minded and informed observer, having considered the relevant facts, would conclude that there was a real possibility that the tribunal was biased.

- Even if Mr. Wang was in a position of conflict, the complaint of bias was not directed at the tribunal making the award against Armco. Such bias could not justify the court to refuse enforcement of the award.

The court made an indemnity costs order against Armco. This is in line with the court's usual practice in dealing with failed attempts in challenging the enforcement of an arbitral award.

C. THE GRANT AND ENFORCEMENT OF INTERIM MEASURES IN INTERNATIONAL ARBITRATION

C.1 Tribunal-Ordered Interim Measures

In Hong Kong, the old Arbitration Ordinance (Cap. 341) did not specifically define the term "interim measures".[11]

---

[11] Arbitrations and related court proceedings which were commenced before the new Arbitration Ordinance (Cap. 609) came into force on 1 June 2011 are governed by the old Arbitration Ordinance (Cap. 341).

The new Arbitration Ordinance (Cap. 609), which came into force on 1 June 2011, adopts the UNCITRAL Model Law amendments in 2006 in respect of interim measures. Pursuant to section 35, interim measure is expressly defined to be any temporary measure, whether in the form of an award or in another form, by which, at any time prior to the issuance of the award by which the dispute is finally decided, the arbitral tribunal orders a party to:

(a) maintain or restore the status quo pending determination of the dispute;

(b) take action that would prevent, or refrain from taking action that is likely to cause current or imminent harm or prejudice to the arbitral process;

(c) provide a means of preserving assets out of which a subsequent award may be satisfied; or

(d) preserve evidence that may be relevant and material to the resolution of the dispute.

An interim measure includes an injunction.[12]

An arbitral tribunal may, in deciding the dispute, award any remedy or relief that could have been ordered by the court if the dispute had been the subject of civil proceedings in the court.[13] Despite this broad right, an arbitral tribunal has no power to make binding awards and orders on third parties to the arbitration.

C.1.1 Conditions for granting interim measures

The conditions for granting interim measures are set out in Section 36 of the Arbitration Ordinance, which adopted Article

---

[12] Section 35(2), Arbitration Ordinance (Cap. 609).

[13] Section 70(1), Arbitration Ordinance (Cap. 609).

17A of the UNCITRAL Model Law. Any application has to satisfy a two pronged test: (i) that harm not adequately reparable by damages is likely to result if the measure is not ordered; and (ii) a reasonable possibility of the applicant's success on the merits. This is intended to serve as a check against frivolous and unfounded applications for interim measures of protection. It bears some resemblance to the English threshold for application for an injunction as set out in *American Cyanamid*, given the test has been derived from the rules governing court ordered interim measures.

The arbitral tribunal may require security from the party requesting an interim measure.[14]

C.1.2 Preliminary orders

Preliminary orders were not previously addressed. Under the new Arbitration Ordinance, there is a specific and detailed regime. These include preliminary orders made on an *ex parte* basis. A preliminary order may be granted if the tribunal considers that prior disclosure of the request for the interim measure to the party against whom it is directed risks frustrating the purpose of the measure.[15]

C.1.3 Emergency arbitrators

As explained in section A.1 above, the revised HKIAC Administered Arbitration Rules expected to come into force in early 2013 will introduce a procedure for appointing an emergency arbitrator to deal with applications for urgent relief before the constitution of an arbitral tribunal.

---

14   Section 40(1), Arbitration Ordinance (Cap. 609).

15   Sections 37 and 38, Arbitration Ordinance (Cap. 609).

The 2012 ICC Arbitration Rules include emergency arbitrator procedures to provide urgent interim or conservatory measures before the constitution of an arbitral tribunal.

C.2 Court-Ordered Interim Measures

Section 45 of the Arbitration Ordinance deals with court ordered interim measures. The powers under section 45 may be exercised by the court notwithstanding that similar powers may be exercised by an arbitral tribunal in the same dispute, illustrating that section 45 is intended to be independent of the other sections which deal with tribunal ordered interim measures.

The section also provides for court ordered interim measures in support of arbitration outside of Hong Kong, although only if the arbitral proceedings are capable of giving rise to an arbitral award (whether interim or final) which may be enforced in Hong Kong and if the interim measure sought belongs to a type or description of interim measure that may be granted in Hong Kong arbitral proceedings.

Leviathan Shipping Co. Ltd. v. Sky Sailing Overseas Co. Ltd.[16] illustrates that Hong Kong courts will be reluctant to interfere in the arbitration unnecessarily. In setting aside two *ex parte* orders for security and a Mareva injunction, the court stated:

> [N]otwithstanding that the plaintiff's action is referred to arbitration, the court has jurisdiction to deal with the applications for interim relief. The question is whether or not the court should exercise this jurisdiction when the arbitral tribunal has the same powers. For a long time now, the court[s] have leaned in favour of making the parties who have agreed to settle their disputes by arbitration stick to that

---

[16]   [1998] 4 HKC 347.

method of dispute resolution rather than resorting to litigation when it suits them to do so. . . . In my view, this jurisdiction should be exercised sparingly, and only where there are special reasons to utilise it. A special reason would be where the arbitral tribunal does not have the power to grant all the relief sought in a single application. Rather than apply to the tribunal for some of the relief and to the court for the other relief, it would obviously be more appropriate for the application to be made in its entirety to the court.

Section 60(1) provides that on the application of any party, the court may, in relation to arbitrations which have been or are to be commenced in or outside Hong Kong, make an order:

- directing the inspection, photographing, preservation, custody, detention, or sale of any relevant property by the tribunal, a party to the arbitral proceedings, or an expert;

- directing samples to be taken from, observations to be made of, or experiments to be conducted on any relevant property.

C.2.1 Tribunal vs. court-ordered interim measures

There are a number of differences between applying to the tribunal or to the courts for interim measures. Advantages of applying to the courts, rather than to the tribunal, include the following:

- a court may grant pre-arbitral relief, whereas such relief is generally not available until the tribunal has been constituted;

- it is generally quicker to obtain a decision from the Hong Kong courts than from a tribunal, especially where it comprises three arbitrators. Interim measures may be obtained in a few hours, without notifying the other side. For injunction applications, there is a Duty Judge available to hear urgent applications, even outside official court hours;

- orders granted by the courts are more likely to be effective against third parties;

- the courts have coercive powers of enforcement, and this is especially useful where the party is within its jurisdiction;

- in some cases, the courts have more extensive or different powers from those of the tribunal.

However, there are also a number of advantages of applying to the tribunal:

- the tribunal is often more familiar with the dispute and able to make a decision that is more appropriate for the case rather than one based on first impression;

- where the counterparty is outside the jurisdiction of the courts, an interim order from the court of the seat may be of limited value. In contrast, although a tribunal may not have coercive powers, parties may be more inclined to comply with an order made by the tribunal, knowing that the tribunal will ultimately be ruling on the merits of the case;

- as illustrated in *Leviathan Shipping Co. Ltd. v. Sky Sailing Overseas Co. Ltd.*, the court will only exercise its jurisdiction to grant interim relief sparingly.

C.2.2 Anti-suit injunctions

Hong Kong courts recognize that they are able to grant anti-suit injunctions, and they have in a small number of cases granted such orders, outside an arbitration context.[17]

In the context of anti-suit injunctions granted in relation to arbitral proceedings, in addition to their general power, it has

---

[17] See, for example, *China Light & Power Co. Ltd. v. Wong To Sau Heung* [1993] 2 HKC 238 involving an interim anti-suit injunction.

been suggested that the courts may also be empowered by section 45(2) of the Arbitration Ordinance to grant such an injunction as it qualifies as an interim measure which the court is empowered to order.

Applications for anti-suit injunctions have failed in a number of Hong Kong cases. In the context of arbitrations, the Hong Kong courts may be prepared to grant such orders more readily, particularly where it is clear that a party has commenced court proceedings overseas in clear breach of an agreement to arbitrate in Hong Kong.

For anti-arbitration injunctions, there is a recent case, *Lin Min & Anor v. Chen Shu Quan & Others*,[18] where the parties took out mirror-image applications to stay the proceedings initiated by the other parties in another forum (court/arbitration) in favor of their own proceedings.

The first Plaintiff ("P1") was the owner of a food processing business in Mainland China. He entered into a Share Purchase Agreement ("SPA") with the 28th Defendant ("D28") for the sale of 1,000 shares in a company known as Win Power, which is wholly owned by P1. The 27th Defendant ("D27") and a company known as Gingero were subsequently assigned portions of the 1,000 shares in Win Power and therefore inherited the same rights and obligations under the SPA as D28.

The SPA contained a put option clause which gave D27, D28 and Gingero the right to sell their shares back to P1 at a contractually agreed price if Win Power was not listed on an internationally recognized stock exchange within 24 months of completion of the SPA. The SPA also contained an arbitration agreement requiring the parties to refer disputes arising out of or relating to the SPA to arbitration.

---

[18]   [2012] 2 HKLRD 547.

Arbitration Proceedings

As the listing did not take place within the stipulated time, D27, D28 and Gingero exercised the Put Option. After P1 failed to pay the purchase price under the Put Option, D27, D28 and Gingero commenced arbitration proceedings against P1 to compel the payment.

Court Proceedings

Shortly after the arbitration was commenced, P1 and the second Plaintiff ("P2," a Mainland company engaged in the food business and wholly owned by P1) commenced court proceedings in Hong Kong against 28 defendants (including D27 and D28). P1 and P2 alleged that the defendants, together with Mainland officials, had unlawfully conspired to take over P1's food business, which included attempts to have P1 and his sister arrested in the Mainland.

Confronted with parallel proceedings in court and arbitration dealing with similar factual issues, P1, D27 and D28 took out mirror image applications to stay the proceedings in the other forum initiated by the other parties.

D27 and D28: Application to Stay Court Proceedings

D27 and D28 took out the typical application to stay the court proceedings pending arbitration of the dispute under Section 20 of the Arbitration Ordinance (Cap. 609), which gives legal effect to Article 8 of the UNCITRAL Model Law. Section 20 reads as follows:

"A court before which an action is brought in a matter which is the subject of an arbitration agreement shall . . . refer the parties to arbitration unless it finds that the agreement is null and void, inoperative or incapable of being performed."

P1: Application for Injunction to Restrain Arbitration Proceedings

The application by P1 involved asking for a novel remedy. P1 applied for an injunction to restrain D27, D28 and Gingero from continuing with the arbitration pending resolution of the Court proceedings. The injunction application was based on the court's general power under Section 21L of the High Court Ordinance (Cap. 4) to grant injunctions when it is just and convenient to do so. Section 21L reads:

"The Court of First Instance may by order (whether interlocutory or final) grant an injunction or appoint a receiver in all cases in which it appears to the Court of First Instance to be just or convenient to do so."

Decision of the Court

With respect to the D27 and D28's application to stay the court proceedings, the court held that it was bound to grant a stay once the conditions set out under Section 20 of the Arbitration Ordinance were satisfied. As the conditions were satisfied, the court granted the stay application.

Turning to P1's injunction application to restrain D27, D28 and Gingero from continuing with the arbitration, the court was content to assume that it had the power under Section 21L of the High Court Ordinance to grant an injunction to restrain parties from continuing with an arbitration, notwithstanding the terms of section 12 of the Arbitration Ordinance which provides that no court shall intervene except where so provided by the ordinance. The court's assumption was in part derived from English case law cited by P1, which was persuasive authority because England has similar legislation carrying the same tension between Section 12 of the Arbitration Ordinance and Section 21L of the High Court Ordinance. However, as the court did not hear full arguments on this point, it declined to express a conclusive view on it.

In any event, the Court exercised its discretion and held that it would not restrain D27, D28 and Gingero from continuing with the arbitration for the following reasons:

- First, the risk of inconsistent findings in parallel proceedings were self-induced by P1 taking out the court proceedings two months after the arbitration had commenced.

- Second, D27 and D28 would suffer an injustice in having to wait for a long time for the court proceedings to be resolved before they could resume the arbitration, as the number of parties and the scope of the issues in the court proceedings is much larger than the arbitration.

- Third, it would not be oppressive, vexatious, unconscionable or an abuse of process to allow the arbitration to continue. This is because D27 and D28 will still have to contend with the court proceedings which will proceed between P2 and the Defendants, including D27 and D28. Accordingly, the inconvenience, expenses and strain on resources suffered by P1 in having to deal with two parallel proceedings will be equally felt by D27 and D28.

- The court has no power to restrain Gingero from continuing with the arbitration as it is not a party to the court proceedings.

C.3 Enforcement of Interim Measures

Under the new Arbitration Ordinance, a new regime for the enforcement of interim measures separate from the recognition and enforcement of awards has been created pursuant to sections 43 and 61. Orders and directions for interim measures made by an arbitral tribunal, whether in or outside of Hong Kong, can be enforced by the court as a judgment.

C. The Grant and Enforcement of Interim Measures in International Arbitration

For an order or direction made outside Hong Kong, leave to enforce will not be granted by the court unless the party seeking to enforce it can demonstrate that it belongs to a type or description of order or direction that may be made in Hong Kong in relation to arbitral proceedings by an arbitral tribunal.

HUNGARY

József Antal,[1] Anna Ménes[2] and Dávid Kovács[3]

A. LEGISLATION, TRENDS AND TENDENCIES

A.1 Legislation

The Hungarian Arbitration Act[4] contains the fundamental rules of domestic and international arbitration procedures[5] as well as related ordinary court procedures. The Hungarian Arbitration Act is in conformity with the UNCITRAL Model Law. In the past year, the legislator has plainly aimed to prevent cases involving Hungarian state entities and/or national assets of Hungary from being resolved before arbitral tribunals.

These amendments may be disadvantageous for foreign investors and companies operating in Hungary and may have a serious impact on Hungary's international commercial and economic relations. The key provisions of the recent legislation are outlined below.

---

[1]   József Antal is a Partner in the Firm's Budapest office and routinely assists clients in litigation, alternative dispute resolution and procurement matters, and has advised clients in numerous industry sectors from transportation to energy and financial services to telecommunications.

[2]   Anna Ménes is an Associate in the Firm's Budapest office and primarily works on civil lawsuits, arbitration cases and out-of-court procedure as well as public procurement issues. She has experience in several fields of law, including the law of damages, competition law, copyright law, banking and finance litigation, fraud investigations and compliance-related matters.

[3]   Dávid Kovács is an Associate in the Firm's Budapest office and works on civil lawsuits and arbitration cases, both domestic and international.

[4]   Act LXXI of 1994 on Arbitration.

[5]   Except for a few provisions, the Hungarian Arbitration Act applies only to those international arbitration procedures in which the place (registered seat) of the arbitration is in Hungary. *See* Section 1 of the Hungarian Arbitration Act.

A.1.1 Arbitrability of disputes related to the national assets of Hungary

Pursuant to the provisions of the National Assets Act,[6] in any civil law contract concerning national assets located within the borders of Hungary, those who are entitled to dispose of such national assets shall only stipulate the jurisdiction of a Hungarian ordinary court and may not stipulate the jurisdiction of any arbitration court in relation to any dispute that may arise in relation to such contract. Further, only Hungarian law and the Hungarian language may govern the contract. The Hungarian Arbitration Act has been amended in line with this provision.

According to leading Hungarian arbitration experts, this provision seems to violate several international treaties and bilateral investment agreements and may have an adverse effect on the international relations of Hungary. Furthermore, in certain cases, the scope of national assets for the purposes of the National Assets Act cannot be clearly determined. This could lead to considerable difficulties in determining whether or not a particular asset is covered under the Act. This uncertainty may also adversely influence certain transactions between the state and foreign investors.

A.1.2 Arbitrability of disputes related to real estate located in Hungary

Another amendment to the Hungarian Arbitration Act that was passed this year excludes foreign arbitration courts from dealing with disputes related to real estate located in Hungary. According to the amendment,[7] only a Hungarian permanent arbitration court with its own rules of proceedings may proceed

---

6   *See* Section 17 (3) of the Act CXCVI of 2011 on the National Assets.

7   *See* Section 2(3) of the Hungarian Arbitration Act.

in any dispute where the following conditions are met: (i) the dispute arises in relation to a contract concluded by parties that have their registered seat or their company seat located exclusively in Hungary; (ii) the dispute concerns rights *in rem* relating to real estate located in Hungary or the dispute relates to a lease or tenancy agreement concluded in relation to a property located in Hungary; and (iii) the agreement is governed by Hungarian law. According to the amendment,[8] the language of such proceedings must be the Hungarian language.

A.1.3 Brief overview of the Hungarian arbitration law

Besides recent legislation, the principal features of Hungarian arbitration law and the four main permanent arbitration courts operating in Hungary are also worth mentioning.

Submission to arbitration

Disputes may generally be settled by arbitration if (i) at least one of the parties is professionally engaged in business activities and the legal dispute arises out of, or in connection with, this activity; (ii) the parties may freely dispose of the subject-matter of the proceedings; and (iii) the parties concluded an arbitration agreement.[9]

Applicable law in international cases

In the absence of a choice of law, the applicable law shall be determined by the arbitration court on the basis of the applicable rules of private international law.[10]

---

[8] *See id.* at Section 2(4).

[9] *See id.* at Section 3.

[10] Such as the Rome I Convention on the law applicable to contractual obligations or Law Decree No. 13 of 1979 on Private International Law.

Rules of proceedings

Each Hungarian permanent arbitration court has its own rules of proceedings, which correspond to generally accepted international standards.

Arbitrators, independence and impartiality of arbitrators

Parties may generally freely agree to the number and person of the arbitrators; however, the number of arbitrators may only be an uneven number. Each Hungarian permanent arbitration court has its own roll of arbitrators. Parties may choose arbitrators from this roll, but usually they also have the option of choosing arbitrators who are not mentioned on the roll.[11] Arbitrators must be independent and impartial, and may not provide representation to either party in the arbitration. Moreover, arbitrators may not accept any instructions in their official capacity.[12] Persons proposed or appointed as arbitrators must disclose all facts and circumstances that may give rise to justifiable doubts as to their impartiality and independence.[13] If any fact or circumstance seems to give rise to justifiable doubts as to an arbitrator's impartiality or independence, or if an arbitrator does not have the qualifications agreed upon by the parties, the adverse party may initiate a challenge procedure against the arbitrator. However, a party that appointed an arbitrator may only challenge the arbitrator if the circumstances giving rise to the challenge occur after the appointment[14] has already been made.

---

[11] In proceedings before the Arbitration Court of Financial and Capital Markets and the Arbitration Court attached to the Hungarian Chamber of Agriculture, parties may only appoint arbitrators who are listed on these courts' rolls of arbitrators.

[12] *See* Section 11 of the Hungarian Arbitration Act.

[13] *See id.* at Section 17.

[14] *See id.* at Section 18.

A. Legislation, Trends and Tendencies

Remedies against arbitral award

The legal effect of an arbitral award is the same as that of a final and binding ordinary court judgment.[15] No appeal is allowed against an arbitral award. The only remedy available is a request to the competent state court for the cancellation of the award. Such request may be filed within sixty days from the delivery of the award,[16] and only on the following grounds:[17] (i) a party to the arbitration agreement was incapacitated; (ii) the arbitration agreement is not valid under the law to which the parties have subjected it or, in the absence of such indication, under Hungarian law; (iii) a party was not given proper notice of the appointment of an arbitrator or of the arbitration proceedings, or was otherwise unable to present its case; (iv) the award deals with a difference not contemplated by or not falling within the terms of the submission to arbitration; or if the award contains decisions on matters beyond the scope of the submission to arbitration (however, if the decisions on matters properly submitted to arbitration are separable from improper submissions, then those parts of the award which refer to matters properly submitted to arbitration are not cancelable on this ground); (v) the composition of the arbitration tribunal or the arbitration procedure was not in accordance with the agreement of the parties, unless such agreement was in conflict with any mandatory provision of the Hungarian Arbitration Act, or—in lack of such agreement—was not in accordance with the Hungarian Arbitration Act; (vi) the subject-matter of the dispute

---

[15] See id. at Section 58.

[16] See id. at Section 55.

[17] These grounds mirror Article V of the New York Convention, which enumerates the circumstances under which the recognition and enforcement of a foreign arbitral award may be refused.

is excluded from resolution via arbitration under Hungarian law; or (vii) the award is in conflict with Hungarian public policy.

Parties have tried to bring cancellation cases many times as a quasi appeal; however, in many decisions, the Hungarian Supreme Court (known today as the Curia) made it clear that state courts can only cancel an arbitral award on the above-listed grounds, which must be interpreted in a restrictive manner.

Enforcement

Parties are required to voluntarily comply with the arbitral award. In the absence of voluntary performance, the enforcement of the arbitral award shall be governed by the rules applicable to the enforcement of ordinary court judgments.[18] The award may be enforced in any foreign country that also ratified the New York Convention.

Costs

The cost of arbitration is determined based on the amount in controversy. Each permanent arbitration court has its own fee chart. The costs include a registration fee, administrative expenses and the arbitrators' fee. The costs of arbitration shall be advanced by the claimant but are borne at the end by the losing party in proportion to its fault established in the case.

Confidentiality

In the absence of an agreement of the parties to the contrary, arbitration proceedings are not public.[19] Arbitrators must keep confidential all information that they receive in the course of the proceedings[20] even after the proceedings have ended.

---

[18]   Act LIII of 1994 on Judicial Execution contains these rules.

[19]   *See* Section 29 of the Hungarian Arbitration Act.

[20]   *See id.* at Section 11.

Relationship of arbitration courts and ordinary courts

In addition to acting in cancellation cases and in the course of the execution of arbitral awards, ordinary courts may also provide legal aid to arbitration courts in evidence taking and ordering interim measures and security injunctions. In certain cases, ordinary courts may also play a role in the appointment of the members of the arbitration panel. Further, if a party requests the exclusion of a panel member and the arbitration court denies the exclusion, the party may turn to the respective ordinary court for a final decision on the exclusion. Ordinary courts may also decide disputes concerning the termination of the appointment of a panel member. In addition, if the jurisdiction of an arbitration court is disputed, but the arbitration court finds that it has jurisdiction, any party to the dispute may turn to the competent ordinary court to challenge the arbitration court's decision.

The four main permanent arbitration courts operating in Hungary[21]

(i) Permanent Arbitration Court attached to the Hungarian Chamber of Commerce and Industry ("HCCI Arbitration Court"); (ii) Energy Arbitration Court; (iv) Arbitration Court of Financial and Capital Markets, and (iv) the Arbitration Court attached to the Hungarian Chamber of Agriculture.

The HCCI Arbitration Court, seated in Budapest,[22] continues to be the most frequently used and most well-known permanent arbitration court in Hungary.

The Energy Arbitration Court, which is also seated in Budapest, started to operate in 2009. The Energy Arbitration Court is non-

---

[21] Note that on 1 January 2012, the Permanent Arbitration Court of Telecommunication Matters ceased its operation.

[22] For further information, visit www.mkik.hu (also in English).

exclusively authorized to proceed in legal disputes on rights and obligations arising from the articles of acts on gas supply and electricity and from contracts concluded between license holders under the scope of these acts, provided that the parties referred such matters to arbitration and that they are free to dispose of the subject-matter of the proceeding.[23] Targeted clients of the Energy Arbitration Court are traders, power stations and industrial costumers. The roll of arbitrators consists of industry experts and lawyers with considerable experience in the energy sector. The Rules of Proceedings[24] of the Energy Arbitration Court is similar to the Rules of Proceedings of the HCCI Arbitration Court. Still, it is worth pointing out that the Energy Arbitration Court endeavors to complete the proceedings within five months from the formation of the arbitral tribunal.[25]

The Arbitration Court of Financial and Capital Markets has exclusive jurisdiction to handle domestic and international arbitration cases arising in these industries. The Arbitration Court attached to the Hungarian Chamber of Agriculture is designed to adjudicate arbitration cases of companies in the agricultural sector.

A.2 Trends and Tendencies

Arbitration has become a well-known dispute resolution mechanism and a true alternative to civil litigation of commercial matters since 1994, when the Hungarian Arbitration Act entered into force. Although *ad hoc* arbitration is also recognized,

---

[23] *See* Section 1.2 of the Memorandum of the Energy Arbitration Court. In our view, the jurisdiction of the Energy Arbitration Court may also be established on the basis of Section 3(1) of the Hungarian Arbitration Act, i.e., not only in energy-related disputes.

[24] *See* www.eavb.hu.

[25] *See* Section 6 of the Rules of Proceedings of the Energy Arbitration Court.

institutional arbitration is more accepted and used in practice. However, the number of cases filed in arbitration continues to be substantially below the number of cases filed in ordinary courts. According to the latest statistics of the HCCI Arbitration Court, its caseload has been more or less stable in the past few years. During the period between September 2011 and September 2012, 239 cases were filed with the HCCI Arbitration Court, 23 of which were international arbitrations.[26] The foreign parties involved in the international cases originated from Norway, Ireland, France, Germany, Russia, Finland, The Netherlands, Italy, Austria, Spain, the Czech Republic, Poland, Slovakia, Albania and Macedonia. The total value of the disputes commenced at the HCCI Arbitration Court in this period amounts to HUF 50 billion (which is approximately EUR 176,522,000).

According to the report of the HCCI Arbitration Court, the disputes in question arise in practically all areas of the economy, as follows: (i) work and services sector (26 percent); (ii) bank sector (20 percent); (iii) agricultural sector (19 percent); (iv) building and construction (16 percent); (v) trade and international trade (9 percent); (vi) commercial representation and agency (5 percent); carriage and transportation (3 percent); (vii) energy sector (2 percent).

B. CASES

Arbitration cases and awards are generally not publicly available in Hungary. The decisions of the HCCI Arbitration Court may only be published in journals or in special publications if the President of the HCCI Arbitration Court grants specific consent for the publication. In 2012, hardly any awards were published

---

[26] With some statutory exceptions, the HCCI Arbitration Court has exclusive jurisdiction over international arbitration proceedings in Hungary.

that would have major significance for foreign and domestic investors operating in Hungary. Nevertheless, a recently published case relating to the recognition and enforcement of foreign arbitral awards in Hungary is worth mentioning.

In its recent judgment,[27] the Supreme Court of Hungary considered the recognition and enforcement of foreign arbitral awards in Hungary. The claimant in the arbitration proceeding requested the Hungarian court to enforce an ICC award. The respondent argued that the award could not be enforced because it was not a party to the agreement that contained the arbitration clause. Furthermore, the respondent initiated a cancellation proceeding in relation to the arbitral award in The Netherlands. Thus, the respondent stated that the award could not be enforced in Hungary based on Article V of the New York Convention. The Supreme Court held that according to the text of the agreement, it could not be concluded that the respondent was not a party to the agreement that contained the arbitration clause. Furthermore, the award had not been set aside or suspended by the competent court; thus, the grounds for refusal defined in Article V of the New York Convention were not met. Consequently, the Supreme Court held that the ICC award was enforceable in Hungary.

C. THE GRANT AND ENFORCEMENT OF INTERIM MEASURES IN INTERNATIONAL ARBITRATION

C.1 Tribunal-Ordered Interim Measures

Under the Hungarian Arbitration Act, unless otherwise agreed by the parties to the arbitration agreement, Hungarian arbitral tribunals may, at the request of a party, order any party to take

---

[27]   *See* decision No EBH 2011. 2419.

such interim measures of protection as the arbitral tribunal may consider necessary in respect of the subject matter of the dispute. This gives arbitral tribunals a much wider discretion in the field of interim measures than the ordinary courts.[28] The arbitral tribunal may require any party to provide appropriate security in connection with such measure.[29]

A party does not have to satisfy any formal tests in order for the arbitral tribunal to order interim measures, although the tribunal will of course consider the circumstances of the case and the interests of the parties. Pursuant to the rules of proceedings of the Hungarian arbitral tribunals, interim measures are only available from the tribunal after the commencement of the arbitration proceeding.[30]

C.2 Court-Ordered Interim Measures

The ordinary courts in the Hungarian jurisdiction have concurrent powers to order interim measures while the arbitration proceeding is pending. The party to the arbitration proceeding does not have to apply to the tribunal first for interim measure once the arbitration proceeding is commenced. The ordinary court renders its decision in relation to the interim measure in an expedited proceeding.[31]

---

[28] According to the provisions of the Hungarian Code of Civil Procedure and the Hungarian Judicial Execution Act, the ordinary courts in Hungary may only order interim measures and security measures if the statutory conditions are met.

[29] *See* Section 26 (1) of the Hungarian Arbitration Act.

[30] We have to note in this regard that if the parties stipulate the rules of proceeding of a foreign arbitration court, interim measures may be available before the commencement of arbitration (e.g., emergency arbitrators).

[31] *See* Section 156(3) of the Hungarian Code of Civil Procedure.

In Hungary, ordinary courts do not have the power to grant anti-suit injunctions. However, particularly if the ordinary court has established its jurisdiction, a party may raise an objection to jurisdiction in any proceeding initiated on the same subject matter before another forum.

Hungarian ordinary courts may grant interim measures in aid of a foreign arbitration (i.e., outside the jurisdiction of the supervisory court) if it is requested by a party to the arbitration proceeding and reciprocal treatment is granted by the country where the arbitration proceeding is pending.[32]

C.3 Enforcement of Interim Measures

Interim measures ordered by the tribunal are not enforceable in the same way as an arbitral award or a court judgment. In this regard, we have to note that the Hungarian Judicial Execution Act is not consistent with the Hungarian Arbitration Act. According to the reasoning of the Hungarian Arbitration Act, interim measures ordered by the arbitral tribunal are not enforceable in the same way as interim measures ordered by the ordinary courts. However, the Hungarian Judicial Execution Act deals with the enforcement of arbitral "decisions," not arbitral "awards." Nevertheless, in our view, the interim measures of an arbitral tribunal are not enforceable in the same way as an arbitral award.

---

[32] *See* Section 46 of the Hungarian Arbitration Act.

ITALY

Gianfranco Di Garbo[1] and Emanuela Banfi[2]

A. LEGISLATION, TRENDS AND TENDENCIES

A.1 The Italian Constitutional Court Declares Compulsory Mediation Illegitimate in Civil and Commercial Disputes

On 24 October 2012, the Italian Constitutional Court declared invalid the provision of Legislative Decree n. 28 dated 4 March 2010, which had implemented a compulsory mediation procedure for the resolution of certain disputes (Article 5.1 of the "Decree").

The Decree—which implemented in Italy the European Mediation Directive (2008/52/EC) published on 21 May 2008 as part of the European initiative to promote and regulate the development of mediation throughout the EU—was aimed at reducing the overload on the Italian legal system by the introduction of a two-fold mediation procedure: (i) a non-compulsory procedure that applies to any civil and commercial litigation (Article 2.1, introduced on 20 March 2010); and (ii) a compulsory procedure that applied to any litigation in relation to insurance, banking and financial agreements, joint ownership, property rights, division of assets, hereditary and family law, leases in general, gratuitous loans, leases of going concerns, medical liability or defamation (Article 5.1, effective since 20

---

[1]   Gianfranco Di Garbo is a Partner in Baker & McKenzie's Milan office and coordinator of the office's Dispute Resolution Practice Group. He is a member of the Firm's European and Global Dispute Resolution Practice Groups. His practice concentrates on litigation and arbitration, and as of January 2013, he is serving as Honorary Judge of the Court of Lecco (Milan).

[2]   Emanuela Banfi is an Associate in Baker & McKenzie's Milan office and a member of the Firm's European and Global Dispute Resolution Practice Groups.

March 2011, or for vehicle insurances and property disputes, effective since March 2012).

The Constitutional Court's ruling that the compulsory mediation procedure is invalid was based on its finding that the Italian government lacked the legislative power to introduce Article 5.1 of the Decree. The government had issued the Decree based on delegated legislative powers flowing from Law no. 69 of 2009 of the Italian Parliament. Law 69 implemented the 2008 EU Directive on certain aspects of cross-border mediation, but granted no specific authority for the government to introduce mediation.

The court ruled that the specific language used in the 2009 law did not empower the government to introduce mediation as a mandatory precursor to trial. It is expected that compulsory mediation will be re-introduced in the form of a bill (which does not require a delegation of power) rather than a legislative decree. A new bill to that effect was proposed on 25 October 2012 and is currently pending.

In general, these mediation requirements do not apply to arbitration. However, Article 5 of the Decree provides that when a contract or the by-laws of a company provide for a two-step settlement mechanism combining mediation and arbitration and no attempt is made to mediate the dispute, the arbitrator, upon request of a party, should invite the parties to attempt to settle their dispute through mediation within 15 days, and shall not decide the case unless the parties have previously tried to resolve the dispute by mediation. Such a provision falls under the non-compulsory mediation procedure and therefore will not be affected by the decision of the Constitutional Court.

B. CASES

The following are the more interesting arbitration-related cases decided in 2012.

B.1 Arbitration Clauses in International Arbitration

The Court of Milan[3] ruled that if a contract includes both an arbitration clause and an exclusive jurisdiction clause, the latter shall prevail. The court held that if there is uncertainty as to the actual intention of the parties, the competence of the ordinary court must be assessed with the consequence that an award issued under these circumstances would be declared null and void and the ordinary court will eventually decide on the controversy.

B.2 Binary Arbitration Clauses in International Arbitration

The Supreme Court[4] held valid and effective a binary arbitration clause (i.e., an arbitration clause providing that each party (in the singular) appoint an arbitrator with a third arbitrator acting as a chairman of the tribunal) inserted in a multilateral contract of franchising in a case where only some of the parties decided to refer their dispute to arbitration. The Supreme Court based its decision on the consideration that, although there were three parties in the contract, the interests of two of them were "polarized": therefore the parties were substantially two and the binary arbitration clause could apply.

B.3 Arbitration Clauses in Corporate Arbitration

The Supreme Court[5] found that an arbitration clause included in the articles of association of a corporation, providing that any

---

3   Judgment of the Court of Milan of 10 September 2012.

4   Judgment of the Court of Cassation 3, 23 July 2012 n. 12825.

5   Judgment of the Court of Cassation 1, 17 July 2012, n. 12333.

disputes arising between shareholders, the company and the shareholders as well as acts of the directors and auditors in relation to the execution of the company's purpose or to the interpretation or execution of the by-laws, should be referred to arbitration, does not include a liability action (under Article 2476 of the Civil Code) against directors, regardless of whether the latter are also shareholders.

B.4 Recourse for Nullity of the Arbitral Award

In an important judgment, the Supreme Court ruled that amendments made to Article 829 of the Italian Code of Civil Procedure by Legislative Decree of 2 February 2006 no. 40 to limit the scope of appeal of an arbitration award, apply only to arbitral proceedings based on arbitral clauses executed after the enactment of the new law.[6] Appeals based on a violation of the law governing the merits were generally permitted by the previous wording of Article 829 of the Code of Civil Procedure, whilst the new provisions require a previous specific agreement of the parties to permit such an appeal. Violations of rules of law continue to be permitted as a ground of appeal against decisions that are contrary to public policy.

B.5 The Interpretation of the Arbitral Clause

The Supreme Court held that an arbitration clause referring generically to "any dispute" arising under the contract, in the absence of express contrary intention, should be interpreted in the sense that the jurisdiction of the arbitrators includes only disputes relating to a cause of action under the contract itself, thus excluding disputes for which the contract represents only a factual precondition.[7] In that case, the court ruled that a non-

---

[6] Judgment of the Court of Cassation of 19 April 2012, n. 6148.

[7] Judgment of the Court of Cassation of 3 February 2012, no. 1674.

contractual claim relating to serious defects in a real estate property was not covered by the arbitral clause included in the property's purchase contract.

C. THE GRANT AND ENFORCEMENT OF INTERIM MEASURES IN INTERNATIONAL ARBITRATION

C.1 Tribunal-Ordered Interim Measures

According to Article 818 of the Italian Code of Civil Procedure ("ICCP"), "[a]rbitrators may not grant attachments or other interim measures of protection, except if otherwise provided by the law."

In other words, this provision prevents arbitrators from granting any interim measures. Thus, whenever an arbitration agreement is in force or arbitration is pending, preliminary relief and interim measures should be requested from—and may be granted by—the ordinary courts. Specifically, Article 669-*quinquies* of the ICCP provides that in such circumstances, interim injunctions have to be requested from the court that would otherwise have had competence on the merits.

However, an exception to the above provision is provided by Article 35.5 of Legislative Decree n. 5/2003, which regulates arbitration in corporate matters, and more specifically, disputes on the validity of shareholders' meeting resolutions. Arbitrators empowered to decide on the validity of the shareholders' meeting resolutions are entitled to suspend the effectiveness of such resolutions. This is the only kind of interim measure admitted in corporate arbitration. Therefore, parties to a corporate arbitration proceeding must refer to the ordinary courts any request for interim measures other than the suspension of the effectiveness of shareholders' meeting resolutions.

Italian ordinary courts have always interpreted Article 818 of the ICCP in a very narrow way, excluding any possibility of arbitrators granting injunctions, attachments or other interim measures. In particular, the prohibition on arbitrators issuing interim measures is interpreted as a general prohibition on granting any measure that, following a summary procedure, grants a party an enforceable title or a decision intended to anticipate a result that could otherwise have been achieved only at the end of a full cognition procedure. This prohibition also covers any injunction provided by special laws.

Finally, it is undisputed that the prohibition under Art. 818 of the ICCP is mandatory in nature. It represents a public policy rule from which the parties and the arbitrators cannot derogate. Its mandatory nature was confirmed by the Italian legislature in the last arbitration reform, which became effective as of March 2006, and treated the law (and not the parties' will) as the only source able to overcome such prohibition.

C.2 Court-Ordered Interim Measures

Article 669-*quinquies* of the ICCP establishes an autonomous rule of jurisdiction for disputes subject to arbitration or compromised in arbitration. It provides that, whenever an arbitration agreement is in force or arbitration is pending, interim injunctions have to be requested from the court that would otherwise have had jurisdiction over the merits of the dispute. Article 669-*quaterdecies* of the ICCP provides that this applies to the following interim measures: (i) pre-trial attachments; (ii) restraint orders concerning new works or threatened damages, and, finally (iii) urgent measures provided by Article 700 of the ICCP.

Preliminary investigation orders, provided by Article 696 of the ICCP, were initially excluded from the application of Article 669-*quinquies* above. However, the Italian Constitutional Court held Article 669-*quaterdecies* of the ICCP to be unconstitutional in that it did not permit recourse to ordinary courts to obtain a preliminary investigation order in cases reserved for arbitration. The Constitutional Court held that this limitation infringed both the right of defense (Article 24 of the Constitutional Charter) and the right of equal treatment (Article 3), since it gave rise to an unjustified disparity between state court and arbitral proceedings with respect to the ability of the parties to obtain evidence. Therefore, since this decision, prior investigation measures in claims submitted to arbitration may be authorized by the ordinary court that would have jurisdiction in the absence of the arbitration clause.

This rule applies both before the commencement of the arbitral proceeding and while the arbitral proceeding is pending. Even during the period allowed for an appeal against an arbitral award, the prevailing opinion asserts the jurisdiction of the court that would have competence over the merits of the dispute.

If the parties refer their dispute to a foreign arbitral proceeding, requests for interim measures should be submitted to the court that would have jurisdiction, on the basis of the nature of the case or of the other ordinary criteria, in the place where the interim measure is to be executed (in accordance with Article 669-*ter, alinea* 3, ICCP).

As to the procedure, the competent judge or court decides on the motion requesting the measure by means of an order after having heard the other party. However, if there is a concrete risk that the enforcement of the measure may be jeopardized as a result of a delay, the judge may issue a decree *ex parte*. In that case, the judge, through the same decree, will fix a hearing within 15 days; the decree and the relevant motion of the applicant must be served on the other party within the following eight days (24 days if the service has to be made abroad) (Article 669-*sexies* ICCP). At that hearing, the judge will confirm, modify or cancel the measure granted in the *ex parte* decree.

In the event the order authorizing the measures is issued before the arbitral proceeding on the merits is commenced, the latter must be commenced within the next 60 days (Article 669-*octies, alinea 5, ICCP*). If this term elapses or the proceeding on the merits is terminated, the provisional measure becomes ineffective. The precautionary measure also loses its effect if the party that applied for it does not seek enforcement in Italy of the foreign arbitration award within the compulsory time limits provided for by law or by international treaties, or if an arbitration award declares the non-existence of the right for whose protection the measure had been issued.

C.3 Enforcement of Interim Measures

Article 818 ICCP is a mandatory provision from which the parties cannot derogate. Therefore, an interim measure issued by arbitrators cannot be enforced as such in Italy.

As the provision is in the nature of a public policy, such interim measures cannot be enforced even if issued by foreign arbitrators. Thus, referring the dispute to foreign arbitrators cannot circumvent the jurisdiction of the Italian courts with regard to procedures for the granting of interim measures. In such a case, the interested party should file a separate motion before the Italian court in order to seek an interim measure, leading to a trial *de novo* where the prior grant of interim relief by the foreign arbitrators may only be taken into account as a factual precedent.

Although the matter has not yet been submitted to the Italian court, it is expected that the above conclusion will apply also to interim measures delivered by an arbitral tribunal under the new Article 29 of the ICC Rules, effective as of 1 January 2012, which offers a procedure for parties to seek urgent interim relief that cannot await the constitution of an arbitral tribunal.

JAPAN

Haig Oghigian,[1] Mami Ohara[2] and Hiroyuki Hamai[3]

A. LEGISLATION, TRENDS AND TENDENCIES

Japan revamped its arbitration system and enacted a new stand-alone arbitration law on March 1, 2004 (the "Arbitration Law"),[4] which is largely based on the UNCITRAL Model Law. At the same time, Japan's leading international commercial arbitration institution, the Japan Commercial Arbitration Association (the "JCAA"), revised its commercial arbitration rules (the "Rules") to bring them in line with the Arbitration Law, the UNCITRAL Arbitration Rules, and the rules of other leading international commercial dispute resolution organizations.

Over the past decade, the use of arbitration has become increasingly more common to resolve international disputes in Japan. Courts in Japan are generally known to be pro-arbitration in making their decisions, and they respect the finality of arbitration awards.

This section will provide a brief summary of the historical background of arbitration law in Japan as well as an introduction

---

[1]   Haig Oghigian is a Partner and co-chair of the Litigation and Dispute Resolution Group at Baker & McKenzie, Tokyo office. In addition to his work in dispute resolution, Mr. Oghigian advises clients on mergers and acquisitions, joint ventures, license agreements and distribution agreements, as well as construction and engineering contracts.

[2]   Mami Ohara is an Associate in the Litigation and Dispute Resolution Group in Baker & McKenzie's Tokyo office.

[3]   Hiroyuki Hamai is an Associate in the Litigation and Dispute Resolution Group in Baker & McKenzie's Tokyo office.

[4]   English translation of the Arbitration Law can be found at http://www.kantei.go.jp/foreign/policy/sihou/arbitrationlaw.pdf.

of the key reforms and unique features of the Arbitration Law and the Rules.

A.1 Historical Background

Before the enactment of the Arbitration Law, there was no stand-alone arbitration law in Japan. Rather, arbitration provisions were provided for under the 8th Book of the old Civil Procedure Law[5] and they had not been amended for over a century. Based on the German Civil Procedure Law of 1877, the old Civil Procedure Law contained provisions governing the procedures for judgments, enforcements, provisional attachments and dispositions, public notices and arbitration. When the current Civil Procedure Law was drafted and came into effect in 1997, provisions concerning arbitration and public notices were not included in the Civil Procedure Law, and were renamed the Public Peremptory Notice and Arbitration Procedure Law. When the Arbitration Law was promulgated, provisions dealing with public notice procedures were then renamed as the Public Peremptory Notice Procedure Law.

In Japan, arbitration was not utilized frequently, and disputes were normally resolved through negotiation and litigation. For a long time, therefore, it was not felt that there was a need for stand-alone arbitration legislation. Nevertheless, interest in arbitration grew and in 1979 an arbitration study group (*Chusai Kenkyukai*) was established.[6] The group undertook comparative studies of major or new arbitration laws in other countries in force at that time, and a draft for a new arbitration law was

---

[5]   Law No. 29 of 1890. The Civil Procedure Law itself was revamped in 1996.

[6]   Toshio Sawada, "The 2004 Japanese Arbitration Law in Relation to the UNCITRAL Model Law and the Japanese ADR and Attorneys Law," *Global Reflections on International Law, Commerce and Dispute Resolution: Liber Amicorum in Honor of Robert Briner*, 2005, ICC Publishing, 726.

produced around 1989 (*Chusaiho Shian*). However, the draft was not adopted. A second draft was produced in 2001, amidst calls for reform and the belief held by some scholars and promoters of arbitration that Japan needed to be promoted as a center for arbitration (*Chusaiho 2001 Shian*).[7] This draft was also not adopted.

Around the same time, as a part of the government's efforts to expand/facilitate the use of alternative dispute resolution ("ADR"), the Office for Promotion of Justice System Reform (*Shiho Seido Kaikaku Shingikai*) called for a new legal framework for arbitration that reflected worldwide developments, and that used the Model Law as the basis for a new arbitration law. As a result, a draft of the Arbitration Law was created and passed by the Diet.

A.2 Main Features of the Arbitration Law

While the Arbitration Law largely follows the provisions of the Model Law, it has made some modifications that are specific to the Japanese context. Below are some of the special features of the Arbitration Law about which potential users should be aware before entering into an arbitration agreement specifying Japan as the place of arbitration:

- In Japan, in principle, only civil disputes that may be resolved by settlement between the parties may be submitted to arbitration.[8] Article 13(1) specifically lists divorce and

---

[7] *Ibid.*

[8] Article 13(1) of the Arbitration Law. This is in line with the Model Law which leaves the issue of what type of dispute may or may not be submitted to arbitration to the laws of individual states (Model Law Article 1(5)). Following the practices in many civil law countries such as Germany, Switzerland, France, Italy and Sweden, Japan therefore prescribes the possibility of settlement as a criteria for whether or not a dispute may be resolved by arbitration.

separation as matters that are non-arbitrable.[9] In the commercial fields, for example, applications for the invalidation of patents,[10] actions for declaratory judgment of absence of a new share issue, actions for declaratory judgment of absence or invalidation of a resolution of a shareholders meeting, or actions seeking revocation of a resolution of a shareholders meeting, are all deemed as matters that cannot be resolved through settlement,[11] and hence are not arbitrable.

- In line with litigation practices in Japan whereby judges are expected to encourage amicable settlements, many arbitration cases were traditionally settled through the active involvement of arbitrators. This has attracted criticism, especially from common law practitioners who do not like the idea of arbitrators acting as mediators. To balance customary practice with the general trend in international commercial arbitration to separate arbitration and mediation proceedings, Article 38(4) of the Arbitration Law provides for the possibility of the involvement of an arbitrator in a mediation, but only after both parties have given their written consent.

- The Arbitration Law contains special provisions concerning consumers and employees. Under the Arbitration Law, consumers can unilaterally cancel an arbitration agreement even when they knowingly entered into it.[12] Further, an

---

[9] Divorce and separation matters relate to changes of personal status the settlement of which was traditionally rejected, and which are normally determined by courts.

[10] As illustrated in Section B below, while the issue of the validity of a patent is considered as non-arbitrable, claims for damages arising out of alleged patent infringement may be subjected to arbitration.

[11] As these are matters may greatly impact on the interests of third parties if arbitration proceedings are allowed, they are therefore deemed as non-arbitrable.

[12] Article 3 of Supplementary Provisions of the Arbitration Law.

arbitration agreement contained in an individual's employment contract will be deemed invalid.[13]

- Perhaps one of the most significant features of the Arbitration Law is the continuance of significant involvement of the courts. First, whether arbitral tribunals should have the power to order interim measures was one of the most debated issues during the drafting process. While the Arbitration Law contains language that would appear to empower tribunals to order interim measures,[14] uncertainties remain over whether interim measures issued by an arbitral tribunal will be enforceable.[15] Second, the Arbitration Law also allows the court to "assist" a party in determining the place of arbitration if it is not clearly set out and where "there is a possibility" that the place of arbitration might be Japan.[16] Third, the Arbitration Law allows the court to appoint an arbitrator, particularly if "either party has a place of business in Japan."[17] Finally, Article 35 of the Arbitration Law allows the tribunal (on its own volition or through application by a party) to seek the assistance of the court in taking evidence.[18]

---

[13] *Id.* at Article 4.

[14] Article 24(1) of New Arbitration Law states that "Unless otherwise agreed by the parties, the arbitral tribunal may, at the request of a party, order any party to take such interim measure of protection as the arbitral tribunal may consider necessary in respect of the subject matter of the dispute."

[15] The uncertainty over the enforceability of interim measures ordered by a tribunal is lessened somewhat by Article 24(2) of the Arbitration Law, which provides that the arbitral tribunal may order any party to provide appropriate security in connection with such measure. The JCAA also blunted the uncertainties regarding this issue by providing, under Rule 48, that the arbitral tribunal may issue interim measures of protection including the requirement to advance security.

[16] Article 8 of the Arbitration Law.

[17] *Id.* at Articles 8 and 17.

[18] As described below in Section B, an application has indeed been made to the court for assistance in taking evidence.

- In the past, arbitration proceedings in Japan were often criticized for being exceedingly lengthy and slow as arbitrators could be reluctant to limit the number of document exchanges. Further, hearings could be akin to court proceedings where numerous short hearings were held weeks apart. This practice has been replaced with single hearings similar to those held in other arbitration centers.

- Article 45(1) of the Arbitration Law allows for enforcement of an arbitral award even if it is rendered in a jurisdiction not a party to the New York Convention. This is particularly relevant for a number of jurisdictions in Asia, such as Taiwan.

- Before the Arbitration Law, Japanese law contained no specific provision dealing with the language of the arbitration. In the past, there were criticisms from non-Japanese parties that they were disadvantaged in arbitration proceedings in Japan due to huge expenses in connection with translation requirements. In an effort to make the law fairer, the Arbitration Law provides that the parties are free to agree on the language or languages to be used in the arbitral proceedings. In the absence of such an agreement, the arbitral tribunal may make such a determination.[19]

As stated above, together with the reform of the Arbitration Law, the JCAA also completely revised its rules and a new set of rules came into effect in 2003.[20] The Rules have balanced and, in some contexts, clarified the provisions contained in the Arbitration Law.[21] Steps were taken to modernize, streamline

---

[19] Article 30 of the Arbitration Law.

[20] The Rules were subsequently amended in 2006 (Rule 11, Language) and 2007 (Rule 28, Impartiality and Independence of Arbitrators). The current Rules are effective as of 1 January 2008.

[21] For example, Rule 28 sets forth both stricter guidelines for ensuring independence of arbitrators and a mechanism to remove an arbitrator for lack of impartiality.

and generally improve the Rules. Examples vary from allowing the tribunal to determine whether an agreement to arbitrate exists,[22] allowing facsimiles and e-mail as evidence of a written arbitration agreement,[23] to allowing parties free choice of representation.[24]

While there are issues that may still be of concern to foreign parties, the Arbitration Law and the Rules allow for a flexible and modern arbitration system in Japan that is compatible with the laws and rules of other leading arbitration centers.

B. CASES

There have been a number of interesting cases thus far regarding the Arbitration Law since it came into force.

B.1 Court Assistance in Taking Evidence

Article 35(1) of the Arbitration Law allows an arbitral tribunal and a party to an arbitration proceeding[25] to apply to a court for assistance in taking evidence by any means that the arbitral

---

There is also greater flexibility to manage the case both by the JCAA and the tribunal, in order to prevent the process from grinding to a halt. For example, JCAA can establish a tribunal even if one of the parties has raised a jurisdictional issue and the tribunal is then charged with ruling on its own jurisdictional power under Rule 16 (reflecting the thinking of *Kompetenz-Kompetenz*). Under Article 35, the tribunal is also permitted to proceed with the arbitral process even where one of the parties has refused to participate.

[22] Rule 16 of the JCAA Arbitration Rules.

[23] Rule 5 of the JCAA Arbitration Rules.

[24] Rule 10 of the JCAA Arbitration Rules. But see below for the implications of the Lawyers' Law on representation on the application of this rule.

[25] The arbitral tribunal must consent to the application before it can be made.

tribunal considers necessary.[26] In this case, an examination of a witness in support of arbitration proceedings was conducted in the Tokyo District Court in accordance with Article 35(1).[27]

Although the procedure was one in support of arbitration proceedings, since it was conducted in court, it was considered a court proceeding rather than an "international arbitration case." It was therefore managed and administered by the court. As such, only a *bengoshi* (a licensed attorney of Japan) could represent the applicant and respondent.

As a result, this case made clear that a *bengoshi* needs to be separately retained for an application for court assistance under Article 35(1) and for conducting any resulting witness examination. Even if a *bengoshi* is retained for the arbitration proceeding from the beginning, the *bengoshi* needs to be retained anew for such an application.

This demonstrates the unfortunate effect of court intervention in international commercial arbitration. More significantly, it evidences the continuous obstacles created by the Lawyers' Law (*Bengoshi Ho*)[28] in relation to international commercial arbitration and, more specifically, in relation to the parties' right

---

[26] Such means include entrustment of investigation, examination of witnesses, expert testimony, and investigation of documentary evidence or inspection prescribed in the Code of Civil Procedure.

[27] Junya Naito, "Examination of Witnesses in Court for Arbitration Proceedings in Japan," (2007) 18 JCAA Newsletter, 5.

[28] Law No. 205 of 1949. Article 72 of the Lawyers' Law states that:

"Persons who are not *bengoshi* or *bengoshi* juridical persons, as a business, may not for the purpose of receiving compensation, deal with legal advice, representation, arbitration or settlement or other legal work, or lend good offices, provided that the foregoing does not apply where there is a provision to the contrary in this or another law."

to be represented by whomever they choose in international commercial arbitration proceedings.

This issue is dealt with in part by Article 58-2 of Special Measures Law Concerning the Handling of Legal Business by Foreign Lawyers (Law No. 66 of 1986), which allows a foreign lawyer to represent clients in procedures for an international arbitration case that he or she was requested to undertake or undertook in a foreign country. However, even outside of court assistance in taking evidence relating to arbitration, doubts remain as to the right of foreign lawyers employed in Japan to represent parties in international arbitrations.[29]

B.2 Separability of Arbitration Agreement

The second case involving the Arbitration Law is more encouraging.[30] In this case, the plaintiff granted the defendant a non-exclusive license of its patents. The plaintiff alleged that the defendant had underreported the amount of sales of the licensed products, thus having underpaid the royalties owed to plaintiff. The defendant asked the court to dismiss the plaintiff's action on the basis that there was an arbitration clause in the license agreement.

The plaintiff argued that it had terminated the license agreement which contained the arbitration agreement and that the arbitration agreement therefore became invalid. The plaintiff further claimed that the defendant, in seeking an invalidation

---

[29] Article 58(2) only deals with representation by a foreign lawyer practicing outside of Japan and specifically excludes a person who is employed and is providing services in Japan, based on his or her knowledge of foreign law. However,, Rule 10 of the JCAA Arbitration Rules explicitly states that a party may be represented by any person of its choice.

[30] Decision by the Tokyo district court handed down on October 21, 2005, 1216 Hanrei Taimuzu 309; 1926 Hanrei Jiho 127.

judgment of two of the patents licensed under the license agreement, had breached the arbitration agreement and rendered it invalid. The court held that even if a contract containing an arbitration agreement is null and void, the validity of the arbitration agreement was not necessarily affected. Furthermore, the patent invalidation judgment was held to be non-arbitrable, and therefore did not infringe the arbitration agreement. Even if it did infringe the arbitration agreement, it would only render the application unlawful, and thus did not necessarily invalidate the arbitration agreement.[31]

The plaintiff then made an appeal to the Intellectual Property High Court[32] on two grounds:

(1) Article 12(2) of the license agreement required a party seeking to contest a termination notice to initiate arbitration proceedings within 40 days from the date it received the termination notice. If the party receiving the termination notice did not initiate arbitration within 40 days from the date it received the termination notice, the arbitration clause expired together with the termination of the license agreement; and

---

[31]   *See* "The First Case Applying the New Japanese Arbitration Law, Tokyo District Court, 21 October 2005" in (2007) 18 JCAA Newsletter, 9-10. The other interesting and encouraging aspect of this case is that although both parties to the license agreement were Japanese, they chose arbitration as the dispute resolution mechanism in their license agreement. Significantly, the parties chose ICC arbitration rather than JCAA, the leading arbitration institution in Japan, even though it concerned a domestic agreement.

[32]   The Intellectual Property High Court was established on 1 April 2005, as a special branch within the Tokyo High Court in accordance with the Law for Establishing the IP High Court enacted in June 2004. The Intellectual Property High Court hears appeals from district courts in Japan on patent actions and suits against appeal/trial decisions made by the Japan Patent Office ("JPO"). It also hears any other cases before the Tokyo High Court, as far as the nature and contents of the case are related to intellectual property.

B. Cases

(2) Even if the arbitration agreement continued to exist after the termination of the license agreement, the defendant continuously breached the license agreement through its unilateral action in stopping royalty payments rather than initiating arbitration proceedings in accordance with the parties' agreements; its failure to initiate arbitration proceedings when there were questions concerning the validity of the termination of the license agreement; and its decision to seek the invalidation of relevant patents rather than initiating arbitration proceedings when there were concerns regarding the validity of the relevant patents. Based on the principles of fairness and equity, the defendant should therefore be barred from seeking a dismissal of the plaintiff's action.

The Intellectual Property High Court found that the 40-day period was a grace period for the correction of a breach under the license agreement, and Article 12(2) only clarified that the 40-day grace period would stop running once arbitration was initiated. It did not place any onus on a party to initiate arbitration proceedings. The Intellectual Property High Court also found that the arbitration agreement only required the parties to submit any differences and disputes to arbitration under the ICC Rules if the parties could not resolve their differences within a reasonable time, and it did not place an obligation on a party to actively pursue arbitration. The Intellectual Property High Court therefore dismissed the appeal.[33]

---

[33] Case No. 10120 of 2005.

B.3 Public Policy

A third recent case is also supportive of international arbitration. The applicant, a Japanese company selling semi-conductor related products between Japan and Korea, entered into an agency agreement with the respondent in 1994. The agreement specified that either party could refuse to renew the agreement upon expiration of the term, with 60 days' notice. The agreement also specified that all disputes arising out of the agreement shall be finally settled by arbitration in accordance with the rules of the Korean Commercial Arbitration Board and the governing law of the agreement was Korean law.

On January 22, 2007, the respondent notified the applicant of its refusal to renew the agreement upon its expiration on March 31, 2007. The applicant filed an application for a provisional injunction in an attempt to preserve its contractual status. It claimed, *inter alia*, that the clauses concerning jurisdiction and governing law were invalid as they were in breach of Japan's public policy to protect continuous contractual relationships,[34] and the jurisdiction and governing law clauses had been inserted into the agreement in order to avoid the protections Japanese laws gave to long-term contractual relationships.

Interestingly, the court found that the principle of party autonomy applied when determining an issue concerning governing law. The fact that the application of the parties' chosen governing law may have a result that is contrary to the public policy of Japan did not mean that the choice of governing law (and jurisdiction) itself would necessarily be deemed invalid. This case demonstrates Japanese courts' willingness to respect

---

[34] In Japan, irrespective of the written agreements of the parties, it is difficult to terminate a long-term contractual relationship, especially one with an automatic renewal provision.

party autonomy and to enforce an agreement to arbitrate whenever possible.

B.4 Enforcement Order

Under Article 45 of the Arbitration Law, an arbitral award has the same effect as a final and conclusive judgment unless any of the following grounds (for refusal of recognition) are present:

(1) The arbitration agreement is not valid due to limits to a party's capacity;

(2) The arbitration agreement is not valid for a reason other than limits to a party's capacity under the law to which the parties have agreed to subject it (or failing such agreement, the law of the country under which the place of arbitration falls);

(3) A party was not given notice as required by the provisions of the country under which the place of arbitration falls;

(4) A party was unable to present its case in the arbitral proceedings;

(5) The arbitral award contains decisions on matters beyond the scope of the arbitration agreement or the claims in the arbitral proceedings;

(6) The composition of an arbitral tribunal or the arbitral proceedings were not in accordance with the provisions of the law of the country under which the place of arbitration falls;

(7) The arbitral award has not yet become binding, or has been set aside or suspended by a court of the country under which the place of arbitration falls;

(8) The claims in the arbitral proceedings relate to a dispute that is not arbitrable under the laws of Japan; and

(9) The content of the arbitral award would be contrary to the public policy or good morals of Japan.

In order to enforce an arbitral award in Japan, an enforcement order from the court is necessary. Under the Arbitration Law, an enforcement order may be obtained through a court hearing called "*Shinjin*," in which the parties are given the opportunity to contest the enforcement, or when the case is more complicated, through a procedure called "*Koutou Benron*" in which public oral arguments along with witness examinations need to be carried out.

The first reported case of an enforcement order being granted under the Arbitration Law occurred in 2008. In that case, summary proceedings under the JCAA Commercial Arbitration Rules had been conducted due to the small monetary value of the claim. After the award was rendered the respondent refused to satisfy the award and therefore claimant filed a petition for an enforcement order with the court of competent jurisdiction. The enforcement order was ultimately rendered and the respondent made the payment without the need for further compulsory enforcement measures.[35]

In the current case, the respondent's attorney did not attend the hearing, asserting that "there is nothing specifically the respondent wishes to claim" and the enforcement order was rendered within 50 days from the filing of the enforcement petition. However, claimant's lawyer expressed concern that had the respondent applied a delay tactic by claiming the attorney's unavailability or fiercely contested the enforcement of the award, then substantial delays could have been foreseen.[36] He therefore

---

[35] Masafumi Kodama, Toshihiko Oinuma and Jiri M. Mestecky, "First Enforcement Order Granted under Japan's Arbitration Act," (2008) 21 JCAA Newsletter, 7-9.

[36] *Ibid.*

believes that this is one area where the court should monitor the practices of the parties and ensure effective progress of the case.[37]

B.5 Grounds for Setting Aside the Arbitral Award

Under the Arbitration Law, arbitration awards may only be set aside under limited circumstances as provided in Article 44.

On June 16, 2011, the Tokyo District Court set aside an arbitral award for the first time under Article 44(1)(viii) of the Japanese Arbitration Act,[38] which provides that a party may apply to court to set aside an award when it is in conflict with the public policy or good morals of Japan. The court held that Article 44(1)(viii) applied to this case because the procedure conducted by the tribunal in the arbitration was in conflict with the "procedural aspect of" the public policy of Japan. It found that the arbitrator's treatment of a disputed issue on the interpretation of the contract as an undisputed fact was in conflict with the public policy of Japan.

The court expressed its reluctance to set aside an award even where the tribunal had engaged in unreasonable fact finding or the legal decision was unreasonable, unless the legal outcome would conflict with the public policy of Japan. Nevertheless,

---

[37] We assisted a client in seeking recognition and enforcement of a foreign arbitral award that was initially contested. During the first hearing, the court explained clearly that it would not reopen the case based on substantive grounds. While the defendant attempted to contest the application for enforcement based on the ground that the arbitration agreement was invalid, after the hearing, the defendant immediately proposed settlement with our client. While no court decision was rendered in that case, the court's attitude in adhering strictly to the limited grounds for refusing recognition and enforcement is encouraging and is demonstrative of the courts' willingness to monitor the parties' practice to ensure effective and efficient enforcement.

[38] Tokyo District Court, June 13, 2011, Heisei 21 (*chu*) No.6.

referring to Article of 338(1)(ix) of the Code of Civil Procedure[39] as an example of the "procedural aspect of" public policy in Japan, the Tokyo District Court held that an arbitration award that was rendered without considering the material issues of fact raised by the parties would violate the procedural aspect of public policy in Japan.

C. THE GRANT AND ENFORCEMENT OF INTERIM MEASURES IN INTERNATIONAL ARBITRATION

C.1 Tribunal-Ordered Interim Measures

Under the Arbitration Law, an arbitral tribunal may, at the request of a party, order any party to take interim measures of protection as the arbitral tribunal may consider necessary with respect to the subject matter of the dispute, unless the parties had otherwise agreed.[40] The arbitral tribunal has the discretion to order interim measures of protection anytime between the commencement and the termination of the arbitral proceedings.

The Arbitration Law does not clearly define the term "interim measure." However, in practice, it is construed to have the same meaning as the term "interim measure" defined in Article 17(2) of the UNCITRAL Model Law.[41]

---

[39] Article of 338(1)(ix) of the Code of Civil Procedure provides that where there is an omission in the determination of material matters that should have been considered, an appeal may be submitted by filing an action for retrial against a final judgment even if it has become final and binding.

[40] Article 24(1) of the Arbitration Law.

[41] Under UNCITRAL Model Law Article 17(2), an interim measure is defined as any temporary measure, whether in the form of an award or in another form, by which, at any time prior to the issuance of the award by which the dispute is finally decided, the arbitral tribunal orders a party to (a) maintain or restore the status quo pending determination of the dispute; (b) take action that would

C. The Grant and Enforcement of Interim Measures in International Arbitration

The Arbitration Law does not provide requirements that an applicant must satisfy in order for the tribunal to order interim measures. However, it is generally considered necessary for the applicant to prove that (i) there is a reasonable possibility that the requesting party will succeed on the merits of the claim; and that (ii) there is a necessity to order such measures.[42]

Under the current legal framework in Japan, interim measures from the arbitral tribunal are not available before commencement of arbitral proceedings (e.g., emergency arbitrators).[43] Likewise, interim measures from the arbitral tribunal are not available before commencement of arbitral proceedings under the JCAA Rules.

C.2 Court-Ordered Interim Measures

The arbitration law allows a party to request a court to grant an interim measure of protection with respect to any civil dispute that is within the scope of the arbitration agreement, before or during arbitration proceedings.[44] There are no court precedents to date that address this issue, and there are different views as to whether the court has concurrent powers to order interim

---

prevent, or refrain from taking action that is likely to cause, current or imminent harm or prejudice to the arbitral process itself; (c) provide a means of preserving assets out of which a subsequent award may be satisfied; or (d) preserve evidence that may be relevant and material to the resolution of the dispute.

[42] Naoki Idei and Nobuyuki Miyaoka, "Q&A Shin Chusai Hou Kaisetsu," *Sanseido*, 2004, 119-120.

[43] The language of Article 24 of the Arbitration Law, which provides that the interim measures should be ordered by the arbitral tribunal (contrary to the language of Article 15, which explicitly provides that the court may grant an interim measure of protection before or during arbitral proceedings), suggests that this provision only applies after the appointment of the arbitrators.

[44] Article 15 of the Arbitration Law.

measures. Moreover, the current Code of Civil Procedure does not address the issue of whether the courts can grant an anti-suit injunction, and there are no court precedents that address this issue. Finally, courts in Japan may grant interim measures in aid of an arbitration outside of Japan.[45]

C.3 Enforcement of Interim Measures

The Arbitration Law does not address the issue of whether interim orders by the arbitral tribunal (either in or outside of Japan) are enforceable by the court in the same way as an award or court judgment.

In practice, interim orders by the arbitral tribunal are not considered to be as enforceable by the court in the same way as an award or a court judgment, and the applicant must rely on the other party's willingness to comply with the interim order issued by the arbitral tribunal. However, the uncertainty in enforceability does not deprive interim measures of practical significance. Parties usually comply with interim orders as the tribunal is empowered to take into account the parties' conduct, including noncompliance with interim orders, when rendering the award.

---

[45]   *Id.* at Article 3(2), which specifically provides that Article 15 applies when the place of arbitration is in or outside the territory of Japan, or when the place of arbitration is not designated.

KAZAKHSTAN

Alexander Korobeinikov[1] and Yekaterina Kolmogorova[2]

A. LEGISLATION, TRENDS AND TENDENCIES

A.1 Domestic Legislation

Arbitration proceedings and the enforcement of foreign arbitral awards are regulated by a number of legislative acts, including the Arbitration Court Law and the International Commercial Arbitration Law. These laws, which were adopted in December 2004, were the first arbitration laws adopted by Kazakhstan following the collapse of the USSR. One of the main objectives of the new legislation was to end the uncertainty and controversy concerning the right to arbitrate and enforce arbitration awards in Kazakhstan.

The Arbitration Court Law applies to disputes between residents of Kazakhstan and permits such disputes to be resolved by "arbitration courts." The law regulates every stage of the arbitration proceedings and provides a mechanism for enforcing awards made by such "arbitration courts" in the state courts. It should be noted that the Arbitration Court Law prohibits the use of arbitration as a means of resolving disputes involving state interests, state enterprises or natural monopolies.

The International Commercial Arbitration Law largely mirrors the UNCITRAL Model Law and applies to disputes where at least one party is not a resident of Kazakhstan. A wholly-owned

---

[1] Alexander Korobeinikov is a Senior Associate in Baker & McKenzie's Almaty office and a member of Baker & McKenzie International Arbitration Practice Group.

[2] Yekaterina Kolmogorova is a Junior Associate in Baker & McKenzie's Almaty office and a member of Baker & McKenzie Dispute Resolution Practice Group.

Kazakhstani subsidiary of a foreign legal entity is considered to be a local resident for the purposes of this law. The International Commercial Arbitration Law regulates arbitration proceedings inside Kazakhstan and also sets out the procedures for the enforcement of foreign arbitration awards in Kazakhstani courts.

In addition to the specific legislation referred to above, international commercial arbitration matters are also governed by:

- the Civil Procedure Code of the Republic of Kazakhstan, dated 13 July 1999, which deals with, *inter alia*, the recognition, enforcement and appeals of foreign arbitral awards; and

- the Law of the Republic of Kazakhstan on Commodity Exchange, dated 4 May 2009, which permits the arbitration of disputes arising out of commodity exchange transactions.

At the end of 2010, Kazakhstan adopted a new law on mediation. Under the new Mediation Law, parties will have the right to resolve the following types of disputes through mediation in accordance with their agreement:

(i) civil disputes involving individuals and legal entities; and

(ii) disputes concerning certain minor criminal offenses.

However, mediation is not available in the context of disputes involving state organizations or incapable persons.

Under the Mediation Law, parties have a right to execute a mediation agreement at any time prior to or after the initiation of legal proceedings. If the parties execute a mediation agreement during civil court proceedings, the court shall stay those proceedings until the mediation has concluded. Where the parties resolve the dispute through mediation, they will execute a settlement agreement and the court proceedings will be terminated. If one of the parties refuses to comply with the terms of the settlement agreement, the other party may seek to enforce the agreement in a state court.

A.2 International Treaties

Kazakhstan is a party to the New York Convention and the European Convention. Kazakhstan is also a party to a number of bilateral and multilateral agreements that grant investors of certain countries the right to arbitrate disputes relating to their investments in Kazakhstan. These treaties include:

1. the ICSID Convention;

2. the Treaty between the United States of America and the Republic of Kazakhstan concerning the Reciprocal Encouragement and Protection of Investment dated 19 May 1992;

3. the Treaty between the Government of the Republic of Kazakhstan and the Government of the United Kingdom of Great Britain and Northern Ireland concerning the Reciprocal Encouragement and Protection of Investment dated 23 November 1995;

4. the Energy Charter Treaty dated 17 December 1994; and

5. a number of regional CIS treaties, including the Convention on Investor Rights Protection dated 28 March 1997.

A.3 Trends

In recent years, Kazakhstan has enacted various legislative amendments designed to confirm the right to arbitrate in Kazakhstan and to facilitate the enforcement of foreign arbitral awards. Pursuant to the Conception of Development of Judicial Administration of Local Courts, which was adopted by the

Committee of Judicial Administration of the Supreme Court in 2010, the Supreme Court intends to encourage the use of arbitration and mediation, as well as courts of *doyens* (a traditional Kazakh means of resolving disputes).

The Kazakh Parliament is currently reviewing amendments to the arbitration legislation that would expand the jurisdiction of domestic and international arbitration. In particular, under these amendments, both contractual and non-contractual disputes as well as monetary and non-monetary claims would become arbitrable. Additionally, international arbitrations will be able to be used to determine civil cases that do not arise out of a commercial activity.

Further, under the proposed amendments, where there is an arbitration agreement between parties, courts will have an obligation to refer parties to arbitration even without a request from one of the parties. These amendments should be adopted during 2013.

B. CASES

B.1 Commercial Arbitration Disputes

A noteworthy aspect of recent commercial arbitration practice in Kazakhstan relates to challenges to domestic arbitral awards.

In April 2012, the Supervisory Panel of the Supreme Court of the Republic of Kazakhstan upheld a decision of the local courts to set aside a domestic arbitration award issued in a dispute between shareholders of a Kazakh company. The Kazakh courts took the position that the award issued in the dispute between two shareholders of the Kazakh company, in connection with the acquisition of shares by one of them, violated pre-emptive rights of the third shareholder. Additionally, the courts reviewed the award on its merits and stated that the arbitral tribunal incorrectly applied relevant provisions of Kazakh legislation.

The above decision of the Supervisory Panel of the Supreme Court illustrates that the Kazakh court's approach in dealing with challenges to domestic arbitral awards is still controversial despite numerous declarations and guidelines issued by the Supreme Court to the lower courts to avoid reconsideration of awards on their merits.

C. THE GRANT AND ENFORCEMENT OF INTERIM MEASURES IN INTERNATIONAL ARBITRATION

C.1 Tribunal-Ordered Interim Measures

Following amendments adopted in February 2010 to the Kazakh arbitration legislation, an arbitral tribunal can order any interim measures it deems necessary for the purposes of a pending dispute.[3] No guidance is given as to the extent that such measures should apply and what test should be used by the tribunal to determine whether to grant such interim measures. However, parties are able to agree in their arbitration agreement to restrict the tribunal from ordering interim measures.

Interim measures ordered by arbitral tribunals (both domestic and international) cannot be directly enforced through the state courts. Instead, parties have to file a separate motion with the state court, seeking interim measures to support the claim that is currently under consideration by the tribunal. It should be noted that the parties have a right to seek interim measures in the court even if they do not raise this issue in front of the tribunal. It is

---

[3] Article 15-1 of the International Commercial Arbitration Law or Article 32 of the Arbitration Court Law.

not possible for the parties to refer to the state courts for interim measures before the commencement of arbitral proceedings and parties have to provide the state court with confirmation of this fact.

C.2 Court-Ordered Interim Measures

As mentioned above, under both the International Commercial Arbitration Law and the Arbitration Court Law, the state courts are granted with concurrent powers to order interim measures, provided that arbitral proceedings have already commenced.[4]

The interim measures, which the state court (and, by probable extension, tribunals) can order include but are not limited to:[5]

- arrest of defendant's property;

- arrest of defendant's bank accounts;

- prohibiting the defendant to take certain actions; and

- prohibiting third parties to transfer any property to the defendant or to perform any obligations due to the defendant.

Where necessary, the court may order other interim measures, provided that they correspond with the scope of the substantive claims and will restrain the defendant from taking any actions that may encumber the enforcement of the arbitral award or make it unenforceable *de facto*.[6]

---

[4] Under both laws, the International Commercial Arbitration Law and Arbitration Court Law, the arbitral proceedings are deemed to have commenced once the claim is filed by the claimant and the tribunal has issued an order on commencement of arbitral proceedings.

[5] Article 159 of the Civil Procedure Code of Kazakhstan.

[6] Normative Regulation of the Supreme Court of Kazakhstan concerning Interim Measures in Civil Cases dated 12 January 2009, No. 2.

C. The Grant and Enforcement of Interim Measures in International Arbitration

An application for interim measures will be considered by the state court on the same day the application is filed, without notifying the defendant or any other parties participating in the dispute. An order (*opredeleniye*) granting interim measures will be issued by the court. There is no provision in Kazakh law permitting the state court to compel arbitration by means of an anti-suit injunction directed at the parties to the dispute, for example in cases where either side files a claim in a foreign court. The state court can compel arbitration by declaring the arbitration agreement valid and operative, and accordingly, terminate its own consideration of a claim. This may occur when one of the parties to the dispute files a claim in a state court in an attempt either to commence parallel court proceedings or to avoid arbitration in general.

The Civil Procedure Code does not differentiate between local and international arbitration when determining a request for interim measures.[7] State courts are not allowed to issue interim measures in relation to financial organizations, non-financial organizations that are part of a bank conglomerate in the capacity of a parent company, or their property when they undergo the process of restructuring.

C.3 Enforcement of Interim Measures

Interim orders issued by the courts are enforceable in the same way as court judgments[8] via the court marshal service. Interim orders can be enforced immediately upon being granted.[9]

---

[7] Article 158 of the Civil Procedure Code of Kazakhstan.

[8] *Id.* at Article 236.

[9] *Id.* at Article 161.

KOREA

June Junghye Yeum[1] and Wonyoung Yu[2]

A. LEGISLATION, TRENDS AND TENDENCIES

A.1 The Korea Arbitration Act

Both international and domestic arbitrations in Korea are governed by the Korea Arbitration Act (the "Arbitration Act"). The Arbitration Act is largely based on the UNCITRAL Model Law (as adopted in 1985, excluding the 2006 amendments). The ability of Korean courts to intervene in the arbitral process is limited to circumstances specified in the Arbitration Act.[3] Parties can request that a court grant interim measures of protection before or during the arbitration.[4]

The Arbitration Act mandates that Korean courts provide assistance in the taking of evidence on written request from an arbitral tribunal.[5] Korean courts are also authorized to intervene to assist arbitration proceedings in the following circumstances:

- To appoint arbitrators on request of either party in circumstances where the parties, a designated appointing

---

[1] June Junghye Yeum is a Partner and co-head of the International Dispute Resolution Practice at Lee & Ko in Seoul, Korea. Prior to joining Lee & Ko, she was a Partner at Baker & McKenzie's New York office and has extensive experience handling cross-border disputes and international arbitrations under various arbitral rules including ICC and ICDR. She is also an arbitrator/neutral on the panel of the KCAB, SIAC and WIPO.

[2] Wonyoung Yu is an Associate of Lee & Ko's International Dispute Resolution Practice Group.

[3] Article 6 of the Arbitration Act.

[4] *Id.* at Article 10.

[5] *Id.* at Article 28(3)-(4).

authority, or the party-appointed arbitrators, as applicable, have failed to do so.[6]

- To decide challenges to arbitrators on appeal from the tribunal.[7]

- To decide requests for termination of an arbitrator's mandate.[8]

- To review the jurisdiction of an arbitral tribunal on request of the objecting party in circumstances where the tribunal has preliminarily ruled that it has jurisdiction.[9]

- To decide challenges to experts appointed by the arbitral tribunal.[10]

Under the Arbitration Act, Korean courts can decide applications for setting aside an arbitral award issued in Korea[11] and applications for recognition or enforcement of domestic or foreign arbitral awards.[12] Pursuant to Article 39 of the Arbitration Act, Korean courts review applications for recognition and enforcement of foreign arbitral awards to which the New York Convention applies in accordance with the Convention. While Articles 36 and 38 set forth the procedures for setting aside an arbitral award, these provisions apply only to domestic and not to foreign arbitral awards. A losing party wishing to challenge a foreign arbitral award should therefore wait for the winning party to bring an enforcement action in Korea. If a vigorous defense is mounted, an enforcement action in Korea may become a full-fledged litigation where both parties

---

[6] *Id.* at Article 12(3)-(5).

[7] *Id.* at Article 14.

[8] *Id.* at Article 15.

[9] *Id.* at Article 17.

[10] *Id.* at Article 27(3).

[11] *Id.* at Article 36.

[12] *Id.* at Article 37.

have the opportunity to present their case before the court. However, as discussed below, courts generally will not engage in a substantive review of the arbitral award. In practice, even a hotly-contested enforcement action typically lasts for only about six months to a year in the first instance court.

While the Arbitration Act primarily applies to arbitrations seated in Korea, Article 2 of the Arbitration Act provides that Articles 9, 10, 37 and 39 shall apply irrespective of the place of arbitration. Article 9 provides for the dismissal of a court action where there is a valid arbitration agreement. Article 10 provides that a party to an arbitration may request interim measures from a Korean court. Articles 37 and 39 set forth, respectively, the procedural requirements for obtaining recognition and enforcement of a foreign arbitral award, and the standards for determining whether a foreign arbitral award will be enforced in Korea. Pursuant to Article 37, a party applying to a Korean court for recognition or enforcement must submit authenticated originals or certified copies of the arbitral award and arbitration agreement. This is the only procedural requirement for recognition and enforcement of a foreign arbitral award in Korea.

Presently, a task force set up by the Korean Ministry of Justice is reviewing the Arbitration Act with a view to introducing amendments to the Act in light of the 2006 amendments to the UNCITRAL Model Law. A draft bill amending the Arbitration Act is expected to be submitted to the Korean National Assembly sometime in 2013.

A.2 The Korean Commercial Arbitration Board

The Korean Commercial Arbitration Board (the "KCAB") is the only arbitral institution in Korea specifically authorized under the Arbitration Act to administer commercial arbitrations. Since its inception in 1970, the KCAB has administered over 4,000 domestic and international arbitrations and is known to be an efficient and responsive arbitral institution. Its International Arbitration Rules ("International Rules") were first introduced in 2007 in an effort to better serve an increasing number of international arbitration cases filed with the KCAB. As originally promulgated the International Rules were not automatically applicable to all international arbitration cases, but only to those in which the parties had agreed in writing to refer their disputes to the International Rules.

As a consequence of this opt-in requirement, the International Rules saw very little use during the first four years of their existence. However, under amendments effective as of September 1, 2011, with respect to arbitration agreements entered into after that date, the International Rules apply by default to all KCAB arbitrations in which any party is from a jurisdiction outside Korea or where the place of arbitration is outside Korea.[13] The International Rules are similar to those of major international arbitral rules such as the ICC and SIAC rules and are designed to reflect the latest standards and best practice in international arbitration.

As of January 2013, a total of 1,224 arbitrators are listed on the KCAB's Panel of Arbitrators, including over 200 arbitrators on its Panel of International Arbitrators. The KCAB, unless otherwise agreed by the parties, appoints arbitrators from a list of candidates recommended by KCAB's Secretariat. The KCAB and its Secretariat employ many internationally trained, knowledgeable arbitration practitioners and case managers, who generally provide efficient, high-quality service of international caliber in a transparent manner. Further, the KCAB offers a wealth of training and education programs on international

---

[13] Articles 2(d) and 3(1) of the International Rules.

arbitration, contributing to Korean companies' increasing knowledge and use of arbitration.

A.3 Latest Developments in Korean Arbitration

Seoul International Dispute Resolution Center

As Korean companies continue to gain leverage in the global market, we are also seeing more arbitrations seated in Korea and an increase in the number of international arbitrations involving Korean companies. There is a consistently growing momentum to enhance the already-strong level of support in Korea for international arbitration to expand its adoption of best international practice and to attain the status enjoyed by SIAC and HKIAC as a competitive Asian arbitration center. Acting upon such a momentum, the Korean Bar Association and Korean legal community have worked together to set up a state-of-the-art arbitration infrastructure (tentatively named "Seoul International Dispute Resolution Center"), which has recently signed memoranda of understanding with major arbitral institutions such as HKIAC and LCIA.

Korea's First Major Investor-State Arbitration Case

The level of investor-state arbitration in Korea has generally been negligible. Until recently, only one reported case was filed with ICSID, which was settled before proceeding to an award.[14] In November 2012, in a much-publicized matter, the holding company of US private equity firm Lone Star, LSF-KEB, filed an ICSID claim for purported unlawful interference of its rights as majority shareholder in the Korean Exchange Bank.[15] Having

---

[14] *Colt Industries Corporation v. Republic of Korea*, ICSID Case No. ARB/84/2.

[15] *LSF-KEB Holdings SCA et al v. Republic of Korea*, ICSID Case No. ARB/12/37.

entered into over ninety BITs[16] and several FTAs, most of which include arbitration as a means of resolving disputes between foreign investors and states, Korea is expected to witness an increasing number of investor-state disputes going forward.

B. CASES

B.1 Reliance on Public Policy for Resisting Enforcement

Application of "International Public Policy" to Foreign Arbitral Awards

The arbitral process in Korea is supported by pro-enforcement courts which seldom refuse to recognize or enforce a foreign arbitral award under the New York Convention. Of the grounds for refusing recognition and enforcement of a foreign arbitral award, one that is most frequently relied upon by the resisting party has been the public policy exception under Article V(2)(b) of the New York Convention. Korean courts routinely have held that the Article V(2)(b) public policy exception should be restrictively interpreted in light of the need for certainty and stability in international commercial transactions.[17] Under this principle, Korean courts have rejected parties' attempts to resist enforcement in Korea on public policy grounds based upon allegations that enforcing the award would be inconsistent with Korean law.[18] The Seoul High Court has held that the same

---

16   United Nations Conference on Trade and Development, "Investment Instruments Online: Bilateral Investment Treaties," viewed on January 15, 2013, http://www.unctadxi.org/templates/DocSearch.aspx?id=779.

17   *See* Seoul High Court Judgment 2000Na23725, 27 February 2001; Seoul High Court Judgment 2003Na5513, 5 December 2003; Seoul Central District Judgment 2011 GaHap29968, 1 June 2011.

18   *See* Supreme Court Judgment 89DaKa20252, 10 April 1990; Seoul Central District Court Judgment 2009GaHap136849, 9 July 2010.

standard applies even where Korean law is the governing law of the arbitration.[19]

Awards in Violation of Mandatory Provisions of Korean Law

In a 2010 New York Convention case, the Seoul Central District Court indicated that certain mandatory provisions of corporate law are not arbitrable and thus any award determining such matters would be unenforceable as contrary to public policy.[20] The district court, however, went on to find that the award was not in violation of mandatory provisions of Korean corporate law at issue in the case, and enforcement of the award could not, therefore, be considered inconsistent with international public policy. While not entirely clear, the court's ruling seemed to imply that had the court found the award in breach of any of those mandatory provisions, it would have refused to enforce the award.

Seoul Central District Court Judgment, 2011KaHap82815, 27 September 2012

In a recent decision issued on September 27, 2012, the Seoul Central District Court did find a foreign arbitral award unenforceable on the ground that the underlying transactions and the plaintiff's activities violated, inter alia, certain mandatory provisions of the Asset-Backed Securitization Act of Korea and, as such, were deemed inconsistent with good morals and the social order of Korea. Interestingly, while the proceeding was a New York Convention case, the district court did not refer to the concept of "international public policy." This case is currently on appeal and if the ruling is sustained, it will mark the second Korean case refusing the recognition and enforcement of a foreign award.

---

[19] *See* Seoul High Court Judgment 2003Na5513, 5 December 2003.

[20] *See* Seoul Central District Court Judgment 2009GaHap136849, 9 July 2010.

B.2 Reliance on Fraud for Refusing Enforcement of a Foreign Arbitral Award

Supreme Court Judgment 2010Da3148, 29 April 2010[21]

The Supreme Court of Korea has held that obtaining an arbitral award by fraud could constitute grounds for refusing recognition and enforcement under the public policy ground of the New York Convention only when the following elements are met: (i) there is clear evidence that a party seeking enforcement of an arbitral award committed fraud in the arbitral proceedings; (ii) the counter-party did not know of the fraud and did not have an opportunity to raise the issue of fraud during the arbitral proceedings; and (iii) there is a causal connection between the fraud and the outcome of the arbitral proceedings. The Supreme Court determined that the first two elements were not satisfied in that case and reaffirmed the limitations to the ability of the courts to review the merits of arbitral awards under the New York Convention.

C. THE GRANT AND ENFORCEMENT OF INTERIM MEASURES IN INTERNATIONAL ARBITRATION

C.1 Tribunal-Ordered Interim Measures

Under the Arbitration Act, unless otherwise agreed by the parties, the tribunal can, at the request of a party, issue a decision granting the interim measures that it considers necessary in respect of the subject matter of the dispute.[22] These interim

---

[21]   Related cases are Ulsan District Court 98GaHap8505, 31 July 2003; Busan High Court Judgment 2003Na12311, 16 February 2006; Supreme Court Judgment 2006Da20290, 28 May 2009 and Busan High Court Judgment 2009Na7618, 25 November 2009.

[22]   Article 18 of Arbitration Act.

measures include preliminary injunctions, provisional attachments and orders seeking preservation of evidence or security for costs. It is generally understood that a tribunal is not entitled to issue injunctive relief with respect to assets of a party that are not the subject matter of the dispute, e.g., by providing a means of preserving assets with which a future favorable award may be satisfied.

Article 18 of the Arbitration Act authorizes the tribunal to grant interim measures in the form of an order or decision, but not in the form of an award. It is generally accepted that a tribunal may grant interim measures of a nature similar to those issued by a Korean court, subject to certain limitations. For example, a tribunal cannot issue preliminary measures with respect to a third party that is not a party to the arbitration.

There are no statutorily defined tests that an applicant must satisfy in order for the tribunal to order interim measures. Korean courts, however, apply the following test: (i) the applicant must have a viable claim that will likely succeed on the merits; and (ii) unless the interim measure is granted, execution of the judgment will be difficult, if not impossible in light of the likelihood that the losing party will dissipate its assets.[23] The 2006 amendments to the UNCITRAL Model Law concerning interim measures and preliminary orders are being considered for potential adoption in 2013.

C.2 Court-Ordered Interim Measures

Under Article 10 of the Arbitration Act, interim measures of protection may be requested from a court before or during arbitral proceedings (where the arbitration has commenced, a court may grant interim measures irrespective of whether the

---

[23]   *See* Articles 276, 278 and 303 of the Civil Enforcement Act.

tribunal has been constituted). Further, under Article 276 of the Civil Enforcement Act, interim measures of protection may also be granted after an award has been rendered and pending its recognition and enforcement. Any court-ordered provisional relief obtained before the constitution of an arbitral tribunal maintains its force even after the tribunal is constituted.

Normally, a Korean court will not issue an injunction against a party to restrain ongoing litigation in a foreign court. Although courts can issue interim measures with respect to assets of third parties to the arbitration, the assets (or subject matter of the provisional attachment) must be located in territory over which the relevant court has jurisdiction, or else the parties must have agreed to confer jurisdiction on the relevant court to issue such relief. Korean courts will likely grant interim measures if the subject matter or assets are located in Korea, even where the place of arbitration is outside Korea. Where neither the subject matter/assets nor the seat of arbitration is in Korea, Korean courts will likely reject the application unless there is a ground for exercising jurisdiction in the case.[24]

C.3   Enforcement of Interim Measures

Interim orders by the tribunal are not enforceable by the court in the same way as an award and/or court judgment. Interim measures issued by tribunals are generally understood to lack enforceability by Korean courts. However, the issuance of such interim measures often serves as persuasive evidence supporting the grant of an injunction or attachment application filed with the court pursuant to Article 10 of the Arbitration Act.

---

[24]   *See* Articles 278 and 303 of the Civil Enforcement Act

KYRGYZSTAN

Alexander Korobeinikov[1]

A. LEGISLATION, TRENDS AND TENDENCIES

A.1 Domestic Legislation

The ability to settle disputes via binding arbitration has been the subject of much uncertainty and controversy in recent years.

While the first international arbitration court was established in Kyrgyzstan in December 1994 by the Presidium of the Chamber of Commerce and Industry of the Republic of Kyrgyzstan, in 1997 the Constitutional Court of Kyrgyzstan ruled that activity of this arbitration court contradicted mandatory provisions of the Constitution. Moreover, in 1999 the Supreme Court of the Kyrgyz Republic proposed amendments to the Civil Procedure Code where provisions relating to parties' rights to solve disputes through arbitration were deleted.

The situation was changed only at the beginning of the twenty-first century after the adoption in 2002 of the Law on Arbitration Courts (mostly mirroring the UNCITRAL Model Law) and amendments to the Constitution in 2003, which set forth the right of parties to solve civil disputes through arbitration. This legislation created the legal framework for arbitration courts in Kyrgyzstan and was a basis for the re-establishment of the International Arbitration Court of the Chamber of Commerce and Industry in 2002.

---

[1] Alexander Korobeinikov is a Senior Associate in Baker & McKenzie's Almaty office and a member of the International Arbitration Practice Group of the Firm's Global Dispute Resolution Practice Group.

In addition to the Law on Arbitration Courts, in August 2001 the President approved the Rules of Out-of-Court Settlement of Disputes Arising in the Agrarian Sector. These rules also regulate the arbitration of disputes relating to ownership of agricultural land plots.

In addition to the above acts, arbitration in Kyrgyzstan is also regulated by the relevant provisions of the Civil Procedural Code, which contains rules regarding arbitration procedure and the enforcement of domestic and foreign arbitration awards relating to non-commercial disputes.

While in general the Kyrgyz legislation is in line with international principles of arbitration, local court practice is still unclear and controversial.

A.2 International Treaties

Kyrgyzstan is a party to a number of international and regional treaties that relate to arbitration proceedings, including the New York Convention and the European Energy Charter Treaty as well as several CIS treaties.

Additionally, it should be noted that while the Parliament of Kyrgyzstan ratified the ICSID Convention, the Kyrgyz government has not filed official notification with the Secretariat of ICSID. Therefore, Kyrgyzstan is not currently recognized as a party to the ICSID Convention.

A.3 Trends and Tendencies

Over the past few years, arbitration became more popular as an alternative method of resolving commercial disputes. It should be noted that after the adoption of Expedited Rules of the Kyrgyz Arbitration Court, most local banks now prefer to solve their disputes with debtors under these rules.

However, court practice in relation to challenging and enforcing local and foreign awards is still unpredictable and sometimes contradicts local legislation and international treaties ratified by Kyrgyzstan.

B. CASES

While recent court decisions relating to the enforcement or setting aside of arbitral awards are generally in line with international practice, it should be noted that the Kyrgyz courts do not have wide experience in connection with arbitration-related cases, and such lack of experience leads to some controversial decisions.

B.1 Refusal to Refer Parties to Arbitration due to Non-Binding Arbitration Clause

In 2007, a Kyrgyz company filed a claim with the Bishkek Inter-District Court against its Kyrgyz counterparty seeking termination of the contract executed between the parties.

This contract had an arbitration clause, which set forth a right of any party to commence arbitration in Denmark, and so the respondent challenged the jurisdiction of the state court arguing that there was a valid arbitration clause executed between the parties.

Ultimately, the respondent's appeal against jurisdiction was reviewed by the Supervisory Panel of the Supreme Court. The Supreme Court rejected the appeal of the respondent on the basis that the above arbitration clause could not be considered as binding.

This decision of the Supreme Court is an example of disputed and controversial decisions of the Kyrgyz courts, which are not in line with recent trends in international arbitration.

C. THE GRANT AND ENFORCEMENT OF INTERIM MEASURES IN INTERNATIONAL ARBITRATION

In accordance with the relevant provisions of the Kyrgyz Law on Arbitration Courts, arbitral tribunals have the discretionary power to issue interim measures. In accordance with the Rules of Arbitration of the Kyrgyz International Arbitration Court, the arbitral tribunal has a right to issue interim measures upon a request of the parties and such decision is issued in the form of an award.

These Rules of Arbitration of the Kyrgyz International Arbitration Court also allow parties to enforce an interim measures award through the state courts in the same way as final awards are enforced. It should be noted that this approach is confirmed by court practice and courts usually enforce interim measures issued by an arbitral tribunal. However, it is not entirely clear whether this approach could be applied for enforcement of interim measures decisions of foreign arbitral tribunals. This issue still has to be clarified in legislation or by court practice.

MALAYSIA

Elaine Yap[1]

A. LEGISLATION, TRENDS AND TENDENCIES

A.1 Legislative Framework

The law and practice of arbitration in Malaysia is governed by the Arbitration Act 2005 ("AA"), which came into force on 15 March 2006. The AA repealed the outdated Arbitration Act 1952, which can be traced historically to the equivalent legislation in England in 1972. In a significant departure from this original framework, the AA is modeled closely on the UNCITRAL Model Law. The main body of the AA can be found in Part II, which follows Articles 3 to 36 of the Model Law almost word for word.

Malaysia has also been a signatory to the New York Convention since 1985. The New York Convention was passed into domestic law in Malaysia through the Convention on the Recognition and Enforcement of Foreign Arbitral Awards Act 1985. It should be noted, however, that this Act was repealed by the AA as of 15 March 2006. The AA now sets out a uniform procedure for the recognition and enforcement of both local and foreign arbitral awards within the same legislation.

A.2 Trends and Tendencies

Consistent with the UNCITRAL Model Law, the AA distinguishes between domestic and international arbitrations and

---

[1] Elaine Yap is a Partner in the Dispute Resolution Practice Group of Baker & McKenzie's Kuala Lumpur office. Her areas of expertise include civil and commercial litigation and arbitration. She serves as a panel arbitrator for the Malaysian Institute of Arbitrators.

an "international arbitration" is defined in the same way it is defined in the Model Law. However, unlike Article 1(2) of the UNCITRAL Model Law, which sets out by reference to specific Articles, which part of the law also applies to arbitrations where the seat of arbitration is not the local territory, Section 3 of the AA only provides for the application of the Act to domestic and international arbitrations where the seat of arbitration is in Malaysia.

In 2008, the High Court in *Aras Jalinan Sdn Bhd v. Tipco Asphalt Public Company Ltd. & Ors*,[2] made a bold decision as concerns the jurisdiction of the courts in matters governed by the AA. The *Aras Jalinan* case involved an application by the plaintiff for an interim injunction pending determination of an arbitration between the parties in Singapore. In opposing this application, the defendants raised a preliminary objection against the jurisdiction of the court to grant the orders sought as the seat of arbitration was in Singapore, citing Sections 3 and 8 of the AA.[3]

The High Court agreed with the defendants and dismissed the plaintiff's application, holding that on a strict construction of Section 3 of the AA, read together with the provision on the restricted extent of court intervention in Section 8 of the AA, the High Court had no inherent or residual powers to intervene in arbitrations where the seat was outside Malaysia. It was also held that such jurisdiction could not be conferred by the agreement of the parties.

The effect of the *Aras Jalinan* decision, which was approved by the Court of Appeal in an unreported decision, left in serious doubt the ability of the High Court to exercise any powers in aid of arbitrations seated outside of Malaysia, including Malaysia's

---

[2]   [2008] 5 CLJ 654.

[3]   Provision on the extent of court intervention in matters governed by the AA.

treaty obligation to enforce all valid arbitration agreements by, *inter alia*, ordering a mandatory stay of parallel court proceedings brought in breach of such agreements.

After much anticipation, the AA was finally amended[4] to address the implications of the *Aras Jalinan* case as well as other shortcomings of the AA. The significant changes made to the AA by the amendments, which came into force on 1 July 2011, can be summarized as follows:

(a) confirmation that all sources of jurisdiction of the courts other than the AA itself, including the inherent jurisdiction of the courts, are excluded, to clearly limit the ability of the courts to intervene in matters governed by the AA;

(b) express provisions were included in the AA on the application of the powers of the court to grant relief in aid of arbitration under Section 10 of the AA (stay of parallel court proceedings) and Section 11 of the AA (interim measures and other relief) to foreign-seated arbitrations;

(c) introduction of specific provisions under Sections 10 and 11 of the AA to govern admiralty disputes in arbitration, such as provisions on the arrest of vessels and the securing of the amount in dispute;

(d) removal of the ground that there is no dispute between the parties with regard to the matters to be referred to arbitration, as a reason for refusal to stay parallel court proceedings;

(e) reinstatement of party autonomy in choice of governing law clauses for domestic arbitrations to enable parties to apply laws other than the laws of Malaysia; and

---

[4]   Arbitration (Amendment) Act 2011.

(f) additional requirement for the reference on questions of law arising out of an award that the question of law substantially affects the rights of one or more of the parties.

While these amendments have taken longer than expected to pass into law, they reflect a positive trend by the legislative arm of the government to respond to calls to harmonize Malaysian arbitration laws with that of the international arbitration community in order to promote Malaysia as another major regional center for arbitration in Asia Pacific.

B. CASES

B.1 Applicable Law to Challenge an Arbitration Award

In *The Government of India v. Cairn Energy India Pty Ltd. and anor*,[5] the Federal Court considered the question of what law should apply in deciding a challenge to an arbitral award. The award in question concerned a production-sharing contract in an oil and gas joint venture between the appellant and the respondents for the development of an area described as "Ravva Field" situated off the coast of India.

The challenge had been submitted by the appellant pursuant to Section 24(2)[6] of the now-repealed Arbitration Act 1952. The High Court had set aside a finding of the arbitral tribunal on a particular issue on grounds that there was a manifest error of law on the face of the award. However, the decision was overturned by the Court of Appeal, and this instigated the further appeal to the Federal Court.

---

5   [2012] 3 CLJ 423.

6   The provision states that where an arbitrator or umpire has misconducted himself or the proceedings, or an arbitration or award has been improperly procured, the High Court may set the award aside.

B. Cases

The parties had chosen Indian law as the proper law of the contract, English law as the law to govern the arbitration agreement, and the seat of the arbitration proceedings was in Kuala Lumpur. Although conceding that the challenge to the award had been made before the Malaysian courts pursuant to Malaysian arbitration law, the appellant argued before the Federal Court that the correct arbitration law to apply should be English law.

As the highest court in Malaysia, the Federal Court granted leave to determine this question: "Where an award from an international commercial arbitration is submitted for review before the Malaysian Courts under Section 24(2) of the Arbitration Act 1952, and the contract provides for the application of one foreign law to govern the contract (namely the laws of India) and another foreign law to govern the arbitration agreement (namely the laws of England), is it proper for the Malaysian Court to apply Malaysian law exclusively to decide the scope of intervention in arbitration awards or the dispute at hand where the seat of arbitration is in Malaysia?"

In submitting that English law should apply, the appellant relied on a decision by the Indian Supreme Court in *Sumitomo Heavy Industries Ltd. v. ONGC Ltd.,*[7] which held that the "curial law" ceases to have effect once the arbitral tribunal has handed down its award. Based on that decision, it was argued that the enforcement process, being independent of the proceedings before the arbitrator, is governed not by the curial law that governed the procedure that the arbitrator followed in the conduct of the arbitration, but by the law governing the agreement to arbitrate and the performance of that agreement.

---

[7]   AIR 1998 SC 825.

The Malaysian Federal Court was not persuaded by the appellant's arguments or the decision of the Indian Supreme Court, and ruled that challenges to an award must be made in the place of the seat of the arbitration. Thus, in applications to set aside arbitral awards, the applicable law is that of the seat of the arbitration, and parties must follow the mandatory rules of that seat.

B.2 Setting Aside of Arbitral Awards on Questions of Law

The decision of the Federal Court in *The Government of India* case also determined several other important questions in connection with Section 24(2) of the now-repealed Arbitration Act 1952.[8] Among other things, Section 24(2) provided that where an award has been improperly procured, the High Court may set it aside. This provision was regularly invoked as a means of setting aside arbitral awards on grounds of errors of law on the face of the award. Although Section 24(2) of the Arbitration Act 1952 has been repealed, the High Court has noted that the authorities that interpret it remain relevant.[9]

The Federal Court in *The Government of India* case considered whether the common law distinction between a specific reference and a general reference (where the question of law arises from findings of fact by the arbitrator on matters or issues

---

[8] *Ibid.*

[9] *See Majlis Amanah Rakyat v. Kausar Corporation Sdn Bhd*, [2009] 1 LNS 1766. In *Majlis*, the High Court discussed Section 42 of the AA, which permits aggrieved parties to refer questions of law arising out of an award to the High Court. The High Court noted that due to the small body of case law in Malaysia interpreting section 42 of the AA and the lack of guidance within the text, relevant jurisprudence established under the Arbitration Act of 1952 will continue to apply. It should be noted that Section 42 of the AA can be found in Part III of the AA which contains additional provisions that are only applicable to domestic arbitrations (unless the parties agree in writing to exclude it) and to international arbitrations (if the parties agree in writing to include it).

B. Cases

referred to it for determination) is applicable in determining the scope of intervention by the High Court, and whether intervention is possible in any event where an illegal act has been committed by the arbitrator. [10]

Relying on prior decisions of the Federal Court in *Intelek Timur Sdn Bhd v. Future Heritage Sdn Bhd*.[11] and the Supreme Court in *Ganda Edibile Oils Sdn Bhd v. Transgrain BV*,[12] the Federal Court in *The Government of India* case concluded that where a specific matter is referred to arbitration, courts may not interfere on grounds that the decision upon the question of law referred is an erroneous one.[13] The Federal Court further concluded that where the question referred for arbitration is a question of construction of a document, which is, generally speaking, a question of law, the arbitrator's decision cannot be set aside merely because the court would itself have come to a different conclusion.

The Federal Court also clarified that whether the reference is specific or general, the court retains discretion to set aside an arbitral award if the arbitrator has proceeded illegally, for instance, by relying on inadmissible evidence or applying principles of construction which the law does not countenance.

B.3 Requirement of a Written Arbitration Agreement

Recently, the Court of Appeal in *Duta Wajar Sdn Bhd v. Pasukhas Constructions Sdn Bhd & Anor*[14] considered whether

---

[10]   *Ibid.*

[11]   [2004] 1 CLJ 743.

[12]   [1987] 2 CLJ 394.

[13]   *Ibid.*

[14]   [2012] 4 CLJ 844.

an arbitration agreement in an unsigned sub-contract under which work had been performed, is sufficient to constitute a written arbitration agreement within the meaning of Section 9 of the AA.

Section 9 of the AA is based on the equivalent 1985 UNCITRAL Model Law provision. Section 9(4) provides that an arbitration agreement is in writing if it is contained in (a) a document signed by the parties, (b) an exchange of letters, telex, facsimile or other means of communication which provide a record of the agreement, or (c) an exchange of statement of claim and defense in which the existence of an agreement is alleged by one party and not denied by the other. Section 9(5) of the AA further explains that a reference in an agreement to a document containing an arbitration clause shall also constitute an arbitration agreement, provided that the agreement is in writing and the reference is such as to make the arbitration clause part of the agreement.

In the *Duta Wajar* case,[15] the defendant had awarded the plaintiff a sub-contract for piling works[16] but the sub-contract document was never signed. The plaintiff commenced work under the sub-contract on 27 August 2007, on the instructions of the defendants, and completed the work on 15 November 2007. The plaintiff first received the sub-contract document containing the arbitration clause on 16 October 2007, but refused to sign it.

The plaintiff subsequently initiated court proceedings to recover outstanding claims for work done. In response, the defendant applied to have the court proceedings stayed on the ground that the parties had agreed to refer disputes to arbitration, relying on

---

[15] *Ibid.*

[16] Work done when a hole is hammered into the ground for concrete to be poured in to make the foundation of a structure.

the arbitration clause in the sub-contract and the fact that the plaintiff had proceeded with work even after receiving the sub-contract document from the defendant.

The High Court agreed with the defendant and held that there was a valid arbitration agreement in writing through the conduct of the plaintiff in bidding for and proceeding with the sub-contract works. According to the High Court, signing the sub-contract agreement was a mere formality, citing an earlier decision of the Court of Appeal in *Bina Puri Sdn Bhd v. EP Engineering Sdn Bhd & Anor.*[17]

Nevertheless, the Court of Appeal unanimously allowed the plaintiff's appeal. On the facts, the Court of Appeal observed that while a contractual relationship between the parties did exist, the relationship existed even before 27 August 2007. Therefore, the sub-contract document which the defendant forwarded to the plaintiff on 16 October 2007 was an attempt to impose another agreement, to which the plaintiff did not agree.

In the judgment of the Court of Appeal, the burden was on the defendant seeking the stay of the court proceedings to prove the existence of an arbitration agreement. The plaintiff's non-response to the sub-contract document sent to it by the defendant meant that there was no exchanges of letters or faxes or other means of communication that could provide a record of an arbitration agreement between the plaintiff and the defendants on or around 16 October 2007.

---

[17] [2008] 3 CLJ 741.

C. THE GRANT AND ENFORCEMENT OF INTERIM MEASURES IN INTERNATIONAL ARBITRATION

C.1 Tribunal-Ordered Interim Measures

Section 19(1) of the AA provides that unless otherwise agreed by the parties, the arbitral tribunal is empowered to grant the following interim measures:

(a) security for costs;

(b) discovery of documents and interrogatories;

(c) giving of evidence by affidavit;

(d) the preservation, interim custody or sale of any property which is the subject matter of the dispute.

The AA does not set out any guidelines on how the powers under Section 19 should be exercised. In practice, it is submitted that the tests that an applicant should satisfy for the tribunal to order interim measures must follow any applicable rules or guidelines that the parties have agreed to and should, but is not bound to, apply the tests formulated by the courts based on the legal traditions and norms familiar to counsel and the arbitral tribunal. For example, parties familiar with the common law tradition may require an applicant to demonstrate that there are serious issues to be tried and that irreparable damage will be caused if a restraining order is not granted in the interim pending a final award.

The authority of the arbitral tribunal to issue interim measures under Section 19 of the AA can only be invoked after the constitution of the arbitral tribunal since no provision is made for emergency arbitrators or any body other than the sole or panel of arbitrators duly appointed in arbitration proceedings. Accordingly, interim measures from the arbitral tribunal are not available before the commencement of arbitral proceedings unless the parties have agreed to a set of institutional rules that allow for emergency arbitrator procedures. The current version of the arbitration rules of the Kuala Lumpur Regional Centre for Arbitration[18] do not provide for such procedures.

C.2 Court-Ordered Interim Measures

The High Courts in Malaysia have concurrent powers to order interim measures in relation to arbitration proceedings under Section 11 of the AA. As noted in Part A of this chapter, the AA was amended on 1 July 2011, to provide that the powers of the court to grant interim measures under Section 11 also apply to foreign-seated arbitrations, i.e., those arbitrations where the seat of arbitration is not in Malaysia.[19]

Section 11(1) of the AA provides that a party may, before or during arbitral proceedings, apply to the High Court for any interim measure and the High Court may make the following orders:

(a) security for costs;

(b) discovery of documents and interrogatories;

(c) giving of evidence by affidavit;

(d) appointment of a receiver;

(e) securing the amount in dispute, whether by way of arrest of property or bail or other security pursuant to the admiralty jurisdiction of the High Court;

---

[18] The Kuala Lumpur Regional Centre for Arbitration (KLRCA) is an international arbitral institution based in Kuala Lumpur and provides support as an independent venue for the conduct of domestic and international arbitration proceedings in the region. Its rules adopt the UNCITRAL Arbitration Rules with modifications.

[19] Section 11(3) of the AA.

(f) the preservation, interim custody or sale of any property that is the subject-matter of the dispute;

(g) ensuring that any award, which may be made in the arbitral proceedings, is not rendered ineffectual by the dissipation of assets by a party; and

(h) an interim injunction or any other interim measure.

The powers of the High Court to issue interim measures under Section 11(1) are thus more extensive than those of the arbitral tribunal. Nevertheless, Section 11(2) explicitly recognizes the limited concurrent powers of the arbitral tribunal to issue measures; it provides that, where a party applies to the High Court for any interim measure and an arbitral tribunal has already ruled on any matter that is relevant to the application, the High Court shall treat any findings of fact made in the course of such ruling by the arbitral tribunal as conclusive for the purposes of the application.

Section 11(2) of the AA also underscores the fact that one objective of the AA is to limit the intervention of the courts in the arbitral process. This principle was applied in *NBC Land Sdn Bhd v. Teras Kiara Gemilang Sdn Bhd*,[20] in which the High Court was asked to order security for costs after a similar application had been made to, and rejected by, the arbitral tribunal. The High Court rejected the application in deference to the prior decision of the arbitral tribunal in the absence of any evidence of any intervening change of circumstances.

In addition, it is well-accepted that where there is concurrent jurisdiction, a party should first seek relief from the arbitral tribunal unless there are countervailing factors, such as where

---

20   [2011] 1 LNS 669.

third parties are involved, where matters are urgent or where the court's coercive powers of enforcement are required.[21]

The urgent need for interim measures is in many circumstances a countervailing factor justifying first resort to the courts. This is particularly true considering that the powers under Section 19 of the AA can only be invoked after the constitution of the arbitral tribunal, which may take several weeks. The courts in Malaysia are highly responsive to urgent applications filed by litigants for interim orders where the circumstances warrant. If necessary, *ex-parte* orders for interim measures can be obtained in a matter of 1-2 days.

Considering the broad language of Section 11(1)(h) of the AA, parties may seek to invoke the power of the court to issue interim measures in a variety of circumstances. One such instance may be the anti-suit injunction. Although there are no reported cases where section 11(1)(h) of the AA has been invoked to restrain an arbitration, the authority of the courts in Malaysia to restrain a defendant from prosecuting a claim in a foreign court (otherwise known as the anti-suit injunction) has long been recognized. [22] Nevertheless, because Section 18 of the AA provides that the arbitral tribunal may rule on its own jurisdiction, including any objections with respect to the existence or validity of the arbitration agreement, it is submitted that the courts should be slow to exercise its power under Section 11(h) to restrain an arbitration.[23]

---

[21] See *Jiwa Harmoni Offshore Sdn Bhd v. Ishi Power Sdn Bhd,* [2009] 1 LNS 849; *Cobrain Holdings Sdn Bhd v. GDP Special Projects Sdn Bhd*, [2010] 1 LNS 1834.

[22] The principles relating to the jurisdiction of the courts to issue anti-suit injunctions were re-stated by the Court of Appeal in *BSNC Leasing Sdn Bhd v. Sabah Shipyard Sdn Bhd & Ors & Anor appeal.* [2000] 2 CLJ 197. The test for the grant of an anti-suit injunction is whether the foreign action brought by the defendant is vexatious or oppressive.

[23] Note a peculiar situation in *Cyber Business Solutions Sdn Bhd v. Elsag Datamat SPA* [2012] 1 CLJ 115 where the High Court issued an interim injunction to

This view finds support in Sections 18(8) and (9) of the AA, which provide that any party may appeal a positive ruling on a jurisdictional objection to the High Court and pending such an appeal, the arbitral tribunal may continue the arbitral proceedings and make an award.

C.3 Enforcement of Interim Measures

Interim orders by the tribunal are enforced by the courts in Malaysia in the same way as an award and/or court judgment. Section 19(3) of the AA provides that unless otherwise agreed by the parties, Sections 38 and 39 of the AA (relating to recognition and enforcement of awards) shall apply to orders for interim measures made by an arbitral tribunal. Section 38(1) provides that on an application in writing to the High Court, an award made in respect of an arbitration where the seat of arbitration is in Malaysia or an award from a foreign state shall, subject to the grounds for refusal of recognition of such an award as set out in section 39, be recognized as binding and be enforced by entry as a judgment in terms of the award or by action.

Apart from the limited grounds found in Sections 38 and 39 of the AA upon which an award may be refused recognition and enforcement, there are no specific types of interim orders that the courts of Malaysia would not enforce. There is also no distinction between enforcement of an award for interim measures made within or outside Malaysia, as Sections 38 and 39 of the AA apply to any award, irrespective of the location in which it is rendered.

---

restrain an ICC arbitration on account of a competing arbitration clause stipulating a KLRCA arbitration for the same dispute. The injunction was granted pending a trial as to which of the two arbitration clauses should prevail.

MEXICO

Salvador Fonseca González[1] and Juan Carlos Zamora Müller[2]

A. LEGISLATION, TRENDS AND TENDENCIES

A.1 2011 Legal Reform

In 2011, the Mexican arbitration law contained within the Mexican Commercial Code and based on the UNCITRAL Model law,[3] was modified to modernize and clarify the role that Mexican courts should take with arbitration proceedings.

This reform is still quite commented upon in the Mexican arbitration community, chiefly because many of the new rules remain untested in the courts. As reported in previous Yearbooks, the reform created a friendlier environment for arbitral proceedings as well as court proceedings associated with or arising out of arbitration.

---

[1]   Salvador Fonseca-González is a Partner in Baker & McKenzie's Mexico City office. He has more than 15 years of experience representing corporate and individual clients in complex international and domestic arbitration and litigation. Mr. Fonseca has participated in cases under the rules of the major arbitral institutions and is familiar with dispute boards and other methods of solving disputes. He has served as sole arbitrator and chairman of arbitral tribunals in several international and local cases. He has lectured on International Commercial Arbitration at the most prestigious universities in Mexico.

[2]   Juan Carlos Zamora Müller is an Associate in Baker & McKenzie's Mexico City office. His practice focuses on dispute resolution, commercial litigation and arbitration. He has meaningful experience representing clients before Mexican courts and arbitral tribunals in *ad hoc* and ICC proceedings. He has served as associate professor in Procedural Law and Arbitration at the School of Law of the Centro de Investigación y Docencia Economicas in Mexico City.

[3]   In Mexico, commercial matters are subject to federal regulation, thus, only a single Commercial Code exists and special commercial legislation governs trade uniformly across the country.

The trend continues in the same fashion: Mexico is growing in significance as a convenient seat of arbitration, while more and more companies and entities, private and public, national and transnational, enter into arbitration agreements related to transactions with Mexico as a venue for the arbitration proceedings.

A.2 Minor Amendments to the Legislation

Since the major 2011 reform, two minor amendments were made to the law, further proving the Mexican legislature's commitment to arbitration.

First, in June 2011, a paragraph was added to Article 1424 of the Commercial Code (Article 8 of the UNCITRAL Model Law) to clarify that if a Mexican court refuses to recognize and enforce an award the parties will be free to exercise their rights either in arbitration or before the courts, as the case may be.

Second, Article 1467 of the Commercial Code was amended to provide that in cases where Mexican courts must appoint an arbitrator they should consult with the relevant commercial chambers or arbitral institutions about the potential candidates.

A.3 Constant Positive Trend

Generally, Mexican judges and practitioners are increasingly becoming familiar with arbitration as a viable option to handle disputes. Judges are now aware that arbitration is not only a way to solve commercial disputes, but a powerful tool of economic growth. Thus, judges show their support of arbitration by referring parties to arbitration, or during enforcement and annulment proceedings.

The main arbitration institutions in Mexico report greater numbers of arbitration cases, as well as a steady increase in the amounts in dispute. Also, the forum has been very active. Mexico has hosted many arbitration-related events that attract foreign expertise and have created a truly international arbitration scene.

Finally, judicial precedence show a clear preference towards arbitration and an inclination to reach consistency between Mexico's internal legal framework and international standards. These factors lead to the conclusion that Mexico has become an arbitration friendly jurisdiction.

B. CASES

B.1 Available Legal Remedies against Decisions Rendered within Proceedings to Set Aside Arbitral Awards

In a recent case[4] that is still pending, the court of first instance made a controversial decision dismissing the petition to set aside an arbitration award based on formal grounds linked to the petition's timeliness. The petitioner was determined to challenge the dismissal; however, given the recent legal reforms and the lack of precedent, the legal remedy available to question the legality of the dismissal was uncertain.

Generally, under Mexican law, court of first instance decisions may be ordinarily challenged before a court of appeals that examines the decision's legality, unless the law provides otherwise, e.g., that the particular resolution is final.

As mentioned in Section A above, the legal reform focused precisely on court proceedings related to arbitration, including

---

[4] Although, we understand that the decision will be issued as public legal precedent, unfortunately, we cannot provide the names of the parties or other identification information as the case is still pending.

enforcement proceedings and those intended to set aside an award. One feature of the reform was to make decisions in enforcement or annulment proceedings impossible to appeal to save time and allow for faster proceedings. In these cases, the only available remedy would be an extraordinary constitutional challenge (*amparo* proceedings), which, as explained below, is not a straight forward issue.

The difficulty in this case was that the decision dismissing the petition to set aside the award did not decide anything on the merits, raising the question as to whether or not the dismissal could be challenged by ordinary means or leaving the *amparo* proceeding as a last alternative.

The complexity of the question lay not in the fact that prior to this case, no other precedent nor clear indication in the law helped to decide the matter, but rather in the practical angle of the problem: choosing the ordinary appeal instead of the *amparo* proceeding would most likely bar the possibility of trying the alternative and vice versa. A poor choice would then mean loosing the opportunity to pursue the original petition to set aside the award.

To complicate matters further, under Mexican law, there are two kinds of *amparo* proceedings: "direct" and "indirect." Although both share many essential characteristics, filing the correct proceeding is very important because the federal court in charge of deciding indirect *amparo* proceedings is different from the one in charge of resolving direct ones. Furthermore, the direct *amparo* is a single instance procedure, while the indirect one could consist of two instances, with the corresponding time and costs. Normally, a direct *amparo* is the legal remedy available against final judgments, while an indirect *amparo* is used to combat a myriad of different acts, including interlocutory trial decisions.

B. Cases

Prior to the reform, the procedural way to obtain enforcement of an arbitral award was very different and certain cases[5] made it fairly clear that the appropriate challenge to a decision on the merits was the indirect *amparo*. In fact, this particularity of Mexican law was a concern during the 2011 reform, which intended to reduce the time of enforcement or annulment proceedings.

As a matter of strategy, the petitioner filed a direct *amparo* against the dismissal, arguing, as to the propriety of the challenge, that (a) the dismissal ended the annulment proceedings, and thus became final, even if the decision was not on the merits and (b) against this kind of resolution (i.e., the ones that end proceedings) the legal remedy available, when no ordinary appeal is allowed, is a direct *amparo* that must be resolved by a Collegiate Tribunal.

In turn, before it analyzed the dismissal's legality the Collegiate Tribunal had to decide if the *amparo* was the appropriate proceeding to challenge the dismissal, and if so, whether the direct *amparo* was the correct type of *amparo* proceeding.

Based on Commercial Code Article 1470, the Collegiate Tribunal reasoned that according to the new regulation, annulment proceedings were in fact a full trial (not an ancillary proceeding). This meant that a resolution rendered on the merits of these kinds of cases would be deemed a judgment. Moreover,

---

5   For example: *LAUDO ARBITRAL. CONTRA LA INTERLOCUTORIA QUE DECLARA SU NULIDAD PROCEDE EL JUICIO DE AMPARO INDIRECTO PRIMERA SALA; Tomo XXVII, Enero de 2008; Pag. 268; Jurisprudencia(Civil). [J]; 9a. Época; 1a. Sala; S.J.F. y su Gaceta* and *RECONOCIMIENTO, EJECUCIÓN Y NULIDAD DE LAUDO ARBITRAL. SON MATERIA DE INCIDENTE Y LA RESOLUCIÓN QUE LO RESUELVE ES RECLAMABLE EN AMPARO INDIRECTO TERCER TRIBUNAL COLEGIADO EN MATERIA CIVIL DEL PRIMER CIRCUITO; Tomo XXIX, Abril de 2009; Pag. 1953; Tesis Aislada(Civil). [TA]; 9a. Época; T.C.C.; S.J.F. y su Gaceta.*

according to Article 1476, a judgment rendered in an annulment or enforcement proceeding is not subject to an ordinary challenge. Thus, these judgments can only be challenged through direct *amparo* proceedings, an extraordinary recourse.

The Collegiate Tribunal considered that, for these purposes, the dismissal's finality amounted to a "judgment," not because it dealt with the merits, but because it materially ended the proceedings. Consequently, it not only allowed the *amparo* to follow its course, it also confirmed that dismissal of a claim to set aside an award is not subject to ordinary challenges.

Clearly, recourses and remedies can be confusing and the annulment or enforcement of an award may depend on them. The Collegiate Tribunal's decision added to the arbitration regulation's certainty and cleared some of the doubts, hindrances and obstacles that came from past practices. At the same time, it helped to clarify the new regulation's reach and scope on the very important issue of the legal remedies available to challenge unfavorable decisions.

B.2 Recent Decision on the Concept of Public Policy (Amparo Proceedings 755/2011)

In June 2012, the Mexican Supreme Court of Justice (the "Supreme Court") decided an *amparo* proceeding arising from enforcement proceedings where the lower courts resolved to set aside an award on several grounds. The main grounds for the lower courts' decision were purported violations of Mexican public policy and the principle of *res judicata*.

As in many jurisdictions, the concept of "public policy" in Mexico is not concrete or clearly defined. Of course, this has led to many complications, and although there are several cases in which the federal judiciary has issued decisions and precedents to clarify its breadth, it is still a concept that is defined on a case by case basis.

In the *amparo* proceedings 755/2011, the Supreme Court again considered the issue and established the criteria to construe the concept of public policy in the context of enforcement or annulment proceedings. In summary, the Supreme Court held that the essence of the dispute and the facts must be considered to determine if they truly concern an issue of public policy.

Additionally, the Supreme Court analyzed the relationship of *res judicata* to arbitration proceedings, and found that the question of whether the arbitral tribunal violated the principle of *res judicata* could be answered from a factual standpoint. After the Supreme Court reviewed the "conflicting" awards it held that there was no violation of *res judicata* and the awards were consistent. In any event, the Supreme Court highlighted the importance of the concept of *res judicata* within the Mexican system. The Supreme Court overturned the lower court's decision and confirmed the challenged award's validity and enforceability.

Needless to say, this case illustrates the Mexican federal judiciary's modern approach towards the enforcement and annulment of arbitral awards and confirms its willingness to further define unclear concepts like public policy to increase certainty in Mexico's arbitration landscape.

C. THE GRANT AND ENFORCEMENT OF INTERIM MEASURES IN INTERNATIONAL ARBITRATION

When examining the most important developments in Mexico's arbitration law, it is essential to consider the 2011 reform that introduced a set of procedural rules intended to (a) obtain interim relief from a court, or (b) enforce an interim measure issued by an arbitral tribunal.

Two main results must be highlighted. First, the scope of judicial interim relief available in the aid of arbitration is completely limitless. This is significant because judges were traditionally quite conservative about the types of interim measures that they allowed. Now, with this legislative reform, which provides courts with the express power to issue the kinds of interim relief deemed fit to the circumstances of a case, a giant step towards modernity has been made.

Second, the 2011 amendment also expressly provided for the enforceability of interim measures issued by arbitral tribunals, and perhaps more importantly, provided for a concrete set of rules to enforce such measures in Mexican courts.

The new regulation is consistent with the UNCITRAL Model Law because it sets forth rules for quick enforcement with essentially the same limitations for exceptions provided in the UNCITRAL Model Law.

In conclusion, the Mexican judiciary has displayed its willingness and enthusiasm to enforce interim relief that arbitral tribunals grant, which adds up to good news for arbitration in Mexico.

THE NETHERLANDS

Frank Kroes[1] and Saskia Temme[2]

A. LEGISLATION, TRENDS AND TENDENCIES

A.1 Legislative Proposal to Amend Dutch Arbitration Act

The current Arbitration Act in the Dutch Code of Civil Procedure ("DCCP") dates from 1 December 1986.[3] Since then, there have been no major legislative changes in Dutch arbitration law.[4] The Ministry of Justice has been indicating for over a decade that the Arbitration Act would undergo major legislative changes.[5] A proposal was in fact published on 13 March 2012 for internet consultation.[6] The consultation closed on 1 June 2012. The proposal is aimed at making arbitration law more

---

[1] Frank Kroes is a Partner in the Amsterdam office of Baker & McKenzie. His practice focus is on litigation and arbitration for financial institutions and other complex commercial disputes.

[2] Saskia Temme is a Senior Associate in the Amsterdam office of Baker & McKenzie. Her practice focus is on commercial litigation and international arbitration.

[3] Legislation of 2 July 1986, *Stb.* 1986, 372.

[4] Amendments since 1986 include minor textual changes, and more fundamentally, the possibility of requesting preliminary witness examinations (Article 1022 DCCP).

[5] *See*, for instance, Parliamentary papers II 1999/2000, 26 855, no. 5, p. 3; Letter from the Minister of Justice, Parliamentary Papers II 2006/07, 30 951, no. 1, p. 31; and *Innovatieagenda rechtsbestel* (Innovation Agenda Legal System), Ministry of Safety and Justice, 31 October 2011, p. 11 (the name of the Ministry was changed as of 14 October 2010). *See also* The *Baker & McKenzie International Arbitration Yearbook 2009*, p. 207, T*he Baker & McKenzie International Arbitration Yearbook 2010-2011*, p. 297 and The *Baker & McKenzie International Arbitration Yearbook 2011-2012*, p. 329.

[6] http://www.internetconsultatie.nl/herzieningarbitragerecht.

attractive by (i) modernizing, for instance by establishing the possibility to use electronic means; (ii) codifying arbitration practice, for instance by specifying the procedures for the written stage of arbitral proceedings; and (iii) reducing costs, for example by offering the parties the possibility of refraining from lodging the arbitral award with a district court.[7] The explanatory memorandum to the proposal notes that it is furthermore aimed at improving the competitive position of The Netherlands by offering high-quality dispute resolution, both in state courts as well as in arbitration proceedings conducted in The Netherlands.[8]

The legislative proposal is currently being further prepared for submission to the Dutch Parliament. The new Arbitration Act is intended to be effective as of 1 January 2014.[9]

A.2 Trends and Tendencies

As discussed in *The Baker & McKenzie International Arbitration Yearbook 2011-2012*,[10] an "e-Court" initiative was launched in the Netherlands in early 2010. E-Court is an arbitration institute within the meaning of Article 1026 DCCP that provides a swift online arbitration.[11] In 2011, case law from the lower courts revealed a number of concerns about the e-Court arbitration practice, which mainly related to the limited ability of respondents to defend themselves against claims. Several lower

---

7   *See* explanation on http://www.internetconsultatie.nl/herzieningarbitragerecht.

8   *See* explanatory memorandum, p. 2 (http://www.internetconsultatie.nl/herzienin garbitragerecht).

9   *See* http://www.rijksbegroting.nl/2013/voorbereiding/begroting,kst173857_25.html.

10 *See The Baker & McKenzie International Arbitration Yearbook 2011-2012*, p. 331.

11 Https://www.e-court.nl (currently only in Dutch).

courts therefore refused to grant an *exequatur* (permission to enforce) for arbitral awards that were rendered by e-Court.[12]

The e-Court arbitration rules have been altered since, and it seems that the tide now is turning in favor of e-Court. On 1 December 2011, the District Court of Almelo granted a request for an *exequatur* for an arbitral award that was rendered by e-Court.[13] That decision, however, did not contain any grounds for the decision rendered. More recently, in a more elaborate judgment dated 5 March 2012, the District Court of Almelo again granted a request for an *exequatur* for an arbitral award that was rendered by e-Court.[14] The court found that as opposed to previous decisions, the respondent in the arbitration tacitly consented to arbitration by accepting general terms and conditions that included an arbitration clause for e-Court arbitration. The court also found that the arbitration clause providing for e-Court arbitration could not be considered to be "unfair," since it provided for arbitration in the Netherlands, which has a solid and secure arbitration law. The court did note that the notification of arbitration—if not served by a bailiff— must be sent by registered mail and not by regular mail, since only then can it be established that the notification was duly delivered to the respondent.

As a reaction to the on-going development of the financial market, P.R.I.M.E. Finance, based in The Hague, has been established to assist judicial systems in the settlement of disputes

---

[12]   *See* District Court of Zutphen, 7 October 2011, LJN: BT7213; District Court of Almelo, 7 October 2011, LJN: BT7088; District Court of Almelo, 7 October 2011, LJN: BT7606; District Court of Almelo, 28 October 2011, LJN: BU2030. All judgments are discussed in *The Baker & McKenzie International Arbitration Yearbook 2011-2012*, p. 331-333.

[13]   District Court of Almelo, 1 December 2011, LJN: BU6895.

[14]   District Court of Almelo, 5 March 2012, LJN: BV8413.

on complex financial transactions.[15] An opening conference was held at the Peace Palace The Hague on 16 January 2012. The organization's core activities will include education and judicial training; providing expert opinions and determinations; risk assessment; and arbitration or mediation. The P.R.I.M.E. Finance Arbitration Rules are based on the 2010 UNCITRAL Arbitration Rules.[16] To reflect the market need for speedy resolution of disputes, several provisions and annexes were included that allow the parties to arbitral proceedings to shorten time frames in several ways. The main additions are the possibility of emergency arbitral proceedings before the tribunal in the main proceedings has been appointed,[17] and referee arbitral proceedings allowing for fast track proceedings that result in an enforceable award within 30 to 60 days.[18]

There seems to have been an increase in arbitrations held in the Netherlands or under Dutch arbitration rules. The Netherlands Arbitration Institute ("NAI") registered a total of 147 arbitrations in 2011 (50 international), as compared to a total of 125 in 2010 (32 international). In 2011, 41 arbitrations involved amounts of more than EUR 1 million. The final statistics for 2012 are not yet known.

---

[15] For all information on P.R.I.M.E. Finance, see http://www.primefinance disputes.org.

[16] The 2010 UNCITRAL Rules are published on http://www.uncitral.org/uncitral/ uncitral_texts/arbitration/2010Arbitration_rules.html.

[17] *See* Article 26a and Annex C to the P.R.I.M.E. Finance Arbitration Rules.

[18] *See* Article 26b and Annex D to the P.R.I.M.E. Finance Arbitration Rules. This fast track option is only open to parties which have agreed that the seat of the arbitration shall be in The Netherlands - see Article 1051(1) Dutch Code of Civil Procedure.

B. CASES

B.1 Court Proceedings: Appeal against *Exequatur* Inadmissible

The Court of Appeal of The Hague had to decide on an appeal that was lodged by a Hungarian company against a decision of the District Court of Rotterdam recognizing two arbitral awards rendered in the United Kingdom[19] and granting an *exequatur* for those two awards.[20] The Dutch entity that had been granted the *exequaturs* claimed that the appeal was inadmissible, since no appeal was available against the District Court's decision. The Court of Appeal first found that if the place of arbitration is in The Netherlands, Article 1062(4) in conjunction with Article 1064(1) DCCP prohibit appeals of decisions recognizing an award and granting an *exequatur*. An appeal can only be lodged against a decision denying a request for recognition and enforcement. The Court of Appeal, basing its decision on the prohibition against discrimination contained in Article III of the New York Convention, found that the prohibition against appealing a decision granting a request for recognition and enforcement in arbitrations in The Netherlands must also be applied to awards rendered in arbitrations seated outside The Netherlands. Consequently, the Court of Appeal found that the appeal of the Hungarian company was in principle inadmissible.

The Court of Appeal also dismissed the Hungarian company's argument that the prohibition on appeals was contrary to Article 6 of the European Convention on Human Rights ("ECHR"), since under the laws of the United Kingdom, it did not have the possibility of opposing the arbitral award after the *exequatur* had been granted in the Netherlands. The court considered that the

---

[19] The arbitral awards were rendered under the rules of the International General Produce Association in London, United Kingdom.

[20] Court of Appeal The Hague, 20 December 2011, *TvA* 2012, 27 and LJN: BU8275.

Hungarian company had had the possibility of opposing the arbitral awards in the United Kingdom pursuant to Part 1, sections 66-71 of the Arbitration Act of 1996. By reference to previous Dutch Supreme Court case law,[21] the court considered that it was not relevant whether this possibility also existed after the *exequatur* in the Netherlands had been granted. The Court of Appeal thus found that the prohibition on appealing was not contrary to Article 6 of the ECHR. It also dismissed the Hungarian company's argument that the prohibition on appealing should be lifted because the Rotterdam District Court did not apply the Brussels I Regulation. The Court of Appeal found that the Brussels I Regulation should in fact not be applied, since it does not apply to arbitration or to recognition and enforcement of arbitral awards.

B.2 Arbitration Proceedings: Acceptance of Jurisdiction in Arbitral Summary Proceedings

In a recently published award of the NAI of 2010, the jurisdiction of an arbitrator in summary arbitral proceedings was at stake.[22] Since the place of arbitration was Amsterdam, Dutch arbitration law applied. The respondent contested the jurisdiction of the arbitrator in the summary arbitral proceedings on the basis that there was no arbitration agreement containing the possibility of such summary proceedings. The respondent argued that it follows from Article 1051 DCCP—which provides for the possibility of agreeing upon summary arbitral proceedings—that jurisdiction in summary proceedings should be conferred explicitly in order to apply. The claimants maintained that there was jurisdiction, referring to the arbitration clause, which provided that all disputes "including claims for provisional

---

[21] Dutch Supreme Court, 25 June 2010, RvdW 2010, 804 (*Rosneft/Yukos*).

[22] Netherlands Arbitration Institute 4 June 2010, *TvA* 2012, 21.

relief' should be settled in accordance with the rules of the NAI. These rules, the claimants continued, provided in Articles 42a–42o for the possibility of summary proceedings, and there was nothing in the arbitration clause suggesting that the parties sought to exclude their application.

Article 42a(4) of the NAI Rules provides that the regulation on summary arbitral proceedings contained therein applies if the place of arbitration is in the Netherlands. Article 42f(1) of the NAI Rules stipulates that the tribunal deciding in summary arbitral proceedings shall consist of a sole arbitrator. The arbitrator in this case found that a reference to claims for provisional relief in the arbitration clause, combined with Articles 42a(4) and 42f(1) of the NAI Rules, amounted to an acceptance of his jurisdiction. The arbitrator found this conclusion supported by the fact that Article 1051 DCCP only applies in the absence of a specific rule pertaining to summary proceedings in the applicable rules. Since the NAI rules applied, the parties should have explicitly excluded the possibility of summary arbitral proceedings in order to prevent the rules pertaining to that possibility from applying. The arbitrator thus assumed jurisdiction.

B.3 Arbitration Proceedings: Document Production Order

As is apparent from an award of the NAI of September 2011, published mid-2012, a sole arbitrator ruled on a document production request in a procedural order dated 10 August 2011.[23] The arbitrator observed that he was authorized to order the production of specific documents (either on his own motion or on the initiative of the parties) pursuant to Article 1039(4) DCCP and Article 42j together with Article 28(2) of the NAI Rules. Upon the respondent's request, the arbitrator ordered the

---

[23] Netherlands Arbitration Institute 23 September 2011, *TvA* 2012, 24.

production of a specific contractual document, but the respondent's request for the production of "any other relevant schedule, annex or side letter" was denied. The arbitrator found the respondent's request too vague and not supported by any evidence to suggest that such further documents even existed.

C. THE GRANT AND ENFORCEMENT OF INTERIM MEASURES IN INTERNATIONAL ARBITRATION

C.1 Tribunal-Ordered Interim Measures

Article 1051 DCCP—which applies only where the (agreed) place of arbitration is in The Netherlands[24]—provides that the parties may agree to empower the arbitral tribunal or its chair to render an award in summary arbitral proceedings within the limits imposed by Article 254 DCCP. Article 254 DCCP governs the authority of state courts to grant interim relief. It requires, *inter alia*, that the interim relief is urgent (the plaintiff cannot be required to await the outcome of proceedings on the merits), and it also requires weighing the parties' interests in deciding whether interim relief should be granted. Article 37 of the NAI Rules of Arbitration provides for a rule similar to Article 1051 DCCP, albeit Article 37 of the NAI Rules only applies to summary arbitral proceedings after the appointment of the arbitral tribunal on the merits, whereas Article 1051 DCCP is generally considered to also enable the parties to agree upon the possibility of summary arbitral proceedings without any pending arbitral proceedings on the merits.[25]

---

[24] Article 1073 DCCP.

[25] See *Tekst & Commentaar Burgerlijke Rechtsvordering* (Text & Comments to Code of Civil Procedure), comment 2 under a to Article 1051 DCCP, and G.J. Meijer, *Overeenkomst tot arbitrage*, Deventer: Kluwer 2011, p. 194.

Numerous types of interim relief are possible, such as an order to retain certain evidence or an injunction to sell goods, depending on the specific situation at hand. Article 38 of the NAI Rules further provides that the tribunal may, at the request of a party, provisionally make any decision or take any measure regarding the subject-matter of the dispute if the arbitral tribunal deems it useful or necessary. Such a decision or measure shall be made or taken in the form of an order. Both Articles 37 and 38 explicitely include the authority to order the provision of security.

Before commencement of arbitral proceedings, in addition to any possibility that Article 1051 DCCP may provide, the parties may initiate summary arbitral proceedings on the basis of Articles 42a-42o of the NAI Rules of Arbitration. These provisions apply if the agreed place of arbitraton is in The Netherlands. A sole arbitrator, considering the interests of the parties, may order an immediate provisional measure that is urgently required. The arbitral award can be obtained within a few weeks.

C.2 Court-Ordered Interim Measures

Where the place of arbitration is in The Netherlands, Article 1022(2) DCCP provides that the arbitration agreement does not prevent parties from requesting a Dutch state court to provide protective measures or requesting summary proceedings under Article 254 DCCP. The court may be directly addressed, regardless of whether arbitration proceedings have already commenced and/or whether the tribunal has already been established. Protective measures may, for instance, include permission for conservatory attachments. Obtaining such permission usually just takes a couple of days. In summary proceedings, considering the interests of the parties, the court may grant interim relief if such relief is immediately required. The standard jurisdiction rules apply in order to assess whether the court has jurisdiction. In the event that the Brussels I

Regulation applies, jurisdiction of the court in summary proceedings can only be based on Article 31, rather than any other provision of the Brussels I Regulation.[26] Obtaining a judgment in state court summary proceedings usually takes a few weeks, but the process can be sped up if urgently required. Where the place of arbitration is outside The Netherlands, Article 1074(2) provides for similar rules.

In the event the parties have validly agreed upon arbitral summary proceedings in accordance with Article 1051 DCCP, the court may refer to the agreed-upon arbitral summary proceedings.[27] Among other considerations, the court will take into account the period of time within which the arbitral tribunal may render its decision.[28]

Various types of interim relief are possible in summary proceedings, such as an advance payment order or any other order depending on the plaintiff's needs in the situation at hand. Anti-suit injunctions have also occasionaly been granted by Dutch lower courts,[29] where such orders were not found to be contrary to case law of the European Court of Justice.[30]

---

[26] *See Tekst & Commentaar Burgerlijke Rechtsvordering* (Text & Comments to Code of Civil Procedure), comment 2 under b and c on Article 1022 DCCP.

[27] Where the agreed place of arbitration is in The Netherlands, this is based on Article 1022(2) DCCP. Where the place of arbitration is outside The Netherlands, this does not have a statutory basis, but the possibility has been argued in literature (*See Tekst & Commentaar Burgerlijke Rechtsvordering* (Text & Comments to Code of Civil Procedure)), comment 2 under e to Article 1074 DCCP.

[28] *See Tekst & Commentaar Burgerlijke Rechtsvordering* (Text & Comments to Code of Civil Procedure), comment 2 under e to Article 1022 DCCP.

[29] *See, e.g.,* District Court of Rotterdam, 27 July 2011, LJN: BR5442, and District Court of Rotterdam, 29 December 2010, LJN: BP1040. These anti-suit orders were not given in summary proceedings, but in proceedings on the merits. Previous anti-suit orders have been given in summary proceedings (see District

C.3 Enforcement of Interim Measures

Where an interim order given in an arbitration seated in the Netherlands actually contains a final decision on any of the claims in the summary proceedings, it will in principle be considered to be a final award, and an *exequatur* can therefore be requested and granted (Article 1061 DCCP). This applies both to separate summary arbitral proceedings and to orders given in an arbitration on the merits.[31] Orders that are merely interlocutory awards without any final decision are not enforceable in The Netherlands.

It has been argued in literature that interim orders given in an arbitration seated outside the Netherlands can equally be enforced on the basis of Article 1076 DCCP, where no relevant treaty is in place.[32] Where a treaty is in place, enforcement of a foreign arbitral award will depend on the contents of the relevant treaty (Article 1075 DCCP).

Court of The Hague, 5 August 2004, *NJ* 2004, 597 and District Court of Amsterdam, 14 December 2004, *NJF* 2005, 27).

[30] ECJ 10 February 2009 (C-185/87), JBpr 2010, 1.

[31] *See Tekst & Commentaar Burgerlijke Rechtsvordering* (Text & Comments to Code of Civil Procedure), comment 5 under d to Article 1051 DCCP.

[32] G.J. Meijer, *Overeenkomst tot arbitrage*, Deventer: Kluwer 2011, p. 1008-1009.

PERU

Ana María Arrarte Arisnabarreta[1]

A.   LEGISLATION, TRENDS AND TENDENCIES

A.1   Legislative Framework—Overview

Legislative Decree No. 1071 has been in force in Peru since September 2008, regulating arbitration (hereinafter, "Peruvian Arbitration Law") and includes the main contributions of the UNCITRAL Model Law to Peru's arbitration practice and experience. This law is the result of a long evolution and consolidation process of arbitration practice in the country.

One of the characteristics of the Peruvian Arbitration Law is the unification of the provisions that regulate both national and international arbitration. The same procedure governs both types of arbitration, except for specific regulations that differ from the general treatment when justified by the arbitration's international nature.

---

[1]   Ana Maria Arrarte Arisnabarreta is a Partner in Estudio Echecopar associated with Baker & McKenzie International in Lima, Peru. Ms. Arrarte represents clients in civil and commercial procedural law matters, including arbitration, negotiation and conciliation. She is a member of the arbitrators' lists at the Center for Local and Foreign Conciliation and Arbitration of the Lima Chamber of Commerce, the State Council on Procurement and Acquisitions, the American Chamber of Commerce, the Center of Arbitration at the Professional Association of Engineers of Peru and the Center of Arbitration at the Pontificia Universidad Católica del Peru. In addition to her practice, for the past 18 years, Ms. Arrarte has been a Professor at Peru's most prestigious universities (Pontificia Universidad Catolica del Peru, Universidad de Lima, Universidad del Pacifico, among others). She has authored several articles on arbitration and litigation in both national and international law reviews, and has co-authored several books on litigation and arbitration.

Also, the consolidation of Peru's arbitration system demonstrates the state's commitment to turn this arbitration into a guarantee, ensuring a due, speedy and efficient dispute resolution process to promote national and foreign investment growth that, in turn, will generate development and progress for Peru.

A.2 Training: A Key Element

A major part of this process involved training key actors on the interrelation between arbitration and judicial activity. One of the most sensitive issues has been fostering understanding of the actors' (the state and the arbitrators) roles and participation to achieve success and efficiency in arbitration. Precautionary measures and their enforcement are particularly important in this context.

B. CASES

Arbitration has been growing consistently in Peru over approximately the past 10 years. For the Firm, 2012 was quite important in terms of the number of cases and the amounts at stake. The Firm is limited in its ability to disclose certain cases and outcomes due to the private nature of arbitration. Nonetheless, some relevant cases, primarily those involving precautionary measures, are briefly addressed below:

B.1 *ENERSUR v. EGEMSA et al.* (pending)

Our clients, EGEMSA, EGASA, EGESUR and SAN GABAN (the "Companies"), power generation plants, were sued by ENERSUR in an arbitration that has implications for all generators and the COES, the system operator that runs and coordinators the Peruvian power system. In this case, plaintiff ENERSUR questions the Regulator's decisions regarding the allotment of energy withdrawals made by distributors without a binding agreement.

The Companies filed several precautionary measures to obtain an order to enjoin the application for the Regulator's decision. Our four clients' subsistence depended upon it. The injunctions were successfully obtained from a court of law and the Constitutional Court, and enabled the Companies to continue operations without jeopardizing their existence.

B.2 *KALLPA and EDEGEL v. COES* (in excess of USD 100 million)

The Firm represents COES, the Peruvian energy system operator that comprises all power generation, power transmission and power distribution companies, as well as industrial users. An arbitration tribunal may annul COES' decisions regarding energy system operations. The Firm represents COES in 10 annulment arbitrations, which represents COES almost its entire arbitration caseload. The relevance of these cases is the amount at stake because granting injunctions could jeopardize the operations of an entire power generation company. This risk led all power generation companies operating in Peru to agree that injunctions will not be enforced in these types of cases.

B.3 *ACTIVOS MINEROS* (settled—USD 140 million)

This is one of the largest arbitration cases, in terms of the amount at stake, ever to be addressed against the Peruvian State and its companies. Minera Ancash Cobre (a subsidiary of Inca Pacific Resources, Inc.) filed arbitration against Firm clients FONAFE, PROINVERSION and ACTIVOS MINEROS for the ownership of the copper mining project *Magistral*, arguing wrongful termination of the exploitation contract and seeking forced continuation and damages.

The plaintiff tried to affect the future sale of concession rights and filed for a precautionary measure: a registry on the public records. The measure was later revoked and the sale of concessions was achieved. The parties later settled on favorable terms, which did not require the our client to pay any moneys and confirmed the termination of the exploitation contract.

C. THE GRANT AND ENFORCEMENT OF INTERIM MEASURES IN INTERNATIONAL ARBITRATION

Origin

To begin, there must be clarification regarding precautionary measures and their enforcement that determines the analysis below about the relationship between arbitration and judicial processes.

It is theorized that arbitration's origin and legitimacy do not arise from its constitutional recognition as "exceptional jurisdiction" (as is the case in Peru), but because it has all of the features inherent to "jurisdiction" and its legitimacy is not granted by the law, but rather by free will.

Parties exercise their free will when they agree that any dispute that may arise between them will be decided by an arbitrator that they vest with the power to resolve the dispute, rather than a member of the judiciary vested by the Constitution.

Thus, the state may not interpose itself to decide a controversy that was referred to arbitration (before, during, or after such proceeding), because its has no *jurisdiction* to do so since it has been deprived of its power to decide, as Osvaldo Gozaíni explained.[2]

Interrelation

This does not mean that the judiciary is barred from valid involvement in a pending national or international arbitration proceeding. Actually, it is allowed to do so, within certain limits, because effective arbitration requires a close and harmonic relation between both devices. This does not signify, however, that the judiciary is vested with the power to settle the dispute. Arbitration and judicial proceedings are validly related in different forms: subsidiary, supplementary and reviewing.

In a subsidiary relationship, the judiciary participates through the issuance of resolutions that an arbitration tribunal may not adopt. For example, this may occur before the tribunal is appointed or when it lacks jurisdiction over a certain decision.

In a supplementary relationship, it is necessary that both the arbitrator and the judge participate to achieve a result. For example, the arbitration tribunal must issue an award for the judiciary to, in exercise of its judicial enforcement power, provide the necessary legal aid for its enforcement.

C.1 Tribunal-Ordered Interim Measures

In the Peruvian arbitration system, an arbitrator's jurisdiction to order precautionary measures, whether in a national or international arbitration, is clear because the powers to order and enforce precautionary measures are set forth by law (Section 43

---

[2] GOZAÍNI, Osvaldo. *Formas Alternativas para la Solución de Conflictos* (Alternative Dispute Resolution Methods). Ed. DEPALMA. Buenos Aires. 1995. P. 147.

of the Peruvian Arbitration Law). It should be noted that public power may not be used to enforce arbitration awards. Therefore, it may be necessary to have the assistance of the judiciary.

The regulations of the different local arbitration centers[3] are in line with the international regulations on this matter.[4]

In certain cases, the parties may deprive the arbitrators of their right to issue precautionary measures. As the arbitrators' jurisdictional power comes from the parties, it is clear that they may act within the bounds of the law and the parties' will, unlike in a judicial proceeding. In this sense, since a legal provision limiting this possibility does not exist, the parties may agree that the arbitrators may not issue precautionary measures regarding a certain controversy.

The fact that the parties to the arbitration may prevent the arbitrators from issuing precautionary measures does not imply a breach of any right or a waiver of precautionary measures, since the party requesting an arbitration procedure may at any time petition the judiciary for a measure securing the effectiveness of the award. In such case, the judiciary's subsidiary role will prevail.

For the issuance of a precautionary measure in Peruvian arbitration, the arbitrators must verify the requirements set forth by procedural law: (i) the plausibility or probability of the right invoked in the claim; (ii) the danger in a delayed response;

---

[3] As for example, the Arbitration Rules of the Arbitration Center of the Lima Chamber of Commerce (Article 50: Conservatory Measures).

[4] As for example, the Arbitration Rules of the Arbitration Center of the International Chamber of Commerce (Article 28: Conservatory and Interim Measures, and the International Dispute Resolution Procedures of the International Center for Dispute Resolution (ICDR) (Article 21: Interim Measures of Protection).

(iii) adaptation, which implies that the precautionary measures be consistent with and proportional to the subject matter of the arbitration; and (iv) an injunction bond, the purpose of which is to guarantee compensation of any damage caused by the enforcement of the precautionary measure.

Regarding the characteristics of arbitration precautionary measures, these are basically the same as those requested before a court. However, it is worth mentioning that, in principle, precautionary measures in arbitration are not *in audita pars*, i.e., that for issuing a precautionary measure it is necessary to hear the other party, unless it is proved that hearing the other party will render the measure ineffective.

Even though the general rule at court is that precautionary measures be issued without hearing the affected party, the reason behind this rule is that the right to challenge is not eliminated, but suspended or delayed until the time of appeal before a second instance by means of an appeal.

If it is considered that in arbitration there is no possibility of appealing a precautionary measure before a higher instance; a precautionary measure may only be validly issued if the other party is given the chance to challenge the measure, unless it is proved that hearing the other party shall render the urgency measure ineffective. Otherwise, the right to due process would be denied.

Title 3, section 47 of the Peruvian Arbitration Law provides that: "Before deciding, the arbitration tribunal *shall inform the opposing party of the request.* However, it may issue a precautionary measure without informing the opposing party in the event that the requesting party justifies it is necessary not to inform the other party in order to guarantee the effectiveness of the measure. Once the measure is issued, the decision *may be challenged.*" (emphasis added)

Consequently, there are two characteristic features of precautionary measures in the new arbitration law: (i) as a general rule, the precautionary measure is issued with prior notification to the other party to guarantee its right of defense, unless the other party proves that giving the other party the possibility of defending itself would render the measure ineffective; (ii) the resolution issuing a precautionary measure may now be challenged by means of a request for reconsideration before the same arbitration tribunal, notwithstanding the fact that the affected party may request that the measure be set aside or modified when it deems appropriate, and prove that the de facto or legal situation that gave rise to the issuance of the measure by the arbitrators has changed.

Notwithstanding the fact that the arbitrators do not have the power to enforce their decisions through public force, some scholars believe that an arbitration tribunal may enforce its decisions provided that the use of the public force is not necessary. Others believe that under no circumstances may the arbitrators enforce the precautionary measures that they issue, since enforcement power is an exclusive state power and is not granted to the arbitrators in any form.

The authors favor the former position, which is more consistent with the Peruvian arbitration system. To fully develop this idea, it is necessary to repeat the concept that arbitration power arises from the parties' will, in compliance with the limits set forth by the law and the Constitution. These sources of arbitration power do not prohibit arbitrators from enforcing their own decisions, except for those cases that require the use of force, which is an exclusive state power.

There are no impediments for arbitrators to enforce precautionary measures that do not imply the use of force, such as a precautionary interim measure or a stay (to maintain the status quo existing at the time the claim was filed). The same happens with an order to innovate (to modify the status quo existing when the measure was requested), such as an order requesting that the effects of an agreement entered into against public order rules be suspended. In order to enforce this decision, the use of force would not be necessary; enforcement would be achieved by sending a notification to the party affected by the arbitration process.

Considering that precautionary measures are intended to ensure the effectiveness of the arbitration award, in the Peruvian arbitration system arbitrators may not only issue precautionary measures to ensure their decisions are enforced, but compliance with such measures is also mandatory for the parties to the arbitration agreement. The Peruvian Arbitration Law provides that arbitrators can enforce their precautionary measures; therefore, they may only resort to the judiciary in those cases in which the judicial enforcement power is necessary.

The following are some conclusions on the enforcement of precautionary measures in arbitration:

In the event that enforcement of the precautionary measure merely implies a notification to the respondent, arbitrators are empowered to enforce such measures although the arbitration agreement does not include an express provision to that effect.

If enforcement of the precautionary measure requires a third party intervention, such as a public (like a public registry) or private institution (a bank or financial institution), it may also be carried out by the arbitrators. Therefore to avoid situations where a third party denies that it entered into a binding arbitration agreement, the Peruvian Arbitration Law includes the following provisions:

(a) As of the effective date of the law all legal references made to judges shall also refer to an arbitration tribunal, which ensures that arbitration awards are treated as judicial decisions (Complementary Provision No. 4).

(b) Arbitration centers may enter into cooperation agreements with public and private institutions in order to enforce arbitration awards (Complementary Provision No. 2).

(c) For precautionary measures that require judicial power for their enforcement, arbitrators may not be granted enforcement powers and the judiciary must intervene and provide necessary assistance.

Finally, the limit to the judiciary's activity in enforcing tribunal rendered precautionary measures is determined by the court's complementary role.

C.2 Court-Ordered Interim Measures

As stated above, an arbitration tribunal may issue precautionary measures that it is empowered to issue, i.e., from the time the tribunal is formed to when the parties grant it the necessary powers in the formation document, until the time an award is rendered.

It is the author's interpretation that the judiciary may only issue precautionary measures in those cases in which the arbitration tribunal may not enforce its decisions, otherwise, the judiciary lacks competence to carry out valid procedural acts. Therefore, the Judiciary may only issue precautionary measures if the Arbitration Tribunal has not been formed and once the arbitration process has finished, that is to say, when the arbitrators do not have enforcement powers or when enforcement is necessary.

With regard to national arbitration, paragraph 47 of section 47 sets forth: "Precautionary measures requested from a judicial authority before formation of the arbitration tribunal are not contrary to arbitration . . . ."

Moreover, judges will not be empowered to order precautionary measures when an arbitration tribunal has been formed, unless expressly agreed by the parties in the arbitration agreements or in the relevant formation document. This is consistent with the "adverse effect" of the execution of an arbitration agreement, whereby the Judiciary "is deprived" of the jurisdiction to validly perform certain acts, in connection with a dispute that has been submitted by the parties to the arbitration authority.

With regard to international arbitration, the Peruvian Arbitration Law sets forth a specific application provision. Thus, paragraph 9 of section 47 provides: "In international arbitration, during the arbitration proceeding, the parties may also request from the competent judicial authority, upon prior authorization by the tribunal, the adoption of the precautionary measures they deem convenient."

The law applicable to international arbitration provides for what is known as "concurrent jurisdiction" for precautionary measures, i.e., judges have jurisdiction to order these measures both before the formation of the arbitration tribunal and during the arbitration proceeding.

Obviously, before the formation of the arbitration tribunal, the matter does require further discussion, but the point in question here is whether the judiciary may order precautionary measures while the arbitration proceeding is pending. The justification for this latter position lies in that taking into account that even when the arbitrators have jurisdiction to order precautionary measures, the judges are in charge of enforcing them, it would be more efficient to directly resort to them in order to request and enforce such measures, especially when the measures are to be enforced in a place other than where the arbitration tribunal is sitting.

In this case, the rule of territorial jurisdiction (Section 8) should be applied, whereby the judge having jurisdiction over the place where the measure is to be enforced or have effects shall be the competent judge. Nevertheless, when such measures need to be adopted or enforced abroad, the treaties on enforcement of foreign precautionary measures shall be applicable (e.g., New York Convention).

D. CONCLUSIONS

Precautionary measures under Peruvian Arbitration Law may be summarized as follows:

- In Peru, it is not necessary that precautionary measures be expressly provided in the arbitration agreement to be ordered.

- The parties may expressly agree to limit the arbitrators' power to order precautionary measures. This does not imply damage to a fundamental right because the parties remain entitled to request these types of urgent measures from the judiciary.

- Precautionary measures in an arbitration proceeding have the same requirements and essentially the same features of those ordered in a court proceeding, except for the *in audita pars* characteristic.

- on the party that the measure will be enforced against. The respondent may object to the measure through an appeal for review, which does not require the measure's prior enforcement.

- Arbitrators are empowered to order and enforce precautionary measures, as follows:

D. Conclusions

o In the event that the enforcement of a precautionary measure merely implies a notification to the respondent, arbitrators are entitled to enforce said measures even though it is not expressly authorized in the arbitration agreement.

o When the enforcement of a precautionary measure requires any action other that service on the respondent, but does not require the use of force, the arbitrators do have enforcement powers. Thus, they may enforce such measures against third parties as long as they do not require the use of force that is reserved to the state.

o When the enforcement of a precautionary measure requires judicial enforcement acts, it is not possible to grant enforcement powers to arbitrators. In this case, the exercise of public force is exclusively reserved to the judiciary, which will enforce the measure.

• When enforcing precautionary measures ordered by an arbitration tribunal, the judiciary acts in a supplementary form and exclusively for the purposes of providing its judicial enforcement power necessary to enforce the arbitration decision. Therefore, it is not necessary to previously serve such measure on the other party, and the judiciary may not clarify, interpret, or allow for any objection to the precautionary measure.

• In domestic arbitrations, the judiciary has no jurisdiction to order precautionary measures if an arbitration tribunal has been formed. Thus, the formed tribunal has jurisdiction to order precautionary measures while an arbitration proceeding is pending. A different scenario is found in international arbitrations where the law provides for concurrent jurisdiction if authorized by the arbitration agreement or arbitration rules.

PHILIPPINES

Donemark J.L. Calimon,[1] Lemuel D. Lopez[2] and
Jay Patrick R. Santiago[3]

A. LEGISLATION, TRENDS AND TENDENCIES

A.1 Special Rules of Court on ADR

After the enactment in 2004 of Republic Act No.
9285, otherwise known as the Alternative Dispute Resolution Act of
2004 ("ADR Act"),[4] and around the same time as the

---

[1] Donemark J.L. Calimon is a Partner in Quisumbing Torres Law Offices, a
member firm of Baker & McKenzie International in Manila. He specializes in
commercial arbitration, both domestic and international. He is a member and an
accredited arbitrator of the Philippine Dispute Resolution Center, Inc. (PDRCI),
an accredited arbitrator of the Philippine Intellectual Property Office, a member of
the Chartered Institute of Arbitrators, East Asia Branch (Philippine Chapter), and
a director/officer of the Philippine Institute of Arbitrators.

[2] Lemuel D. Lopez is an Associate in Quisumbing Torres Law Offices, a member
firm of Baker &McKenzie International in Manila. A member of the Chartered
Institute of Arbitrators, East Asia Branch, he has been involved in several
arbitrations and has worked on projects and cases with international and foreign
elements involving banking and financial institutions, energy, mining,
manufacturing and agricultural industries. He received his Master of Laws in
International Law and Master of Diplomacy from the Australian National
University under the Australian Leadership Awards. He also teaches Private
International Law.

[3] Jay Patrick R. Santiago is an Associate in Quisumbing Torres Law Offices, a
member firm of Baker & McKenzie International in Manila. His practice covers
commercial arbitration, both domestic and international, as well as general
litigation. He is a member of the Chartered Institute of Arbitrators, East Asia
Branch (Philippine Chapter), a member of the Philippine Institute of Arbitrators
and a member of Young ICCA.

[4] *See The Baker & McKenzie International Arbitration Yearbook 2008,*
Developments in Philippine Arbitration Law, at pp. 47-50.

promulgation in 2009 of the Implementing Rules and Regulations of the ADR Act ("IRR of the ADR Act"),[5] the Supreme Court issued the Special Rules of Court on Alternative Dispute Resolution ("ADR Rules").[6]

The issuance of the ADR Rules was a significant development in Philippine arbitration law as it was intended to define the objectives and limits of court intervention in arbitration proceedings, whether international or domestic. Notably, in the limited instances in which courts can intervene, courts are to assist and cooperate with arbitral tribunals. Thus, in addition to the courts' duty to refer parties covered by an arbitration agreement to arbitration, the ADR Rules allow courts to issue interim measures of protection in aid of arbitration proceedings.

With respect to the granting of interim measure of protection, the ADR Rules set out important rules which courts are required to observe, including the following:

- The arbitral tribunal shall be accorded the first opportunity or competence to rule on the issue of whether or not it has jurisdiction.[7]

- When exercising its power to determine whether the arbitration agreement is null and void, inoperative or incapable of being performed, the court must make no more than a *prima facie* determination of that issue.[8]

---

[5]   *See The Baker & McKenzie International Arbitration Yearbook 2010*, Philippines, at pp. 84-86.

[6]   *See The Baker & McKenzie International Arbitration Yearbook 2011-2012*, Philippines, at pp. 345-347.

[7]   ADR Rules, Rule 2.4.

[8]   *Ibid.*

- The court must not enjoin arbitration proceedings during the pendency of the petition involving the jurisdiction of the arbitral tribunal.[9]

- Courts may issue interim measures of protection when there is an urgent need and only to the extent that the arbitral tribunal has no power to act or is unable to act effectively.[10]

- Court orders granting or denying interim measures of protection may subsequently be modified or revoked by the arbitral tribunal.[11]

- The court shall assist in the enforcement of an interim measure of protection issued by the arbitral tribunal that it is unable to enforce effectively.[12]

- The court shall assist in enforcing an interim measure of protection ordered by an arbitral tribunal even if it was granted *ex parte*, or the party opposing the application found new material evidence not previously considered, or it amends, revokes, modifies or is inconsistent with an earlier measure of protection issued by the court.[13]

- An order of the court on a petition for an interim measure of protection is generally immediately executory.[14]

---

[9]   *Id.*, Rule 3.3.

[10]   *Id.*, Rule 5.2.

[11]   *Id.*, Rule 5.13.

[12]   *Id.*, Rule 5.16.

[13]   *Id.*, Rule 5.11.

[14]   *Id.*, Rule 5.10.

A.2 Executive Order No. 78 (series of 2012)

On 4 July 2012, acknowledging the need to provide a more attractive climate for private investments, the Office of the President issued Executive Order No. 78 ("EO 78") requiring certain contracts with the Philippine government to include provisions on the use of ADR mechanisms. EO 78 was intended to make the resolution of disputes less expensive, tedious, complex and time-consuming, especially for large-scale, capital-intensive infrastructure and development contracts.

The government contracts covered by EO 78 include: (a) those involving public-private partnership projects; (b) those entered into under Republic Act No. 6957, entitled *The Act Authorizing the Financing, Construction, Operation and Maintenance of Infrastructure Projects by the Private Sector, and for Other Purposes*, as amended by Republic Act No. 7718, or the *Build-Operate and Transfer Law*; and (c) certain joint venture agreements between government and private entities issued by the National Economic and Development Authority. EO 78 also encourages parties who enter into similar contracts with local government units to stipulate on the use of ADR mechanisms, in accordance with their own joint venture rules, guidelines or procedures.[15]

What is notable under EO 78 is that while it requires the inclusion of ADR provisions in covered contracts, it expressly gives the parties to freedom to agree on: (a) the venue[16] or forum[17] of the arbitration; and (b) the applicable rules or

---

[15] EO 78, § 1.

[16] It is possible that EO 78 meant to refer to the "Place of Arbitration," instead of just the venue thereof.

[17] It is possible that EO 78 meant to refer to the arbitral institution which will administer the arbitration.

procedures. This potentially conflicts with the exclusive and original jurisdiction of the Construction Industry Arbitration Commission to resolve disputes relating to construction when the parties are bound by an arbitration agreement.[18] The implementing rules of EO 78, which is being drafted by the National Economic Development Authority, will hopefully provide guidance on this matter.

A.3 Executive Order No. 97 (series of 2012)

On 18 October 2012, the Office of the President also issued Executive Order No. 97 ("EO 97") which expands the powers and responsibilities of the Office for Alternative Dispute Resolution ("OADR").

EO 97 transfers from the Office of the President to the OADR all powers, functions, and duties over the development, use, implementation, promotion, monitoring, coordination, expansion, evaluation, and study of ADR programs and services in the Executive Branch, including all its departments, administrative offices, quasi-judicial agencies, and government-owned or controlled corporations.[19]

---

[18] Section 4 of EO 1008 provides:

The CIAC shall have original and exclusive jurisdiction over disputes arising from, or connected with, contracts entered into by parties involved in construction in the Philippines, whether the disputes arises [sic] before or after the completion of the contract, or after the abandonment or breach thereof. These disputes may involve government or private contracts. For the Board to acquire jurisdiction, the parties to a dispute must agree to submit the same to voluntary arbitration.

The jurisdiction of the CIAC may include but is not limited to violation of specifications for materials and workmanship; violation of the terms of agreement; interpretation and/or application of contractual provisions; amount of damages and penalties; commencement time and delays; maintenance and defects; payment default of employer or contractor and changes in contract cost.

[19] EO 97, § 1.

EO 97 requires the Executive Branch to continue to promote the use of ADR including, but not limited to, arbitration, mediation, conciliation, and early neutral evaluation as part of their practice in resolving disputes filed before them[20] and puts in place certain requirements to allow the OADR to monitor the use of ADR by the Executive Branch.[21]

A.4 ADR Accreditation Guidelines and Training Standards

The Department of Justice, through the OADR, recently issued Department of Justice Circular No. 49, otherwise known as the *Accreditation Guidelines for Alternative Dispute Resolution Provider Organizations and Training Standards for Alternative Dispute Resolution Practitioners* ("Guidelines"). The Guidelines apply to all private ADR Provider Organizations ("APOs")[22] and ADR Practitioners[23] which offer ADR training programs or dispute resolution services to the general public, to government agencies, or in partnership with said agencies.[24]

Accreditation[25] is mandatory only for private APOs and ADR practitioners offering ADR services[26] to government agencies or

---

[20]   *Id.* at § 3.

[21]   *Id.* at §§ 4, 5, and 6.

[22]   "ADR Provider Organizations" means institutions, associations, centers or organizations which provide ADR services to the general public through a roster of neutrals serving as mediator, conciliator, arbitrator, neutral evaluator, or any person exercising similar functions in any Alternative Dispute Resolution system. Guidelines, § 1[c].

[23]   "ADR Practitioners" or "ADR Neutrals" shall refer to individuals acting as mediator, conciliator, arbitrator, neutral evaluator or any person exercising similar functions in any Alternative Dispute Resolution system. Guidelines, § 1 [b].

[24]   Guidelines, § 2, in relation to § 1(j).

[25]   "Accreditation" or "Certification" means a process whereby an individual or organization engaged in, or a program relating to, the delivery of ADR services undergoes evaluation for the purpose of determining whether it meets the

in partnership with said agencies.[27] Essentially, the Guidelines provide that government agencies shall only partner with or engage the services of OADR-accredited private APOs and ADR Practitioners.[28]

As the Guidelines are generally intended to elevate the quality of the services provided by APOs and ADR Practitioners, they prescribe standards that apply to the training of ADR Practitioners to enable them to serve as neutrals in ADR proceedings, such as arbitration, mediation, conciliation, early neutral evaluation, mini-trial or any other ADR process.[29]

A.5 Trends and Tendencies

Arbitration, whether domestic or international, continues to become more popular as a means of dispute resolution in the Philippines. However, the slow development of jurisprudence on arbitration-related issues, particularly on the enforcement of arbitral awards, tends to delay this process as many stakeholders continue to take a wait-and-see attitude towards arbitration. Nevertheless, though development may be slow, there appears to be a bright future ahead for arbitration in the Philippines. The recent issuances from the Executive Department indicate genuine efforts to institutionalize its use and to make Philippine arbitration laws more responsive to the changing times.

---

minimum standards on qualifications, competence and performance in regard to those services. Guidelines, § 1[a].

[26] "ADR Services" shall include but not be limited to serving as an ADR practitioner; providing ADR trainings; conducting program and system design; and managing, overseeing or administering ADR programs. Guidelines, § 1[d].

[27] Guidelines, § 3 and 10.

[28] *Ibid.*

[29] Guidelines, § 22.

B. CASES

B.1 Foreign Corporations Doing Business in the Philippines without a License May Seek to Enforce Foreign Arbitral Awards

In *Tuna Processing, Inc. v. Philippine Kingford, Inc.*, G.R. No. 185582, 29 February 2012, the Philippine Supreme Court allowed the enforcement of a foreign arbitral award in favor of a foreign corporation doing business in the Philippines without a license.

The dispute involved a Memorandum of Agreement between Philippine Kingford, Inc. ("PKI") and several parties for the establishment of Tuna Processing, Inc. ("TPI"). PKI eventually withdrew from TPI, and consequently, reneged on its obligations. TPI submitted the dispute for arbitration before the ICDR in the state of California, United States and was able to obtain an award against PKI.

TPI sought to enforce the award in the Philippines. PKI opposed enforcement and filed a motion to dismiss on the ground that TPI, as a foreign corporation doing business in the Philippines without a license, lacked the legal capacity to file suit in a Philippine court. PKI cited Section 133 of the Corporation Code, which provides in part that "no foreign corporation transacting business in the Philippines without a license, or its successors or assigns, shall be permitted to maintain or intervene in any action, suit or proceeding in any court or administrative agency of the Philippines."

On appeal to the Philippine Supreme Court by TPI, after the trial court and the court of appeals agreed with the position of PKI, the enforcement of the foreign arbitral award was allowed. The court ruled that the Corporation Code, a general law, does not apply and that the ADR Act, a special law, should govern. The court further held that a losing party cannot invoke grounds other than those enumerated in Article V of the New York Convention in opposing the recognition or enforcement of an arbitral award in the Philippines. Significantly, in upholding the enforcement of the foreign arbitral award, the court stated:

> Indeed, it is in the best interest of justice that in the enforcement of a foreign arbitral award, we deny availment by the losing party of the rule that bars foreign corporations not licensed to do business in the Philippines from maintaining a suit in our courts. When a party enters into a contract containing a foreign arbitration clause and, as in this case, in fact submits itself to arbitration, it becomes bound by the contract, by the arbitration and by the result of arbitration, conceding thereby the capacity of the other party to enter into the contract, participate in the arbitration and cause the implementation of the result.

B.2 An Agreement to Submit Any Dispute to Arbitration May Be Construed as an Implicit Waiver of Immunity from Suit

In *China National Machinery & Equipment Corp. (Group) v. Hon. Cesar D. Santamaria, etc., et al.*, G.R. No. 185572, 7 February 2012, the Supreme Court construed an arbitration clause as an implicit waiver of immunity from suit.

The case involved a railway project where China National Machinery & Equipment Corp. (Group) ("CNMEG") was designated as prime contractor. A complaint for annulment of contract and injunction was filed against CNMEG and various Philippine government agencies. CNMEG filed a motion to dismiss arguing, *inter alia*, lack of jurisdiction over its person, on the grounds that it was an agent of the Chinese government and therefore immune from suit. The trial court denied the motion, which denial was upheld by the Court of Appeals.

On appeal, the Supreme Court agreed with the lower courts that the trial court had jurisdiction. The Supreme Court noted that under the arbitration clause, if any dispute arises in relation to the project, both parties are bound to submit the matter to the HKIAC for arbitration. The enforcement of any arbitral award resulting therefrom, the court further noted, would be subject to the ADR Rules. According to the Supreme Court, these show that CNMEG agreed that it would not be afforded immunity from suit.

The Supreme Court also referenced the Foreign Sovereign Immunities Act of 1976 of the United States, which provides for waiver by implication of state immunity. Under that law, the agreement to submit disputes to arbitration in a foreign country is construed as an implicit waiver of immunity from suit. According to the Supreme Court, although there is no similar law in the Philippines, the legal reasoning behind the US law was applicable.

C. THE GRANT AND ENFORCEMENT OF INTERIM MEASURES IN INTERNATIONAL ARBITRATION

C.1 Tribunal-Ordered Interim Measures

Interim measures which may be issued by an arbitral tribunal include, without limitation, the issuance of a preliminary injunction directed against a party, appointment of receivers, or detention, preservation, inspection of property that is the subject of the dispute in arbitration.[30]

The ADR Act and its IRR provide that interim or provisional relief may be granted for any of the following reasons: (i) to

---

[30] ADR Act, § 29 and IRR of ADR Act, Art. 4.17.

prevent irreparable loss or injury, (ii) to provide security for the performance of any obligation, (iii) to produce or preserve any evidence, or (iv) to compel any other appropriate act or omission.[31] However, there is yet no jurisprudence, rule or legislation which prescribe more specific tests or guidelines that an applicant must satisfy in order for a tribunal to issue interim measures.

The Arbitration Rules of the Philippine Dispute Resolution Center, Inc. ("PDRCI"), the leading arbitral institution in the Philippines, do not provide for available interim measures that an arbitral tribunal may issue before commencement of the arbitration. Specifically, the PDRCI does not yet have in place rules for appointment of emergency arbitrators.

C.2 Court-Ordered Interim Measures

Courts may also grant interim measures: (a) before arbitration is commenced, (b) after arbitration is commenced, but before the constitution of the arbitral tribunal, or (c) after the constitution of the arbitral tribunal and at any time during arbitral proceedings, but at this stage, only to the extent that the arbitral tribunal has no power to act or is unable to act effectively.[32] Thus, as a rule, once the arbitral tribunal has been constituted, petitions for interim measures must be filed with it and not with the court.

Strictly applying the ADR Rules, applications for interim measures should be resolved within 30 to 45 days from date of application. If the petition appears to be urgent and the court finds the grounds meritorious, the court may even hear the petition without need of notice to the other party. The other party is given a period of 15 days from service of the petition/

---

[31]   ADR Act, § 28 (b) (2) and IRR of ADR Act, Art. 4.17 (c) (ii).

[32]   ADR Act, § 28 (a) and ADR Rules, Rule 5.2.

application to file its comment or opposition, and the court is given a maximum of 30 days from: (a) submission of the opposition, or (b) upon lapse of the period to file the same, or (c) from termination of the hearing, to resolve the matter.

The question of whether courts may grant anti-suit injunctions is not provided for under Philippine law. However, whether or not a court will issue an injunction to prevent a party from commencing or maintaining a proceeding in another jurisdiction or forum will likely depend on whether the requirements for issuance of injunctive relief under Philippine rules are present. To be entitled to a writ of injunction, a party must generally establish the following: (a) the right of the complainant is clear and unmistakable, (b) the invasion of the right sought to be protected is material and substantial, and (c) there is an urgent and paramount necessity for the writ to prevent serious damage.[33]

Philippine courts may grant interim measures in aid of a foreign arbitrations. Under the ADR Rules, a party to an arbitration agreement, without distinction as to whether the arbitration is in the Philippines or abroad, may petition the court for interim measures of protection.

C.3 Enforcement of Interim Measures

Interim measures issued by an arbitral tribunal may be enforced through the courts. A court shall not deny an application for assistance in implementing or enforcing an interim measure of protection ordered by an arbitral tribunal on any of the following grounds:

---

[33] *Boncodin v. National Power Corporation Employees Consolidated Union (NECU)*, G.R. No. 162716, 27 September 2006.

C. The Grant and Enforcement of Interim Measures in International Arbitration

(a) The arbitral tribunal granted the interim relief *ex parte*;

(b) The party opposing the application found new material evidence, which the arbitral tribunal had not considered in granting in the application, and which, if considered, may produce a different result;[34] or

(c) The measure of protection ordered by the arbitral tribunal amends, revokes, modifies or is inconsistent with an earlier measure of protection issued by the court.[35]

However, while courts may assist in enforcing interim measures, there is no authority supporting the position that interim measures may be enforced in the same way as final awards or as court judgments. Notably, the Supreme Court has applied the New York Convention only to foreign arbitral awards, not to foreign interim measures. On the other hand, interim measures also cannot be considered as judgments, as they do not finally dispose of a dispute.[36]

Currently, there are no legal provisions or cases that identify the types of interim measures that courts will not enforce. Nevertheless, interim measures are likely to be refused enforcement if they are contrary to Philippine public policy.

---

[34] If the court finds that an interim measure should not be enforced under letter (b) above, it shall refer the matter back to the arbitral tribunal for appropriate determination. ADR Rules, Rule 5.11.

[35] ADR Rules, Rule 5.11.

[36] Interim measures are interlocutory because they deal with preliminary matters and the trial on the merits is yet to be held and the judgment rendered. The test to ascertain whether or not an order or a judgment is interlocutory or final is: does the order or judgment leave something to be done in the trial court with respect to the merits of the case? *See Pahila-Garrido v. Tortogo, et.al.*, G.R. No. 156358, 17 August 2011.

Finally, with respect to enforcement of interim measures, a distinction should be made between arbitrations conducted within and those conducted outside the Philippines. While interim measures issued in the Philippines may be enforced through the courts, the Philippine Supreme Court has yet to address the issue of whether interim measures issued in arbitrations outside the Philippines may be enforced in the Philippines by the courts.[37] Given that the New York Convention is only applied to the enforcement of foreign arbitral awards, and considering that interim measures may not be considered foreign judgments, it remains to be seen whether or not a Philippine court will enforce foreign interim measures.

---

[37] The Philippines has not adopted the 2006 Amendments to the UNCITRAL Model Law, which expressly allow the enforcement of foreign interim measures. Article 17H, 2006 UNCITRAL Model Law.

POLAND

Marcin Aslanowicz[1] and Sylwia Piotrowska[2]

A. LEGISLATION, TRENDS AND TENDENCIES

A.1 Sources of Arbitration Law in Poland

The main source of law in Poland regarding arbitration is the Civil Procedures Code ("CPC"), which dates back to 1964 and applies to both domestic and international arbitration. The CPC underwent a significant amendment in 2005, so that it now mirrors the UNCITRAL Model Law to a large extent. Arbitration issues are regulated in Part V of the CPC (Articles 1154 to 1217).

International conventions, in particular the New York Convention and the 1961 European Convention on International Commercial Arbitration, are other sources of arbitration law in Poland. Poland is also bound by agreements with numerous countries regarding access to justice and the protection of foreign investments that provide for the settlement of disputes by arbitration.

A.2 Arbitrability

According to Article 1157 of the CPC, unless a particular provision states otherwise, and except for child maintenance claims, parties may arbitrate any dispute regarding proprietary or

---

[1] Marcin Aslanowicz is a Partner in Baker & McKenzie's Warsaw office and heads the Litigation and Dispute Resolution Practice Group in Warsaw. Mr. Aslanowicz represents multinational and domestic clients in civil and commercial disputes before common courts and arbitral tribunals.

[2] Sylwia Piotrowska is an Senior Associate in Baker & McKenzie's Warsaw office and a member of the Firm's Global Dispute Resolution Practice Group.

non-proprietary rights that would otherwise be eligible for settlement in court. Arbitrators can hear a request for an order requiring performance or a dispute as to whether a legal relationship or right exists.

A.3   Arbitration Agreement

According to Article 1162(1) of the CPC, an arbitration agreement must made be in writing and signed by both parties in order to be enforceable. An oral arbitration agreement is not enforceable. An exchange of correspondence or other documents indicating the intent to be bound to arbitration may be sufficient to establish the requirement of the written form. However, an agreement on arbitration cannot be inferred through the performance of acts or a course of dealings. Where an arbitration agreement is lost, evidence may be introduced through the testimony of witnesses and the examination of the parties to prove its existence.

In the arbitration agreement, the parties must specify precisely the object of the dispute or the legal relationship giving rise to or which could give rise to the dispute that is to be the subject of the arbitration. An inequitable arbitration clause, in particular an arbitration clause that gives only one party the right to pursue a claim in arbitration, is unenforceable.

An arbitration clause contained in the articles of association or statutes of a commercial company relating to disputes arising from the company's internal relations is binding on the company and its shareholders. This also applies to the statutes of cooperatives and associations. Because of the specific nature of labor disputes, an arbitration clause applicable to that kind of dispute may only be entered into in writing once the dispute has arisen (See Article 1164 of the CPC).

Unless otherwise provided for, a power of attorney granted by a commercial entity to perform legal actions also includes the authorization to enter into an arbitration agreement with respect to disputes arising from that legal action.

A.4 Arbitrators

Article 1170 of the CPC provides that any individual having full capacity to perform legal acts may be an arbitrator, regardless of citizenship. Polish law only contains one restriction regarding the capacity to fulfill the function of arbitrator: according to Article 1170(2) of the CPC, a state judge cannot be an arbitrator. This rule does not apply to retired judges.

The parties may set out specific requirements as to the selection of the arbitrators or the chair in their arbitration agreement. Provisions of an agreement that grant a party disproportionate rights in the appointment of an arbitral tribunal are unenforceable. Unless the parties agree otherwise, the procedure for appointing arbitrators and the chair should comply with Article 1171 and the provisions that follow it.

The parties may define the procedure for excluding an arbitrator and may make a joint statement in writing at any time to dismiss any of the arbitrators. A state court may dismiss an arbitrator on the motion of either party if it is obvious that the arbitrator is not fulfilling his/her duties within the appropriate deadline or if he/she delays the performance of those activities without cause.

Arbitrators are entitled to compensation for their activities, as well as the reimbursement of expenses incurred in connection with the performance of those activities (Article 1179(1) of the CPC). The parties are jointly and severally liable for these costs. If the parties do not reach an agreement on the compensation of the arbitrators, this compensation will be set by a state court.

A.5 Jurisdiction of an Arbitral Tribunal

As in the case of the UNCITRAL Model Law, an arbitral tribunal may rule on its own jurisdiction, as well as on the existence, validity, or effectiveness of an arbitration clause (the so-called Kompetenz-Kompetenz principle). The invalidity or expiry of the underlying agreement containing the arbitration clause, however, will result in the invalidity or expiry of that clause.

In general, an objection regarding the jurisdiction of an arbitral tribunal should be made in the response to the statement of claim, and not later. An arbitral tribunal may rule on an objection as to its own jurisdiction in a separate ruling, against which an appeal may be filed with a state court.

Articles 1181 and 1182 award the right to an arbitral tribunal to grant conservatory measures (such as injunctive relief or the provision of security). According to Article 1181(3), such a decision is implemented after a state court has ordered its enforcement.

A.6 Proceedings before an Arbitral Tribunal

The essence of arbitration proceedings is contractual freedom, and therefore the parties may agree the procedure to be followed. Neither the parties nor the arbitral tribunal are bound by the judicial civil procedure. The arbitral tribunal adopts whichever procedure it considers appropriate, subject to certain mandatory provisions of the law. For example, the parties cannot exclude the right to petition a state court to overrule an arbitral award.

An arbitral tribunal may examine witnesses and experts and swear in witnesses, but may not use coercive measures (Article 1191(1) of the CPC). In proceedings before an arbitral tribunal, the parties should be granted equal rights. Each of the parties has the right to present and have its statements and related evidence heard (Article 1183).

A.7 Conclusion of Arbitral Proceedings

The arbitral tribunal issues an award after comprehensively examining the case. The award requires a majority, unless agreed otherwise by the parties (Article 1195(1) of the CPC). If it is impossible to achieve the required unanimity or majority of votes, the arbitration clause will be deemed unenforceable in such a respect. The award issued by the arbitral tribunal may be an award for a specific performance or one that determines the existence or form of legal relationships or rights. An arbitral tribunal may issue interim, partial or final awards.

The award should be issued in writing and signed by the arbitrators. When signing the award, the arbitrator who voted against the majority opinion may cast a *votum separatum*. A copy of the signed award should be made available to the parties to the proceedings.

Proceedings before an arbitral tribunal are completed upon a final award being issued. After the award is served to the parties, an *ad hoc* arbitral tribunal must submit the case files to a state court together with the original of the award and other documents relating to the case (Article 1204(1) of the CPC). Only permanent arbitration courts are released from this obligation. Permanent arbitration courts keep the case files in their own archives and are required to provide them to the state courts upon demand. The state court to which such documents are sent is the court that would have had jurisdiction over the case had the parties not agreed to arbitrate.

A.8 Appeals against Arbitration Awards

Standard grounds for appeal are not available for arbitral awards. Instead, under Article 1206(1) of the CPC, a party may demand that the arbitral award be overruled on the following grounds:

(a) there was no arbitration clause or if the arbitration clause was invalid or no longer enforceable;

(b) the party was not duly notified of the appointment of an arbitrator or of the proceedings before the arbitral tribunal or was otherwise prevented from defending its rights;

(c) the award of the arbitral tribunal applies to a dispute not covered by the arbitration clause or extends beyond the scope of such a clause;

(d) the requirements regarding the composition of the arbitral tribunal or the general rules applicable to procedures before an arbitral tribunal were not respected;

(e) the award is obtained as a result of a criminal act or the award was issued on the basis of a counterfeit or modified document; or

(f) a final judgment of a state court has already been issued in the same matter between the same parties.

In addition to the grounds listed above, which may be raised by a party to the proceedings, the state court considering a petition filed *ex officio* shall overrule an arbitral award if it ascertains that:

(a) the dispute is not arbitrable under Polish law; or

(b) the award of the arbitral tribunal is in conflict with the basic rules of the legal order in Poland (public policy clause).

Petitions for overruling an award must be filed with the state court within three months of the award being issued. A petition to overrule the award may be made outside the three-month limitation period in certain cases, for instance, if a party discovers there are grounds for overruling the arbitral award after the three-month limitation period has passed (e.g., if it discovers that a final judgment of a state court has already been issued in the same matter) but, in any event, a party cannot demand that the award be overruled after five years from the date on which it is issued. Unless otherwise agreed by the parties, overruling an arbitral award will not result in the termination of the arbitration clause.

A.9 Recognition and Enforcement of an Arbitral Award

Arbitral awards have the same legal force as verdicts of state courts upon recognition or enforcement by the state court. Those arbitral awards which do not require any performance by a party but, for example, only determine the validity of a legal obligation, must be recognized or acknowledged (as opposed to "enforced") by the court. All other arbitral awards (such as those requiring the payment of damages) must be enforced by the state court. The court will recognize or enforce an arbitral award on the motion of a party. Motions for the recognition of awards are reviewed in closed hearings. A state court can refuse to acknowledge an arbitral award *ex officio* or declare it (or the underlying agreement) enforceable in the event that:

(a) the provisions of Polish law provide that the dispute cannot be settled by an arbitral tribunal; or

(b) the acknowledgement or implementation of the award or the underlying agreement would be in conflict with the basic rules of the legal order in Poland (public policy clause).

There are certain differences in the CPC regarding the acknowledgement and enforceability of arbitral awards issued by a foreign arbitral tribunal. In such cases, the state court will adjudicate on the matter after conducting a hearing. Article 1215 §2 of the CPC provides the grounds on which the state court may, on the request of a party, refuse to recognize a foreign arbitral award or declare it enforceable. The reasons for refusal provided in these regulations are similar to the reasons provided in the UNCITRAL Model Law and the New York Convention on the recognition and enforcement of foreign arbitral awards.

B. CASES

The Polish Supreme Court/Court of Appeal and the Court of Arbitration at the Polish Chamber of Commerce passed several important rulings in 2009 and 2011 regarding arbitration.

In its ruling of January 28, 2011 (I CSK 231/10), the Supreme Court confirmed that it would only be possible to assess any possible breaches of the procedural regulations made by the Court of Arbitration after previously establishing that an appeal may be filed with the state court against the award issued in the proceedings in which these breaches allegedly took place.

In the judgment of the Court of Appeal dated November 10, 2011 (I ACz 1608/11, I ACz 1687/11), the court confirmed that, since it clearly arises from the wording of the settlement agreement that the previous agreement (which included an arbitration clause) had been terminated in whole and that the intention of the parties was to regulate all relationships arising from the earlier agreement, it cannot be accepted that the arbitration clause remained effective. This is because it can be accepted that since the parties did not re-introduce an arbitration clause into their settlement agreement, they agreed that any possible disputes would be settled by the state court.

In its award of July 30, 2009 (SA 128/08), the Court of Arbitration at the Polish Chamber of Commerce confirmed that the written form of the provision regarding the court should also include the name of the permanent arbitration court (or its equivalent description enabling the certain identification and designation of the particular permanent arbitration court), and not just the elements of the wording of the provision specified in Article 1161 § 1 of the CPC. Therefore, the provision of Article 1161 § 1 of the CPC does not constitute a statutory definition of the obligatory (minimum) scope of the wording of every arbitration clause from the point of view of the observance of its form, as specified by law.

C. THE GRANT AND ENFORCEMENT OF INTERIM MEASURES IN INTERNATIONAL ARBITRATION

C.1 Tribunal-Ordered Interim Measures

Prior to the 2005 amendment of the CPC, only the state courts could order interim measures securing claims pursued by a party to arbitration proceedings.

One significant change introduced by the 2005 amendment of the CPC was the adoption of Article 1181 of the CPC which provides that, unless the parties agree otherwise, the arbitral tribunal may decide to order an interim measure. According to Article 1181 § 1 of the CPC, unless the parties agree otherwise, the arbitral tribunal may, at the request of a party that has demonstrated the legitimacy of its claim, order such measures as it deems appropriate given the subject matter of the dispute.

Article 1181 of the CPC is a non-mandatory provision. The parties decide whether to empower the arbitral tribunal to grant interim measures. The parties may exclude this right of the arbitral tribunal, but they may also freely define the grounds for initiating proceedings to secure claims and how such proceedings are to be conducted. Unless the parties agree otherwise, one of the parties must file a request for an interim measure and must demonstrate the legitimacy of the claim it is pursuing. Demonstrating the legitimacy of the claim is therefore the only ground for the arbitrators to order interim measures.

As is the case with proceedings conducted before the state courts, the arbitral tribunal is not bound by the request of the parties and may refuse to order an interim measure.

The requirement of demonstrating legitimacy of the claim is connected with Article 730§ 1 of the CPC which regulates the granting of interim measures by the state courts. A party asking the state court to grant an interim measure is required to demonstrate that the party has legal standing and the claim is legitimate. The requirement to show the existence of legal standing is not repeated in Article 1181 of the CPC. However, academic legal writers and commentators take the view that the requirement that the requesting party have a legal interest should be a condition of eligibility to seek an interim measure.

The arbitral tribunal may grant an interim measure only against a party to the arbitration agreement, that is *inter partes*. Should an interim measure be requested against a third-party, it may be granted only by the state courts.

The arbitral tribunal orders appropriate forms of interim measure by a decision.

Article 1181 of the CPC does not impose any time limits within which a party may file a request for an interim measure. Hence, one has to assume that an interim measure may be ordered both before a statement of claim is filed with the arbitral tribunal (but after a request for arbitration has been filed) and during the arbitration proceedings. However, a request for an interim measure submitted before the appointment of the arbitral tribunal may not be examined until the tribunal is appointed.

The regulations relating to the granting of interim measures by arbitral tribunals prior to the initiation of arbitration do not fix (as is the case with the granting of such measures by the state courts) any time limit in which to start arbitration. In cases when interim measures are granted by the state courts prior to the initiation of arbitration, the state courts set a time limit for the requesting party in which to submit a statement of claim. If no arbitration is opened within such time limit, the interim measures terminate by the operation of law. However, it seems that considering the need to protect the interests of both parties to the arbitration and the ban on discrimination of parties to arbitration, the arbitral tribunal should also fix a time limit within which the parties should be required to initiate arbitration when it grants an interim measure prior to the initiation of arbitration.

C.2 Court-Ordered Interim Measures

The state courts are also empowered to grant measures securing claims that also may be sought before arbitral tribunals.

Since the amendment of the Civil Procedure Code in 2005, this right stems from two provisions of the Civil Procedure Code: Article 730, according to which interim measures may be sought in any civil-law case that is heard by the state courts or an arbitral tribunal, and Article 1166 § 1, according to which a referral of a dispute for resolution to an arbitral tribunal does not exclude the option to seek interim measures from the state courts.

In addition, Article 1181 of the CPC is non-mandatory (Article 1181 of the CPC provides "[u]nless the parties agreed otherwise..."), which means that it is up to the parties to decide whether the arbitral tribunal may grant interim measures.

It should be stressed that even if the parties agree to empower the arbitral tribunal to grant interim measures, the state court is still competent to grant interim measures. In theory, a request for an interim measure may be submitted concurrently to both forums. Practically speaking such a situation is possible if different types of interim measures are sought. The CPC does not require parties that have submitted a request for an interim measure to the state court to exhaust their remedies before the arbitral tribunal or vice versa. Earlier submission of a request to the arbitral tribunal (or to the state court) does not result in the case becoming pending before the state court (or the arbitral tribunal).

Since it is legally permitted to seek interim measures simultaneously before the state court and the arbitral tribunal, it is likely that each of these forums will issue a different order. This is because the state courts and the arbitral tribunals rely on different grounds to decide whether or not to grant an interim measure (as indicated in C.II above). In addition, each of these forums enjoys judicial independence.

It follows from the wording of Article 1181 § 1 of the CPC that parties may exclude the powers of the arbitral tribunal to decide whether they may grant orders securing claims. It is disputed whether party autonomy encompasses the ability to contractually exclude the powers of the state court in this respect. According to the prevailing views and opinions of academic writers and law commentators, Article 730 of the CPC, which empowers state courts to grant interim measures, is a mandatory provision, and therefore cannot be contractually excluded.

C.3 Enforcement of Interim Measures

According to Article 1181 § 3 of the CPC, an arbitral tribunal's decision to order interim measures is subject to enforcement once it is declared enforceable by the state court. When viewed in this context, one has to make a distinction between decisions to grant interim measures of arbitral tribunals in Poland and foreign arbitral tribunals.

The state court declares as enforceable a decision of the arbitral tribunal to grant an interim measure at the request of a party. If a decision to grant an interim measure is issued by a Polish arbitral tribunal, in principle, such decision is declared enforceable in a closed court session.

Article 1214 § 3 of the CPC specifies cases when the state courts may refuse to declare as enforceable an award of the arbitral tribunal. According to this article, the court shall refuse to recognise or shall refuse to declare as enforceable an award of the arbitral tribunal or a settlement concluded before the arbitral tribunal in the following cases:

1) the dispute is not arbitrable under Polish law,

2) the recognition or declaration of enforceability of the arbitral tribunal's award or of the settlement concluded before the arbitral tribunal would be in conflict with the basic rules of the legal order of the Republic of Poland (public policy clause).

The "basic rules of the legal order" are defined by academic law commentators as the set of fundamental (constitutional) rules and as the basic rules in force in specific areas of law. For example, the arbitral tribunal's decision to grant an interim measure which is aimed at satisfying the claim could be deemed contrary to the basic rules of the legal order. This is because one of the basic rules of any proceedings to secure claims before the state courts is the requirement that interim measures must not lead to a claim being satisfied.

Decisions to grant an interim measure, taken by foreign arbitral tribunals, are declared enforceable by the state court after a hearing. The state court may refuse to declare as enforceable the foreign arbitral tribunal's decision to grant an interim measure (save for the cases specified in Article 1214 § 3 of the CPC) also in the cases specified in Article 1215 § 2 of the CPC, that is when:

(a) there was no arbitration clause, the arbitration clause is invalid, ineffective or has become invalid according to the applicable law,

(b) a party was not duly informed of the appointment of an arbitrator or of the proceedings being conducted before the arbitral tribunal, or was otherwise deprived of the ability to defend its rights before the arbitral tribunal,

(c) the composition of the arbitral tribunal or the proceedings conducted before the arbitral tribunal were not in compliance with the agreement of the parties or—in the absence of such agreement—were not in compliance with the law of the country in which the proceedings were conducted before the arbitral tribunal.

C.3.1 Sanctions Applicable in Cases When Interim Measures are Enforced without Legitimate Reasons.

According to Article 1182 of the CPC, when it is obvious that the interim measure ordered by the arbitral tribunal has been used without legitimate reasons, the party in whose favor the measure has been used shall be liable for any resulting damage. A claim for reparation of damage also may be pursued during an action conducted before the arbitral tribunal.

The provision of Article 1182 is equivalent to the provision of Article 746 of the CPC, which applies in proceedings to secure claims conducted before the state courts. The cited provision regulates the liability of the party in whose favor the decision to grant an interim measure has been issued for damage caused by such measure.

To be able to claim damages, one has to demonstrate (i) that the interim measure was clearly used without legitimate reasons; (ii) the damage which occurred as a result of the enforcement of the decision to grant an interim measure; and (iii) the causal link between the decision and the damage.

Liability for damages rests on the individual in whose favor the interim measure has been granted. The provisions of the CPC do not regulate issues connected with arbitrators' liability for damages (if any).

Finally, Article 1182 of the CPC does not fix any time limit in which claims for reparation of damage may be raised; hence the general rules governing the statute of limitations apply.

RUSSIAN FEDERATION

Vladimir Khvalei[1] and Irina Varyushina[2]

A. LEGISLATION, TRENDS AND TENDENCIES

Amendments to the Russian law governing international commercial arbitration[3] (also the "ICA Law") passed their first reading in the State Duma (the lower chamber of Russian legislature) on 25 January 2012. These amendments aim at incorporating the changes made to the UNCITRAL Model Law in 2006 and mainly concern issues of the arbitration agreement and interim measures.

B. CASES

B.1 *Novolipetsk Steel OJSC v. Maksimov Nikolay Victorovich*[4]

Novolipetsk Steel OJSC ("NLMK") and Mr. Maksimov were parties to a Share Purchase Agreement dated 22 November 2007 (the "SPA") under which Mr. Maksimov was to transfer ownership of 50% plus one share of OJSC "Maxi-Group" to NLMK against payment of the purchase price. The SPA

---

[1] Vladimir Khvalei is a Partner in Baker & McKenzie's Moscow office and heads its CIS Dispute Resolution Practice Group. He is also a steering committee member of the Firm's International Arbitration Practice Group. Mr. Khvalei serves as a Vice President of the ICC International Court of Arbitration and is included in the list of arbitrators of the arbitration institutions in Austria, Russia, Belarus and Kazakhstan and Dubai.

[2] Irina Varyushina is a Professional Support Lawyer in Baker & McKenzie's Moscow office.

[3] Russian Federation Law of 7 July 1993 N 5338-1 "On International Commercial Arbitration."

[4] Case A40-35844/11-69-311.

provided for arbitration under the Rules of the International Commercial Arbitration Court at the Russian Chamber of Commerce and Industry (the "ICAC"). Mr. Maksimov was successful in this arbitration claiming the recovery of the purchase price plus interest. NLMK challenged the award, alleging, *inter alia*, violation of the public order of the Russian Federation and non-arbitrability of the dispute resolved by the ICAC.

Violation of public order

The courts set aside the award,[5] finding that it violated public order in that it violated the fundamental principles of Russian law, namely the procedural principles of independence and impartiality of the court and the principle of legality.

The principles of independence and impartiality of the court were breached as two of the arbitrators failed to disclose in the course of arbitration the fact that they were employed by the same university as Mr. Maksimov's experts, despite an explicit obligation to do so imposed by the ICA Law,[6] the ICAC Rules and the Rules of Impartiality and Independence of Arbitrators.[7] The courts dismissed the arguments of Mr. Maksimov that NLMK had prior knowledge of the facts to be disclosed, and failed to file a challenge within the time limits provided by the ICAC Rules and that there were no grounds for granting the challenge.

---

[5]   Ruling of Moscow City Arbitrazh Court of 28 June 2011; Resolution of the Federal Arbitrazh Court of the Moscow Circuit of 10 October 2011.

[6]   Article 12 of the ICA Law.

[7]   These rules were approved by Order #39 of the President of the RF Chamber of Commerce and Industry of 27 August 2010 and recommended for use by, *inter alia*, the Presidium of the ICAC. The rules, *inter alia*, impose an obligation to disclose the fact of an arbitrator, a party's representative, expert or consultant of a party to the arbitral proceedings, being employed by one and the same organization.

B. Cases

The cassation court stated that:

> It is the fact of the arbitrators' failure to perform the legal
> duty of disclosing circumstances that could give rise to
> justifiable doubts, that is the breach of the judicial principle
> of impartiality and independence. Such violation of the law
> by arbitrators is irreversible and derogates from the legality
> of an arbitral award.[8]

The courts also reasoned that by agreeing to ICAC arbitration the
parties had agreed on the procedure under the ICAC Rules,
including the standards for constituting the tribunal and the
grounds for challenging arbitrators. The breach of the duty of
disclosure thus resulted in the arbitral procedure being
inconsistent with the agreement of the parties, which is a
separate reason for setting aside the award under the ICA Law.[9]

A violation was also found in the failure of the arbitral tribunal
to apply the mandatory Russian Federation civil law rules on
determination of a purchase price. The court reasoned that the
arbitral tribunal breached this principle when instead of
determining the price based on the contract terms, and failing
that, on the price of similar goods in comparable circumstances,
it calculated the price as the sum of two numbers put forward by
the parties divided by two. The cassation court upheld the
conclusions of the lower court and dismissed the appeal based on
allegations that the trial court entered into the merits of the
dispute. The cassation court expressly distinguished between
failure to apply specific substantive law rules and compliance of
tribunals with the fundamental principles of the law that
constitute public order. As these principles were breached by the

---

[8]　Resolution of the Federal Arbitrazh Court of the Moscow Circuit dated 10
　　October 2011.

[9]　Article 34(2) of the ICA Law.

arbitral tribunal in determining the price of the transaction, the court found it to be in violation of public order.

Non-arbitrability of corporate disputes

The courts also held that the dispute in question (transfer of ownership of shares) was a non-arbitrable corporate dispute. The courts relied on provisions[10] of the Code of Arbitrazh Procedure of the Russian Federation (also the "CAP") establishing the special jurisdiction of state arbitrazh (commercial) courts over corporate disputes. The special jurisdiction, in the courts' view, was justified due to the special registration procedures for the ownership, transfer and issuance of shares, as well as the involvement of the issues of establishment, participation and management of a Russian legal entity.

The court drew a distinction in the case between the private law nature of the part of the transaction concerning the sale of shares, and the public law nature of the remaining part that concerned issues of the ownership to the shares, observance of specific pre-sale conditions that involved corporate management issues and issuance of additional shares. Having established that these two parts of the transaction could not be separated, the court concluded that the dispute in question could not be resolved by arbitration:

> Taking into account the mixed nature of the agreement of 22.11.2007 and the complex nature of transaction B provided for in the agreement, it is impossible to separate the private issue of payment of the share price only without determining whether preliminary conditions of the transaction have been complied with, conducting an additional share issuance, complying with the payment terms and considering the issue of ownership to such shares. Therefore, it is improper to speak of the separability of a private law arbitrable dispute

---

[10]   Article 33 of the CAP; Article 225(1) of the CAP.

B. Cases

regarding the payment for the shares from the public law non-arbitrable disputes regarding the transfer of ownership of the shares as a result of performing the set of conditions of transaction B regarding corporate management.

The panel of judges of the RF Supreme Arbitrazh Court refused to transfer the case for supervisory review, thus implicitly agreeing with the conclusions of the lower courts.[11]

These decisions caused a lot of concern in the Russian legal community, because in essence the courts found a dispute arising out of a contract for the sale of shares to be non-arbitrable as they qualified it as a corporate dispute. The legal basis for such conclusions is pretty vague, because the courts relied on the provisions of the CAP, which specifically state that corporate disputes fall within the exclusive jurisdiction of state arbitrazh courts.

However, these provisions of the CAP were aimed at differentiating between disputes falling under the jurisdiction of state arbitrazh (commercial) courts and those that were to be referred to the state courts of general jurisdiction. A similar interpretational issue related to the arbitrability of real estate disputes was finally resolved last year by the Russian Federation Constitutional Court in favor of arbitrability.

Nonetheless, for some reason the Constitutional Court of the Russian Federation decided not to intervene in the Maximov case and not to express its view on the arbitrability of corporate disputes.[12] Mr. Maksimov argued, inter alia, that the provisions

---

[11] Ruling of the Supreme Arbitrazh Court of the Russian Federation VAS-15384/11 of 30 January 2012.

[12] *See* RF Constitutional Court Ruling N 1804-O-O of 21 December 2011 (also the "First Ruling") and RF Constitutional Court Ruling N 1488-O of 17 July 2012 (also the "Second Ruling").

of the CAP establishing the special jurisdiction of arbitrazh courts over corporate disputes, as applied in this particular case, infringe upon his constitutional rights by excluding corporate disputes related to the transfer of ownership of shares from the possibility of referring such disputes to arbitration.

The Constitutional Court of the Russian Federation refused to accept this case for consideration stating that the CAP provisions cited above are aimed at establishing a procedure whereby violated rights can be judicially protected and thus cannot infringe the applicant's constitutional rights in the particular case.

Therefore, the Constitutional Court did not take a clear position with regard to the arbitrability of corporate disputes. Given the reluctance of the Supreme Arbitrazh Court to clearly state its position with regard to the arbitrability of corporate disputes, the issue remains open.

B.2 *Russian Telephone Company v. Sony Ericsson Mobile Communications Rus LLC (RF)*[13]

This case deals with the interpretation by Russian courts of asymmetric dispute resolution clauses. Russian Telephone Company ("RTC") and Sony Ericsson Mobile Communications Rus LLC ("Sony Ericsson") were parties to a general agreement containing a clause that referred any dispute in connection with the agreement to arbitration in London under the ICC Rules. However, Sony Ericsson (and only it) was entitled to submit disputes for recovery of funds owed to it by RTC to a competent court.

---

[13]   Case A40-49223/2011.

B. Cases

RTC filed a claim for specific performance with the Moscow City Arbitrazh Court despite the arbitration agreement, arguing that the arbitration agreement could not be performed as the parties had failed to agree on the rules to govern the arbitration proceedings. The trial court dismissed the case due to the existence of a valid arbitration agreement and the second and third level courts supported this view.[14] However, the Supreme Arbitrazh Court reversed the decisions of the lower courts as it found the arbitration agreement invalid as breaching the principle of procedural equality of the parties.[15]

This fundamental procedural principle means that both sides must have equal procedural rights, including equal opportunities to state their case and equal access to any procedural remedies. This serves as a guarantee of fair trial and effective judicial protection. The court concluded that a dispute resolution clause cannot provide an option of referring disputes to a competent court for one party only. Such agreement, if made, would be invalid as violating the balance of the parties' rights. At the same time, interestingly, the court added that the party affected by such a clause would be entitled to refer to the competent court as well, thus eliminating the inequality of procedural rights.

The Supreme Arbitrazh Court reversed the lower courts' acts and sent the case for re-trial to the first level court, thus leading to speculation as to the effect it intended to give to the dispute resolution provisions of the general agreement. Based on the reasoning of the Supreme Arbitrazh Court, one can distinguish the following options: (1) invalidation of the clause as a whole as

---

[14] *See* Ruling of Moscow City Arbitrazh Court of 08 July 2011; Resolution of the Ninth Arbitrazh Court of Appeal of 14 September 2011; Resolution of the Federal Arbirazh Court of Moscow Circuit of 05 December 2011.

[15] Resolution of the Supreme Arbitrazh Court of the Russian Federation VAS-1831/12 of 19 June 2012.

violating the principle of equality of the parties; (2) invalidating the unilateral option to refer to a competent court; (3) eliminating the inequality by extending the unilaterally granted right to the other party.

The first possibility seems a logical implication of the Supreme Arbitrazh Court's actions of reversing the lower court acts and sending the case for retrial to the first level court of competent jurisdiction. Moreover, it is clearly in line with the explicit statements the court made in its resolution regarding the invalidity of unilateral clauses that violate fundamental principles of the law. The second possibility is unlikely, as in this case the court should have terminated proceedings giving full effect to the valid part of the dispute resolution clause (i.e., the arbitration agreement, as this part does not result in unequal procedural rights).

The third possibility was expressly stated in the Resolution of the Supreme Arbitrazh Court. Literally applying the statements made by the Supreme Arbitrazh Court, one would have to conclude that the party that does not have a right to apply to a court should also have such a right. In order to give effect to this statement, the court should have modified and expanded the agreement of the parties, which is possible only in very limited cases under Russian law.

Therefore, taking into account both the conclusions of the Supreme Arbitrazh Court and its actions in the case, it is difficult to predict the position of the court with regard to unilateral dispute resolution's clauses. At the same time, the first option has more chance of being implemented by lower courts. However, this option is also the most dangerous, because it provides the basis for setting aside arbitral awards issued in the Russian Federation and refusing recognition and enforcement of arbitral awards issued in Russia and abroad when an asymmetrical dispute resolution clause is involved.

Considering also that the Resolution of the Russian Federation Supreme Arbitrazh Court specifically stated that previous court decisions in other cases could be reconsidered based on new circumstances, the implications of this position could adversely affect the development of arbitration in Russia.

B.3 *Kubik LLC v. Regus Business Center Metropolis LLC*[16]

Kubik LLC ("Kubik") and Regus Business Center Metropolis LLC ("Regus") agreed in a preliminary lease agreement on submitting all disputes the parties fail to settle amicably to be finally resolved in accordance with the Rules of the ICAC,[17] with such rules incorporated into the clause by reference; the tribunal to consist of three arbitrators, each party appointing one arbitrator and the two arbitrators appointing the chairman of the tribunal.[18] Regus filed for arbitration at the ICAC, which granted

---

[16]   Cases A40-21119/11-68-183 and A40-29251/11-68-256 (consolidated).

[17]   International Commercial Arbitration Court at the Russian Chamber of Commerce and Industry.

[18]   *Note:* this wording of the clause was analyzed during the first round of the court review. The wording of the entire clause (as specified in Ruling of Moscow City Arbitrazh Court during the second round of the court review is as follows:

> All disputes arising out this agreement or in connection with it, are to be resolved by the parties via negotiations. If the parties fail to settle the dispute amicably within ten (10) days after one party notifies the other party in writing of the existence of a dispute, any such dispute, disagreement or claim arising out of this agreement or in connection with it, including any issue concerning the existence, validity or termination thereof are submitted to a commercial court and are finally resolved by it in accordance with the Rules of the International Commercial Arbitration Court at the Chamber of Commerce and Industry of the Russian Federation, and such Rules are considered to be incorporated into this clause. The tribunal shall consist of three arbitrators. Each party appoints one arbitrator and the two arbitrators so appointed appoint the third arbitrator, who will act as chairman. The place of the arbitration proceedings is Moscow, the language of the arbitration proceedings is English.

its claims against Kubik and dismissed Kubik's counterclaims. Regus filed an application with Moscow City Arbitrazh Court for a writ of execution, while Kubik filed for setting aside the ICAC award based, *inter alia*, on the absence of an agreement to arbitrate the dispute at the ICAC.

The first level court set aside the ICAC award finding that no agreement to arbitrate at the ICAC had been reached by the parties. The court considered the reference to the ICAC Rules in the clause to be insufficient to conclude on the existence of such an agreement. Rather, in the court's view, by incorporating the ICAC Rules into the clause, the parties had agreed only on the procedure for constituting the arbitration court. Thus, the court concluded the parties had reached an agreement to resolve the dispute in accordance with the ICAC Rules, as opposed to resolving it at the ICAC.[19]

The Cassation court sent the case for retrial on formal grounds, finding that the first level court failed to specify on which of the grounds stipulated in the ICA Law[20] it had set aside the award. Upon the second round of review the first level court set aside the award on the grounds that the composition of the court was not in accordance with the agreement of the parties.[21] This time, as instructed by the cassation court, the trial court analyzed in closer detail the correctness of the translation into Russian of the dispute resolution provisions (the English wording of the parties' agreement prevailing over Russian). It found that in English the clause provided for submitting the dispute to "a commercial court" to be resolved thereby in accordance with the ICAC Rules. The use of the indefinite article led the court to conclude

---

[19]   Ruling of Moscow City Arbitrazh Court of 31 May 2011.

[20]   Article 34(2)(1).

[21]   Ruling of Moscow City Arbitrazh Court of 11 January 2012.

that the parties meant not any particular commercial court (which would have called for a definite article) but a type of court (commercial court versus court of general jurisdiction, military court etc.).

Interestingly, this prompted the court to conclude that the arbitration agreement was invalid for failing to name the particular court that was to resolve the dispute. The cassation court in upholding the ruling, corrected the trial court in this regard, referring to Article 4 of the European Convention on International Commercial Arbitration that enables the parties to submit their dispute to *ad hoc* arbitration and establish in this case the rules of the procedure to be followed by arbitrators.[22] The court added that the ICAC Rules do not expressly prohibit their use in *ad hoc* arbitration proceedings.

The Supreme Arbitrazh Court agreed with the lower courts' findings that the parties did not specify the ICAC as the place for considering the dispute, and the reference to the ICAC Rules was not sufficient for the ICAC to have jurisdiction. It refused to submit the case for supervisory review to its Presidium.[23]

C. THE GRANT AND ENFORCEMENT OF INTERIM MEASURES IN INTERNATIONAL ARBITRATION

C.1 Tribunal-Ordered Interim Measures

The ICA Law does not specify the types of interim measures that can be ordered by the arbitral tribunal. According to Article 17 of the ICA Law (following the wording of the 1985 UNCITRAL Model Law) the tribunal has discretion to order the measures

---

[22] Resolution of the Federal Court of Moscow Circuit of 13 March 2012.

[23] Ruling of the Supreme Arbitrazh Court of the Russian Federation #VAS-8147/12 of 09 July 2012.

with regard to the subject-matter of the dispute that it considers to be necessary. Thus, there are no express limitations on the power of the arbitral tribunal to order interim measures.

The ICA Law is also silent with regard to the tests to be met by a party requesting party interim measures, leaving it to the discretion of the tribunal. However, the amendments to the ICA Law awaiting approval of the Russian legislature do contain such provisions. Thus, according to the bill, the party requesting an interim measure [other than an order to preserve evidence] must satisfy the arbitral tribunal that failure to grant the measures will result in harm to the requesting party that cannot be adequately repaired by an award of damages, and that such harm substantially outweighs the harm likely to be inflicted on the party against whom the measure is directed. Therefore, the bill incorporates two of the three conditions for granting interim measures stipulated in the UNCITRAL Model Law (as amended in 2006).

There are no provisions in the law dealing with an emergency arbitrator.

C.2   Court-Ordered Interim Measures

According to Article 9 of the ICA Law, the parties to arbitration proceedings may request interim measures from the court before the commencement of arbitration proceedings, as well as during the course of arbitration. There is no requirement to approach the arbitral tribunal on the issue first. However, if the tribunal has ordered interim measures and the party complied with them, the court may consider such measures to be sufficient and refuse to order further interim measures.[24]

---

[24]   *See* ¶24 of Information Letter of the Presidium of Supreme Arbitrazh Court #78 of 07 July 2004 "Digest of Arbitrazh Court Case Law on the Application of Preliminary Interim Measures."

C. The Grant and Enforcement of Interim Measures in International Arbitration

The procedure and conditions for granting interim measures and the types of interim measures available are set out in the CAP.

An application for interim measures in support of arbitration proceedings, if filed by a party to those arbitration proceedings, must be accompanied by a copy of the statement of claim with evidence that it was duly filed and certified by the head of the permanent arbitration institution (in the case of arbitration under the rules of such arbitration institution) or a notarized copy of such statement of claim or a duly certified copy of the corresponding arbitration agreement (in the case of *ad hoc* arbitration). An application for preliminary interim measures may be filed even before the commencement of arbitration proceedings.[25] However, it will only be considered by the court if accompanied by the confirmation of counter-security for the equivalent amount, provided by the applicant. Once the court awards preliminary interim measures, the applicant has 15 days to file a statement of claim.

The court must consider an application for interim measures on the day following the date of filing the application. The court takes a decision on interim measures by issuing a court ruling to be sent to the parties on the day following its issuance. The decision is taken *ex parte* by the same judge who is to hear the case.

Interim measures may include, among others:

(1) attachment of funds or other assets of the respondent and held by the respondent or another party;

(2) a prohibition on the respondent or another party committing certain acts relating to the subject matter of the action;

---

[25]   Article 99 of the CAP.

(3) an order that the respondent must commit certain acts to prevent the spoilage or other deterioration of an asset in dispute;

(4) an order for the transfer of assets in dispute to the claimant or other party for storage;

(5) a stay of execution under a writ of execution or other document challenged by the claimant that enables uncontested recovery; and

(6) the suspension of the sale of assets in an action to have an attachment of assets lifted.

The list of interim measures is not exhaustive, and the court may take other measures, as well as several of them. A court may, on its own initiative, order additional interim measures be taken when granting an application for interim measures.

It should be noted that in practice, when a judge hears an application for preliminary relief, in addition to the formal grounds on which such application may be granted, he/she also takes into account the extent to which the claims in the statement of claim are well-founded (by reference to the evidence attached to the case file at the date of hearing the application).

According to an imperative CAP provision where security measures are applied for, they may not be denied if the applicant provides counter-security.[26] At the same time, this provision should not be interpreted strictly to mean that in such cases security measures will be granted automatically, even when no grounds for granting the measures have been established.

Security measures may be granted even if no counter-security is provided by the applicant. However, the court may instruct the

---

[26]   Article 93(4) of the CAP.

claimant to provide counter-security for any damage that may be caused to the respondent by security measures (usually by a bank deposit or a bank guarantee). The amount of such counter-security may be fixed within the total amount of the claimant's claims as stated in its statement of claim including accrued interest thereon. The amount of counter-security may not be less than one-half of the total amount of the claim.

Counter-security may also be provided by a respondent in lieu of measures to secure an action, if the action is for the recovery of money, by transferring funds in the amount of the claim to the account of the court.

The court may replace one interim measure with another one upon an application by the respondent. Although there are no restrictions in the CAP as to the types of interim measures that can be ordered by state courts, as a matter of practice, the courts in the Russian Federation do not grant anti-suit injunctions, as there is no tradition in Russian procedure of intervening in proceedings of other courts.

When a party files a claim with a court in breach of the arbitration agreement, the court must leave the claim without consideration, unless it finds that the arbitration agreement is invalid, or has become inoperative and incapable of being performed and the other party has filed the relevant objection before its first submission on the merits.[27]

As Article 9 of the ICA Law, dealing with the power of the court to order interim measures, also applies to international arbitration proceedings seated abroad, the court can also order interim measures in aid of foreign arbitrations. Such measures were granted in a recent case in support of an ICC arbitration in

---

[27] Article 148(1)(5) of the CAP.

London.[28] Nevertheless, case law on the granting of such measures is scarce.

C.3 Enforcement of Interim Measures

Interim measures ordered by a state court are enforceable through the court bailiff with sanctions stipulated in case of non-compliance. However, in practice, non-compliance is not often sanctioned by the law enforcement agencies. Nevertheless, the attachment of monetary funds, immovable property or shares can be effective, as this is normally done by notifying banks, the registry of property or shares of such restrictions. Finally, Russian law does not contain provisions allowing interim measures taken by tribunals to be enforceable through the system of state courts as final awards.

---

[28] Resolution of the Presidium of the Supreme Arbitrazh Court of the Russian Federation #17095/09 of 20 April 2010.

SINGAPORE

Gerald Kuppusamy[1] and Jennifer Fong[2]

A. LEGISLATION, TRENDS AND TENDENCIES

A.1 Amendments to the International Arbitration Act

The International Arbitration Act[3] ("IAA") provides the legislative framework that governs the conduct of international arbitrations in Singapore. On 1 June 2012, amendments to the IAA came into effect in order to:

(a) clarify that awards and orders given by emergency arbitrators are enforceable by the High Court;

(b) clarify that certain orders and directions of interim measures made by arbitral tribunals in arbitrations outside Singapore are enforceable by the High Court;

(c) permit an appeal to the High Court and the Court of Appeal on a tribunal's ruling that it does not have jurisdiction;

(d) expand an arbitral tribunal's powers to award interest; and

(e) expand the definition of "arbitration agreement" by providing that the requirement that it "shall be in writing" is met if "its content is recorded in any form," however the arbitration agreement was concluded.

---

[1]   Gerald Kuppusamy is a Senior Legal Consultant in Baker & McKenzie, Wong & Leow in Singapore. He advises clients on cross-border litigation and international arbitration in a wide variety of commercial disputes, and is a Fellow of both the Chartered Institute of Arbitrators and the Singapore Institute of Arbitrators.

[2]   Jennifer Fong is an Associate in the Dispute Resolution Group of Baker & McKenzie, Wong & Leow in Singapore.

[3]   Cap 143A, 2002 Rev Ed.

The amendments concerning emergency arbitrators and interim measures are the most noteworthy. The rules of many arbitral institutions provide for appointment of an emergency arbitrator, prior to the appointment of an arbitral tribunal, with the power to order or award interim relief, such as an interim injunction.[4] Uncertainty existed as to the enforceability of an emergency arbitrator's orders and awards because it was unclear whether an emergency arbitrator was an "arbitral tribunal" as defined in the IAA, and whether an emergency arbitrator's order or "award" was enforceable, since the IAA defines an award as "a decision . . . on the substance of the dispute and includes any interim, interlocutory, or partial award but excludes any orders or directions made under section 12." The excluded Section 12 provides, among other things, for an arbitral tribunal's power to make orders or give directions for various interim measures, including interim injunctions. These uncertainties are, for the most part, removed by the amendments.

An amendment to the definition of "arbitral tribunal" removes uncertainty by expressly extending the definition to include emergency arbitrators. Also revised is the definition of "arbitral award" in the section of the IAA that governs the recognition and enforcement of awards in arbitrations made outside Singapore.[5] This provides that certain interim orders or directions of arbitral tribunals are included in the definition of arbitral award. Orders for security for costs and discovery of documents are not included in the definition of an arbitral award, as they have

---

4   *See, e.g.,* SIAC Rules 2010 Rule 26 and Schedule 1; ICC Rules 2012 Article 29 and Appendix V; ICDR Rules Article 37; SCC Rules Article 32 and Appendix II; Swiss Rules of International Arbitration Article 43.

5   Part III; *see* Section 27(1).

similarly been excluded from the court's powers to order interim measures in aid of arbitration.[6]

Uncertainty remains as to the enforceability outside Singapore of orders and awards by emergency arbitrators and awards for interim measures (whether by an emergency arbitrator or other tribunal). But, in Singapore, the amendments provide for the enforceability of such orders.

B. CASES

We set out below an overview of noteworthy decisions of the Singapore courts in 2012.

B.1 Lack of Jurisdiction May Not Be Invoked as Grounds for Resisting Enforcement of a Singapore Award after the Time Limits in Articles 16 and 34 of the Model Law

In *Astro Nusantra International BV v. PT Ayunda Prima Mitra* [2012] SGHC 212, the Singapore High Court held that lack of jurisdiction could not be invoked as a ground for resisting enforcement of an award made by a tribunal seated in Singapore

---

[6] It is debatable whether security for costs and discovery orders may properly be considered interim measures, but for present purposes, they are taken to be interim measures. When IAA Section 12A(2) was introduced by way of amendment to the IAA in 2009, the Minister for Law in describing the powers of the court stated:

> The scope of the new powers is limited to interim measures in support of arbitration, for example, interim injunctions to preserve assets. They do not extend to procedural or evidential matters dealing with the actual conduct of the arbitration itself—like discovery, interrogatories or security for costs. These procedural matters fall within the province of the arbitral tribunal and must be decided by the tribunal itself. This is similar to the position taken in the UK Arbitration Act.

Singapore Parliamentary Debates, Official Report (19 October 2009) vol. 86 at col 1628.

(a "Singapore Award") after the timelines for challenges under Articles 16 and 34 of the Model Law have expired. In this case, the respondents in the arbitration (including non-parties to the disputed contract) unsuccessfully challenged the jurisdiction of the tribunal to join them as parties to the arbitration. However, they did not challenge the tribunal's decision on jurisdiction in the manner prescribed by Article 16(3) of the Model Law—by seeking a review from the High Court within 30 days of receipt of notice of the ruling that the tribunal has jurisdiction. Instead, the respondents—under protest—proceeded to defend the merits of the arbitration, and even lodged a counterclaim. The respondents were unsuccessful, but did not take any steps to set aside awards on the merits against them until long after the time limit for doing so had elapsed,[7] presumably because they did not have any assets in Singapore at the time.

The High Court reasoned that Section 19, read with Section 19B of the IAA, renders an arbitral award final and binding and enforceable with leave of court, subject only to the grounds within the IAA and the Model Law for setting aside or refusing recognition of an award, which are prescribed in Article 34 of the Model Law and Section 24 of the IAA.[8] The court held that there was no "hook" in the statutory provisions for the inclusion of grounds prescribed in Article 34 of the Model Law after they are time-barred. With reference to the statutory schemes of other

---

[7] Article 34(3) of the Model Law provides that an application for setting aside an award may not be made after three months have elapsed from the date on which the party making the application had received the award, or if a request for correction or interpretation is made, from the date on which that request had been disposed of by the tribunal.

[8] Section 24 of the IAA adds to the grounds familiar under the New York Convention, that an award may be set aside if the award was induced or affected by fraud or corruption, or a breach of natural justice occurred in connection with the award by which the rights of any party have been prejudiced.

B. Cases

Model Law jurisdictions (Germany and Quebec),the court concluded that the non-adoption of Articles 35 and 36 of the Model Law meant there are no other grounds remaining to challenge the enforcement of an award after the time limit in Article 34.

More specifically, the High Court held that Article 16 of the Model Law provides the exclusive route to challenge a tribunal's award on jurisdiction, and that it makes a "mockery of the finality and effectiveness of arbitral awards on jurisdiction" if a party can revive its jurisdictional challenge at a later stage should it prove to be unsuccessful in the arbitration.[9] Accordingly, "[t]here is no avenue under the Model Law to participate in a hearing on the merits under protest without having lodged an appeal under Article 16(3) if a party wishes to properly and effectively retain its right to raise an objection to the tribunal's jurisdiction."

This decision, from which an appeal is expected, has significant implications for a party that has lost a preliminary challenge to jurisdiction. Prior to this decision, some authors took the view that an unsuccessful party had the option to resist enforcement when enforcement proceedings were brought, instead of applying to set aside the award on jurisdiction.

B.2   Award Will Be Set Aside for Breach of Natural Justice if Material Excluded Could Reasonably Have Made a Difference

In *LW Infrastructure Pte Ltd. v. Lim Chin San Contractors Pte Ltd.* [2012] SGCA 57, Singapore's apex court set aside an additional award worth approximately SGD274,000 in pre-award interest against LW Infrastructure Pte Ltd ("LW") on the basis that there had been a breach of natural justice. The annulled

---

[9]   *Astro Nusantra International BV v. PT Ayunda Prima Mitra* [2012] SGHC 212 at [147].

additional award was made by the arbitrator without granting a pre-award interest and without hearing further submissions from the parties.

The Court of Appeal held that the test for setting aside an award for breach of natural justice is whether the material that had not been placed before the arbitrator because of the breach of natural justice "could reasonably have made a difference; rather than whether it would necessarily have done so." The court held that the failure to hear further submissions on the issue of whether or not an additional award was to be issued, and among other things, the rate and amount of interest, was a breach of natural justice that resulted in real prejudice to LW.

B.2.1 Background

The sole arbitrator had granted post-award interest but not pre-award interest in his award. Nearly four weeks after the award was issued, Lim Chin San's solicitors wrote to request an additional award for "pre-award interest."

Three days later, the arbitrator issued an additional award of SGD274,114.61 covering 13 January 2003 to the date of his award against LW. When LW's solicitors wrote to protest, stating that they had been intending to write to the arbitrator that very day objecting to Lim Chin San's request, the arbitrator replied in writing that he had waited for three days and since there had been no objection from the plaintiff, he had proceeded to deal with the application.

B.2.2 The court's decision

Although this arbitration was governed by the Arbitration Act (the "AA"),[10] Singapore's legislative framework for domestic

---

[10]   Cap 10, 2002 Rev Ed

B. Cases

arbitration, this decision is equally applicable to arbitrations governed by the IAA because the court relied on the legislative intention that the two acts should be "broadly consistent," and relied on authorities interpreting identical language in the IAA and the UNCITRAL Model Law to interpret the AA.

First, the court rejected the argument that the additional award should be declared a nullity, rather than set aside, under the court's inherent jurisdiction to interfere in arbitral proceedings. The court emphasized that, in situations expressly regulated by the IAA, it would not interfere with an arbitral award except where provided by the IAA. Having regard to the need for a broadly consistent approach in interpreting the AA and the IAA, the same reasoning applies to the AA.

In this case, sub-section 48(1)(a)(v) and 48(1)(a)(vii) of the AA expressly provided that the court may set aside an award if the arbitral procedure was not in accordance with the agreement of the parties or if there was a breach of rules of natural justice.

Second, the Singapore Court of Appeal refined the test for setting aside an award due to a breach of natural justice, rejecting the argument that an application to set aside an award is bound to fail if there is a possibility that the same result might have been reached even if the breach of natural justice had not occurred.

In an earlier decision, the Court of Appeal had stressed that the principal requirement was the "demonstration that there has been some actual or real prejudice caused by the alleged breach." In this decision, the court explained that if a court must be satisfied that a different result would have been reached, it would have to put itself in the position of the arbitrator and consider the merits with the benefit of materials that had not been placed before the arbitrator. This was not the court's role.

Thus, "the real inquiry is whether the breach of natural justice was merely technical and inconsequential or whether as a result of the breach the arbitrator was denied the benefit of arguments or evidence that had a real as opposed to a fanciful chance of making a difference to his deliberations . . . [or] whether the material could reasonably have made a difference . . . rather than whether it would necessarily have done so."

On the facts, the court considered that the arbitrator breached the rules of natural justice by failing to give the parties an opportunity to be heard on:

(a) whether the additional award should or should not be made, i.e., whether section 43(4) of the AA (empowering the tribunal to make an additional award as to claims presented during the arbitrations but omitted from the award) could be invoked. In particular, the court considered that LW's intended argument, that the original award had impliedly rejected the claim of pre-award interest by only awarding post-award interest could have reasonably made a difference to the outcome of the case; and

(b) the rate of interest, the date from which interest should accrue, the amount on which interest would be levied, as well as whether or not there was a reasonable basis for him to adopt a different approach in the additional award towards pre-award interest, as opposed to post-award interest. In this respect, the Court of Appeal noted that LW had submitted that pre-award interest should have been reduced as the defendant had used inordinate delay in prosecuting the arbitration.

Interestingly, the court rejected the argument that LW was prejudiced because it did not have a chance to argue that Lim Chin San had, by claiming "interest," not claimed "pre-award interest." The court determined that this argument could not reasonably have made a difference.

On the facts, the Singapore Court of Appeal found that prejudice had been caused by the breach of natural justice and set aside the award. This case illustrates that Singapore courts can and will control and supervise the integrity of the arbitration process, while not interfering in the process by substituting their views on the merits over those of the arbitrator.

B.3 The Role of Pleadings in Arbitration

In *PT Prima International Development v. Kempinski Hotels SA*,[11] Singapore's Court of Appeal reinstated awards set aside on the grounds that the arbitrator decided issues that had not been formally pleaded, and therefore, were beyond the scope of submission to arbitration. The decision gives important guidance on the role and rules of pleadings in arbitration. In the court's view the crucial point was whether the un-pleaded issue was part of, or directly related to the dispute the parties submitted for arbitration. The court held that any new fact or change in the law arising in the course of the arbitration that would affect the claimant's right to the remedies it had sought all along must fall within the scope of the parties' submission to arbitration. The court also held that "any new fact or change in the law arising after a submission to arbitration which is ancillary to the dispute submitted for arbitration and which is known to all the parties to the arbitration is part of that dispute and need not be specifically pleaded."

B.3.1 The arbitration

The respondent, Kempinski entered into a contract to manage a hotel owned by the appellant, Prima, in Jakarta. The Indonesian Ministry of Tourism subsequently issued three decisions that made it compulsory for the contract to be carried out by a company incorporated in Indonesia (the "Three Decisions").

---

[11] [2012] SGCA 35. The High Court decision was discussed in last year's *Yearbook*.

Nonetheless, Kempinski remained the company managing the hotel pursuant to the contract. Prima terminated the contract. Kempinski commenced a SIAC arbitration for alleged wrongful termination. In the course of the proceedings, Prima applied for and was granted leave to amend its defense to include a plea of supervening illegality, namely, that the contract had become illegal due to the Three Decisions. The issues of illegality were heard in two tranches. The tribunal's first award found the contract valid but incapable of being performed except in a manner consistent with the Three Decisions. In a second award, the tribunal ruled out *force majeure* because the contract might still be performed through alternative methods consistent with the Three Decisions. Accordingly, Kempinski could claim damages. Thereafter, Kempinski entered into a new contract for the management of another hotel with a third party in Indonesia (the "New Venture") in breach of the contract with Prima. Prima wrote to the tribunal to seek "clarification" on the first and second awards in light of this fact, prompting further discovery of documents, written submissions and exchanges of expert evidence on Indonesian law pertaining to this issue.

The Tribunal then published a third award holding, among other things, that the alternative methods to perform the contract consistently with the Three Decisions were no longer possible in light of the New Venture. In a fourth award, the Tribunal ruled that it was contrary to Indonesian public policy to award damages for the period between the date of the alleged wrongful termination by Prima and the date of the New Venture (the "Intervening Period").

Dissatisfied, Kempinski commenced proceedings in the Singapore High Court to set aside the awards on the basis that, amongst other grounds, the tribunal dealt with issues that had not been formally pleaded.

B. Cases

B.3.2 The High Court sets aside the awards

The High Court agreed with Kempinski that the award should be set aside on the ground that failure to plead the New Venture resulted in the tribunal making a decision that was beyond the scope of the submission to arbitration. Article 34(2)(a)(iii) of the Model Law provides that an award which decides matters not falling within the terms of the submission to arbitration may be set aside. The High Court reasoned that to determine whether matters in an award were within or outside the scope of submission to arbitration, a reference to the pleadings would usually have to be made. The High Court rejected the submission that the jurisdiction in a particular reference to arbitration was not limited to the pleadings or that there was no rule of pleading that requires all material facts to be stated and specifically pleaded as would be required in court litigation.

The High Court held that PT Prima should have amended its pleadings to raise the argument that the fact of the New Venture made it impossible for Kempinski to perform the contract, and therefore, to claim damages from the point the New Venture came into existence. This would have allowed Kempinski to amend its own pleading. The arbitrator would then have been able to take evidence and establish the facts necessary to make a decision as to whether or not the existence of the New Venture made it impossible for Kempinski to perform the contract.

The High Court also set aside the fourth award on the ground that it was not based on any pleaded case nor had evidence been admitted in relation to whether an award of damages for the Intervening Period would be contrary to public policy.

B.3.3 The Court of Appeal reinstates the awards

The Court of Appeal disagreed with the narrow approach taken by the High Court in determining the scope of the arbitrator's jurisdiction under the parties' submission to jurisdiction. The Court of Appeal agreed that pleadings do play a role in defining the jurisdiction of the arbitrator by setting out the precise nature and scope of the disputes sought to be adjudicated. However, the Court of Appeal took the view that "any new fact or change in the law arising after a submission to arbitration which is ancillary to the dispute submitted for arbitration and which is known to all the parties to the arbitration is part of that dispute and need not be specifically pleaded." In particular, the Court of Appeal took the view that since Kempinski was seeking either damages or specific performance, "any new fact or change in the law arising in the course of the Arbitration which would affect Kempinski's right to these remedies must fall within the scope of the parties' submission to arbitration." The Court of Appeal also found it immaterial that PT Prima did not amend its pleadings to specifically include the issue of the legal effect of the New Venture, because Kempinski was given ample opportunity to address the issue and did not suffer any prejudice.

The Court of Appeal also disagreed with the High Court on the setting aside of the fourth award. The court held that the arbitrator was correct in holding that he had no power to award any damages to Kempinski for the intervening period as doing so would have been contrary to the public policy of Indonesia.

B.4 Interim Orders Cannot Be Set Aside as They Are Not Awards

In *PT Pukuafu Indah v. Newmont Indonesia Ltd*[12] the High Court refused an application to set aside a tribunal's order of an interim anti-suit injunction against court proceedings in Indonesia. The court held that the order of interim anti-suit injunction was not an "award." Accordingly, it had no jurisdiction to set aside the order. That case is further discussed below.

---

[12]   [2012] SGHC 187.

C. THE GRANT AND ENFORCEMENT OF INTERIM MEASURES IN INTERNATIONAL ARBITRATION

C.1 Tribunal-Ordered Interim Measures

In an international arbitration governed by the IAA,[13] a tribunal has wide powers to make orders for any interim measure.[14] Section 3 of the IAA gives Article 17 of the UNCITRAL Model Law the force of law in Singapore, which means that unless otherwise agreed by the parties, the tribunal may, at the request of a party, order any party to take such interim measure of protection as the tribunal may consider necessary in respect of the subject-matter of the dispute. The arbitral tribunal may require any party to provide appropriate security in connection with such measure.

The interim measures that may be ordered by the tribunal include the following:

(a) security for costs;[15]

(b) discovery of documents and interrogatories;

(c) giving of evidence by affidavit;

(d) the preservation, interim custody or sale of any property which is or forms part of the subject-matter of the dispute;

(e) samples to be taken from, or any observation to be made of or experiment conducted upon, any property which is or forms part of the subject-matter of the dispute;

---

[13] Parties may opt out of the IAA, in which case the AA applies.

[14] IAA § 12(1); Model Law Article 17 given the force of law pursuant to the IAA § 3(1). For example, see SIAC Rules r 26.

[15] *Dermajaya Properties Sdn Bhd v. Premium Properties Sdn Bhd* [2002] 1 SLR(R) 492, HC. The arbitral tribunal's has authority to order security for costs even if the rules of arbitration adopted by the parties do not provide for this power.

(f) the preservation and interim custody of any evidence for the purposes of the proceedings;

(g) securing the amount in dispute;

(h) ensuring that any award, which may be made in the arbitral proceedings, is not rendered ineffectual by the dissipation of assets by a party; and

(i) an interim injunction or any other interim measure.

In contrast, in domestic arbitrations or where parties have opted out of the IAA, the tribunal does not have the power to grant injunctions or freezing orders (unless it is conferred on the arbitral tribunal by agreement of the parties).[16]

C.1.1 Standards to be met in order for the Tribunal to order interim measures

Neither the IAA nor AA mandates a tribunal to apply any particular tests that an applicant must satisfy in order for the tribunal to order interim measures. However, the IAA does impose one statutory constraint on the tribunal's power to order security for costs, namely, that the tribunal shall not exercise its power to order a claimant to provide security for costs solely because the claimant is:

(a) an individual ordinarily resident in Singapore; or

(b) a corporation or association incorporated or formed under the law of a country outside Singapore, or whose central management and control is exercised outside Singapore.[17]

---

[16] AA § 28.

[17] *See* IAA § 12(4). A similar restriction is found under AA § 28(3).

But, the tribunal can still take into account the issue of residence, amongst other factors, when deciding whether to grant security for costs.[18]

C.1.2 Obtaining interim measures prior to the commencement of arbitral proceedings—application to an emergency arbitrator

Where parties have adopted rules that allow for an emergency arbitrator to be appointed,[19] they may apply to the emergency arbitrator for emergency relief prior to the commencement of the arbitration proceedings. As exemplified by the SIAC Rules, applications brought before the emergency arbitrator are usually heard *inter partes* and it is debatable whether the emergency arbitrator (or the tribunal) has the power to hear applications on an *ex parte* basis. Parliament specifically avoided adopting Articles 17A to 17J of the 2006 Model Law, which allow for the tribunal to grant *ex parte* interim measures,[20] on the basis that "industry opinion was on balance against the adoption of those articles."[21]

The SIAC Rules also provide that the tribunal may reconsider, modify or vacate the interim award or order of emergency relief issued by the emergency arbitrator and is not bound by the actions of the emergency arbitrator. Further, any order or award issued by the emergency arbitrator ceases to be binding if the tribunal is not constituted within 90 days of such order or award,

---

[18]   *Zhong Da Chemical Development Co. Ltd. v. Lanco Industries Ltd.* [2009] SGHC 112 at [12].

[19]   *See* fn 4 above.

[20]   Article 17B(1) of the 2006 Model Law provides for a party to make a request for an interim measure without notice to another party.

[21]   *See* Singapore Parliamentary Debates, Singapore Parliament Reports (9 April 2012) vol 89, Parliament No. 12, Session No. 1, International Arbitration (Amendment) Bill, Second Reading.

or when the tribunal makes a final award, or if the claim is withdrawn.[22]

Since the amendment to the SIAC Rules introducing emergency arbitrators, at least ten emergency arbitrator applications have been received by the SIAC.[23]

C.2 Court-Ordered Interim Measures

In Singapore, the High Court has the same powers as a tribunal to order any interim measure, except security for costs and discovery of documents and interrogatories,[24] irrespective of whether the seat of arbitration is in Singapore.[25] Although the court may order interim measures to aid, promote or support foreign arbitration, it may refuse to make such an order if, in its opinion, the fact that the place of arbitration is outside or likely to be outside Singapore makes such an order inappropriate.[26] Importantly, the High Court shall exercise its power to order interim measures "only if and to the extent that the arbitral tribunal, and any arbitral or other institution or person vested by the parties with power in that regard, has no power or is unable for the time being to act effectively."[27]

---

[22]   SIAC Rules Sch 1 para 7.

[23]   Professor Michael Pryles, *Singapore: The Hub of Arbitration in Asia*, available at http://www.siac.org.sg/index.php? option=com_content&view=article&id=405:singapore-the-hub-of-arbitration-in-asia&catid=56:articles&Itemid=171.

[24]   IAA § 12A(2). However, where the law governing the arbitration is not the IAA, the power to order security for costs and discovery orders is not excluded. *See* AA § 31(1).

[25]   IAA § 12A(1)(b).

[26]   *Id.* at § 12A(3).

[27]   *Id.* at § 12A(6). This restriction does not apply where the governing law is not the IAA. Where the IAA does not apply, the High Court only needs to have regard to

C.2.1 Applications for urgent relief

From 1 June 2012, the definition of "arbitral tribunal" was amended in the IAA to include emergency arbitrators. This raises the question whether the limit to the court's jurisdiction— inability of the arbitral tribunal or institution to act effectively — can be satisfied. However, during the Parliamentary Debates on the recent amendment to the IAA, the Minister for Law described the emergency arbitrator procedure as an "additional option"[28] to the court's power to make interim conservatory orders in support of arbitration, suggesting that parties have a choice between making an application to the courts or to the emergency arbitrator for emergency interim relief. It remains to be seen whether the Singapore courts will decline any applications for urgent interim relief on the basis that parties should have appointed an emergency arbitrator instead.

C.2.2 Applications for non-urgent relief

If the case is not one of urgency, the court can only make an order for an interim measure with the permission of the tribunal or the agreement in writing of the other parties (and upon notice

---

any application before or order made by the arbitral tribunal in respect of the same interim measure when exercising its powers to make interim orders. See AA § 31(3).

[28] *See* Singapore Parliamentary Debates, Singapore Parliament Reports (9 April 2012) vol 89, Parliament No. 12, Session No. 1, International Arbitration (Amendment) Bill, Second Reading, where the Minister for Law stated:

The last time the International Arbitration Act was amended, the court was granted the power under section 12A to make certain interim conservatory orders in support of arbitrations. With the passage of the Bill, a party involved in an arbitration conducted in Singapore who requires such relief now has *the additional option of applying to an emergency arbitrator* who would be able to exercise the full range of powers available to arbitral tribunals, and the proposed amendment to section 2 would ensure that such orders would be enforceable by the Singapore courts. [emphasis added]

to the other parties and the tribunal).[29] Any interim order made by the High Court ceases to have effect in whole or in part (as the case may be) once the tribunal makes an order which expressly relates to the High Court's order.[30]

C.2.3 Length of time needed to obtain an interim measure

Interim measures may be obtained on an urgent basis fairly quickly (sometimes in a matter of days) if the applicant has a good reason why the measure should be granted urgently. Applications made to emergency arbitrators under the SIAC Rules have been heard fairly quickly, with relief granted within three days in one case, and within ten days in another.[31] The SIAC Annual Report 2011 describes a further instance when an order was made the day after the application for emergency interim relief, which was made just before the Chinese New Year holidays in respect of a deteriorating cargo of coal in a Chinese port.[32]

It is also possible to obtain urgent interim relief from the courts in a fairly short time. In the appropriate case, it is not unusual for the court to grant a holding injunction while the parties are heard on the application for the interim measure. As both parties will be given an opportunity to be heard, and to introduce evidence if necessary, the application for an interim measure could take a few weeks or a couple of months before it is finally heard and decided.

---

[29] IAA § 12A(5).

[30] *Id.* at § 12A(7); AA § 31(2).

[31] *See* Vivekananda N. and Ankit Goyal, "Interventionist, No More?," 30 November 2011; available at http://www.siac.org.sg/index.php?option=com_content&view =article&id=327:interventionist-no-more&catid=56:articles&Itemid=171.

[32] *See* Singapore International Arbitration Centre (SIAC) Annual Report 2011; available at http://www.siac.org.sg/index.php?option=com_content&view=article &id=288&Itemid=148.

C.3 Enforcement of Interim Measures

Interim orders made by an arbitral tribunal are enforceable in the same manner as a court order.[33]

C.3.1 Enforcement of interim measures for arbitrations seated in Singapore

Interim orders by the tribunal are not awards[34] and therefore they are not subject to appeal or to be set aside. The party seeking to enforce the interim order must apply for leave from the High Court to do so, pursuant to § 12(6) of the IAA, which provides that: "All orders or directions made or given by an arbitral tribunal in the course of an arbitration shall, by leave of the High Court or a Judge thereof, be enforceable in the same manner as if they were orders made by a court and, where leave is so given, judgment may be entered in terms of the order or direction."[35]

At the same time, the definition of arbitral awards in Part I and II of the IAA relating to international arbitrations seated in Singapore expressly "excludes any orders or directions made under section 12." It is therefore clear that orders and directions made by an arbitral tribunal are not an "award."[36]

The effect of § 12(6) of the IAA is that the court has no jurisdiction under the IAA to set aside interim measures made by an arbitral tribunal for arbitrations seated in Singapore. This was considered in the case of *PT Pukuafu Indah v. Newmont*

---

[33] IAA § 12(6); AA § 28(4).

[34] *PT Asuransi Jasa Indonesia (Persero) v. Dexia Bank SA* [2007] 1 SLR(R) 597, CA at [62].

[35] IAA s 12(6); AA s 28(4); Rules of Court O 69A r 5 and O 69 r 13.

[36] However, an "arbitral tribunal" is defined to include an emergency arbitrator under the IAA § 2(1). *See* AA § 2(1) for a similar definition of "arbitral tribunal."

Indonesia Ltd.[37] ("PT Pukuafu"), where the court observed that an order made under § 12 of the IAA cannot be set aside because it is not an award. The legislative rationale for this was that procedural issues should be decided only by the tribunal, who was in a better position to consider the substantive context of the dispute and the merits of the grounds for ordering the interim relief, and that "[l]imiting challenges only to awards that decide the substantive merits of the case would reduce the risk of delay and prevent tactical attempts to obstruct the arbitration process by bringing challenges on interim orders."[38]

However, the court in PT Pukuafu also considered, without expressing a concluded view, that the court's power to refuse leave could provide some measure of protection for the rights of both parties.[39] Further, where the tribunal's order is in the nature of an interim injunction, leave shall be granted only if the applicant undertakes to abide by any order the court or the tribunal may make as to damages.[40]

The Singapore courts have not set out the circumstances where leave will be refused. However, in one instance, the court declined to enforce interim orders that the tribunal had no powers to make. In *Bocotra Construction Pte Ltd. and others v. Attorney-General*,[41] the court declined to grant interim declaratory relief confirming an arbitrator's order restraining the call on a performance bond until the respondent's right to call on the bond was determined in the arbitration. The court considered that the arbitrator had incorrectly relied on his power to grant

---

37   *PT Pukuafu Indah v. Newmont Indonesia Ltd.* [2012] SGHC 187 at [27].

38   *Id.* at [25].

39   *Id.* at [27].

40   Rules of Court O 29 r 5(2).

41   [1995] 2 SLR(R) 262.

security for costs as a basis for restraining a call on the performance bond.

C.3.2 Enforcement of interim measures granted by a tribunal in the territory of a Convention country other than Singapore.

The definition of "award" in part III of the IAA, which concerns the enforcement of foreign awards (i.e., awards for arbitrations seated in New York Convention countries other than Singapore), includes orders and directions given by a tribunal in respect of any of the interim measures set out in § 12(1)(c) to (i) of the IAA.[42]

This means that all orders and directions given by a tribunal seated outside of Singapore (and in a New York Convention country) except for orders for security for costs, discovery of documents and interrogatories are enforceable in a Singapore court. Such orders and directions are therefore subject to closer scrutiny of the courts and may be set aside on any of the usual grounds for refusal of enforcement under the New York Convention.[43]

---

[42] IAA § 27(1).

[43] *Id.* at § 31.

SOUTH AFRICA

Gerhard Rudolph[1] and Darryl Bernstein[2]

A. LEGISLATION, TRENDS AND TENDENCIES

A.1 Legislation

The law of arbitration in South Africa derives from common law, legislation and the Constitution of the Republic of South Africa 1996. It is primarily regulated by the Arbitration Act 42 of 1965 (the "Arbitration Act").

This Act, extensively influenced by the English Arbitration Acts of 1889 and 1950, recognizes the binding effect of an agreement to arbitrate and the referral of a dispute for determination by way of arbitration. The Arbitration Act follows traditional English principles, essentially reflecting English law as it stood in 1965. While the English statutes have since been amended to accommodate the development of international commercial law, the Arbitration Act remains unchanged.

The Arbitration Act applies to both international and domestic arbitration proceedings. Parties are essentially free to adopt procedures of their choice within the framework of the Arbitration Act. Indeed, the arbitration agreement may itself specify the rules of procedure to be followed, or the parties may

---

[1] Gerhard Rudolph is a Partner in Baker & McKenzie's Johannesburg office. His practice involves dispute resolution and arbitration for a broad range of areas of practice, including banking, insurance, construction and engineering, mining and resources, and general primarily commercial corporate and commercial issues.

[2] Darryl Bernstein is a Partner in Baker & McKenzie's Johannesburg office. He regularly represents clients in international litigation and arbitration proceedings, often in the spheres of banking, insurance, information technology, mining and resources, and insolvency.

leave it to the arbitrator to decide the procedure, subject essentially to the principles of natural justice and broad procedural framework envisaged by the Arbitration Act.

Domestic arbitrations are typically conducted in terms of comprehensive rules adopted by agreement between the parties, importing either the Uniform Rules of Court[3] or the rules published and administered by the Arbitration Foundation of Southern Africa ("AFSA") or the Association of Arbitrators ("ASA"), being the major private arbitral institutions within South Africa. International disputes are typically governed by the rules of the ICC or the LCIA.

The enforcement of foreign arbitral awards is governed by the Recognition and Enforcement of Foreign Arbitral Awards Act 40 of 1977 (the "Enforcement Act"), which incorporates and ratifies the New York Convention. Although the Enforcement Act deals comprehensively with the enforcement of foreign awards, it fails to deal expressly with their recognition. In order for a foreign arbitral award to be enforced, the Enforcement Act requires that an application be made to court for its recognition and enforcement. The court may decline the application where the content of the dispute is such that arbitration would not be permitted under South African law, or where the enforcement of the award is contrary to public policy.[4]

A.2   Proposed Changes to the Arbitration Act

During 2001, in the face of almost universal adoption of the UNCITRAL Model Law by countries in the process of updating

---

[3]   The Uniform Rules of Court are a set of rules regarding the conduct of proceedings of the several provincial and local divisions of the Supreme Court of South Africa.

[4]   Sections 4(1)(a)(i) and (ii) of the Enforcement Act.

their arbitration legislation and the ongoing development of international commercial law, the South African Law Reform Commission (the "SALC") submitted a comprehensive report on the status of its domestic arbitration[5] in which it was recommended, *inter alia*, that a new domestic arbitration statute be added to the Arbitration Act, combining the best features of the UNCITRAL Model Law and the English Arbitration Act of 1996, while retaining otherwise effective provisions of the Arbitration Act.[6] To date, however, the legislature has taken no steps to implement the SALC's recommendations.

No amendment has been made to the Arbitration Act since its inception in 1965. The legal profession in South Africa, including the judiciary, is presently under considerable pressure to deal with transformation in order to address historic inequality based on racial and gender discrimination. The SALC has suggested that a reason for the delay in bringing the Arbitration Act into line with international best practice is the perception by the government that the arbitration process amounts to "privatized litigation," allowing both corporate entities and legal professionals to circumvent formal court process and compromise the government's efforts to transform the judiciary.

Accordingly, arbitration reform is a politically contentious issue in South Africa, receiving nominal priority among legislators.

A.3 Trends and Tendencies

Commercial arbitration is a long-established mechanism for dispute resolution in South Africa. It has become increasingly popular in the last decade due to the relative speed and certainty

---

[5] Project 94: Domestic arbitration report dated May 2001, available at www.justice.gov.za/salrc/reports/r_prj94_dom2001.pdf.

[6] P. Ramsden, *The Law of Arbitration* at 19.

with which resolution of disputes may be obtained, particularly in comparison to the staffing and resource constraints in the court system, which has resulted in backlogged court trial rolls and increasingly unaffordable access to courts. Arbitration is viewed in South Africa as a particularly flexible procedure for resolving disputes—the parties are at liberty to modify the procedure in accordance with the nature and extent of the particular dispute as well as the amount at stake.[7]

Arguably the most significant development in recent years affecting cross-border commercial dispute resolution in South Africa was the October 2009 launch of Africa ADR, an initiative of the Southern African Development Community ("SADC"). Africa ADR is a regional dispute resolution forum for the determination of cross-border disputes within the SADC region, established in conformity with the resolutions of the General Assembly of the United Nations, which encourage the use of alternative and appropriate methods for the resolution of civil disputes.[8] It is hoped that this forum will result in substantial change in respect of the manner in which cross-border arbitration agreements are concluded between parties within South Africa. The value and efficacy of the forum, however, is yet to be determined.

B.   CASES

The most significant recent decisions rendered by South African courts in relation to arbitration proceedings are summarized below.

---

[7]   Butler & Finsen, *Arbitration in South Africa: Law and Practice,* at 2.

[8]   Accessed via www.africaadr.com.

B. Cases

B.1 *Lufuno Mphaphuli & Associates (Pty) Ltd. v. Andrews and Another*

In *Lufuno Mphaphuli & Associates (Pty) Ltd. v. Andrews and Another*,[9] the court dealt with an application for leave to appeal to the Constitutional Court (the highest court in South Africa with respect to constitutional matters) from a decision of the Supreme Court of Appeal ("SCA") enforcing an arbitral award and dismissing an application to set aside the award.

The party opposing enforcement argued that the application for leave to appeal raised a number of constitutional issues regarding the relationship between arbitrations, the courts and the Constitution, insofar as Section 34 of the Constitution stipulates that "everyone has the right to have any dispute that can be resolved by the application of law decided in a fair public hearing before a court or, where appropriate, another independent and impartial tribunal or forum." The issue before the Constitutional Court was the extent to which the courts are entitled and required to exercise control over arbitral awards before sanctioning them, and whether in concluding an arbitration agreement a party may be said to have waived its Section 34 right to a fair hearing.

A majority of the court considered that, in determining the correct constitutional approach to private arbitration, it must be borne in mind that litigation before ordinary courts can be a rigid, costly and time-consuming process. The court held that it was not inconsistent with the Constitution for parties to seek a quicker and cheaper mechanism for the resolution of disputes. Section 33(1) of the Arbitration Act, which provides for the circumstances under which an arbitration award may be set aside, may be interpreted in a manner that restricts the power of

---

9   2009 (4) SA 529 (CC).

courts to set aside private arbitral awards without compromising the values of the Constitution.

In reaching its conclusion, the court drew heavily on international jurisprudence (in particular, the UNCITRAL Model Law) suggesting that courts should be careful not to undermine the achievement of the goals of private arbitration.

B.2 *Road Accident Fund v. Cloete NO and Others*

In *Road Accident Fund v. Cloete NO and Others*,[10] the SCA was requested to consider and apply Section 20(1) of the Arbitration Act, which permits an arbitrator at any time during the course of an arbitration to refer "any question of law" to the High Court in the form of a special case "for the opinion of the court."

Claimants, a Belgian doctor and her curators, initiated an arbitration in Belgium against the Road Accident Fund (the "RAF") to recover damages from a motor vehicle accident that left the doctor unable to practice medicine. The primary issue in dispute was whether the doctor was entitled to claim certain damages from the RAF in light of benefits she would continue to receive from the Belgium Social Security System. The curator had in fact undertaken to refund the Belgium insurance institutions for such benefits should they be received from the RAF.

The claimants relied on the precedent of *Zysset and Others v. Santam Ltd.*[11] for their entitlement to payment. In *Zysset* the Cape Provicial Division of the High Court had already decided in favor of four Swiss resident claimaints in similar circumstances *vis-à-vis* a variety of Swiss compulsory social security insurance schemes. The Cape Court held that there

---

10   2010 (6) SA 120 (SCA).

11   1996 (1) SA 273 (C).

could be no question of a deduction if the plaintiffs were not doubly compensated and the effect of a similar agreement to refund the Swiss schemes ensured that the plaintiffs would not be doubly compensated in respect of patrimonial loss if they were awarded their full damages.

The RAF contended that the case had been wrongly decided and requested that the arbitrator, under Section 20(1) of the Arbitration Act, refer certain questions of law for the opinion of the court in the form of a special case.

The arbitrator was not prepared to refer the questions of law on the basis sought by the RAF, however. Relying on the English Arbitration Act of 1996, the arbitrator instead formulated the question for the court as "whether on the facts stated therein the order in the *Zysset* matter was correctly made or not. If not, the court is requested to state what the order should have been."

The SCA first noted that, while the English Arbitration Act contains wording that is materially different from the South African Act, the position in South African law is similar. However, the court held that the mere fact that an arbitrator refers a question of law for the opinion of the court does not oblige the High Court to furnish such opinion. For example, if the court considers the question of law to be irrelevant to the issues in the arbitration or if the facts in the record do not support adjudication of the question of law, the court would be justified in declining to decide the point.[12]

---

[12] The court, in determining the factors to be taken into account before exercising its power in terms of Section 20(1) of the South African Arbitration Act, relied on the equivalent Sections of the English Arbitration Act, and held that a court may determine any question of law arising in the course of arbitration proceedings if the application for determination was made without delay and the court is satisfied that the determination would substantially affect the rights of one or more of the parties and would produce a substantial saving in costs.

The SCA also held that the court's powers under Section 20 of the Act should be exercised sparingly, since Section 20 constitutes an exception to the general principle that it is for the arbitrator to finally decide all matters referred to him, including questions of law.

Consequently, the SCA refused to make the determination sought on the basis that it would be unusual and inappropriate to do so where the very issue stated by the arbitrator had already been decided in the courts. The court found that, in this particular case, the parties agreed to have their dispute resolved by arbitration, and arbitration was not the proper procedure through which to request the court to review or change the substantive law.

C. THE GRANT AND ENFORCEMENT OF INTERIM MEASURES IN INTERNATIONAL ARBITRATION

Interim measures—orders issued by the arbitral tribunal or a national court intended to preserve evidence, protect assets, or in some other way maintain the *status quo* pending the outcome of the arbitration proceedings—are fairly indicative of South Africa's failure to update its legislation in line with international best practice and the development of international arbitration law.

C.1 Tribunal-Ordered Interim Measures

The authority of the arbitral tribunal and the extent of its powers are subject to the provisions of the arbitration agreement[13] and the provisions of the Arbitration Act.[14] The tribunal does not

---

[13] Butler & Finsen, *Arbitration in South Africa: Law and Practice* at 97.

[14] *Ibid.*, at 98.

C. The Grant and Enforcement of Interim Measures in International Arbitration

have the power to impose duties and confer rights for which no foundation can be found in the arbitration agreement and, in the absence of agreement between the parties, the tribunal does not have wider powers than a court would have in adjudicating upon a claim.[15]

The general powers of the arbitral tribunal contained in the Arbitration Act do not include the power to order interim measures of protection in relation to the subject matter of the dispute.[16] As such, the tribunal is not in a position to order such measures (including security for costs) unless the power is conferred on the tribunal in the arbitration agreement. In the absence of such provision, the party requiring the interim measures will have no choice but to approach the court.[17]

Section 14(1) of the Arbitration Act provides that the tribunal may order procedural measures such as requiring parties to, *inter alia*, make discovery of documents, deliver pleadings, and appoint a commissioner to take the evidence of a person outside the Republic. In addition, the Act provides that unless there is a contrary provision in the arbitration agreement, the arbitral tribunal may determine the time, location and place of the arbitration proceedings.

In this regard, the Arbitration Act differs substantially from the UNCITRAL Model Law, which defaults to vesting the tribunal with the power to grant interim measures "unless otherwise agreed."

---

[15] Statutory powers of arbitration tribunal *LAWSA* 579; *Meyerowitz .v Lieberman* 1940 WLD 40 42; *Melman v. Engelman* 1940 WLD 151 154.

[16] Section 14(1) of the Arbitration Act.

[17] *Id.* at Section 21(1)(a) and (e) to (g).

C.2 Court-Ordered Interim Measures

Although the parties to an arbitration agreement agree to resolve their dispute outside of the courts, the effect of the agreement does not exclude the jurisdiction of the courts.[18] For instance, the court retains certain powers in respect of the proceedings both before, during and after the arbitration award, classified as powers of assistance, which include the faculties of recognition, enforcement, supervision and intervention.

In respect of impending arbitration proceedings, the court has the power to grant relief by way of an interdict where an applicant can show that the impending arbitration proceedings would be invalid.[19] It has been held that it would be unrealistic and inconvenient to expect an applicant in such circumstances to partake in arbitration proceedings under protest, or await the conclusion of the proceedings, and incur the costs thereof in the interim, and thereafter oppose the award being made an order of court.[20]

During the arbitration proceedings, and in accordance with Section 21 of the Arbitration Act, the court has the power to order discovery of documents and security for costs, grant an interim interdict or an order for the inspection or protection of goods in dispute, require a question of law to be referred to counsel or to the court and, in certain circumstances, can set aside an arbitrator's appointment or remove the arbitrator from

---

[18] *Parekh v. Shah Jehan Cinemas (Pty) Ltd* 1980 1 SA 301 (D) 305F–H.

[19] *Compagnie Iterafricaine de Travaux v. South African Transport Services and Others* 1991 (4) SA 217 (A).

[20] *Inter-Continental Finance and Leasing Corporation (Pty) Ltd. v. Stands 56 and 57 Industria Ltd. and Another* 1979 (3) SA 740 (W).

office.[21] The court also has the statutory power to extend certain time limits.[22]

After the arbitration award has been made, the court has the power to enforce it, (or to decline to do so),[23] set it aside or remit it to the arbitral tribunal so that the tribunal can rectify certain defects.[24] Should the court choose to enforce the award, this will be done in the same manner as a judgment of the court.[25]

Although silent on the granting and enforcing of interim measures, the Enforcement Act does provide that the court's willingness to enforce a foreign arbitral award will depend on whether the content of the award is in conflict with the provisions of the Enforcement Act (see Section A.1, *supra*). Apart from those interim measures contained in Section 21(1) of the Arbitration Act, and unlike Article 17J of the UNCITRAL Model Law, the Arbitration Act does not specifically provide that interim measures in aid of a foreign arbitration may be granted.

However, it is possible that an arbitration agreement and/or the rules governing the arbitration proceedings could clarify a South African court's jurisdiction in this respect.

---

[21] Section 13(2) of the Act.

[22] *Id.* at Section 38.

[23] *Id.* at Section 31.

[24] *Id.* at Section 32.

[25] Section 2(3) of the Enforcement Act.

SPAIN

José María Alonso,[1] Alfonso Gómez-Acebo,[2]
José Ramón Casado,[3] and Víctor Mercedes[4]

A. LEGISLATION, TRENDS AND TENDENCIES

A.1 Arbitration Regulations for Tourist Agreements

Law 4/2012 of 6 July regulates the marketing, sale, resale and use of time-share agreements for tourist purposes and the so-called acquisition agreements for long-term vacation products and those for the resale and exchange thereof. The new law not only regulates basic substantive aspects such as pre-contractual advertising and information, the right to withdrawal, prohibition of advance payments, and the form and contents of the agreements, but also expressly states that the parties can submit their disputes to consumer arbitration or to other systems for non-judicial dispute settlement included in the European Commission's list of alternative dispute settlement systems.

---

[1] José María Alonso is a Partner and Head of the Litigation & Arbitration Department in Baker & McKenzie's Madrid office. He is a member of the Steering Committees of the Global Arbitration Practice Group and the International European Disputes Practice Group.

[2] Alfonso Gómez-Acebo FCIArb is a Partner in Baker & McKenzie's Madrid office. He practises in the area of international arbitration.

[3] José Ramón Casado is a Partner in Baker & McKenzie's Madrid office. He practises in the areas of corporate, commercial and civil litigation and arbitration.

[4] Víctor Mercedes is a Partner in Baker & McKenzie's Barcelona office and Co-Head of the Litigation & Arbitration Department. His practice includes domestic and international litigation and arbitration, especially in regulated sectors and in connection with insolvency.

A.2 Mediation in Civil and Commercial Matters

Spanish legislators have decided to introduce and regulate mediation to relieve courts from overwhelming litigation. The new regulation contained in Law 5/2012 of 6 July completes and confirms the earlier Royal Decree-Law 5/2012.

Mediation will be applicable to civil and commercial matters, including cross-border disputes, unless they affect rights and obligations not subject to disposal by the parties. Spanish legislation will be applicable when a party is domiciled in Spain and the mediation occurs in Spain. Criminal matters, cases related to Public Administrations, labor cases and consumer cases are expressly excluded from the scope of mediation.

A.3 Arbitration in the Electrical Power Production Market in Spain: Decision of 23 July 2012 Adopted by the Secretary of State for Energy

A recent decision adopted on July, 23 2012 by the Secretary of State for Energy of the Spanish Ministry of Industry determined the new operating rules for the daily and intra-day market of electrical power production by developing the provisions of the law and regulations for the electricity sector in Spain in which Spanish and foreign companies operate (Law 54/1997 of 27 November and Royal Decree 2019/1997 of 26 December). The decision expressly states that disputes arising related to application of these rules can be submitted to arbitration by the National Energy Commission, pursuant to the law governing the Electricity Sector, or to arbitration in Madrid, according to the UNCITRAL arbitration rules, subject to the Spanish Arbitration Act., with limited exceptions related to matters of public order.

A.4 Arbitration Related to Royalties for Private Copies in Intellectual Property Law

Following judgments by the European Court of Justice dated June 16, 2011 and October 21, 2010 on the compensation payable to authors of works subject to intellectual property rights for the harm caused by their being copied for private purposes, Royal Decree 1657/2012 of 7 December regulates the proceedings and objective criteria to determine the annual amount payable for the aforementioned compensation (royalties) for private copies. The possibility is expressly granted that disputes relating to these matters, which are increasingly frequent in Spain, may be submitted to arbitration by the so-called Intellectual Property Commission, an administrative body with representatives of the various agents in the market of intellectual property rights, or to any other court or arbitral tribunal assigned for such purpose.

B. CASES

B.1 Review of Arbitrator's Competence

Article 22 of the Spanish Arbitration Act contains the so-called "Kompetenz-Kompetenz" rule, by which arbitrators are exclusively competent to decide on their own competence to solve a specific dispute. Recent judgments issued by the Court of Appeal of Madrid on May 10, 2012 (JUR 2012/247150) and the Court of Appeal of Barcelona on February 16, 2012 (AC 2012/376) state clearly that the decision on whether or not an arbitrator is competent is not subject to further review by the courts on a request for annulment. A full review of the case and the award is not permitted.

B.2   Judicial Designation of Arbitrators

Interesting judgments issued by the Higher Court of the Balearic Islands on June 20, 2012 (RJ 2012/8801) and the Higher Court of Valencia on April 20, 2012 (RJ 2012/8778) remarked that the judicial designation of arbitrators, under Article 15 Spanish Arbitration Act, is only applicable when the parties have agreed on the appointment by mutual agreement or if no agreement exists to appoint arbitrators.

B.3   Annulment of Awards

Judgments issued by the Higher Court of the Balearic Islands on July 9, 2012 (AC 2012/1387) and by the Higher Court of Castilla-León on October 9, 2012 (AC 2012/1389) confirmed that the legal grounds for the annulment of awards are limited to those listed under Article 41 of the Spanish Arbitration Act, and a full review of the merits of the arbitrator's decision is not permitted.

B.4   Form of the Arbitration Clause

A recent judgment issued by the Appeal Court of Valencia on January 13, 2012 (AC 2012/608) states that the arbitration agreement should have the form of a clause incorporated into a contract or an independent agreement and should express the intent of the parties to submit to arbitration all or some of the disputes arising from certain legal relationships, whether in contract or in tort. This requirement may not be fulfilled in standard form contracts due to the unilateral determination of their terms and lack of individual negotiation. In such cases, the arbitration clause should be deemed null and void based on the fact that it damages the fair balance of rights and obligations and the interests of the parties.

According to a judgment issued by the Court of Appeal of León on February 3, 2012 (AC 2012/337), a clause of adhesion included in a contract is not abusive by itself unless the requirements detailed in the above-mentioned judgment are present in the case.

B.5 **Failure to Serve Notice or Improper Notice of the Designation of the Arbitrator or the Arbitral Proceedings**

According to a ruling issued by the Higher Court of Justice of Catalonia dated March 15, 2012 (AC 2012/6120), a defective notice of the designation of the arbitrator does not provide grounds for annulment of an award if the party was able to participate during the proceedings and did not raise any objection on that issue in the course of the case. This ruling invokes criteria stated by the Supreme Court in its judgment dated March 13, 2001 (RJ 2001/3978).

B.6 **Scope of Arbitration Clauses**

According to a judgment issued by the Court of Appeal of Barcelona on July 24, 2012, an arbitration clause that expressly covered all the conflicts and disputes arising from a contract, its interpretation, execution and enforcement also included disputes on the nullity or validity of the contract, due to the general nature of the terms used by the parties. One magistrate dissented, invoking a more restrictive interpretation of the scope of arbitration clause. On a similar topic, a judgment issued by the Court of Appeal of Barcelona (AC 2012/376) states that the terms of the arbitration clause may not be interpreted in a restrictive sense because the interpretation of a contract extends to the analysis of its validity.

Finally, a ruling issued by the Court of Appeal of Girona on February 28, 2012 (AC 2012/377) held that the arbitration clause in that case included disputes alleging nullity based on error as a defect in consent. Such a dispute would require an interpretation of the nature, content, performance and enforcement conditions of the contract, all expressly covered by the arbitration agreement.

B.7 Matters Not Open to Arbitration

A recent judgment issued by the Court of Appeal of Madrid on May 10, 2012, JUR 2012/247150) remarks arbitrable matters should be open to disposal by arbitration according to the law, except where expressly prohibited by law. The imperative nature of certain legal provisions does not mean that disputes arising in connection with such provisions may not be submitted to arbitration. The same criterion is reflected in a recent judgment issued by the Higher Court of Justice of Cantabria on May 8, 2012 (AC 2012/1382).

B.8 Public Policy

A recent judgment issued by the Higher Court of Justice of Castilla-Léon on October 9, 2012 addresses public policy infringement as a legal ground for annulment. According to the judgment, an award is contrary to public policy when its decisions violate the fundamental legal principles of the State and may not be assumed by the public authorities and upheld by the Administration of Justice. The judgment remarks that this ground may be considered *ex officio*.

B.9 Lack of Independence and Impartiality of the Arbitral Institution

The Higher Court of Justice of Catalonia set aside an arbitral award for lack of independence and impartiality of the arbitral institution[5]. This institution was designated in the arbitration clause of a standard-form contract that a mobile phone supplier used with its clients. The Court found that the links between the arbitral institution and the mobile phone supplier's counsel made the institution partial. The Court reasoned that the impartiality and independence of the arbitral institution, even though they were not expressly required by law (unlike those qualities in the arbitrators), were necessary in arbitral proceedings.[6]

B.10 Lack of Reasoning of the Award

Three recent judgments have addressed the requirement that the award must state the reasons upon which it is based. In each case, a party claimed the nullification of an arbitral award on the grounds that the award lacked sufficient reasoning. In the first case, the Higher Court of Justice of Valencia rejected the nullification claim, noting that non-existent, irrational or arbitrary reasons may go against public policy and serve as valid grounds for setting aside an arbitral award, but also noting that state courts cannot review and amend the mistakes that the arbitrator may have made in the interpretation and application of legal norms at the time of deciding on the merits of the dispute.[7] In the second case, the Higher Court of Justice of the Basque Country also refused to set aside the award, noting that what the applicant presented as a lack of reasoning was actually just a manifestation of the applicant's disagreement with the arbitral

---

[5]   Judgment 29/2012 of 10 May 2012.

[6]   In the same line: Court of Appeal of Madrid (Section 11), judgment of 16 February 2004; Court of Appeal of Madrid (Section 14), judgment of 2 April 2004; Court of Appeal of Barcelona (Section 14), ruling of 11 December 2004; Court of Appeal of Barcelona (Section 15), judgment of 15 May 2007.

[7]   Judgment 14/2012, of 26 April 2012.

decision.[8] In the third case, the Higher Court of Justice of Galicia set aside the arbitral award.[9] In this case, the Court found that the arbitrator's reasoning was so scant that it was not possible to know why some claims had been upheld and others had not.

B.11 Breach of a Party's Right of Defense

The Higher Court of Justice of the Canary Islands set aside an arbitral award because of the infringement of the claimant's right of defense.[10] The original dispute arose out of a contract between a company and a tennis player. Following the latter's decision to terminate the contract, the company claimed an amount of compensation that it determined, by applying contractual provisions, as a function of the WTA's ranking of the player at the time the contract was terminated. The claimant in the arbitration contended that the termination had taken place in 2007 and presented documentary evidence that the player's ranking that year was #169. In its statement of defense, the respondent claimed that the termination had taken place in 2006 and that the claimant was not entitled to any compensation, while also acknowledging that the ranking in 2007 was the one that the claimant had stated. However, at a later stage of the arbitration, the respondent argued, on the basis of a witness's oral declaration, that the claimant had not proven that the ranking in 2007 was #169. In the award, the arbitrator found that the termination had occurred in 2007, but did not award any compensation to the claimant because it had not proven the respondent's ranking at the time of the contract termination. According to the Court, the arbitral decision, as well as being illogical, had violated the claimant's right of defense.

---

8   Judgment 3/2012, of 12 June 2012.

9   Judgment 18/2012, of 2 May 2012.

10   Judgment 3/2012, of 9 July 2012.

B.12 Action to Set Aside an Award Brought after Expiry of the Limitation Period

Pursuant to Article 41.4 of the Spanish Arbitration Act, an action to set aside an arbitral award must be brought within two months of its notification. Article 135.1 of the Civil Procedure Act ("CPA") allows procedural actions to be brought until 3pm of the next working day after the expiry of the limitation period. The Spanish Constitutional Court upheld the claim of a party against a court of appeal's decision not to admit an action to set aside an award because the action had been brought before 3pm on the day after the expiry of the 2-month limitation period.[11] The Constitutional Court found that the court of appeal's decision was based on a too rigoristic and unbalanced interpretation of procedural rules, which was against the fundamental right of access to justice.

B.13 Effects of the Declaration of Nullity of an Award

If an arbitration clause is declared null and void, the dispute will remain without decision because the tribunal is not allowed to review the merits of the case, as stated in a recent judgment issued by the Higher Court of Justice of Cantabria on May 8, 2012 (AC 2012/1382).

B.14 Electronic Records and Service

A court order issued by the Higher Court of Justice of Catalonia on March 15, 2012 (RJ 2012/6120) recognized an award granted in an arbitration conducted in London in a dispute over maritime charter contracts, rejecting an allegation that the award violated Spanish public order since there was no arbitration agreement,

---

[11] Judgment 76/2012, of 16 April 2012.

no arbitrator designated, and no arbitration proceeding. The Court recalled that, pursuant to Article II of the New York Convention and the UNCITRAL recommendation regarding interpretation (of July 7, 2006), there are informal methods of recording of an arbitration agreement, e.g., an exchange of letters, telegrams, telexes, faxes, or other telecommunications media which leave a record of the agreement. These means are not exhaustive and may be supplemented with those mentioned in Article 9 of the Spanish Arbitration Act. In the case considered, electronic correspondence was submitted. This evidence showed the business agreements of the parties. Among these were that disputes were expressly submitted to arbitration and that the agreements were subject to English law. The Court further points out that defects in the arbitration agreement should have been objected to within the framework of the arbitration proceedings. The court also rejects the allegation that notice of the designation of an arbitrator and of the proceedings was not served. There was a record of the sending of faxes to the defendants, and sending faxes is accepted by Spanish procedural legislation for notices served by courts. The Court added that, in any event, failure to serve notice is only relevant when it leaves one of the parties either effectively or materially defenseless. This did not occur in the case tried, since there was no privation of the defendants' power to submit allegations and evidence.

B.15 Award for Less Than Was Petitioned For

A court order issued by the Higher Court of Justice of Catalonia on May 30, 2012 (JUR 2012/248238) examines a petition for the exequatur of an arbitration award by the Sports Arbitration Court regarding a dispute over the agreement on the economic rights due to the transfer of a professional soccer player from a Spanish to an English club. The Spanish club was ordered to pay compensation for damages arising from breach of contract. .The court concludes that there was no incongruence such as to make the award unreasonable. It adds that incongruence with the basis of petition exists when a decision breaches the factual basis of the petition, understood as the set of events on which the petition is based, with certain legal consequences. On the other hand, there is a change of the basis of petition, showing unreasonable incongruence, when facts other than those for which the proceedings have been brought (the relevant individual causes for initiating arbitration proceedings) are taken into consideration.

B.16 Adoption of an Arbitration Clause by Joint Owners

In a case examined by a judgment issued by the Court of Appeal of Madrid on March 227, 012 (AC 2012/805) in connection with arbitration in real estate ownership, the arbitration clause was included in the minutes of a meeting of the owners. Some owners, duly informed about the issues of the meeting, did not attend, but did not challenge the decision to adopt the clause. The Court of Appeal states that the failure to challenge the decision may not be considered an implicit declaration of intention, which needs more evident signals. The judgment examines the legal value of silent declarations, recalling the doctrine that silence is only equivalent to an express statement when the circumstances impose a specific response.

C. THE GRANT AND ENFORCEMENT OF INTERIM MEASURES IN INTERNATIONAL ARBITRATION

C.1 Tribunal-Ordered Interim Measures

Spanish law and the arbitration rules of Spanish arbitral institutions grant arbitrators the power to order interim measures.[12] No restrictions on the types of interim measures that may be adopted by arbitrators are imposed by law. An arbitral tribunal, like a state court, may order any type of interim measure that may be necessary to ensure the effectiveness of a final judgment or award upholding the claims on the merits of the requesting party. Even though Article 727 CPA contains a list of specific interim measures that may be granted (e.g., preventive attachment of assets, seizure and deposit of income or temporary deposit of goods), Section 11 of the same provision makes it clear that this list is not exhaustive.

The Arbitration Act does not set out the requirements that an applicant must satisfy in order for the arbitral tribunal to order interim measures, save for the possible need for the applicant to provide appropriate security.[13] From a substantive standpoint, it is generally accepted that the test should be the same as that applicable in civil proceedings before state courts.[14] An applicant for interim relief must justify that it has a prima facie case (*fumus boni iuris*) and that, in the case at hand, failure to order the interim measures could, during the course of the proceedings, lead to situations preventing or hindering the effectiveness of the protection that may be granted if an affirmative judgment is eventually passed (*periculum in mora*).[15] The applicant should also satisfy the court that the requested measures cannot be replaced by another measure equally effective for the purposes of

---

[12] Arbitration Act of 2003 ("AA"), Art. 23.1 and, e.g., Madrid Court of Arbitration Arbitration Rules, Article 36; Barcelona Arbitral Tribunal Rules, Article 22; Spanish Court of Arbitration Procedural Rules, Article 15.1.

[13] Article 23.1 AA and similarly Article 728.3 CPA.

[14] Fernández-Ballesteros, Miguel Ángel, "*Comentarios a la Nueva Ley de Arbitraje 60/2003, de 23 de diciembre*", various authors, Julio González Soria (coord.), Aranzadi, 2004, pp. 270-271.

[15] Article 728 CPA.

interim relief, but less burdensome or damaging for the defendant (proportionality.)[16]

Most arbitration rules of Spanish arbitral institutions do not yet provide for any arbitral mechanism to obtain interim measures before the commencement of the arbitral proceedings or before the constitution of the arbitral tribunal.[17] A party to an arbitration agreement may, however, seek interim relief from state courts before the commencement of the arbitral proceedings.[18] We would expect that most Spanish arbitral institutions will include such a mechanism in future versions of their rules, in line with what some prominent arbitral institutions in the international context have done in recent years.[19]

C.2 Court-Ordered Interim Measures

State courts can order interim measures in support of an arbitration, even before the commencement of the arbitral proceedings and even if the place of arbitration is outside Spain.[20] There is well-established case law in this regard.[21] The court that is competent to adopt interim measures is that of the place where the award is to be enforced and, failing this

---

[16] Article 726.1.2ª CPA.

[17] By way of exception, Spanish Court of Arbitration Procedural Rules, Article 15.4.

[18] Article 722 CPA.

[19] *E.g.*, provisions on 'emergency arbitrator' in the AAA-ICDR International Arbitration Rules (Article 37), the SCC Arbitration Rules (Appendix II) and the ICC Arbitration Rules (Article 29 and Appendix V).

[20] Article 722 CPA and Articles 1.2, 8.3 and 11.3 AA.

[21] *E.g.*, Court of Appeal of Madrid (Section 20), Ruling 205/2012, of 21 September 2012; Court of Appeal of Santa Cruz de Tenerife (Section 3), Ruling 154/2011, of 19 July 2011; Court of Appeal of Barcelona (Section 15), Judgment 55/2010, of 4 March 2012; Court of Appeal of Zaragoza (Section 5), Ruling 542/2009, of 20 October 2009.

determination, that of the place where the measures are to have effect.[22] State courts and arbitrators have concurrent powers to adopt interim measures, and these powers remain in place even if the arbitral proceedings have already started.[23] Under the Arbitration Act, parties are not obliged to apply to the arbitral tribunal first once arbitral proceedings have commenced.

The time required to obtain interim measures from a state court may vary significantly from one case to another, depending on various factors. In cases of extreme urgency, where the measures are normally requested and granted *ex parte*, it may be a matter of a few days. In most cases, though, a hearing with the parties will be held and an overall 3- or 4-week period between the request for interim relief and the court ruling may be deemed normal.

Spanish courts are unlikely to grant anti-suit injunctions. Spanish law grants arbitrators the power to rule on their own jurisdiction in the first instance, including any objections with respect to the existence or validity of the arbitration agreement or any other objections which, if upheld, would prevent the arbitrators from deciding on the merits of the dispute.[24] State courts are prevented from hearing disputes submitted to arbitration, provided that the concerned party invokes the arbitration agreement by means of a plea objecting to the jurisdiction of the court.[25] Courts are also expressly enjoined from intervening in matters governed by the Arbitration Act except where so provided by law.[26] Anti-suit injunctions seem even more unlikely in international arbitrations,

---

[22] Article 8.3 AA.

[23] Articles 23 and 11.3 AA.

[24] Article 22.1 AA. State courts may review the existence or validity of the arbitration agreement at the stage of nullification of the arbitral award (Article 41.a AA)

[25] Article 11.1 AA.

[26] Article 7 AA.

given the special protection that the validity of the arbitration agreement is granted in such cases by the Arbitration Act.[27]

C.3 Enforcement of Interim Measures

Interim orders by arbitrators are enforceable by state courts in the same way as an arbitral award and regardless of the form that such orders may take (e.g., "award," "decision," "ruling," "order").[28] When the place of arbitration is in Spain, the court that is competent to enforce an award or an arbitral decision is that of the place of arbitration.[29] An arbitral order for interim measures is also enforceable in Spain when the seat of arbitration is outside Spain. Foreign interim orders fall under basically the same legal regime of enforcement as domestic orders. In one of the few exceptions to the territorial scope of application of the Arbitration Act, Article 23 (granting arbitrators the power to order interim measures and allowing the enforcement of these measures in the same way as domestic arbitral awards) applies even when the place of the arbitration is outside Spain.[30] In such a case, the court that is competent to enforce an award or an arbitral decision is the court of first instance of the domicile or place of residence of the party against whom the enforcement is sought, or of the domicile or place of residence of the person affected by the decision, or of the place where the decision is to have effect.[31]

---

[27] Article 9.6 AA: "In an international arbitration, the arbitration agreement shall be valid and the dispute shall be capable of being subject to arbitration if the requirements contained in the rules of law chosen by the parties to govern the arbitration agreement, *or* in the rules of law applicable to the merits of the dispute, *or* in Spanish law are met" (emphasis added).

[28] Article 23.2 AA

[29] Article 8.4 AA.

[30] Article 1.2 AA.

[31] Article 8.6 second para. AA.

SWEDEN

Jonas Benedictsson,[1] Stefan Bessman,[2] Magnus Stålmarker[3] and Gustav Ståhl[4]

A. LEGISLATION, TRENDS AND TENDENCIES

No significant legislative changes in relation to arbitration have occurred in Sweden during 2012. The present Arbitration Act entered into force in 1999.

The present arbitration rules of the Arbitration Institute of the Stockholm Chamber of Commerce entered into force on 1 January 2010.

There have been no significant trends or tendencies with respect to Swedish arbitrations during 2012.

B. CASES

In 2012, the Swedish Supreme Court and the courts of appeal rendered a number of decisions in arbitration matters. Some of these decisions are described below.

[1] Jonas Benedictsson is a Partner in Baker & McKenzie's Stockholm office. His practice includes various aspects of arbitration, litigation, alternative dispute resolution and insolvency. He leads Baker & McKenzie's Dispute Resolution Practice Group in Stockholm.

[2] Stefan Bessman is a Partner in Baker & McKenzie's Stockholm office. He focuses in particular on dispute resolution in the fields of banking, finance, insurance and reinsurance.

[3] Magnus Stålmarker is an Associate in Baker & McKenzie's Stockholm office. As a member of Stockholm's Arbitration & Litigation Group, he has acted as counsel and co-counsel in various national and cross-border matters.

[4] Gustav Ståhl is an Associate in Baker & McKenzie's Stockholm office and a member of Stockholm's Arbitration & Litigation Group.

B.1   The Doctrine of Assertion[5]

Concorp Scandinavia AB ("Concorp") filed a lawsuit against Karelkamen Confectionary AB ("Karelkamen") at the District Court of Södertörn, Sweden on the basis that Concorp had granted Karelkamen a loan and Concorp now requested repayment of this loan including interest.

Karelkamen moved to dismiss the lawsuit on the grounds that there existed an arbitration agreement between the parties. The agreement in question was a cooperation agreement under which a third party, the company Xcaret Confectionery Holding AB, had purchased Karelkanen from Concorp (the "Agreement"). Karelkamen argued that the Agreement, including the arbitration clause, was binding in relation to and between all three companies, i.e., Karelkamen, Xcaret Confectionery Holding AB and Concorp.

It was undisputed that the Agreement existed and that it contained an arbitration clause, but Concorp objected that Karelkamen was not a party to the Agreement and the arbitration clause was not applicable as to the dispute between Concorp and Karelkamen.

The district court dismissed Karelkamen's claim and found that it had jurisdiction to try the merits of the case. Karelkamen appealed this decision, and Svea Court of Appeal, rejected the lawsuit due to lack of jurisdiction because of the arbitration clause. Concorp appealed to the Supreme Court, which subsequently ruled that the district court's original decision that it was competent to try the lawsuit should be reinstated.

The Supreme Court concluded that Concorp had not based its lawsuit on the Agreement and that it did not rely on the

---

[5]   Decision by the Supreme Court on 5 April 2012 in Case No. NJA 2012 s. 183.

B. Cases

Agreement at all. Instead, Concorp had asserted that the matter now in question was a claim for repayment of a loan that the parties had agreed upon before the Agreement was signed. According to the Supreme Court, the assessment regarding the jurisdictional question and the court´s competence to try the lawsuit has to be made on the basis of what Concorp asserts regarding its right (the "doctrine of assertion"). Since Concorp had asserted that the claim was based on, and was a result of, a different legal relationship than the Agreement, the arbitration clause in the Agreement was not applicable.

The Supreme Court referred the matter to the district court to try the case on the merits.

B.2 Request for Production of Documents[6]

In an arbitration between the company Euroflon Tekniska Produkter ("Euroflon") and the individual, Bengt Andersson, Euroflon claimed that Mr. Andersson—through his company Flexiboys i Motala AB ("Flexiboys")—had violated a competition clause in an agreement between the parties. The arbitrator had granted Euroflon permission to file a request for production of documents against Flexiboys at the competent district court. The request for production of documents concerned numerous invoices.

Euroflon subsequently filed a request for production of documents at the District Court of Linköping, Sweden. Among other things Mr. Andersson objected and pleaded that the documents were subject to trade secrets. The district court, however, allowed Euroflon's request for production of documents and ordered Flexiboys to produce the requested invoices. The decision was appealed to the Göta Court of

---

[6] Decision by the Supreme Court on 10 May 2012 in Case No. Ö 1590-11.

Appeal, which dismissed the request for production of documents. The Supreme Court upheld the district court's decision.

The Supreme Court concluded that if an arbitrator has granted a party permission to file a request for production of documents at the district court, this means that the arbitrator has made the assessment that the relevant documents are significant as evidence. The court shall only examine the legal conditions for the measure: whether the arbitrator indeed has given the permission; whether the request for production of documents has been made to the court which has jurisdiction; whether the request is sufficiently specified so that it can be enforced; and whether the documents include any trade secrets.

Accordingly, the Supreme Court did not investigate whether the documents were significant as evidence. Instead, and as elaborated above, the Supreme Court concluded that the arbitrator had given the relevant permission, that the request for production of documents was filed with the correct court of jurisdiction and that the request was specific enough to be enforced. The remaining question was whether the documents were subject to trade secrets and thus confidential, but the Supreme Court concluded that they were not subject to any trade secrets. Against this background, the Supreme Court allowed Euroflon's request for production of documents.

B.3 Ordre Public[7]

In 2003, the Ukrainian company Naftogaz of Ukraine ("Naftogaz") and the Italian company Italia Ukraina Gas S.P.A ("IUGAS") entered into an agreement regarding gas delivery (the "Agreement"). The Agreement stated among other things

---

[7]   Decision by the Svea Court of Appeal on 2 July 2012 in Case No. T 611-11

that Naftogaz should sell natural gas to IUGAS during a certain period of time. Naftogaz did not, however, deliver any gas to IUGAS. IUGAS therefore initiated an arbitration against Naftogaz.

The arbitration proceedings were split into two parts. In the first part, the arbitral tribunal assessed whether the Agreement was valid, whether the arbitral tribunal was authorized to try the case, and whether Naftogaz in such case was obliged to deliver natural gas and/or pay a conditional fine and/or damages to IUGAS in accordance with the Agreement. In the second part, the arbitral tribunal was asked to establish the quantum of the conditional fine and/or damages. The arbitral tribunal ruled that the Agreement was valid and that Naftogaz was obliged to deliver gas to IUGAS.

Naftogaz filed a lawsuit against IUGAS at the Svea Court of Appeal and requested that the award be annulled. The ground for the claim was that Ukrainian law prohibited both exportation of gas with Ukrainian origin and re-export of gas with Central Asian origin. Nevertheless, the arbitral tribunal had ordered Naftogaz to fulfill the delivery of gas. Naftogaz also challenged the award and claimed the arbitral tribunal had not considered Naftogaz's assertion that Naftogaz, because of Ukrainian law, was prevented from delivering gas with Central Asian origin.

The Svea Court of Appeal rejected Naftogaz's cause of action. As regards the invalidity claim, the court stated that the assessment of *ordre public* in international arbitrations was narrower than the corresponding assessment under national legislation. The court ruled that Ukrainian law did not contain a total prohibition against the export of natural gas, regardless of its origin, and that the award therefore did not oblige Naftogaz to take illegal actions. Consequently, the award did not violate international or national *ordre public*. As regard the challenge, the court found that the arbitral tribunal had not failed to consider Naftogaz's assertion that it was prevented from delivering gas. As a result, the court concluded that the arbitral tribunal had not committed any administrative errors or excess of mandate.

B.4 Conflict of Interest[8]

After a dispute had arisen between Tidomat AB ("Tidomat") and Relacom AB ("Relacom") regarding outstanding work, Relacom initiated arbitration proceedings against Tidomat. The parties appointed an attorney as arbitrator. The award was given on 21 November 2011.

Tidomat challenged the award at the Svea Court of Appeal claiming that there existed a conflict of interest because the arbitrator had previously had a client relationship with the bank Nordea which now was a part-owner of Relacom. Relacom disputed the claim.

The Svea Court of Appeal ruled that the arbitrator's relationship with Nordea was relatively far back in time and that the relationship had been limited in scope. The court found that these circumstances could not, on an objective basis, undermine confidence in the arbitrator's impartiality, and concluded that the arbitrator was not biased.

B.5 Scope of an Arbitration Agreement[9]

In another interesting case, the Ukrainian company UKRNAFTA filed an action for a negative declaration that there was no binding arbitration agreement between UKRNAFTA and a US

---

[8]   Decision by the Svea Court of Appeal on 29 November 2012 in Case No. T 9620-11.

[9]   Decision by the Svea Court of Appeal on 30 November 2012 in Case No. T 221-12.

company, Carpatsky Petroleum Corporation ("CPC"), which had commenced arbitration against UKRNAFTA in 2007.

In 1995 UKRNAFTA entered a contract with an arbitration agreement with CPC, a company incorporated in the state of Texas since 1992 ("CPC 1"). Allegedly unbeknownst to UKRNAFTA, CPC 1 thereafter merged into another company with exactly the same name, incorporated in the state of Delaware in 1996, ("CPC 2"). As a result of the merger shortly after the formation of CPC 2, CPC 1 ceased to exist as a legal entity.

Prior to the arbitration that was initiated by CPC 2, in reliance on the arbitration agreement entered with CPC 1, there was some confusion as to the proper address of CPC and UKRNAFTA allegedly believed that CPC 2 and CPC 1 were one and the same legal entity. Some time into the arbitration, however, suspicions grew and UKRNAFTA conducted a comprehensive investigation, finding out that there had been two CPC entities and that the entity with which it had contracted, CPC 1, did not exist anymore and was not the same entity as CPC 2. An objection was filed in the arbitration, but disregarded by the arbitrators.

UKRNAFTA then filed parallel proceedings in court seeking the declaration mentioned above. However, both the district court and the Svea Court of Appeal denied the claim for a declaration. The district court took the position that the arbitration agreement survived the merger of the two CPC entities, but the Svea Court of Appeal chose another line of reasoning.

In essence, the Svea Court of Appeal concluded that UKRNAFTA was precluded from objecting that CPC 2 was not the party to the arbitration agreement, since it was too late in finding out the facts and objecting. The court stated that the fact CPC 2, as early as in the request for arbitration, was identified as an entity "registered in the state of Delaware" should have triggered the investigations that UKRNAFTA commenced much later. By not investigating what the court called an "indication of an important change in the legal status of CPC," and thus by not objecting in time by raising the issue more than a year after the request for arbitration, UKRNAFTA had effectively waived its right to dispute the existence of a valid arbitration agreement.

The case was appealed to the Supreme Court, but the Supreme Court has not yet rendered a decision and the case is thus still pending.

C. THE GRANT AND ENFORCEMENT OF INTERIM MEASURES IN INTERNATIONAL ARBITRATION

In Sweden, it is possible to obtain interim measures in two ways: (1) from an arbitral tribunal and (2) from the general courts and the governmental enforcement authority.

C.1 Tribunal-Ordered Interim Measures

C.1.1 Ad hoc arbitration

Unless the parties have agreed otherwise, it is possible (according to Section 25(4) of the Swedish Arbitration Act) for each of the parties to an arbitration to request that the arbitral tribunal compels another party to take certain actions in order to secure the claim that is being examined by the tribunal. The arbitral tribunal may prescribe the requesting party to provide reasonable security for the damage which the counterparty may suffer. As regards preservation of evidence, it is possible to request a third party to provide certain evidence, under the condition that the third party agrees to do so.

The rule is inspired by Article 17 of the UNCITRAL Model Law. The kind of interim measures that are of relevance for a

Swedish arbitration procedure are therefore inspired by the Model Law, and include orders to:

(a) maintain or restore the status quo pending determination of the dispute;

(b) take action that would prevent, or refrain from taking action that is likely to cause, current or imminent harm or prejudice to the arbitral process itself;

(c) provide a means of preserving assets out of which a subsequent award may be satisfied; or

(d) preserve evidence that may be relevant and material to the resolution of the dispute.

The arbitral tribunal's decision on interim measures is not enforceable and a general court cannot make the decision enforceable. However, if a party disregards the tribunal's decision it is possible that the tribunal will consider this when trying the case on the merits.

C.1.2 SCC arbitration

According to Article 32 of the SCC Rules, an arbitral tribunal may, at the request of a party, grant any interim measures it deems appropriate. As well as under an *ad hoc* arbitration, the arbitral tribunal may (under the SCC Rules) order the party requesting interim measures to provide appropriate security in connection with the measure. A request for interim measures by a party to a judicial authority is not incompatible with the arbitration agreement or the SCC Rules.

According to Appendix II of the SCC Rules, it is also possible for each of the parties to apply for the appointment of an emergency arbitrator until the case has been referred to an ordinary arbitral tribunal. The powers of such emergency arbitrator are those set out in Article 32 of the SCC Rules as described above. Any emergency decision on interim measures shall be made no later than five days from the date upon which the application was referred to the emergency arbitrator. Under some circumstances it is, however, possible for the emergency arbitrator to extend this time limit. It should be noted that the emergency decision ceases to be binding if, *inter alia*, the arbitration is not commenced within 30 days from the date of the emergency decision, or the case is not referred to an arbitral tribunal within 90 days from the date of the emergency decision.

C.2 Court-Ordered Interim Measures

According to Section 4(3) of the Swedish Arbitration Act it is possible for general courts to render decisions on interim measures both before and during an arbitration procedure. An arbitration agreement cannot prevent that such procedure is initiated at the competent general court and the applicant is not in breach of the arbitration agreement when it is applying for the interim measure.

A party who wants to apply for an interim measure must file the application with the competent court of jurisdiction in accordance with Section 10 of the Swedish Code of Judicial Procedure. As a general rule, the application shall be filed at the district court in the judicial district in which the counterparty has its domicile. An application must be made in writing, and as a general rule, the counterparty must be served with the application before the decision is rendered. However, if there exists imminent danger it is possible for the court to render a decision before the application has been communicated to the counterparty.

The most commonly used interim measure is sequestration in accordance with Chapter 15 of the Swedish Code of Judicial

Procedure, which the court can decide upon under certain circumstances. The sequestration can be based upon the following grounds: (i) that there exist a claim against the counterparty and it is reasonable to suspect that the counterparty, by absconding, removing property, or other action, will evade payment of the debt; (ii) that someone has a superior right to certain property and it is reasonable to suspect that the opposing party will conceal, substantially deteriorate, or otherwise deal with or dispose of the property to the detriment of the applicant; or (iii) that someone has a claim towards another and it is reasonable to suspect that the counterparty, by carrying on a certain activity, by performing or refraining from performing a certain act, or by other conduct, will hinder or render more difficult the exercise or realization of the applicant's right or substantially reduce the value of that right.

The applicant must substantiate that it is probable that it has a claim or superior right and that the claim or superior right is, or may be, subject to a court action or another similar procedure (such as arbitration). The last condition is that it is reasonable to suspect that the counterparty will make it difficult for the applicant to exercise its claim or superior right. As a general rule, the applicant must provide security for the damage that the counterparty may suffer. If the applicant has not already initiated an arbitration procedure, such procedure must be initiated within one month from the date of the decision on interim measures. Otherwise the sequestration will be cancelled.

As regards non-Swedish arbitration proceedings, there is a requirement, in addition to the requirements described above, that the award is enforceable in Sweden (Section 60 in the Swedish Arbitration Act). Anti-suit injunctions do not exist under Swedish law.

Normally, the interim measure procedure is in writing and the court's decision will be based on the documents provided by the parties. It is possible to request an oral hearing even though it is very unusual. An application for interim measures shall be handled by priority in court. Exactly how long it takes to obtain an interim measure depends on how extensive the application is. In general, it normally takes between a few days and two weeks.

A decision on interim measure may subsequently be enforced by the Swedish governmental enforcement authority and the procedure to initiate enforceable action is regulated in the Swedish Enforcement Act.

SWITZERLAND

Joachim Frick,[1] Urs Zenhäusern,[2] Anne-Catherine Hahn,[3] and Luca Beffa[4]

A. LEGISLATION, TRENDS AND TENDENCIES

A.1 Revised Swiss Rules of International Arbitration

On 1 June 2012, the revised version of the Swiss Rules of International Arbitration (the "Swiss Rules") entered into force. The main goals of the revision were to enhance efficiency in terms of time and cost and to give certain additional powers to the bodies administrating the proceedings. At the same time, the revision was limited to keep the basic structure and principles of the previous version entered into force on 1 January 2004, under which almost 600 cases have been successfully conducted. The fact that many international practitioners are familiar with the Swiss Rules is one of the biggest advantages of Switzerland as a place for arbitration.

---

[1] Joachim Frick is a Partner in Baker & McKenzie's Zurich office. He regularly represents clients in arbitration proceedings as a party-counsel. He has written various publications on Swiss and international commercial arbitration proceedings and teaches as honorary professor at Zurich University.

[2] Urs Zenhäusern is a Partner in Baker & McKenzie's Zurich office. He regularly represents clients in arbitration proceedings as a party-counsel and acts also as an arbitrator.

[3] Anne-Catherine Hahn is a Partner in Baker & McKenzie's Zurich office. She practises mainly in the area of international commercial arbitration and litigation and also acts as a Lecturer at the University of Fribourg.

[4] Luca Beffa is a Senior Associate in Baker & McKenzie's Geneva office. His practice focuses primarily on international and domestic arbitration as well as commercial litigation, sports and public law.

In particular the expedited procedure foreseen in Article 42 of the Swiss Rules, which applies if the parties agree or the amount in dispute does not exceed CHF 1 million, has proven to be very popular and successful. Under the Swiss Rules of 2004, more than a third of all proceedings were conducted under the expedited procedure. The key features are the appointment of a sole arbitrator (unless agreed otherwise), one exchange of written briefs and normally only a single hearing; the award shall be made within 6 months from the date when the arbitral tribunal receives the file. The only change which the 2012 Swiss Rules introduce in this respect is the requirement that the claimant must now pay a provisional deposit of CHF 5,000 immediately upon filing for arbitration.

The new rules continue to be a fairly detailed but clearly understandable set of rules. Some new features ensure that they keep pace with an ever more competitive international market for arbitration services. The new version of the Swiss Rules applies to all arbitrations commenced on or after 1 June 2012, unless the parties agree otherwise. The key revisions can be summarized as follows:

- Further Improvements in Efficiency

  Lack of efficiency is today seen as one of the biggest threats to international arbitration. Accordingly, the revised Swiss Rules, in their aim to maintain the attractiveness of Switzerland as a place of arbitration, introduced additional features to improve efficiency: They foresee that if the respondent does not file an answer to the notice of arbitration or raises a jurisdictional objection, the Arbitration Court shall administer the case unless there is manifestly no agreement to arbitrate under the Swiss Rules (Article 3(12)). Also, the Arbitration Court is given the power to shorten (or extend) a number of time limits (Article 2(3)). To further enhance efficiency, the new Rules require the designation of party appointed arbitrators already in the notice of arbitration and the answer (Articles 3(3)(h) and 3(7)(f)). They foresee a deadline of only 15 days after the relevant circumstances become known for the challenge of an arbitrator (Article 11), and a general requirement that the statement of claim and defense include all documents and other evidence on which the parties want to rely (Articles 18(3) and 19(2)).

• Joinder and Consolidation

In some circumstances, the consolidation of different arbitral proceedings or the participation of third persons may improve efficiency. Accordingly, the new Swiss Rules have amended the powers of the Arbitration Court in this respect (which go further than for instance under the 2012 ICC Rules). They will make the Swiss place of arbitration attractive especially for multi-contract or multi-party arbitrations (Articles 4(1) and (2)).

A decision on participation of a third person is made by the arbitral tribunal upon request by one of the parties or by the third person. The third person can participate not only as an additional party (joinder) but also in other forms (amicus curiae briefs; third party notices). Consolidation may be ordered even when not all of the parties are identical; if consolidation is ordered, the court is empowered to constitute an entirely new arbitral tribunal for the consolidated proceedings.

• New provisions on interim measures

The Swiss Rules now expressly state that arbitral tribunals and state court both have jurisdiction to grant interim measures and that the parties do not waive any right in this respect by agreeing to arbitration (Article 26(5)). The arbitral tribunal may modify, suspend or terminate any interim measures granted at any time (Article 26(1)). It has jurisdiction to award compensation for any damage caused by an interim measure which later proves to be unjustified (Article 26(4)).

Interim relief can be granted, in exceptional circumstances, in the form of preliminary orders before the request has been communicated to any other party (Article 26(3)). The right to be heard is guaranteed by the requirement that the communication of the request is made at the latest together with the preliminary order and the other party is given an immediate opportunity to be heard (Article 26(3)).

* New emergency relief procedure

Similar to other modern rules of international arbitration,[5] the Swiss Rules now foresee emergency relief prior to the constitution of the tribunal to be granted by a so-called emergency arbitrator (Article 43).

Applications for emergency relief are heard by a sole emergency arbitrator, who can also issue ex parte preliminary orders (Article 26(3)). He shall decide within 15 days of receiving the file from the Secretariat. Where appropriate, the court can refuse to appoint an emergency arbitrator, in which case it will be for the arbitral tribunal to decide on interim measures after its constitution. Unless agreed otherwise by the parties, the seat of the emergency relief proceedings is determined by the Court without prejudice to the final determination of the seat under Art. 16(1) (Art. 43(5)). In case the request for emergency relief was filed before the notice of arbitration was submitted, Article 43(3) foresees a 10 day time limit after the receipt of the application by the Secretariat to

---

[5]   *See, e.g.,* Art. 20 and Appendix V ICC Rules; Art. 26 and Schedule I SIAC Rules; Appendix II of the Arbitration Rules of the Stockholm Chamber of Commerce.

file the notice of arbitration. It will be for state court practice to decide on whether or not an award rendered by an emergency arbitrator is an enforceable arbitral award under the New York Convention.

In principle, the new Article 43 applies to all arbitrations in which the notice of arbitration is submitted on or after 1 June 2012 (Article 1(3)). It remains to be seen if a party could successfully argue, however, that the new provisions shall not apply to the extent the arbitration agreement was concluded under the previous version of the Swiss Rules which did not include any provisions on emergency arbitrators.

• New provisions on costs

In expedited proceedings the Arbitration Court (and not the sole arbitrator) will demand a provisional deposit of CHF 5,000 to be paid by the claimant and the file is only transmitted to the arbitrator after payment. A party applying for emergency relief shall pay a non-refundable registration fee of CHF 4,500 and a deposit as an advance for the costs of the emergency relief proceedings of CHF 20,000.

Costs for a secretary to the tribunal are now covered by Art. 38(a) and (b) and shall remain within the limits set out for the total fee range of the arbitrators. As an important new feature, the Arbitration Court has now to approve and if necessary adjust the determination made by the arbitral tribunal in relation to the fees and expenditures of the arbitral tribunal, the secretary and the emergency arbitrator (Article 40(4)).

In order to speed up proceedings, the arbitral tribunal can now set deadlines for parties to pay advances on costs not paid by a party after 15 days instead of 30 days (Art. 41(4)). In case of non-payment, the arbitral tribunal may order the suspension or termination of the proceedings.

In sum, the amendments to the Swiss Rules are not as substantial as those made recently to other institutional arbitration rules such as the 2012 ICC Rules, simply because the prior version of 2004 was already quite modern and did not require major improvement. Also the revision of the ICC Rules had the focus on an increase of efficiency and cost control.[6] The Swiss Rules will continue to provide a professional but lean institutional administration and flexible proceedings, with strong emphasis on efficiency. They appear to be a successful attempt to enhance competitiveness of the Swiss place of arbitration. The Swiss Rules remain suitable for a wide range of arbitrations from small cases to very complex multi-party disputes, allowing for tailor-made and cost effective procedures.

A.2 Pending Legislative Motions

For arbitrations seated in Switzerland, the provisions of Chapter 12 (Articles 176–194) of the Private International Law Act ("PILA") apply, if, at the time when the arbitration agreement was entered into, at least one of the parties had neither its domicile nor its habitual residence in Switzerland. The PILA entered into force in 1989 and it contained at that time (and still contains) a very modern set of international arbitration rules. The Swiss Federal Parliament has now mandated the Swiss government to prepare a bill for a slight revision of Chapter 12 of the PILA. The purpose of the intended revision is to preserve and enhance the most attractive features of the Swiss law of international arbitration, by nevertheless keeping the simple overall structure and the reader-friendly style and language. Michael Schöll as the head of the unit of private international law in the Federal Department of Justice has expressed its support for a review.

---

[6] Sessler/Voser, Die revidierte ICC Schiedsgerichtsordnung – Schwerpunkte; SchiedsVZ 2012, p.120ff.

A proposal to amend Art. 7 of the PILA[7] is still pending. It seeks to add a second paragraph to Art. 7 PILA according to which Swiss courts would postpone their decision on jurisdiction until the arbitral tribunal has decided on its own jurisdiction, except when a summary (prima facie) examination reveals that the arbitration clause is invalid. It was decided to postpone a decision on the motion, this given the above-mentioned motion to review not only Art. 7 PILA but the entirety of Chapter 12 PILA, with a goal to maintain attractiveness of the Swiss seat of arbitration (motion 12.3012).

A.3 Institutional Revisions, Swiss Arbitration Center

The new Swiss Rules provide for important facilitations concerning the institutional organization. The Swiss Chambers Court of Arbitration and Mediation of the seven participating Chambers of Commerce has become the Swiss Chambers Arbitration Institution with its own legal personality. The Arbitration Committee has become the Arbitration Court (in German "Gerichtshof"). The Arbitration Court is granted full power to supervise arbitral proceedings to the fullest extent permitted under applicable law (Art. 1 Sect. 4).

It would only be logical if in due course a Swiss Arbitration Center becomes a reality, i.e., an organization under one roof consisting of arbitration premises with a full-time provisional marketing staff and regular educational offerings (*see Baker & McKenzie International Arbitration Yearbook 2011/2012*). Now that the Swiss Rules are up to date, this would probably be the most important next step to enhance attractiveness of the Swiss set of arbitration. The third pillar could then be the above described revision of Chapter 12 of the PILA.

---

[7] *See Baker & McKenzie International Arbitration Yearbook 2011/2012*, p. 449.

A.4 Swiss Arbitration Association Appoints Executive Director

On 1 September 2012, Alexander McLin was appointed executive director of the Swiss Arbitration Association ("ASA"). In ASA's 35 years of existence, Mr. McLin (who practised for two years also as an attorney in the New York office of Baker & McKenzie before going in-house) is the first employee of ASA. He is based in Geneva, and his principal task is to further promote arbitration as a dispute resolution mechanism, and Switzerland as a place for international arbitration.

A.5 General Trends

The past year has confirmed the general trends in arbitration which have been noted in previous years. Among these are an increasing number of arbitration proceedings, accompanied by an increasing number of (in over 90% of cases unsuccessful) requests to set aside arbitral awards.

Also, an increased judicialization and aggressiveness in the manner proceedings are conducted has been noted[8], in particular with an increased number of objections to appointments of arbitrators.

New arbitration institutions have opened, showing the ever increasing competition for traditional places of arbitration such as Switzerland. This includes for instance the Scottish Arbitration Center; the Bangladesh International Arbitration Center; the Cyprus Eurasia Dispute Resolution and Arbitration Center; the Mauritius International Arbitration Center developed by the LCIA with the goal to be the leading African arbitral institution; the Atlanta International Arbitration Society, etc.[9]

---

[8] *See* for instance Wilske/Markert, Entwicklungen in der Internationalen Schiedsgerichtsbarkeit 2011 und Ausblick auf 2012, SchiedsVZ 2012, p. 58/p. 59.

[9] Wilske/Markert, SchiedsVZ 2012, p. 61.

Other trends important for Switzerland include the fact that the CAS (Court of Arbitration for Sports) has continued to develop as the world's leading sports arbitration institution with its own characteristics.

B. CASES

The Swiss Federal Tribunal rendered more than 30 decisions in 2012 in international arbitration matters. The following is an overview of the most interesting cases.

B.1 Conformity of a Waiver to Appeal against an Award with Article 6 ECHR

In a landmark decision dated 4 January 2012,[10] the Swiss Federal Tribunal confirmed for the very first time that Article 192(1) of the PILA, which allows parties that have neither a domicile nor an habitual residence or an establishment in Switzerland to waive any right of appeal against the awards of an arbitral tribunal, is consistent with Article 6 of the European Convention for the Protection of Human Rights and Fundamental Freedoms ("ECHR").

The relevant arbitration clause provided that: "The decision of the arbitration shall be final and binding and neither party shall have any right to appeal such decision to any court of law." After considering this clause as a valid and binding waiver of any appeal against the award at stake in accordance with Article 192(1) PILA, the Swiss Federal Tribunal rejected the argument of the appellant pursuant to which the exclusion in advance of any appeal against an international arbitral award would be inconsistent with the right to a fair trial guaranteed by Article 6(1) ECHR.

---

[10] Decision 4A_238/2011.

According to the Swiss Federal Tribunal, the renunciation of the right to appeal prevents the losing party from arguing that the award under appeal was issued in breach of the fundamental procedural guarantees contained in the treaty provision. However, neither the letter nor the spirit of Article 6(1) ECHR prevent a person from renouncing such guarantees on his own volition as long as such renunciation is not equivocal and does not conflict with any important public interest.

The Swiss Federal Tribunal held in this respect that Article 192(1) PILA meets these requirements as it requests an express and bilateral renunciation from both parties. Moreover, a renunciation which a party would make not of its own free will but by vitiated consent could be invalidated on that ground. Finally, as arbitration is a contractual method of resolving disputes by recourse to private judges—the arbitrators—that the parties may choose, one does not see *a priori* which important public interest a renunciation of the right to appeal in advance could possibly harm in such a procedural context.

B.2 Consequences of the Failure by an Arbitral Tribunal to Take into Consideration the Post-Hearing Brief of a Party

In a decision dated 31 January 2012,[11] the Swiss Federal Tribunal had to decide about the consequence of the failure by an arbitral tribunal to take into consideration the post-hearing brief validly submitted by a party.

Said party was ordered to pay damages to its adverse party in an ICC arbitration. The Sole Arbitrator admitted that he issued the award without taking into consideration the post-hearing brief validly submitted by the losing party, explaining his oversight by a succession of incidents connected to the introduction of a new

---

[11]   Decision 4A_360/2011.

software by his firm. The losing party moved to set aside the award before the Swiss Federal Tribunal, claiming a breach of both the equality of the parties and its right to be heard.

In its decision, the Swiss Federal Tribunal held first that, by disregarding the post-hearing brief of a party, the Sole Arbitrator did not violate the equality of the parties. The Swiss Supreme Court confirmed in this regard the dominant opinion among Swiss scholars pursuant to which the scope *ratione temporis* of the guarantee of equality of the parties is limited to the examination phase, including hearing and arguments, and does not encompass the deliberation phase of the arbitral tribunal.

However, the Swiss Federal Tribunal also held that such an inadvertence may violate the right to be heard of the relevant party if the brief disregarded by the arbitral tribunal contains statements, arguments, evidence or offers of evidence pertinent to decide the case which are totally overlooked in the award. The Swiss Federal Tribunal found that this was the case in the matter at hand with respect to two of the arguments raised by the Appellant in its post-hearing brief, and therefore annulled the award.

B.3 Jurisdiction of the CAS, WADA's Standing to Appeal, and *Lis Pendens*

In a decision dated 13 February 2012,[12] the Swiss Federal Tribunal confirmed its very liberal approach regarding the incorporation by reference of arbitration agreements in sports arbitration, and clarified its case law with respect to both the legal nature of the question whether a non-signatory to the arbitration agreement can challenge the arbitral tribunal's decisions in sports arbitration, and the possibility to challenge decisions on suspension of arbitral proceedings.

---

[12] Decision 4A_428/2011.

The Doping Tribunal of the Flemish Tennis Federation pronounced a one year ban against two Belgian professional tennis players for breach of anti-doping rules. Both players and the World Anti-Doping Agency ("WADA") appealed this decision to the Court of arbitration for sport ("CAS"). The two players challenged the jurisdiction of the CAS to hear the appeal filed by WADA. In parallel, they initiated several procedures in the Belgium state courts and before the European authorities, requesting the CAS to suspend the appeal proceedings until a decision in these parallel proceedings would be rendered.

In a partial award, the CAS admitted its jurisdiction to hear all of the appeals filed, rejected the suspension of the proceedings and consolidated them. The two players moved to set aside this partial award before the Swiss Federal Tribunal, arguing first that the CAS lacked jurisdiction to decide upon the appeals filed by WADA. The Swiss Federal Tribunal rejected this first argument, confirming that arbitration clauses contained in the regulations of a sport federation bind their affiliates even if they did not expressly agree to be bound by the arbitration clause, and irrespective of whether the federation adopted the regulations and the arbitration clause contained therein on its own initiative or pursuant to a requirement of the state in which it is based.

Concerning WADA, the Swiss Federal Tribunal confirmed that a party's ability to appeal the decision taken by a body of a sport federation (pursuant to its statutes and to the applicable legal provisions) does not relate to the issue of jurisdiction of the arbitral tribunal (as it would in commercial arbitration), but to the issue of *locus standi*. Therefore, according to the Swiss Supreme Court, the issue as to whether or not WADA had standing to appeal the decisions at stake did not involve the jurisdiction of the arbitral tribunal but merely a procedural issue—WADA's standing to appeal—which is not capable of review by the Swiss Federal Tribunal. The latter specified in this respect that, assuming that the CAS did not specifically deal with WADA's standing to act, the players should have challenged the award arguing a violation of their right to be heard, which imposes upon the arbitrators a minimal duty to review and deal with the pertinent issues, and not for lack of jurisdiction as they did.

The Swiss Federal Tribunal also rejected the last argument raised by the players, who blamed the CAS for having failed to suspend the proceedings. The decisions of arbitral tribunals as to a temporary stay of arbitral proceedings are capable of appeal when, in issuing them, the arbitral tribunal implicitly decided on its own jurisdiction. Following this case law, the Swiss Supreme Court held that the players had not proven that the three cumulative requirements justifying a stay of the proceedings under the PILA (i.e. the fact that the two concurrent proceedings concern the same parties and the same dispute, that the case in front of the ordinary state court has been initiated before the CAS was seized, and that some serious grounds justify staying the proceedings) were actually met in the present case.

B.4 Substantive Public Policy

In a landmark decision dated 27 March 2012,[13] the Swiss Federal Tribunal set aside, for the first time in over twenty years, an international arbitration award on the basis of a violation of substantive public policy.

A Brazilian football player, Francelino da Silva Matuzalem, was ordered to pay, together with the Spanish football club Real Saragossa SAD, damages of over EUR 11 million to the Ukrainian football club FC Shakhtar Donesk for terminating his contract with the latter club without notice nor just cause, in order to join the former. As neither Matuzalem nor Real

---

[13] Decision 4A_558/2011.

Saragossa paid this amount to Shakhtar Donesk, the Disciplinary Committee of the International Federation of Football Associations ("FIFA"), on the basis of Article 64 of the FIFA Disciplinary Code, ordered the player and the club to pay a fine of CHF 30'000 and disposed a last time limit of 90 days to pay the amount due, under penalty for the player of a prohibition of any football activity. This decision was confirmed by the CAS upon appeal filed by Matuzalem and Real Saragossa.

Matuzalem moved to set aside the CAS award before the Swiss Federal Tribunal. He argued that the CAS award violated substantive public policy insofar as it subjected him to an unlimited and worldwide prohibition of working as a football player. The Swiss Federal Tribunal upheld the challenge. In its reasoning, the Swiss Federal Tribunal confirmed that the substantive adjudication of a dispute violates public policy when it disregards some fundamental legal principles and consequently becomes totally inconsistent with the important, generally recognized values which, according to the dominant opinion in Switzerland, should be the basis of any legal order. This is the case, for instance, when a sanction imposed by sports federation gravely impacts the personal right to economic development of its members and is not justified by a greater interest of the federation.

The Swiss Supreme Court found that FIFA's interest of enforcing compliance by football players with their duties to their employees expressed in Article 64 of the FIFA Disciplinary Code could not justify the unlimited (both in time and space) professional ban imposed on the player. Furthermore, the sanction was not necessary to enforce the damages awarded, as Shakhtar Donesk could easily enforce the CAS award against Matuzalem and Real Saragossa under the New York Convention on the Recognition and Enforcement of Arbitral Awards.

B. Cases

B.5 Lack of Challenge against a Decision of the *Juge d'Appui* to Reject the Challenge of an Arbitrator

In another landmark decision dated 2 May 2012,[14] the Swiss Federal Tribunal confirmed its long standing but criticized case law pursuant to which, when the ordinary court at the seat of the arbitral tribunal (*"juge d'appui"*) is entitled to, and decides a challenge of an arbitrator, its decision is final and cannot be appealed, either directly or indirectly, before the Swiss Supreme Court.

In the case at hand, an *ad hoc* arbitral tribunal seated in Geneva rendered an award overlooking the arguments raised by one of the parties concerning the fact that the claims of its adverse party were time-barred by an absolute limitation period. The Swiss Federal Tribunal annulled the award without formally sending back the case to the arbitral tribunal. The latter nevertheless seized itself of the matter.

The party having raised the arguments overlooked by the arbitral tribunal challenged the jurisdiction of the arbitral tribunal to render a new award, and argued that the arbitral tribunal was no longer independent and impartial because it had already expressed its opinion as to the limitation period defense. Thus, it demanded that the arbitral tribunal recuse itself *in corpore*. The arbitral tribunal failing to do so, the same party applied to the Court of First Instance of Geneva to challenge the three members of the arbitral tribunal, in vain. Eventually, in its final award, the arbitral tribunal found that it had jurisdiction to resume and bring to an end the arbitral proceedings and rejected the argument concerning the absolute limitation period.

The party having raised such argument moved to set aside the award before the Swiss Federal Tribunal, arguing inter alia that

---

[14] Decision 4A_14/2012, published under the reference ATF 138 III 270.

the arbitral tribunal should not have seized itself again after its first award had been annulled by the Federal Tribunal because it no longer presented the guarantees of independence and impartiality. Hence, according to the appellant, the arbitral tribunal was irregularly composed. Moreover, it would have breached procedural public policy by failing to issue an independent judgment on the legal and factual submissions made.

The Swiss Federal Tribunal rejected this challenge by holding that the issue of the regular composition of the arbitral tribunal had already been decided by the Geneva Court, and that the Swiss Supreme Court was not capable of reviewing this decision. The Swiss Federal Tribunal rejected the criticism expressed in this respect by several legal scholars, by stating that, while any legal order must reserve the possibility to review the awards or the arbitral proceedings from the point of view of their conformity with its fundamental legal principles, among which the right to an independent and impartial arbitrator, when a state court already reviewed whether the arbitrator challenged met these requirements or not, there is no need for new state control. This is consistent with the goal of Swiss law on international arbitration, which is to limit the possibilities to challenge arbitral proceedings.

The Swiss Federal Tribunal also confirmed that there is no objection to the same arbitrators deciding the matter again when their final award was annulled, irrespective of any specific empowerment by the law, the Federal Tribunal or the parties, provided of course that the grounds of annulment do not concern the irregular composition of the arbitral tribunal or the lack of jurisdiction, and provided that they were not validly challenged in the meantime.

B. Cases

B.6 Arbitrability

In a decision dated 23 May 2012,[15] the Swiss Federal Tribunal confirmed that arbitrability in Switzerland is governed exclusively by Article 177(1) PILA and that it must be accepted that some awards of international arbitral tribunals sitting in Switzerland finding a matter arbitrable may conceivably be unenforceable in a specific country.

The Football Association of Serbia ("FAS") moved to set aside a CAS award ordering it to pay more than EUR 2 million to the former coach of the Serbian national team. The FAS argued that the matter was not arbitrable because the Serbian Statute on Private International Law provided that the parties may only confer jurisdiction to a foreign court if at least one of the parties is a foreign citizen. According to FAS, this condition was not met in the present case, as both parties were domiciled in Serbia.

The Swiss Federal Tribunal rejected the challenge holding that FAS had not proven that the coach was domiciled in Serbia. More interestingly, the Swiss Supreme Court also held that the argument that the matter is not arbitrable would have been unfounded in any event, even if the coach was domiciled in Serbia. Indeed, according to the Swiss Federal Tribunal, arbitrability in Switzerland is governed exclusively by Article 177(1) PILA, which provides that any dispute involving an economic interest may be the subject-matter of an arbitration. This provision contains a substantial regulation of arbitrability; the Swiss legislator consciously renounced adopting a conflict rule in order to avoid difficulties in determining the applicable law that would be connected with such a solution.

The Swiss Federal Tribunal nonetheless admitted that the arbitrability of a specific matter may be rejected to the extent that

---

[15]   Decision 4A_654/2011.

foreign provisions provide for the mandatory jurisdiction of state courts and should be taken into consideration from the point of view of public policy. However, the Swiss Supreme Court found that, in the case at hand, the FAS had not proven that the provision of the Serbian Statute on Private International Law mentioned above provided for the mandatory jurisdiction of Serbian State Courts, nor that the adjudication by the CAS would violate public policy.

The Swiss Federal Tribunal further held that the mere fact that the CAS award might be unenforceable in Serbia does not justify its annulment. Indeed, according to the intent of the Swiss legislator, which opted for a substantial regulation of arbitrability, it must be accepted that some awards of international arbitral tribunals sitting in Switzerland finding a matter arbitrable on the basis of Article 177(1) PILA may conceivably be unenforceable in a specific country.

B.7 Negative *Kompetenz-Kompetenz*

In a decision dated 6 August 2012,[16] the Swiss Federal Tribunal confirmed and clarified its case law regarding the negative effect of the principle of *Komptenz-Kompetenz*.

A German businesswoman entered into a Mandate and Trust Agreement with a Swiss asset management company which was already managing her own assets. Pursuant to the Agreement, the asset management company had to constitute a Panama foundation and act as manager of its assets, while continuing to manage the assets of the businesswoman in a separate account. The Agreement contained an arbitration clause in favor of the Zurich Chamber of Commerce.

---

[16] Decision 4A_14/2012, published under the reference ATF 138 III 270.

Further to both the businesswoman and the foundation incurring important losses, the businesswoman sued the asset management company for damages in front of the ordinary courts of Zurich. The company invoked the arbitration clause contained in the Mandate and Trust Agreement and submitted that the claim should be declared inadmissible. The ordinary courts of Zurich decided however that only the claims concerning the management of the assets of the foundation derived from the Mandate and Trust Agreement fell under the scope of the arbitration clause contained therein, to the exclusion of the claims concerning the management of the assets of the foundation not based on the Mandate and Trust Agreement.

On a challenge brought by the asset management company, the Swiss Federal Tribunal held that this decision violated Article 7 PILA, pursuant to which the Swiss court before which the action is brought must decline jurisdiction if the parties have concluded an arbitration agreement as to an arbitrable dispute, unless (a) the defendant proceeded to the merits without contesting jurisdiction, (b) the court finds that the arbitration agreement is null and void, inoperative, or incapable of being performed or (c) the arbitral tribunal cannot be constituted for reasons for which the defendant in the arbitration proceedings is manifestly responsible.

The Swiss Federal Tribunal confirmed in this respect its case law pursuant to which, when a jurisdictional defense based on the arbitration agreement is raised before the state court, the state court's power of review is limited. The court must deny jurisdiction, unless a summary review of the arbitration agreement leads to the conclusion that it is void, inoperative or incapable of being performed. However, this principle applies only when the arbitral tribunal has its seat in Switzerland. If the arbitral tribunal has its seat abroad, the Swiss state court seized with such a defense has a full power to review the validity of the arbitration clause.

With this decision, the Swiss Supreme Court rejected the criticism of both the scholars who pleaded for a full review power irrespective of the seat of the arbitral tribunal, and of those who pleaded for a limited review power to be applied also to arbitrations taking place abroad. Furthermore, it clarified that the limited review of the state courts concerns not only the case in which the occurrence or the validity of the arbitration clause is in dispute, but also the case in which there is disagreement as to whether or not the arbitration clause extends to the claims submitted to the state court.

As to the specifics of the case, the Swiss Federal Tribunal considered that the fact that the arbitration clause contained in the Mandate and Trust Agreement encompassed also disputes "in connection with" the agreement, showed that the parties presumably intended to submit all related claims to the exclusive jurisdiction of the arbitral tribunal, including the claims the businesswoman could raise on the basis of another contractual relationship or due to actions performed without due authority in connection with the assets of the foundation.

B.8 Multiple Appointments of an Arbitrator

In an unfortunate decision dated 9 October 2012,[17] the Swiss Federal Tribunal rejected the challenge brought by a Belgian mountain biker, Roel Paulissen, against an arbitrator who had been appointed by the Union Cycliste Internationale ("UCI") in seven cases dealing with the same legal issue in less than two years.

---

[17] Decision 4A_110/2012.

B. Cases

Paulissen was banned by the Belgian federation from all competitions for two years and fined with EUR 7,500 for breach of anti-doping rules. The UCI appealed against this decision to the CAS, requesting a higher fine. It appointed an arbitrator it had already appointed in several recent cases in which the Arbitral Tribunal had to decide about the financial sanction for doping offenses. Paulissen's counsel was aware of the involvement of the arbitrator in three cases. At the hearing, he therefore asked the arbitrator if he nevertheless deemed himself sufficiently open-minded to hear the Parties' arguments and discuss them with his co-arbitrators without prejudice. Satisfied with the arbitrator's response, Paulissen's counsel confirmed that he had no problem with the composition of the Arbitral Tribunal.

Later on, however, Paulissen's counsel learned that the same arbitrator had been appointed by the UCI in two other similar cases concluded in the same year. He therefore asked both the UCI and the CAS to disclose the Tribunals' composition in all the pending cases concerning the same legal issue, but both the UCI and the CAS refused to do so. In the meantime, the CAS issued its award, increasing the fine due by Paulissen. Paulissen moved to set aside the CAS award before the Swiss Federal Tribunal for bias of the arbitrator appointed by the UCI. During the appeal proceedings, Paulissen learned that the UCI had appointed the same arbitrator for at least seven times in about two years in cases concerning the very same legal issue.

This was not enough for the Swiss Federal Tribunal to uphold the challenge. Indeed, the Swiss Supreme Court found that Paulissen's counsel, who is a renowned specialist in CAS arbitrations, should have expressly asked the arbitrator at the hearing how many times he had been appointed by the UCI in cases dealing with the question of financial sanctions for doping offenses; depending on the answers, he should also have requested the arbitrator to immediately step down. As

Paulissen's counsel never specifically asked the arbitrator to disclose whether or not he had been appointed by the UCI in other cases, his challenge was belated.

The Swiss Federal Tribunal also held that the arbitrator could not be blamed for not having spontaneously disclosed his involvement in other, similar cases, as this duty applies only to facts an arbitrator reasonably believes are unknown to the party affected. The Swiss Supreme Court found that this was not the case in the matter at hand, as the arbitrator could believe, in good faith, that Paulissen's counsel was aware of the UCI having appointed him in several other cases.

C. THE GRANT AND ENFORCEMENT OF INTERIM MEASURES IN INTERNATIONAL ARBITRATION

C.1 Tribunal-Ordered Interim Measures

For arbitrations before an arbitral tribunal in Switzerland, the provisions of Articles 176–194 of the PILA apply if, at the time when the arbitration agreement was entered into, at least one of the parties had neither its domicile nor its habitual residence in Switzerland. Article 183 Section 1 of the PILA provides that, "unless the parties have agreed otherwise, the arbitral tribunal may, at the request of a party, grant interim relief and conservatory measures." In Switzerland, arbitral tribunals, once constituted, are thus deemed to have jurisdiction to order interim relief, unless the parties in their arbitration agreement expressly excluded such competence. An arbitral tribunal's power to order interim relief is, however, limited to the parties to the arbitration.

With regard to the content of interim measures, the arbitral tribunal first has to look as to whether the parties, in their contract, have explicitly agreed on the rules applicable to orders for interim relief. Often, parties choose a set of arbitration rules;

the arbitral tribunal must then consult these rules, although they mostly do not contain detailed provisions on the issue of interim measures.[18] A second source is the law applicable to the merits of the case (*lex causae*) which may offer detailed specific measures that can be ordered.[19]

In general, the arbitral tribunal does not have to consider procedural rules applicable to proceedings before state courts at the place of arbitration. It is, in principle, free to order the relief requested by one of the parties, even if this relief would otherwise not be available in the Swiss courts. However, to the extent that interim measures have to be enforced in Switzerland, it is advisable to limit the relief to what is available under Swiss procedural law or to what may at least be adapted to Swiss law.[20]

Under Swiss law, interim measures may be ordered to preserve the status quo, for example with regard to goods in peril of destruction. They may also be used to order the temporary performance of certain obligations, other than obligations for the payment of money.[21] This form of interim relief is particularly common in the area of intellectual property law or in relation to non-compete obligations, where temporary restraining orders may be imposed, based on prima facie evidence only.

Under Swiss domestic law, measures which are targeted at preserving funds in view of the future execution of monetary obligations are only available in the form of an attachment in the sense of Article 271 *et seq.* of the Swiss Debt Enforcement Act, and only subject to specific statutory conditions. According to

---

[18]   Girsberger/Voser, International Arbitration in Switzerland, Zurich 2008, ¶ 827.

[19]   *Id.* at ¶828.

[20]   *Id.* at ¶ 860.

[21]   Wirth, Interim or preventive measures in support of International Arbitration in Switzerland, Bulletin ASA, Bâle 2000, p. 31 ss.

prevailing opinion, these limitations apply also in international arbitration, with the consequence that tribunals seated in Switzerland cannot order interim measures akin to an attachment or freezing of assets.[22]

A Swiss arbitral tribunal may, in exceptional cases, also grant *ex parte* measures, i.e., interim relief without hearing the party against whom the measure is directed.[23]

Interim measures may only be ordered by an arbitral tribunal if it has, *prima facie*, jurisdiction over the relevant claims. In addition, there must be a reasonable probability that the requesting party will, on the basis of the *lex causae*, succeed on the merits of the claim. Furthermore, the order must, on balance, appear necessary to prevent harm which would be very difficult to repair. Finally the tribunal may make the order dependent on the provision of adequate security.[24]

The requirement of *prima facie* jurisdiction implies that the arbitral tribunal is already constituted. If this is not the case, a party in urgent need of interim relief may—apart from addressing a state court—request interim measures from a so-called "emergency arbitrator" if the arbitration agreement provides for institutional arbitration under arbitration rules providing for the possibility of an emergency arbitrator. This possibility is offered, for instance, by the newly revised Swiss Rules of International Arbitration or the 2012 ICC Arbitration Rules.[25]

---

[22] Girsberger/Voser, International Arbitration in Switzerland, Zurich 2008, ¶862.

[23] *Id.* at ¶ 821.

[24] Article 261 Swiss Code of Civil Procedure, *cf.* Wyss, Vorsorgliche Massnahmen und Beweisaufnahme – die Rolle des Staatlichen Richters bei Internationalen Schiedsverfahren aus Schweizer Sicht, SchiedsVZ 2011, p. 196.

[25] Article 43 Swiss Rules of International Arbitration; Article 29 and Appendix V of the ICC Rules (2012).

C.2   Court-Ordered Interim Measures

According to the prevailing view, arbitral tribunals seated in Switzerland do not have exclusive jurisdiction to order interim measures.[26] Unless otherwise agreed by the parties, local state courts have concurrent jurisdiction, such that the parties may request interim measures either from the arbitral tribunal or the local court at any time during the arbitral procedure, without such request being considered as a waiver of the arbitration agreement. In principle however, a party may not seek interim measures from one instance after such measures have been denied by the first, unless there has been a considerable change in circumstances since the first denial.[27]

In Swiss state courts, interim measures are dealt with in summary proceedings. There are no statutory deadlines for dealing with requests for interim measures but generally 2-4 weeks should suffice to obtain a first instance decision. In particularly urgent cases, the requesting party can request *ex parte* measures, which are without prior hearing of the opposing party.

According to the prevailing view in Switzerland, which has been confirmed by the Federal Supreme Court with regard to proceedings falling within the scope of the Lugano Convention,[28] anti-suit injunctions (as well as anti-arbitration injunctions) are

---

[26]   Girsberger/Voser, International Arbitration in Switzerland, Zurich 2008, para. 862.

[27]   Wyss, Vorsorgliche Massnahmen und Beweisaufnahme – die Rolle des Staatlichen Richters bei Internationalen Schiedsverfahren aus Schweizer Sicht, SchiedsVZ 2011, p. 196; Lembo/Guignet, Interim Measures of Protection, The Concurrent Jurisdiction of Courts and Abritral Tribunals in Switzerland, 2011, p. 5; this view basically coincides with the ICC Procedural Order of 2 April 2002, ASA Bull 4/2003, p. 810.

[28]   Swiss Federal Supreme Court, 5 April 2012, 4A_589/2011, para. 5.3.

not available under Swiss law.[29] Swiss courts can thus not grant anti-suit injunctions, nor will a Swiss court be bound by any such injunction ordered by a foreign court or arbitral tribunal. With regard to the powers of Swiss arbitral tribunals the situation is less clear; the Swiss doctrine is divided on whether an arbitral tribunal may order anti-suit injunctions to protect an arbitration from interference.[30]

The provision of Article 183 PILA applies only to international arbitrations with their seat in Switzerland. As is stated in Article 10 PILA, Swiss courts generally have the power to grant interim relief even if they do not have jurisdiction over the merits of the case, if the measure requested is to be enforced in Switzerland. A party of a foreign arbitration procedure may, therefore, directly apply to a Swiss local court for interim measures.[31] According to Swiss doctrine and case law, the same applies for requests made

---

[29] Tribunal de première instance du Canton de Genève, C/1043/2005-15SP; Scherer/Jahnel, Anti-Suit and Anti-Arbitration Injunctions in International Arbitration: A Swiss Perspective, Int. A.L.R. 2009 Issue 4; Stacher, Prozessführungsverbote zur Verhinderung von sich widersprechenden Entscheiden, Schweizerische Zeitschrift für Zivilprozess- und Zwangsvollstreckungsrecht 2006, p. 78 s.; Liatowitsch, Schweizer Schiedsgerichte und Parallelverfahren vor Staatsgerichten im In- und Ausland, Basel 2002, p.152; s.; Jegher, Abwehrmassnahmen gegen ausländische Prozesse, Zurich 2003, p. 103. The same is true on the European level, for which the European Court of Justice has declared anti-suit injunctions to be invalid, European Court of Justice, *Turner v. Grovit*, 27 April 2004, C-159/02.

[30] *Cf.* Wyss, Vorsorgliche Massnahmen und Beweisaufnahme – die Rolle des Staatlichen Richters bei Internationalen Schiedsverfahren aus Schweizer Sicht, SchiedsVZ 2011, p. 199, Scherer/Jahnel, Anti-Suit and Anti-Arbitration Injunctions in International Arbitration: A Swiss Perspective, Int. A.L.R. 2009 Issue 4.

[31] Contrary to what applies within the scope of Article 183 PILA, the Swiss judge will, in this case, not apply "its own law" when deciding on the requirements of an interim measures being met; instead, the general conflict of law rules of the PILA apply.

by foreign arbitral tribunals, provided that the Swiss court would have been competent for ordering the respective measures had an application been made directly by one party.[32]

C.3 Enforcement of Interim Measures

In case an interim measure ordered by an arbitral tribunal is not voluntarily complied with, Swiss law allows the arbitral tribunal to request the assistance of the competent local court, which will generally be the court at the place where the measure is sought to be enforced.

While the local court may not examine the substance, for instance the practicability and suitability of the measures ordered, it does have the power to review their conformity with Swiss public policy.[33] Furthermore, the local court will only enforce measures known and provided for by Swiss law. If the measures ordered are not foreseen under Swiss law, the state court will, to the extent possible, transform the order of the tribunal into a measure available under Swiss law. In case no such measure exists under Swiss law, the Swiss court will refuse its enforcement.[34]

Swiss courts only provide enforcement assistance with regard to interim measures ordered by arbitral tribunals having their seat in Switzerland. Interim measures ordered by foreign tribunals are not enforceable in Switzerland, because they do not fall under the New York Convention.

---

[32] Wyss, Vorsorgliche Massnahmen und Beweisaufnahme – die Rolle des Staatlichen Richters bei Internationalen Schiedsverfahren aus Schweizer Sicht, SchiedsVZ 2011, p. 200.

[33] Berti, *International Arbitration in Switzerland*, Article 183, ¶18.

[34] Wirth, "Interim or preventive measures in support of International Arbitration in Switzerland," *Bulletin ASA*, Bâle 2000, p. 31 ss.

In contrast, interim measures ordered by foreign courts, in connection with arbitral proceedings, are enforceable in Switzerland if they were ordered by a court in country which is a member to the Lugano Convention. It is, however, disputed whether this will apply also in cases where the local court has not been directly seized but has only transformed an interim measured originally ordered by an arbitral tribunal in order to render it directly enforceable against a party.[35] Interim measures ordered by foreign courts of non-member states to the Lugano Convention do not, according to prevailing opinion, constitute enforceable decisions under Swiss law.[36]

---

[35] *Cf.* Girsberger/Voser, International Arbitration in Switzerland, Zurich 2008, ¶ 874.

[36] *Cf.* Lembo/Guignet, Interim Measures of Protection, The Concurrent Jurisdiction of Courts and Abritral Tribunals in Switzerland, 2011, p. 14; Girsberger/Voser, International Arbitration in Switzerland, Zurich 2008, para. 875.

TAIWAN

Tiffany Huang[1] and Amber Hsu[2]

A. LEGISLATION, TRENDS AND TENDENCIES

A.1 Overview

The Commercial Arbitration Act of Taiwan was promulgated on 20 January 1961, amended on 11 June 1982 and 26 December 1986, and subsequently renamed as the Arbitration Law on 24 June 1998. Thereafter, the Arbitration Law was further amended on 10 July 2002 and 30 December 2009. The Arbitration Law, which contains eight chapters (namely, Arbitration Agreement, Constitution of Arbitral Tribunal, Arbitral Proceedings, Enforcement of Arbitral Awards, Revocation of Arbitral Awards, Settlement and Mediation, Foreign Awards, and Additional Provisions), embodies the fundamental principles of international arbitration. Pursuant to Article 1 of the Arbitration Law, arbitrable matters are not limited to commercial disputes and parties may enter into an arbitration agreement to arbitrate any disputes that may be resolved by settlement.

There are existing laws which provide for compulsory arbitration mechanisms, under which a party may refer a dispute to arbitration even if it has not entered into an arbitration agreement with the counterparty. For example, Article 166(1) of the Securities and Exchange Act states that any disputes arising between the stock exchange and securities firms, or between securities firms themselves, shall be resolved by arbitration even

---

[1] Tiffany Huang is the Managing Partner of Baker & McKenzie's Taipei office, where she heads the Energy & Environment & Infrastructure group.

[2] Amber Hsu is a Senior Associate in the Dispute Resolution and Energy & Environment & Infrastructure groups of Baker & McKenzie's Taipei office.

in the absence of an executed arbitration agreement. In the event that a party to a dispute files a legal action in violation of this provision, the other party may petition the court to dismiss such action as provided by Article 167.

Article 85-1 of the Government Procurement Law, which took effect on 6 February 2002, also provides for arbitration as an alternative dispute resolution mechanism. This provision gives contractors under procurement of construction work from government agencies the right to arbitrate disputes when mediation fails because the relevant government agencies do not agree with the proposal or with the resolution for mediation proposed by the Complaint Review Board for Government Procurement.

A.2 Arbitration Associations

There are four arbitration associations registered with the Ministry of the Interior of Taiwan: the Arbitration Association of the Republic of China[3] (the "CAA"), the Taiwan Construction Arbitration Association (the "TCAA"), the Chinese Construction Industry Arbitration Association (the "CCIAA"), and the Labor Dispute Arbitration Association of the Republic of China (the "CLDAA").

The CAA is the oldest and the most active arbitration association in Taiwan. It administers different disputes, ranging from construction, maritime, securities, international trade, intellectual property rights, insurance, cross-strait disputes, information technology, and the like. Disputes involving construction and infrastructure projects represent a substantial percentage of the total cases administered under the auspices of the CAA. The

---

[3] "Republic of China" is the formal country name of Taiwan.

CAA currently does not administer arbitration proceedings under the rules of foreign arbitration institutions.

The TCAA and the CCIAA focus primarily on the administration of arbitrations of disputes concerning various construction projects. Compared to the CAA, these two associations are relatively small in terms of the number of arbitration cases.

A.3 Recent Developments across the Taiwan Strait

Due to political sensitivity between Taiwan and the People's Republic of China (the "PRC"), the Act Governing Relations between the People of Taiwan Area and the Mainland Area (the "Relations Act") came into effect in 1992. The PRC is referred to in the Relations Act as the Mainland Area, and PRC arbitral awards may be recognized and enforceable in Taiwan, provided that: (a) the PRC arbitral award is not contrary to the public order of good morals of Taiwan, and (b) an arbitral award made in Taiwan will be recognized and enforceable in the PRC on a reciprocal basis.[4]

The Act Governing Relations with Hong Kong and Macau, promulgated in 1997, stipulates that the Arbitration Law shall apply, *mutatis mutandis*, to the validity, petition for court recognition, and suspension of compulsory execution proceedings for arbitral awards made in Hong Kong or Macau.[5] Since the promulgation of this Act, Taiwan courts have recognized a number of arbitral awards made in Hong Kong,[6] but have also, in

---

[4] Article 74 of the Relations Act.

[5] Article 42(2) of the Act Governing Relations with Hong Kong and Macau.

[6] *See,* e.g., Taiwan Taipei District Court, Ruling 87-Chung-Sheng-Tze No. 4 (30 November 1998).

some cases, dismissed the petition to recognize the arbitral award because of a defect in service of notice.[7]

After the Relations Act was enacted, the PRC issued a rule in 1998, stipulating to the recognition and enforcement of Taiwan arbitral awards in the PRC. Reported cases indicate that an arbitral award made by CIETAC South China Sub-Commission has been recognized in Taiwan.[8] Nevertheless, a Taiwan court has also refused to recognize an arbitral award made by CIETAC, Shanghai Commission on the basis of inadequate service of notice.[9]

On 29 June 2010, Taiwan and the PRC concluded the Economic Cooperation Framework Agreement (the "ECFA"). Under the ECFA framework, Taiwan and the PRC agreed, among other things, to commence comprehensive negotiations on several critical issues, including dispute resolution procedures, within six months after the ECFA became effective. After two years of negotiation, Taiwan and the PRC finally signed the Cross-Strait Bilateral Investment Protection and Promotion Agreement (the "Cross-strait BIA") on 9 August 2012.

In relation to the disputes between investors and local governments, Article 13 of the Cross-strait BIA provides for five dispute resolution mechanisms: amicable settlement between the parties, negotiation on site or by the parties' higher organizations, resolution by the Investment Working Group of the Cross-Strait Economic Cooperation Committee, mediation by a third party, and administrative remedy or legal procedure.

---

[7] *See, e.g.,* Taiwan High Court, Kaohsiung Branch Court, Ruling 89-Zai-Tze No. 76 (30 January 2001).

[8] Taiwan Taoyuan District Court, Ruling 97-Chung-Jen-Tze No. 1 (31 July 2009).

[9] Taiwan Taipei District Court, Rulings 95-Kung-Tze No. 71 (28 July 2006) and 93-Chung-Sheng-Tze No. 15 (6 December 2005).

Arbitration is not included, which was different from what Taiwan originally expected.

In terms of the investment commercial disputes between an investor and an investor from either side of the Taiwan Strait, the dispute may be settled via arbitration if the parties have an arbitration agreement, as provided by Article 14 of the Cross-strait BIA. The arbitration may be administered by arbitration institutions in Taiwan, the PRC or Hong Kong. Arbitration hearings and meetings may be conducted at any location mutually agreed by the parties. The courts on either side of the Taiwan Strait may adjudicate on enforcement of arbitral awards.

B.   CASES

B.1   Definition of a Valid and Effective Arbitration Agreement

Under the Arbitration Law, an arbitration agreement must be in writing.[10] An oral agreement between the parties will not suffice. An agreement to arbitrate reached by way of an exchange of fax messages, telegrams, letters or any other similar means can be treated as an arbitration agreement in writing.[11]

The parties may determine the rules governing the arbitral proceedings, the place of arbitration and the language of arbitration. The Arbitration Law empowers the arbitral tribunal to rule on its own jurisdiction and competence, on the existence or validity of the arbitration agreement, and on irregularities in the proceedings.[12]

---

[10]   Article 1(3) of the Arbitration Law.

[11]   *Id.* at Article 1(4).

[12]   *Id.* at Articles 22 and 30.

The Arbitration Law expressly stipulates that the validity of an arbitration clause that forms part of a principal contract may be determined separately from the rest of the contract. An arbitration clause continues in force and effect after the contract is rendered null, void, revoked, rescinded or terminated, in accordance with the principle of severability.[13]

In the event that one of the parties to an arbitration agreement commences a legal action in conflict with the arbitration agreement, the court shall, upon application by the adverse party, stay the legal proceedings and order the plaintiff to submit the dispute to arbitration within a specified time period, unless the defendant proceeds to respond to the legal action.[14] The civil section of the Taiwan Supreme Court passed a resolution on 13 May 2003, ruling that even if an arbitration requires the arbitration venue to be outside the territory of Taiwan, the defendant will be entitled to raise the above procedural objection.

An arbitral award can be annulled if there is no effective arbitration agreement between the parties. In some countries, if an arbitration clause provides an option of arbitration or litigation, such clause is ineffective, meaning an effective clause must refer to arbitration as the sole dispute resolution method of first recourse.

The Taiwan Supreme Court, however, opined that where the parties had agreed that the dispute be resolved by either arbitration or litigation, the agreement would grant an option to the parties to choose between the two methods.[15] In addition, as

---

[13] *Id.* at Article 3.

[14] *Id.* at Article 4.

[15] Taiwan Supreme Court, Judgment 96-Tai-Shang-Tze No. 1491 (5 July 2007) and Ruling 96-Tai-Shang-Tze No. 2246 (11 June 2007).

soon as one party chooses one method over the other, the other party must be bound by this choice. Consequently, after a party initiates litigation, the respondent may not raise a procedural objection that the dispute must be resolved by arbitration,[16] and vice versa.

Taiwan courts have ruled that an arbitration clause is still effective and enforceable if it is silent on matters such as the arbitral institution, the governing substantive law or the place of arbitration.[17] Where an arbitration clause states that the dispute shall be determined by arbitration administered by an international arbitral institution that in fact does not exist, such clause has still been held effective on the basis that the parties only failed to reach agreement on arbitration rules and procedures.[18] After one party has referred the dispute to arbitration, it may then invoke the Arbitration Law to fill in the missing parts of the clause.

B.2 *Ad hoc* Arbitration

Another issue is whether an *ad hoc* arbitration award has the same legal force and effect as an institutional award. Some Taiwan courts appear to question the effect and enforceability of a non-administered award.[19] In its Ruling 99-Fei-Kang-Tze No. 122 (15 September 2010), the Taiwan High Court approved the Taipei District Court's Ruling 99-Kang-Tze No.63 (2 July 2010),

---

[16] Article 4 of the Arbitration Law.

[17] Taiwan Supreme Court, Judgment 93-Tai-Shang-Tze No. 2008 (30 September 2004) and Ruling 87-Tai-Kang-Tze No. 324 (12 June 1998), Taiwan High Court, Rulings 86-Kang-Tze No. 1183 (26 May 1997) and 73-Kang-Tze No. 1798.

[18] *See, e.g.,* Taiwan Taipei District Court, Judgment 88-Chung-Sue-Tze No. 8 (9 May 2000).

[19] Taiwan Supreme Court, Judgment 94-Tai-Shang-Tze No. 433 (10 March 2005), and Ruling 90-Tai-Kang-Tze No. 213 (27 April 2001).

which held that the *ad hoc* arbitral award was not enforceable, and opined that the *ad hoc* arbitral tribunal was not an arbitration institution established under Article 54 of the Arbitration Law, so an *ad hoc* arbitral award did not have the same effect as that of a final court judgment, and was therefore not enforceable. However, after the respondent filed a complaint to revoke the same *ad hoc* arbitral award, the Taiwan courts were silent on whether the *ad hoc* nature of the award constituted grounds for revocation.[20]

On the other hand, some opinions hold that the Arbitration Law allows for both institutional arbitration and *ad hoc* arbitration. This was the case, for instance, in the ruling of the Ministry of Justice, Executive Yuan dated 9 October 2007 with Reference No. Fa-Lu-Tze 0960038134. Also, the Executive Yuan and the Judicial Yuan jointly promulgated the Rules on Arbitration Institution, Mediation Procedures and Fees, under which Article 38 states that the fees of an arbitration, which is not handled by an arbitration institution, may be collected, *mutatis mutandis*, in accordance with those rules. This suggests that an *ad hoc* arbitration shall be acceptable under the Arbitration Law.

B.3 Appointment of Arbitrators by the Court or Arbitration Association

Parties to a dispute may appoint a single arbitrator or an odd number of arbitrators to constitute an arbitral tribunal.[21] If the parties do not have an agreement on whom shall be appointed and the method of such appointment, the tribunal will be

---

20 Taiwan Taipei District Court, Judgment 98-Chung-Sue-Tze No. 7 (5 March 2010), Taiwan High Court, Judgment 99-Chung-Shang-Tze No. 700 (26 April 2011) and Taiwan Supreme Court, Judgment 100-Tai-Shang-Tze No. 1875 (27 October 2011).

21 Article 1(1) of the Arbitration Law.

composed of three arbitrators, with one arbitrator appointed by each party and the appointed arbitrators jointly designating a third arbitrator as chairman of the arbitral tribunal. The arbitral tribunal shall notify the parties, in writing, of the final appointment.[22]

If the arbitrators appointed by the parties fail to agree on a chair within thirty (30) days of their appointment, the final appointment shall be made by a court upon application by either party; however, if the parties have agreed that the arbitration shall be administered by an arbitration institution, the third arbitrator shall be appointed by such arbitration institution.[23] Despite this rule, there is one reported case where the court held that if the parties merely agreed to refer a dispute to an arbitration institution without expressly empowering such arbitration institution to appoint the third arbitrator, only the court could make the appointment.[24]

B.4 Challenge and Withdrawal of Arbitrators

According to Article 16(1) of the Arbitration Law, a party may challenge an arbitrator if:

1. there is a cause requiring a judge to withdraw from a judicial proceeding in accordance with Article 32 of the Code of Civil Procedure;

2. there is or was an employment or agency relationship between the arbitrator and a party;

---

[22] *Id.* at Article 9(1).

[23] *Id.* at Articles 9(2) and (4).

[24] Taiwan Shihlin District Court, Ruling 90-Chung-Sheng-Tze No. 1 (29 March 2002).

3. there is or was an employment or agency relationship between the arbitrator and an agent of a party or between the arbitrator and a key witness;

4. there are other circumstances which raise any justifiable doubts as to the impartiality or independence of the arbitrator; and

5. the arbitrator does not meet the qualifications agreed by the parties.

If a challenge of an arbitrator is accepted, such arbitrator shall withdraw. The arbitral tribunal shall decide on the admissibility and the merits of a challenge, but there have been many cases where the Taiwan courts held that the arbitrator being challenged should not be involved, and a new arbitrator should be appointed so that he/she together with the arbitrators who are not challenged would form another tribunal to decide on the challenge.[25] The Taiwan High Court held a seminar on 16 November 2011, which concluded that the arbitrator being challenged could be involved in the decision making process. Whether the Taiwan Supreme Court would change its position and uphold the above conclusion remains to be seen. A party may apply to the court for a judicial ruling within fourteen days of receiving the tribunal's decision, but a party shall not challenge the ruling of the court. In a case where the tribunal is constituted by a sole arbitrator, the court will decide on the challenge.

If an arbitrator breaches the provisions of the Code of Ethics for Arbitrators of the CAA, the Ethics Committee of the CAA may:

---

[25] Taiwan Supreme Court, Judgment 96-Tai-Shang-Tze No. 1845 (23 August 2007) and Taiwan Taipei District Court, Ruling 100-Chung-Shen-Tze No. 7 (19 July 2011).

1. advise the arbitrator to make corrections;

2. suspend the arbitrator from acting as an arbitrator of the CAA for six months to three years;

3. prohibit the arbitrator from acting as an arbitrator of the CAA and cancel his/her registration; or

4. demand that the arbitrator withdraw from a certain case if a party of such case files a complaint of the arbitrator's breach of the Code.[26]

B.5 Notification of and Intervention in the Arbitration

In civil proceedings, a third person who is legally interested in an action between the parties may, for the purpose of supporting a specific party, intervene in the action. Alternatively, either party may notify such third party to intervene in the proceeding. After intervening in the proceedings or being duly notified of the litigation, the third party shall not dispute the correctness of the decisions made in the action against the party who has notified the third party of the litigation, except where the third party has been denied a means of attack or defense, either due to the progress of the litigation at the time of the intervention, or by an act of the notifying party, or where the party who gives notification of the litigation has willfully, or through gross negligence, failed to employ certain means of attack or defense unknown to the third party.[27]

With respect to arbitration, the arbitral tribunal has the discretion to allow or disallow the third party to intervene or to be

---

[26] Article 26 of the Code of Ethics for Arbitrators of the CAA.

[27] Articles 58, 63, 65, and 67 of Code of Civil Procedures.

notified.[28] The Taiwan Supreme Court, in Judgment 95-Tai-Shang-Tze No. 2277 (13 October 2006), held that where the third party voluntarily applied for intervention in an arbitration and was permitted by the arbitral tribunal to intervene, relevant articles of the Code of Civil Procedures should apply, *mutatis mutandis*, so such third party was not allowed to dispute the correctness of the arbitral award rendered against the assisted party.

However, if the third party did not voluntarily apply for intervention, but was passively notified to intervene in the arbitration, it remains disputed whether such third party is obliged to intervene and whether the third party will be barred from disputing the correctness of the arbitral award against the party who made the notification.

B.6 Time Limit for Rendering Arbitral Awards

According to Article 21 of the Arbitration Law, the arbitral tribunal shall render an arbitral award within six months of commencing the arbitration; provided that if the circumstances so require, the arbitral tribunal may extend the decision period for another three months. Such time limit shall start from the date the last arbitrator is notified of the appointment.[29] The arbitral tribunal shall still meet the time limit even where the respondent makes a counterclaim.[30]

---

[28] Taiwan High Court, Judgment 97-Chung-Shang-Tze No. 497 (28 April 2009) and Taiwan High Court, Kaohsiung Branch Court, Judgment 95-Chung-Shang-Tze No. 64 (23 January 2008), approved by Supreme Court, Judgment 97-Tai-Shang-Tze No. 2094.

[29] The ruling of the Ministry of Justice, Executive Yuan dated 6 May 2004 with reference No. Fa-Lu-Chueh-Tze 0930017621.

[30] *Ibid.*

B. Cases

If the arbitral tribunal fails to render and serve the arbitral award to the parties[31] within this time period, either party may refer the dispute to the court, unless the matters are required to be resolved by arbitration. In such case, the arbitral proceedings shall thereafter be deemed terminated.[32] Nevertheless, if neither party brings the dispute to the court, the arbitration agreement is still binding and effective, and the arbitral award shall not be revoked solely because the arbitral tribunal failed to meet the time limit.[33]

Any time period during which the arbitration cannot proceed (because the arbitrator has died, has resigned or is unable to perform his or her duty for some reason, or the parties agree to stay the procedure, or because of a *force majeure* or other unavoidable events preventing the arbitral tribunal from performing its duties) shall, however, be excluded from the calculation of the time limit.[34]

B.7 Enforceability of Arbitral Awards

Under Article 37 of the Arbitration Law, an arbitral award is binding on the parties and has the same force as a final judgment of a court. However, an award may not be enforceable unless a competent court has, on application of a concerned party, granted an enforcement order. The court will only reject an application for enforcement under certain conditions, as set forth in Article 38 of the Arbitration Law. However, the court does not render a new judgment in respect of the matter in dispute. Whether the

---

[31] Taiwan Supreme Court, Ruling 93-Tai-Kung-Tze No. 798.

[32] Article 21(3) of the Arbitration Law.

[33] Taiwan Supreme Court, Judgments 81-Tai-Shang-Tze No. 2578 (6 November 1992) and 89-Tai-Shang-Tze No. 2677 (24 November 2000).

[34] Taiwan Supreme Court, Ruling 95-Tai-Kung-Tze No. 449 (20 July 2006).

opinion of the arbitrators is proper and whether the award is proper in terms of substance are matters to be determined by the arbitrators at their sole discretion. The court will not review the substantive aspects of the arbitral award.

In principle, the court's enforcement order is required to enforce an arbitral award. By virtue of Article 38 of the Arbitration Law, however, a court shall not grant an enforcement order if:

1. the arbitral award concerns a dispute not contemplated by the terms of the arbitration agreement, or exceeds the scope of the arbitration agreement, unless the inconsistent portion of the award may be severed and the severance will not affect the remainder of the award;

2. no reasons are stated in the arbitral award (unless subsequently amended by the arbitral tribunal); or

3. the arbitral award commands a party to do an act prohibited by law.

Either before or after the court grants an enforcement order,[35] a party who has petitioned the court for revocation of an arbitral award may apply to such court to stay the enforcement of the arbitral award once the applicant has paid a suitable and certain security to the court.[36]

In addition, after the compulsory execution proceedings commence and in case a party has filed an appeal against the enforcement order, the court may render a ruling to stay the compulsory execution if the court deems it necessary, or upon application with adequate security.[37]

---

[35] Taiwan Supreme Court, Ruling 93-Tai-Kung-Tze No. 821 (28 October 2004).

[36] Article 42(1) of the Arbitration Law.

[37] Article 18(2) of the Compulsory Execution Law.

B.8 Revocation of Arbitral Awards

A party may bring a lawsuit in the court for revocation of an arbitral award based on the following grounds:[38]

1. The circumstances stipulated in Article 38 of the Arbitration Law (see above) exist.

2. The agreement to arbitrate is null and void, has been invalidated or has not taken effect before the arbitration proceedings are closed.

3. The arbitral tribunal fails to direct either or both of the parties to present its or their contentions, or if either or both of the parties are not lawfully represented in the arbitration proceeding.

4. The composition of the arbitral tribunal or the arbitration proceedings is in violation of the stipulations of the arbitration agreement or law.

5. Arbitrators who evidently lack independence violate the obligation of disclosure stipulated in Article 15(2) of the Arbitration Law or are challenged by the parties but still participate in the arbitration proceedings, unless the challenge has been rejected according to the Arbitration Law;

6. Any participating arbitrator violated his or her duty in the arbitration, and such violation amounts to criminal liability.

7. Either of the parties or its agent has committed a criminal offense in respect of the arbitration.

8. Any of the evidence upon which the arbitration is based is found to be forged or fraudulently altered.

---

[38] Article 40 of the Arbitration Law.

9. The criminal or civil judgment, court order, or administrative decision upon which the arbitration is based has been rescinded or modified by a subsequent judgment, duly affirmed by an appellate court, or by a subsequent administrative decision.

Paragraphs (f) to (h) are applicable only where a conviction has been confirmed, or where criminal proceedings have not been started or have been discontinued owing to insufficient evidence. Paragraphs (d) and (e) to (i) are applicable only when the arbitration result can be adversely affected.

Once an arbitral award is revoked by a final judgment of a court, a party may bring the dispute to the court unless the parties agree to arbitrate, as provided by Article 43 of the Arbitration Law. An issue arises as to whether a party may refer the dispute to arbitration based on the arbitration agreement upon which the revoked arbitral award relies. The Taiwan High Court, Tainan Branch Court in its Judgment 98-Shang-Yi-Tze No. 203 (30 March 2010) has ruled that a party was not allowed to arbitrate the dispute after the arbitral award had been revoked by a final court judgment. This suggests that if the parties do not reach another arbitration agreement after the arbitral award is revoked, neither party may arbitrate on the same dispute.

B.9 Enforcement of Foreign Arbitral Awards

Taiwan is not a signatory to the New York Convention, but it still follows the spirit thereof. Enforcement of foreign arbitral awards in Taiwan is governed by the Arbitration Law and involves application to a Taiwan court for recognition. As the recognition is non-litigious, open hearings and oral arguments are normally required, unless there are exceptional circumstances.

B. Cases

The Arbitration Law defines foreign arbitral awards as an arbitral award that is rendered outside the territory of Taiwan, or that is rendered within the territory of Taiwan but pursuant to the "foreign laws," which include: (a) foreign arbitration laws, (b) rules of a foreign arbitral institution (such as the ICC Rules), and (c) rules of an international organization (such as the UNCITRAL Arbitration Rules).[39]

Article 49(1) of the Arbitration Law provides that a court shall dismiss the plea for recognition of a foreign arbitral award if:

1. the recognition or enforcement of the arbitral award will run counter to public order or the good morals of Taiwan; or

2. the dispute is not arbitrable under the laws of Taiwan.

In addition, a court may dismiss a plea for recognizing a foreign arbitral award if the place or state where the arbitral award was made does not recognize Taiwan arbitral awards on a reciprocal basis, as provided by Article 49(2) of the Arbitration Law.

As Taiwan is not a signatory of the New York Convention, the Article 49 reciprocity requirement can be an impediment to the recognition of foreign awards. However, Article 49 does not make such a clause compulsory. The courts have given a liberal interpretation to the term "reciprocity" in some cases.[40]

The Supreme Court has held that even though the foreign jurisdiction where the arbitral award was made does not recognize and enforce arbitral awards made in Taiwan, the court, rather than dismissing the plea, may still decide to recognize and

---

[39] Taiwan Taipei District Court, Judgment 88-Chung-Sue-Tze No. 8 (9 May 2000).

[40] *See, e.g.,* Taiwan High Court, Ruling 94-Kung-Tze No. 433 (30 March 1995) and Taiwan Taipei District Court, Ruling 80-Chung-Chih-Geng-Tze No. 39 (28 April 1992).

enforce the foreign arbitral award at its discretion for the purpose of enhancing international judicial cooperation.[41]

If a party applies to the court for recognition of a foreign arbitral award concerning any of the following circumstances, the respondent may request the court to dismiss the application within twenty days from the date of receipt of the notice of the application:

1. The arbitration agreement is invalid as a result of the incapacity of a party according to the law chosen by the parties to govern the arbitration agreement.

2. The arbitration agreement is null and void according to the law chosen to govern said agreement or, in the absence of choice of law, the law of the country where the arbitral award was made.

3. A party is not given proper notice either of the appointment of an arbitrator or of any other matter required in the arbitral proceedings, or any other situations which give rise to lack of due process.

4. The arbitral award is not relevant to the subject matter of the dispute covered by the arbitral agreement or exceeds the scope of the arbitration agreement, unless the inconsistent portion can be severed from and cannot affect the remainder of the arbitral award.

5. The composition of the arbitral tribunal or the arbitration procedure contravenes the arbitration agreement or, in the absence of an arbitration agreement, the law of the place of the arbitration.

---

[41] Taiwan Supreme Court, Ruling 75-Tai-Kung-Tze No. 335 (7 August 1986).

6. The arbitral award is not yet binding upon the parties or has been suspended or revoked by a competent court.[42]

Taiwan courts have recognized and enforced foreign arbitral awards made in a number of US states, and various countries, such as the UK, France, Switzerland, South Korea, Japan, Finland, Russian Federation, South Africa and Vietnam, as well as awards made in accordance with various rules, including the arbitration regulations of the London Metal Exchange, the arbitration rules of the Liverpool Cotton Association Limited,[43] the arbitration rules of the Singapore Commodity Exchange Limited, the AAA Rules, the ICC Rules and the UNCITRAL Arbitration Rules. However, there is no court precedent recognizing arbitral awards rendered in countries that have substantial commercial and cultural interests with Taiwan, such as Germany and Canada. This uncertainty is one of the reasons that contracting parties may be reluctant to choose a foreign country as their venue for arbitration.

C. THE GRANT AND ENFORCEMENT OF INTERIM MEASURES IN INTERNATIONAL ARBITRATION

C.1 Tribunal-Ordered Interim Measures

Pursuant to Article 36(1) of the CAA Arbitration Rules, a tribunal, at the request of either party, may order any interim measures as agreed by the parties in respect to the subject-matter of the dispute for purposes of preserving perishable goods or providing immediate protection, such as ordering their sales or other interim measures the tribunal considers appropriate. Article

---

[42] Article 50 of the Arbitration Law.

[43] On 9 December 2004, the Association was renamed "The International Cotton Association."

43 of the CCIAA Arbitration Rules contains a similar provision. These rules are unclear as to whether such interim measures are available before the commencement of arbitral proceedings.

C.2 Court-Ordered Interim Measures

According to Article 39(1) of the Arbitration Law, only the court can order provisional attachment or provisional injunction. The court at the request of the respondent shall order the applicant to refer the dispute to arbitration by a certain time period if the applicant has not done so. Should the applicant fail to do so, the court may, pursuant to a petition by the respondent, invalidate the order for provisional attachment or provisional injunction.

The Taiwan court can grant interim measures in aid of a foreign arbitration, as suggested by the conclusion made in the seminar held by Taiwan Shihlin District Court on 16 November 1995.

C.3 Enforcement of Interim Measures

Under Article 36(2) of the CAA Arbitration Rules, where the arbitral tribunal orders an interim measure for purposes of preserving perishable goods or providing immediate protection as agreed by the parties and where the parties have an arbitration agreement, the arbitral tribunal may record such agreement on the interim measure in the form of an arbitration settlement, which, according to Article 44(2) of the Arbitration Law, has the same force and effect as that of an arbitral award. The arbitration settlement may be enforced only after the court has issued an enforcement order.

TURKEY

Ismail G. Esin[1] and Ali Yesilirmak[2]

A. LEGISLATION, TRENDS AND TENDENCIES

The International Arbitration Law, Law No. 4686 ("IAL"), continues to be the applicable law in relation to international arbitrations conducted in Turkey. There have been no legislative amendments in 2012.

B. CASES

B.1 The Incorporation of an Arbitration Clause by Reference

In a recent case, the 11th Civil Division of the Court of Appeal[3] had to decide whether or not an arbitration clause contained in a charter-party was validly incorporated into a bill of lading. The contract in question was for the delivery of wheat by the claimant. The voyage was from the port of Sevastopol, Ukraine to the port of Samsun, Turkey. Upon arrival of the goods at the

---

[1]   Dr. Esin is the Managing Partner of Esin Attorney Partnership now associated with Baker & McKenzie in Istanbul, Turkey. He has advised various international companies on their dispute resolution matters in Turkey and abroad. He is the author of seven books published in English, German, and Turkish on mergers and acquisitions and international arbitration. Dr. Esin is a frequent speaker at conferences and symposia on international arbitration and litigation, as well as on mergers and acquisitions and real estate investments.

[2]   Dr. Yesilirmak is a member of the Istanbul Bar Association and of the Faculty of Law, Istanbul Sehir University and a visiting lecturer at Queen Mary College, CCLS. He has published extensively on international commercial and investment law as well as on dispute resolution. He has acted as an arbitrator and counsel for over 20 institutional and *ad hoc* arbitrations.

[3]   Case No. 2012/5132, Decision No. 2012/7052, Decision Date 02 May 2012.

port of discharge, a deficiency of 86 tons was discovered, with a value of TRY 52,140. An injunction was obtained by the claimant to prevent the vessel from sailing without the damages being compensated for. The claimant then commenced proceedings against the defendant before the commercial court of first instance. One of the defenses raised by the defendant was that the matter should be heard by an arbitral tribunal due to the fact that the bill of lading contained a clause incorporating the terms of the charter-party, which contained an arbitration clause. The arbitration objection, as it is referred to under the IAL, was accepted by the court and the claim was dismissed on the grounds of lack of jurisdiction. The court reasoned that since the bill of lading incorporated the charter-party by way of reference, (which in turn contained an arbitration clause) the arbitration clause was validly incorporated and that any dispute arising therefrom should be referred to arbitration.

The importance of this judgment is self-explanatory. In relation to an issue which is controversial in many jurisdictions known to be arbitration friendly, such a decision demonstrates that the Turkish courts have embraced the idea that Turkey has the potential of becoming arbitration friendly by adhering to the parties' agreement to arbitrate.

B.2   The Fees Payable for the Enforcement and Recognition of a Foreign Arbitral Award

In a case before the 19th Civil Division of the Court of Appeal,[4] the enforcement of an arbitral award rendered by an arbitral tribunal constituted pursuant to the International Arbitration Rules of the Korean Commercial Arbitration Board was sought by the claimant. Although the enforcement proceedings were

---

[4]   Case No. 2012/1885, Decision No. 2012/5598, Date 04 April 2012.

contested by the defendant, the court of first instance concerned found for the claimant. However, upon appeal, the judgment of the lower court was set aside on the basis that the application to enforce the arbitral award was subject to progressive court fees. The court of appeal reasoned that as the enforcement which was being applied for was that of a foreign arbitral award relating to the collection of a specified amount, the court should have determined the Turkish Lira equivalent of the amount concerned and then calculated the court fee payable, in proportion to that amount, instead of determining that fixed court fees be paid by the claimant. It should be noted that the determination of the court fees payable is to be made in accordance with the Law on Fees, Law No. 492, and Tariff No. 1. In accordance with Tariff No. 1, the proportionate fee is the equivalent of 5.94 percent of the amount claimed, while the fixed court fee is TRY 21.15 (see, Rule A (III) (1) (a) and (2) (b)).

B.3 The Timing of an Arbitration Objection

In a dispute arising from an architectural services agreement, the 11th Civil Division of the Court of Appeal[5] was provided with the opportunity to clarify the law on when an arbitration objection can be raised. Under the IAL, where a party refers its dispute to the court despite the existence of an arbitration agreement between the parties, an arbitration objection can be raised by the defendant requesting that the claim be dismissed and the dispute be referred to arbitration. Under Article 5(1) of the IAL, the mechanism applicable to such scenarios is that contained in the Code of Civil Procedure, Law No. 6100 ("CCP"). The CCP provides that an arbitration objection must be raised no later than two weeks from the date the statement of claim is notified to the defendant (Articles 127 and 413 of the

---

[5] Decision No. 2012/178, Date 16 February 2012.

CCP), which is the same time period within which the statement of defense must be filed.

In the dispute that was the subject matter of this case, the arbitration objection was raised for the first time on the date of the hearing. On a literal interpretation of the provision relating to arbitration objections, it is apparent that the arbitration objection advanced by the defendant should have been dismissed. Although this interpretation was adopted by the Intellectual and Industrial Property Court of Izmir (the court of first instance), upon appeal the judgment was reversed. The court of appeal adopted a purposive approach and reasoned that an arbitration objection should not be considered as an initial objection, in the technical sense, but rather as a "defense tool". Since under Turkish law the restriction of not being able to advance a defense after a certain stage in the proceedings is subject to the exception of consent of the other party, the court of appeal held that where an arbitration objection is raised after the submission of the defense, the objection may nevertheless stand valid if consented to by the other party. It was noted that the consent may be expressed or implied and will be assumed if advanced by one party and not objected to by the other.

B.4 The Timely Issuance of an Arbitral Award

A decision handed down by the Kadıköy 2nd Civil Court of First Instance demonstrates the importance of arbitral awards being issued within the applicable time period. Unless otherwise agreed, an award rendered under the IAL must be rendered within one year from the date of appointment of the arbitrator, in the case of a sole arbitrator, or, in the case of an arbitral tribunal, from the date when the minutes of the tribunal's first meeting are kept (Article 10(B)). Non-compliance with this provision constitutes a reason for an award to be set aside (Article 15(A)(1)(c)).

In the instant case, the award was set aside by the court and one of the reasons expressed for setting aside the award was non-compliance with the above specified provision. One must therefore always be conscious of local laws that may have a fundamental effect. It should be noted that despite the fact that this decision was overturned on appeal, the ground for overturning the decision related to the fact that the application for the setting aside of the award was not made to the competent court. The court of first instance's reasoning in relation to time limits thus continues to be applicable.

C. THE GRANT AND ENFORCEMENT OF INTERIM MEASURES IN INTERNATIONAL ARBITRATION

C.1 Tribunal-Ordered Interim Measures

The IAL dictates that the arbitral tribunal is entitled to grant interim measures upon application by either of the parties. This entitlement does not extend so far as to include the granting of interim measures that are considered as being within the exclusive jurisdiction of governmental authorities or to include the granting of interim measures against governmental authorities or third parties (Article 6(2)). The types of interim measures that may be granted by an arbitral tribunal have not been specified and is only mentioned in general terms.

The IAL does not specify the test that is to be considered by the arbitral tribunal in the determination of whether or not to grant the interim measure requested. However, since Article 17 of the IAL provides that the CCP is not applicable where a provision to the contrary is contained in the IAL, this should be interpreted to mean that where the CCP does not contravene the IAL, the provisions of the CCP could be used to fill gaps. Therefore, the test contained in Article 389(1) of the CCP could be resorted to by the arbitral tribunal. The provision states the following;

"An interim measure may be granted in relation to a dispute where it is feared that an entitlement to a right will become more difficult to an important extent or completely impossible or where material loss or damage or danger will arise due to delay as a result of a change in the circumstances."

It should be noted that the IAL contains no provisions relating to emergency arbitrators.

C.2 Court-Ordered Interim Measures

In Turkey, the courts have the power to grant interim measures before and after the commencement of arbitral proceedings (Article 6 of the IAL). Such applications usually take between 7 and 10 days if made after the commencement of the proceedings, but may take longer depending on the case. In relation to the time period within which interim measures requested before the commencement of the proceedings are granted, the general rule is to determine such applications as soon as possible; in practice this tends to be within 3 days of making the application. However, it should be noted that where an application is made before the arbitral tribunal is properly constituted, the party making the application is obliged to initiate arbitration within 30 days of the interim measure being granted, failing which the interim measure will cease to have effect (Article 10 (A)(2) of the IAL).

In relation to anti suit injunctions, there is no legislative provision nor case-law concerning this matter. Therefore, whether or not such an application will be granted depends on the approach taken by the court in question. Moving on to the issue of granting interim measures in aid of foreign arbitration, Article 432 of the CCP provides that assistance may be requested from the court by either party, with the arbitral tribunal's consent, in the gathering of evidence. This provision becomes applicable to arbitrations conducted under the IAL, for the reasons stated above. It should be noted that the IAL applies only to arbitrations with its seat in Turkey; whether or not such assistance will be provided to a foreign arbitration with its seat outside of Turkey is therefore unclear. However, it is likely that such assistance will be provided with the application of the provisions of the CCP.

C.3 Enforcement of Interim Measures

In relation to an interim order made by an arbitral tribunal with its seat in Turkey, the IAL provides that, where the order is not complied with, an application may be made by either party to the court for compliance with such an order (Article 6(3) of the IAL). In relation to the enforcement of an interim order granted by an arbitral tribunal seated outside of Turkey, the Turkish International Private Law, Law No. 5718 ("TIPL") provides that arbitral awards that are final or capable of being enforced may be enforced by the Turkish courts (Article 60(1)). Thus, there is no distinction made in the legislative provisions between interim and final arbitral awards. Interim measures that may be enforced by the Turkish courts exclude the granting of interim measures that are considered as being within the exclusive jurisdiction of governmental authorities or the granting of interim measures against governmental authorities or third parties.

UKRAINE

Igor Siusel,[1] Olga Shenk,[2] Taras Aleshko[3] and
Kseniia Pogruzhalska[4]

A.   LEGISLATION, TRENDS AND TENDENCIES

A.1   Introduction

Ukraine is a civil law country and issues of international
arbitration are governed primarily by international conventions
and treaties (which, upon their ratification by the Verkhovna
Rada [Ukrainian Parliament], have priority over national
legislation) and by applicable national legislation. Court
precedents are not considered to be the source of binding law in
Ukraine, except for decisions of the Supreme Court of Ukraine
taken in cases regarding different application of the same
provision of the material law by cassation courts, as foreseen by
Ukrainian procedural legislation, amended in July 2010. Decisions
of the European Court of Human Rights are considered as source
of law and are mandatory and binding for Ukraine.

---

[1]   Igor Siusel is a Counsel in the Kyiv office of Baker & McKenzie. He advises
and represents clients from various industries in domestic and international
arbitration and litigation, recognition and enforcement of arbitral awards,
enforcement of court judgments and bankruptcy proceedings. He is a member of
the Ukrainian Bar Association.

[2]   Olga Shenk is an Associate in the Kyiv office of Baker & McKenzie, and a
member of the Firm's Global Dispute Resolution, Compliance and Employment
Practice Groups.

[3]   Taras Aleshko is an Associate in the Kyiv office of Baker & McKenzie, and a
member of the Firm's Global Dispute Resolution, Energy, Mining &
Infrastructure.

[4]   Kseniia Pogruzhalska is a Junior Attorney in the Kyiv office of Baker &
McKenzie, and a member of the Firm's Global Dispute Resolution Practice
Group.

Ukraine is a party to the New York Convention, European Convention and a number of bilateral investment treaties, many of which provide for arbitration under the UNCITRAL Arbitration Rules or before ICSID.

The Verkhovna Rada ratified the ICSID Convention in 2000, and in 2006, the President of Ukraine adopted the Decree On Procedure for Appointment of Representatives from Ukraine to be Included in the Conciliators' List and the Arbitrators' List of the International Centre for Settlement of Investment Disputes.

Additionally, Ukraine is a party to the Energy Charter Treaty of 17 December 1994 (the "ECT"), which declares the main principles of investment protection in the energy sector and covers all aspects of commercial energy activities through the extension of national treatment or most-favoured nation principles. Being a party to the ECT since 1998, Ukraine assigned, in particular, to the dispute settlement mechanism, set forth therein, which provides for referring disputes with investors for consideration under ICSID Rules, ICSID Additional Facilities Rules, UNCITRAL *ad hoc* Rules or Arbitration Rules of the Stockholm Chamber of Commerce.

Ukraine has also adopted separate laws on domestic and international arbitration, namely, the Law of Ukraine On Domestic Arbitration, dated 11 May 2004, and the Law of Ukraine On International Commercial Arbitration, dated 24 February 1994 (the "Arbitration Law"). The Arbitration Law closely follows the UNCITRAL Model Law as of 1985, except for the following two peculiarities. First, unlike most Model Law countries, the Arbitration Law provides that the President of the Ukrainian Chamber of Commerce and Industry (the "UCCI") shall serve as the appointing authority when there is a failure to appoint an arbitrator. Consequently, the UCCI President is also the authority for challenging arbitrators, as envisaged by the

Arbitration Law. Second, two arbitration institutions are established by the Arbitration Law, namely, the International Commercial Arbitration Court of the Ukrainian Chamber of Commerce (the "ICAC") and the Maritime Arbitration Commission of the Ukrainian Chamber of Commerce (the "MAC"). At present, these are the oldest existing arbitration institutions in Ukraine.

A.2 Short Overview of Ukrainian Legislation regarding Arbitration

A.2.1 Arbitrability

The Arbitration Law provides that upon agreement of the parties, following types of disputes may be referred to international commercial arbitration: (i) disputes arising from contractual and other civil relationships in connection with foreign trade and other kinds of economic relations, if at least one party is located abroad; (ii) disputes involving companies with foreign investments and international organizations and associations, organized or incorporated in Ukraine, among themselves, between members of such organizations, and between such organizations and other Ukrainian entities.

Ukrainian legislation does not contain an integrated list of non-arbitrable disputes or a clear mechanism for determining of dispute's arbitrability. References to non-arbitrable disputes can be found separately in some international agreements and national laws.

At the same time, Ukrainian legislation expressly defines the certain types of disputes as non-arbitrable, namely, (i) disputes arising from corporate relations between a legal entity and its participant (founder, shareholder), including a former participant, or between participants relating to establishment, activity, management or termination of such legal entity (pursuant to

Article 12 of the Commercial Procedure Code of Ukraine); (ii) disputes that, according to the Civil Procedure Code of Ukraine, are reviewed within "non-contentious proceedings" (generally, such disputes relate to the establishment of legal facts, disclosure of bank secrets, restoration of rights for lost securities, etc.); (iii) disputes concerning the invalidation of the acts of state authorities (pursuant to Article 12 of the Commercial Procedure Code of Ukraine); (iv) disputes concerning the execution, change, termination and fulfillment of state procurement contracts (pursuant to Article 12 of the Commercial Procedure Code of Ukraine); and (v) disputes concerning bankruptcy of a Ukrainian debtor.

It is worth mentioning that, pursuant to Article 16 of the Commercial Procedure Code of Ukraine, the disputes involving central state authorities are referred to the exclusive competence of the Kyiv City Commercial Court.

Additional disputes may be defined as non-arbitrable in other legislation regulating specific areas of legal relationships. In 2005, the Law of Ukraine On Private International Law was adopted to regulate the choice of law rules and jurisdiction over disputes with a foreign element. However, the adoption of this law has not solved one of the most important problems, namely, the scope and the extent of the arbitrability of international commercial disputes. In fact, this law has caused some discrepancies in determining the arbitrability of disputes concerning immovable property, intellectual property and securities disputes. Thus, Article 77 of the above law provides for the exclusive jurisdiction of the national courts of Ukraine over disputes concerning immovable property, intellectual property and securities disputes. Recent legal practice demonstrates that there is a tendency to apply this provision to avoid arbitrating these types of disputes.

A.2.2 Court assistance in taking evidence

The Arbitration Law expressly allows arbitral tribunals and parties to address relevant state courts for assistance in gathering evidence for arbitral proceedings, however such evidence must be gathered in accordance with court rules established for taking evidence in court proceedings. At the same time, the applicable procedural rules are silent in respect of the practical implementation of such gathering of evidence for arbitral proceedings by the state courts.

A.2.3 Setting aside arbitral awards

Under applicable legislation, district courts of common jurisdiction at the place of arbitration have jurisdiction to set aside arbitral awards. In particular, the Arbitration Law establishes the procedure of cancellation of an arbitral award by the state court on limited grounds and as an exceptional measure. However, such procedure is only applicable to arbitral awards where the place of arbitration is in Ukraine.

A.2.4 Recognition and enforcement

Ukraine recognizes and enforces arbitral awards issued in member countries of the New York Convention. Otherwise, recognition and enforcement is possible only on the basis of reciprocity.[5]

The procedure for the enforcement of foreign judgments and foreign arbitral awards, is set forth in the Civil Procedure Code of Ukraine, according to which the interested party must file a motion for recognition and enforcement of the award with court of common jurisdiction at the debtor's domicile or at the location

---

5   Under provisions of the Civil Procedure Code of Ukraine, such reciprocity exists by default, unless otherwise established.

of the debtor's assets within three (3) years from the day of entry into legal force of the arbitral award. Generally, the decision on the enforcement of an arbitral award should be taken within two (2) months with a possibility to extend this time period. Court's decision on the enforcement and recognition of arbitralaward can be appealed on general grounds, according to the Civil Procedure Code of Ukraine.

Upon recognition of a foreign arbitral award by the competent Ukrainian court, the ruling on enforcement is rendered by the court and must be submitted by the interested party to the state enforcement authorities. The procedure of such enforcement is governed by the Law of Ukraine *On Enforcement Procedure*, dated 21 April 1999.

A.2.5 Insolvency issues

The bankruptcy proceedings in Ukraine are regulated under the Law of Ukraine on Restoring of a Debtor's Solvency or Recognizing It as Bankrupt, dated 14 May 1992 (the "Bankruptcy Law").

In case if bankruptcy proceedings were commenced by the state commercial court against a party to pending arbitration proceedings, a creditor must immediately apply with its claims to the court considering the bankruptcy case within the thirty (30) day period from the date of official publication of initiation of the debtor's bankruptcy proceedings in press.

It should be noted that the new edition of the Bankruptcy Law, which will become effective on 19 January 2013, provides for official publishing of the announcement on initiation of bankruptcy proceedings on the web-site of the Supreme Commercial Court of Ukraine starting from 19 January 2014.

Before 19 January 2013, under the Bankruptcy Law, if a creditor fails to duly apply, the court will dismiss claims filed after expiration of this period and will consider debtor's liabilities to the defaulting creditor as discharged. The new edition of the Bankruptcy Law foresees possibility to satisfy creditor's claims declared after expiration of thirty (30) day period or those, non-declared at all, although only in course of last turn of order of satisfaction of creditor's claims.

Once the debtor is recognized as a bankrupt by the court, all active enforcement proceedings initiated against the bankrupt debtor are closed, enforcement documents are sent to the liquidator (to the court—starting from 19 January 2013). Therefore, any recovery of the debt in favor of the creditor will be carried out within the bankruptcy proceedings, and the creditor's claims will be satisfied from the liquidation pool of the debtor's assets in the order of priority established by the Bankruptcy Law.

Where a Ukrainian debtor's bankruptcy is initiated after issuance of the final arbitral award, the creditor should apply with its claims to the state court considering bankruptcy case within the same term, providing the court, in particular, with a certified copy of translated arbitral award into Ukrainian and a court's resolution on its recognition and enforcement.

All creditors, whose claims matured after initiation of the debtor's bankruptcy proceedings, are considered to be current creditors, who have a special status in the bankruptcy proceedings, as they are entitled to apply to the court with their claims against the debtor and recover the debt from the latter in general order outside the pending bankruptcy proceedings.

It's worth mentioning that Ukrainian bankruptcy legislation is silent regarding effect of bankruptcy proceedings on pending arbitration proceedings initiated under the same creditor's claims. However, pending bankruptcy proceedings do not *per se* terminate, postpone or otherwise suspend arbitration of the same dispute.

A.2.6 Public policy considerations

As a general rule, according to the Law on Arbitration, public policy considerations may be invoked within the procedure of recognition and enforcement of an arbitral award in Ukraine. Accordingly, recognition and enforcement of an arbitral award may not be granted if such award is found violating public policy of Ukraine. Under the Civil Procedure Code of Ukraine, state court may refuse to grant recognition and enforcement if such enforcement may harm the interests of Ukraine. The Law on Arbitration also provides for possibility to request cancellation of arbitral award on the grounds of public policy violation, though only if place of arbitration was in Ukraine.

The notion of "interests of Ukraine" is vague due to absence of legislative definition (i.e., except for the decision of the Constitutional Court of Ukraine No. 3-рп/99, dated 8 April 1999, in which the "state interests" are analyzed in the context of scope of powers of the prosecutor's authorities while applying to the court to protect such state interests). Also, Supreme Court of Ukraine defines the concept of "public policy" as the legal order of the state and leading principles and foundations that constitute the basis of the social order in it (e.g., concerning independence, integrity and immunity of the state, main constitutional rights, freedoms and guarantees).

In absence of legislative distinction between "domestic" and "international" public policy, it can be noted that as regards the international commercial arbitration, legislative rules refer solely to the concept of "public policy of Ukraine," i.e., "domestic public policy".

Ukrainian courts in their turn tend to interpret the concept of "public policy" broadly providing for possibility to refuse in recognition and enforcement of the award on relatively large scope of grounds, specifically undetermined by legislation.

It's noteworthy that the Ukrainian arbitration legislation does not set forth any specific requirements for reliance on public policy at the enforcement stage.

Alleged breach of public policy may be considered at the court's initiative while considering motion on recognition and enforcement of the arbitral award. At the same time, there may not be a *révision au fond* (i.e., reconsideration of the arbitral award on merits), as demonstrated by Ukrainian court practice and specifically confirmed by the Supreme Court of Ukraine.

A.3 Recently Adopted Ukrainian Legislation regarding Arbitration

Interim Measures May be Granted at Any Stage of Enforcement Proceedings

Under amendments to the Civil Procedure Code of Ukraine, introduced by the Law of Ukraine of 22 September 2011 (effective since 19 October 2011), state courts were permitted to grant interim measures in the course of recognition and enforcement of international arbitral awards (please see section C.2 for more details).

A.4 International Commercial Arbitration Court of Ukrainian Chamber of Commerce ("ICAC")

While Ukraine was a part of the USSR it did not have any separate arbitration institutions. Instead, there was only one Arbitral Tribunal and Maritime Arbitration Commission at the Chamber of Commerce and Industry of the Soviet Union. After

Ukraine became an independent state, in 1992, the Ukrainian Chamber of Commerce and Industry established the ICAC. According to the ICAC's statistics, 303 cases were considered and decided by ICAC during 2011, 406 cases involving parties from 58 countries were accepted by ICAC for consideration.

The ICAC arbitrators' list includes arbitrators from Ukraine, Azerbaijan, Austria, Belarus, Bulgaria, Croatia, Czech Republic, Finland, France, Germany, Great Britain, Hungary, Latvia, Macedonia, Moldova, the Netherlands, Norway, Poland, the Russian Federation, Serbia, Slovakia, Slovenia, Sweden and the USA.

According to the ICAC, the average timeframe for consideration of cases in 2011 was 2-6 months in 74% of its cases; 7-9 months in 18% of its cases and more than 10 months in 8% of its cases.

B. CASES

B.1 Investment Disputes

Since Ukraine obtained its independence, and especially after the Orange Revolution, the amount of foreign investments in the Ukrainian economy has increased significantly. At the same time, however, Ukraine is frequently mentioned as a party to investment disputes considered by ICSID. To date, Ukraine has participated in the following concluded cases: *Joseph C. Lemire v. Ukraine* (Case No. ARB(AF)/98/1), *Joseph C. Lemire v. Ukraine* (Case No. ARB/06/18), *Generation Ukraine Inc. v. Ukraine* (Case No. ARB/00/9), *Tokios Tokeles v. Ukraine* (Case No. ARB/02/18), *Alpha Projektholding GmbH v. Ukraine* (Case No. ARB/07/16), *Western NIS Enterprise Fund v. Ukraine* (Case No. ARB/04/2), *GEA Group Aktiengesellschaft v. Ukraine* (Case No. ARB/08/16); *Global Trading Resource Corp. and Globex International, Inc. v. Ukraine* (Case No. ARB/09/11);

B. Cases

Bosh International, Inc. and B&P, LTD Foreign Investment Enterprise v. Ukraine (Case No. ARB/08/11) and *Inmaris Perestroika Sailing Maritime Services GmbH and others v. Ukraine* (Case No. ARB/08/8).
Except for obligation to pay certain amounts under awards rendered in Case No. ARB/07/16 and Case No. ARB/08/8, Ukraine has not lost any other concluded ICSID cases, and two of them were settled. At the same time, while considering *Joseph C. Lemire v. Ukraine* (Case No. ARB/06/18), the ICSID tribunal rendered its preliminary decision in case finding that Ukraine violated fair and equitable treatment provision of the Agreement between Ukraine and United States of America On Promotion and Mutual Protection of Investments on several occasions, and dismissed investor's other claims. However, on 28 March 2011 the tribunal issued an award on determination of damages obliging Ukraine to pay compensation to the claimant in the amount of approximately USD9,500.00.

B.2 Arbitration Disputes against Ukraine

The most recent official list of disputes pending before foreign courts (including arbitration institutions) involving Ukraine as a party was published by the Ministry of Justice of Ukraine on 24 July 2010. As of this date, following arbitration disputes included in that list are still pending.

Naftrac Limited (Cyprus) v. the National Agency for Ecological Investment

On 25 November 2009, Naftrac Limited applied to the Permanent Court of Arbitration in Hague seeking to charge Ukraine for quotas on greenhouse emissions of almost 20 million AAU (Assigned Amount Units) under the Kyoto Protocol and USD185 million in compensation for projects not realized in Ukraine. The matter concerns agreements, in particular those of

Naftrac, with Ukrainian regional gas companies, which envisaged modernization projects. Cypriot companies were to have installed energy saving technologies at Ukrainian enterprises in exchange for greenhouse emissions quotas. Upon formation of the arbitral tribunal on 8 April 2010, Naftrac requested interim measures, but was refused by the tribunal. A number of submissions were provided by the parties during 2010-2011 with last oral hearing held on 28 September 2012.

OSJC Tatneft (Russia) v. Ukraine

On 21 May 2008, Russian Tatneft filed a notice on arbitration and a statement of claim with an *ad hoc* arbitration tribunal created under the UNCITRAL Arbitration Rules. Tatneft accused Ukraine of violating of rights of Tatneft as a shareholder of Ukrainian CJSC "Uktatnafta" (i.e., an entity controlling the Kremenchuk oil refinery).

Tatneft increased its compensation claims to USD2.4 billion due to inferred losses caused by the sale of those shares. After the rejection of Ukraine's jurisdictional objections, further schedule of submissions and hearings on the matter was approved on 29 November 2010. Accordingly, certain submissions of both parties were to be provided in 2011-2012. Currently Ukraine was to respond to Tatneft's statement of claim by 12 December 2012.

Vanco Prykerchenska Ltd. (British Virgin Islands) v. Ukraine

This dispute was initiated by Vanco Prykerchenska, Limited ("Vanco") in April 2008, after the Ministry of Environmental Protection of Ukraine annulled a special permit issued to Vanco for exploration of the Prykerchenska part of the Black Sea shelf. Consequently, the Cabinet of Ministers of Ukraine ("CMU") unilaterally withdrew from the Production Sharing Agreement earlier concluded with Vanco International, which at a later stage assigned its contractual rights to Vanco.

B. Cases

While this dispute was pending at the Arbitration Institute of the Stockholm Chamber of Commerce (the "SCC"), Vanco tried to approach the Ukrainian government with proposals to resume the cooperation under the Production Sharing Agreement. In particular, on 1 October 2009, Vanco officially submitted for consideration by the CMU a work program and the budget in the amount of USD57 million for the purposes of implementing the first phase of development of the Prykerchenska part of the Black Sea shelf in 2010, as provided for in the agreement.

On 12 May 2010, the Government of Ukraine proposed an amicable agreement to be signed with Vanco. The parties started negotiations in July 2010; the arbitration proceedings were suspended. Upon the agreement of the parties regarding extension of the postponement of the arbitration process until April 2011 in order to sign an amicable agreement, on 11 April 2011 the CMU reported that the project of such agreement was approved by Ruling No. 627-r. Further, both parties agreed to prolong suspension until 31 December 2012. The parties settled the dispute in December 2012.

Torno Global Consulting Spa and Beta Funding SrL (Italy) v. Ukrainian Transport and Communications Ministry and the State Automobile Road Service of Ukraine

In September 2009, Italian-based Torno Global Contracting S.P.A. and Beta Funding S.R.L. filed a claim at the ICC against the Ukrainian Transport Ministry and the State Road Service. The amount claimed is approximately EUR45 million. Claimants accuse the Ukrainian government of violating the conditions of a general agreement, signed on 9 October 2008, on cooperation during the reconstruction and operation of the Kyiv-Odessa highway.

As of March 2011, the schedule of submissions and hearings in the case was approved. Accordingly, a number of submissions are to be made throughout 2011 and 2012; oral hearings were scheduled for March 2012.

In addition to the above disputes, on 8 June 2010, an SCC tribunal ordered NJSC "Naftogaz" to return 11 billion cubic meters of natural gas to RosUkrEnergo (a gas supply company owned by the Russian Gazprom and Ukrainian individuals). In addition, the tribunal ordered that RosUkrEnergo should receive from Naftogaz further 1.1 billion cubic meters of natural gas in lieu of RosUkrEnergo's entitlement to penalties for breach of contract. The recognition and enforcement of this award was granted by the decision of the first instance court (Shevchenkivskiy District Court of Kyiv City) on 13 August 2010, which was upheld by the Ruling of the Appellate Court of Kyiv City of 17 September 2010. On 24 November 2010, the Supreme Court of Ukraine refused to satisfy the cassation complaint of Naftogaz, and upheld the decisions of the lower courts.

B.3 Shares Sale and Purchase Agreement Is Not a "Corporate Relationship" under Ukrainian Law

In 2010, the tribunal acting under the Rules of Arbitration of the International Arbitral Centre of the Austrian Federal Economic Chamber (the "Vienna Centre Tribunal") resolved a dispute pertaining to the validity of several agreements on transfer of ownership rights on shares of Ukrainian company to a non-resident company (the "Transaction Agreements"). Notably, prior to commencement of arbitration, the respondent, a former shareholder of the Ukrainian company, initiated several proceedings in Ukrainian courts seeking to invalidate the Transaction Agreements with subsequent restitution.

Given the fact that the dispute arose between the non-resident company, which was a current shareholder of the Ukrainian company, and the Ukrainian respondent, a former shareholder of the same Ukrainian company, the latter objected to jurisdiction of the Vienna Centre Tribunal by referring to the nonarbitrability of the dispute. The reference was made to Articles 12 and 16 of the Commercial Procedural Code of Ukraine establishing nonarbitrability of corporate disputes (i.e., disputes arising from corporate relations between a company and its participant (founder, shareholder), including a former participant, or between the participants (founders, shareholders) relating to the establishment, activity, management or termination of their company) and exclusive jurisdiction of Ukrainian courts over such disputes.

However, the Tribunal dismissed these arguments and recognized its jurisdiction over all disputes arising out of the Transaction Agreements since (i) the Transaction Agreements were governed by Austrian Law, and the issue of arbitrability should be governed by Austrian Law, and (ii) the claim in the dispute was of a contractual nature and, therefore, did not concern any corporate relations between the parties as defined in Article 12 of the Commercial Procedural Code of Ukraine.

The Vienna Centre Tribunal resolved the dispute in favor of the claimant. The claimant further applied to Ukrainian court for the recognition and enforcement of the arbitral award. The respondent in its turn, filed objections to the recognition and enforcement of the arbitral award with reference to the breach of public policy (public policy rules were addressed specifically in Section A.2.6 above). Recognition of the award is still pending in the Ukrainian courts.

B.4 Refusal to Recognize and Enforce an Arbitral Award against a Ukrainian Debtor for Failure of Notice

An American company "Sea Emerald S.A. Panama" (Claimant) applied to a Ukrainian court for recognition and enforcement of an arbitral award for collection of a debt (the "Enforcement Request") owed by a Ukrainian company, "Sudnobudivnyi Zavod im. Komunara" (Respondent).

In the proceedings, the Respondent stated that it was not informed about the arbitration proceedings. According to the Claimant, the Arbitral Tribunal informed the respondent on every procedural action in the arbitration by e-mail and by facsimile. The Respondent, however, argued that it had no official registered e-mail addresses and, unless the Claimant could prove otherwise, the arbitral award should not be recognized and enforced in Ukraine.

Thus, although the Respondent (during its performance under the contract) used certain e-mail addresses and facsimile numbers, the Claimant could not prove that such contact details were officially registered in the Respondent's name. As a result, the Ukrainian court dismissed the Claimant's request for recognition and enforcement of the arbitral award against the Respondent.

B.5 Ukrainian State Enforcement Service Refused to Enforce Arbitral Award against a Ukrainian Debtor on a Technicality

A German grain trading company filed an application for recognition and enforcement of the arbitral award rendered under the Rules of the Grain and Feed Trade Association in London. The award was rendered against the Ukrainian grain company (Debtor) and provided for collection of a debt. Percherskyi District Court of Kyiv City by its ruling, granted the enforcement of the award.

Further, the German grain company filed the enforcement order with the State Enforcement Service requesting enforcement of the award. However, the application was returned due to the fact that the enforcement order did not provide for specific enforcement measures, such as collection of debt, but rather obliged the State Enforcement Service to enforce the foreign award.

Despite the fact that Ukrainian legislation provides enforcement authorities with an option to take any actions prescribed by Ukrainian courts, it is clear that these authorities may use formal excuses to obstruct enforcement of foreign arbitral awards.

C. THE GRANT AND ENFORCEMENT OF INTERIM MEASURES IN INTERNATIONAL ARBITRATION

C.1 Tribunal-Ordered Interim Measures

As follows from Article 17 of the Arbitration Law, unless parties agree otherwise, upon request of any party to a dispute, arbitral tribunal may order interim measures in relation to the subject-matter of the dispute, which measures shall be taken by either party.

Application of interim measures by ICAC and MAC is also envisaged by the regulations on the functioning of the ICAC and the MAC, set forth in Appendices 1 and 2 to the Arbitration Law (the "Regulation on the ICAC" and the "Regulation on the MAC" accordingly), and the rules of these institutions.

Arbitration Rules of the ICAC entitle the head of the ICAC (before institution of the tribunal) and the arbitral tribunal (upon the institution), to adopt resolutions on application of interim measures, which resolutions are binding upon the parties to the dispute and are valid until the final arbitral award is rendered. The same provision referring, however, only to the head of the institution, is contained in the MAC Rules.

At the same time, the Arbitration Law is silent on the particular types of interim measures to be applied in arbitration proceedings. However, the Regulation on the MAC provides that the MAC may, in particular, take resolution on the precautionary seizure of a vessel or cargo of other party, which vessel or cargo stays in Ukrainian port.

In order to obtain a resolution on interim measures, a party to the proceedings should apply to the ICAC or the MAC with the relevant request. The interim measures may be granted by the arbitration institution or the tribunal (upon institution of the tribunal), if it finds that the party's request is reasonable. It should be noted that neither the Arbitration Law nor the arbitration rules of the ICAC and the MAC provide any rules as to the establishment of the reasonability of a party's request for interim measures.

C.2 Court-Ordered Interim Measures

Although the Arbitration Law allows the parties to the arbitration proceedings to apply to the Ukrainian state courts for the introduction of interim measures, the Ukrainian procedural rules do not provide the mechanism for consideration of such applications and granting interim measures in aid of the international arbitration (domestic or foreign). As a matter of Ukrainian procedural law, interim measures may be granted by the court for the purpose of securing of the forthcoming or the existing trial on the merits in the same state court. Insignificant court practice in this regard is rather contradicting, namely, courts in some cases granted interim measures in respect of pending proceedings in foreign arbitration under general provisions of Ukrainian procedural law, whereas in other cases courts refused to consider applications on interim measures at all due to lack of jurisdiction.

It should be noted that the Ukrainian courts cannot grant an anti-suit injunction, since it is not envisaged by Ukrainian procedural rules and in any event it would violate the basic right of the parties to trial established by the Constitution of Ukraine.

C.3 Enforcement of Interim Measures

Ukrainian law does not provide the mechanism for the enforcement of awards/orders on interim measures issued by arbitral tribunals in contrast to the recognition and enforcement of final arbitral awards. Since there is no legal basis for the enforcement of arbitral awards/orders on interim measures, the Ukrainian courts are reluctant to enforce them.

UNITED KINGDOM

Edward Poulton,[1] Thomas Yates[2] and Carinne Maisel[3,4]

A. LEGISLATION, TRENDS AND TENDENCIES

International arbitration in England and Wales[5] continues to be governed by the Arbitration Act 1996 (the "Arbitration Act"), to which no legislative amendment was made in 2012.[6]

---

[1] Edward Poulton is a Partner in Baker & McKenzie's London office. He practices all forms of dispute resolution and specializes in international arbitration. His experience ranges from contract and M&A disputes to claims in the banking sector and investment treaty claims.

[2] Thomas Yates is a Senior Associate in Baker & McKenzie's London office and a Member of the Chartered Institute of Arbitrators. He practices all forms of dispute resolution, including international arbitration, and has acted in arbitrations under the LCIA, ICC, UNCITRAL and FOSFA Rules. He specializes in corporate disputes, such as M&A and shareholder claims, and carbon trading disputes.

[3] Carinne Maisel is an Associate in Baker & McKenzie's London office. She acts in broad range of matters including both litigation and arbitration.

[4] The authors gratefully acknowledge the assistance of Thomas Courtney and Anuj Moudgil.

[5] England and Wales are two of the four countries that make up the United Kingdom. They have a common legal system, whereas the other two countries in the United Kingdom (Scotland and Northern Ireland) have separate systems. For the purposes of the current publication we intend only to refer to the laws of England and Wales. Any reference to "England" or "English" in this section should also be taken to include "Wales" or "Welsh."

[6] *See also:* the Civil Procedure Rules and Practice Direction, Part 62; the Arbitration Act 1996 (Commencement No. 1) Order 1996 SI 1006/3146; the High Court and County Courts (Allocation of Arbitration Proceedings) Order 1996 SI 1996/3 125; The Unfair Arbitration Agreements (Specified Amount) Order 1996 SI 1996/3211; Arbitration Act 1950, Part II Enforcement of Certain Foreign Awards.

B. CASES

B.1 Governing Law of Arbitration Agreements

B.1.1 *Sulamerica Cia Nacional de Seguros and others v. Enesa Engenharia SA and others* [2012] EWCA Civ 638

The English Court of Appeal confirmed that the governing law of an arbitration agreement is not necessarily the same as the substantive law of the contract in which the arbitration agreement is contained. This is due to the doctrine of the separability of an arbitration agreement from the contract in which it is contained. While the governing law of the arbitration agreement might be the same as the substantive law of the contract in which it is contained, where this is not expressly specified it might alternatively be the law of the agreed seat of the arbitration. The practical consequence of this decision is that where the substantive law of the contract is different from the seat of the arbitration, the governing law of the arbitration agreement should be expressly specified.

Enesa Engenharia SA ("Enesa") and Sulamerica CIA Nacional de Seguros ("Sulamerica") were in dispute over an insurance contract between them. The contract expressly specified the law of Brazil as its governing law and included an exclusive jurisdiction clause in favor of the courts of Brazil. However, it also contained an arbitration clause that provided that London should be the seat of arbitration. When Sulamerica gave notice of arbitration in England, Enesa in turn obtained from the court in São Paulo an injunction restraining Sulamerica from proceeding with the arbitration. Sulamerica in turn succeeded in getting an anti-suit injunction from the Commercial Court in England to stop the proceedings in Brazil. Enesa appealed this decision to the Court of Appeal.

B. Cases

The Court of Appeal dismissed Enesa's appeal and held that the proper law of an arbitration agreement is to be determined by undertaking a three-stage enquiry, in the following order: (i) express choice of law; (ii) implied choice; and (iii) the law with which the arbitration agreement has its closest and most real connection (noting that the second stage often merges into the third). As the parties had not made an express choice as to the law of the arbitration agreement, it was necessary to consider which law the parties had impliedly chosen.

The two key factors indicating the parties' choice of law were that: (i) the choice of London as the seat of arbitration implied acceptance that the arbitration would be conducted and supervised according to the Arbitration Act 1996; and (ii) Brazilian law would have required both parties to consent to arbitration after the dispute arose, notwithstanding the arbitration agreement, which the court considered was not in accordance with the parties' intention. The choice of London as the seat of arbitration was also a strong indicator of English law being the law with which the arbitration agreement had its closest and most real connection.

B.2 Anti-Suit Injunctions

B.2.1 *Joint Stock Asset Management Co Ingosstrakh-Investments v. BNP Paribas SA* [2012] EWCA Civ 644

This case involved consideration of whether an anti-suit injunction could be obtained against a nonparty to an arbitration agreement to prevent it from pursuing court proceedings that would have the effect of undermining an arbitration. In contrast to the decision in the similar *Star Reefers* case,[7] the Court of Appeal upheld the anti-suit injunction against the non-party

---

[7]   Star Reefers Pool Inc. v JFC Group Co ltd [2012] EWCA Civ 14.

("D2"), because there was evidence of collusion with the party to the arbitration agreement ("D1") such that the foreign proceedings were unconscionable and vexatious. This case shows that the court will consider the specific facts before it when considering whether to grant an anti-suit injunction against a nonparty. If the nonparty is able to show, as in *Star Reefers*, that it has a good reason for bringing proceedings in its own right and not just to gain a collateral advantage for the party to the arbitration, the court will not grant a anti-suit injunction.

B.3 Enforceability of Awards under Section 66 of the Arbitration Act 1996

B.3.1 *West Tankers Inc. v. Allianz SpA* (The Front Comor) [2012] EWCA Civ 27

In this case, the Court of Appeal confirmed that an award granting a negative declaration could be enforced, thereby creating an issue estoppel. Following the initial dispute, the charterer's claim against the ship owners, West Tankers Inc. ("West Tankers"), was referred to arbitration in London. While the reference was progressing, the charterers' insurers Allianz SpA ("Allianz") became subrogated "to their right of action. Despite the arbitration agreement, Allianz brought a claim in the Italian courts, which resulted in an anti-suit injunction being granted by the English High Court. However, the European Court of Justice ruled that the Italian court should rule on its own jurisdiction and that an anti-suit injunction granted by one court within the EU affecting another EU court would be inconsistent with the Brussels Regulation.

Meanwhile, the London arbitration resulted in an award in West Tankers' favor in the form of a negative declaration stating that West Tankers was not liable. West Tankers succeeded in obtaining permission in England to enforce the negative declaration under Section 66(1) of the Arbitration Act and to enter judgment in terms of the award under Section 66(2). The effect would be to ensure that any subsequent judgment made by the Italian courts would not be recognized in England due to EU Regulation 44/2001.

Section 66(1) states that an award "... may, by leave of the court, be enforced in the same manner as a judgment or order of the court to the same effect." Allianz appealed against the decision to enforce the negative declaration on the basis that negative declaratory judgments, which do not require a party to actually do anything, could not be "enforced" within the meaning of the word in Section 66, and that the court only had jurisdiction to enforce positive, as opposed to negative, declaratory awards.

The Court of Appeal approved the decision in *African Fertilizers*[8] that a declaratory award is enforceable under Section 66. The court determined that the creation of an effective issue estoppel was a legitimate reason to enforce a negative declaratory award.

B.4 Impact of Decisions of Foreign Courts to Enforce Awards

B.4.1 *Yukos Capital Sarl v. OJSC Rosneft Oil Co* [2012] EWCA Civ 855

The English Court of Appeal held that a decision by a Dutch court to refuse to recognize a judgment by the Russian Arbitrazh Court to set aside an arbitral award did not create an issue estoppel. As a consequence, despite the Dutch courts enforcing the arbitral award, the English courts were not necessarily bound to find the award had not been validly set aside when enforcement was sought in England.

---

[8] *African Fertilizers and Chemicals NIG Ltd (Nigeria) v. BD Shipsnavo GmbH & Co Reederei KG* [2011] EWHC 2542 (Comm) (reported in the 2011 edition of this publication).

Yukos had obtained an arbitral award in Russia against Rosneft. However, Rosneft succeeded in applying to the Russian Arbitrazh Court to set aside the award. Yukos succeeded in enforcing the award in the Netherlands by arguing before the Amsterdam Court of Appeal that the award was valid and the decision to set aside the award by the Russian Arbitrazh Court should not be recognized on the basis that it was partial and dependent. Yukos then brought a claim in England to enforce the award. Yukos argued that the decision of the Amsterdam Court of Appeal created an issue estoppel between the parties, thereby preventing Rosneft from seeking to argue that the decision by the Russian Arbitrazh Court to set aside the award was not partial and dependent. The English court found that this did not create an issue estoppel between the parties because what was contrary to Dutch public policy was not necessarily the same as what was contrary to English public policy.

C. THE GRANT AND ENFORCEMENT OF INTERIM MEASURES IN INTERNATIONAL ARBITRATION

C.1 Tribunal-Ordered Interim Measures

Although tribunals can, in theory, order any type of interim measure permissible under the powers conferred on them by the parties (e.g., by agreeing to arbitration rules that include such powers) and the Arbitration Act, in practice the parties and the tribunal rely on the support of the court and its powers under the Arbitration Act. Section 38 of the Arbitration Act confers certain general powers on tribunals (unless otherwise agreed by the parties), including the power to give directions for the preservation of any property that is subject to the arbitral proceedings. Moreover, Section 39 of the Arbitration Act expressly allows the parties to agree that the tribunal will have

C. The Grant and Enforcement of Interim Measures in International Arbitration

the power to grant on a provisional basis any relief that it would have power to grant in a final award. However, tribunals lack the coercive powers of the English courts to ensure any interim award is complied with.

Section 48(5)(a) of the Arbitration Act provides that, unless otherwise agreed, the tribunal has the same powers as the court to order a party to do or refrain from doing anything, whilst Section 39 of the Act states that "parties are free to agree that the tribunal shall have power to order, on a provisional basis, any relief which it would have the power to grant in a final award." There has been considerable debate as to whether these provisions allow parties to agree to confer on a tribunal the power to make a freezing order. In *Kastner v. Jason,*[9] Lightman J held that whilst the former provision did not provide tribunals the power to grant freezing injunctions, the latter did confer such a power. The Court of Appeal subsequently expressed no view either way, but Rix LJ noted that, whilst it was generally agreed that Lightman J's approach to Section 48(5) was correct, there was significant disagreement among commentators over Lightman J's reasoning in relation to Section 39.[10] The situation has been further clouded by the decision in *Econet Wireless Ltd. v. Vee Networks Ltd.,*[11] where Morison J appeared to assume that the London Court of International Arbitration (LCIA) Rules would permit a tribunal to make an order equivalent to a freezing injunction. However, as the point was not discussed as point of principle, the position remains unclear. The authors question whether a freezing order could ever be granted in a final award and therefore whether it can be granted as an interim award under Section 39(1).

---

9   [2004] EWHC 592 (Ch).

10   [2004] EWCA Civ 1599, at paragraphs 16-19.

11   [2006] EWHC 1568.

C.2 Court-Ordered Interim Measures

C.2.1 The English courts' supportive powers

Although a key aim of the Arbitration Act is to minimize the intervention of the courts in arbitral proceedings, the Act does grant the English courts certain supportive powers where either a tribunal has not been properly constituted, or there are gaps in the powers of the tribunal, such as in relation to the issue and enforcement of interim measures. This is particularly important since the tribunal's own general powers will not be effective against third parties. In particular, Section 44 of the Act allows the English courts to make orders in relation to, among other things, (i) the preservation of property, assets and evidence, and (ii) the grant of interim injunctions. The permission of the tribunal may or may not be required, depending on the urgency of the case: Section 44(3) states that a party may apply to the court to exercise its supporting powers under Section 44 "*if the case is one of urgency.*" In *Cetelem SA v. Roust Holdings Limited*[12] the Court of Appeal confirmed that the court will only intervene without notice if the matter is urgent and the order sought is necessary to preserve evidence or assets (broadly defined). If the matter is not urgent, however, it will be necessary to obtain the permission of the tribunal or the written agreement of the other parties.[13] The courts have tended to adopt a strict approach to the urgency requirement, with Morison J noting that an applicant would need to show "a very good reason" for making an application without notice.[14]

---

[12] [2005] EWCA Civ 618.

[13] Section 44(4) of the Act.

[14] *Econet Wireless Ltd. v. Vee Networks Ltd.* [2006] EWHC 1568 (Comm).

The courts' supportive powers are further limited by Section 44(5) of the Act, which states that the court may only intervene where the tribunal "has no power or is unable for the time being to act effectively," and Section 44(6), which states that the court has the discretion to order that its own order shall cease to have effect once the tribunal has the power to act.

C.2.2 Length of the application period

The courts do not treat applications in relation to arbitral proceedings any differently to standard applications relating to litigation: the speed at which an application for an interim measure will be heard will depend largely on the urgency of the application. Therefore, in urgent cases, a party could apply for and obtain an interim order on the same day.

C.2.3 Anti-suit injunctions

The English courts have power under Section 37 of the *Senior Courts Act 1981* (the "SCA") and Section 44 of the Act to grant anti-suit injunctions to restrain a party to an arbitration agreement from bringing or continuing proceedings in the courts of another jurisdiction, and do so regularly. This power has recently been limited, preventing the English courts from issuing anti-suit injunctions in connection with proceedings being brought in another EU state.[15]

Under Section 37 of the SCA, the courts have the power to grant an injunction simply "where it appears to the court just or convenient," meaning that the court need not pay regard to the powers of an arbitral tribunal when exercising its discretion to grant an anti-suit injunction. On the other hand, under Section

---

[15] *See Allianz SpA (formerly Riunione Adriatica Di Sicurta SpA) and Others v. West Tankers Inc.* (C-185/07).

44, the courts are subject to the same restrictions as set out above (i.e., the consent of the tribunal is required unless the matter is urgent, and the tribunal must be unable to act). It has been noted by the Court of Appeal that some tension exists between the statutes.[16] The current approach of the courts, as evinced in *Starlight Shipping Co. v. Tai Ping Insurance Co. Ltd. (Hubei Branch),*[17] is to have regard to issues that arise under Section 44 of the Arbitration Act when exercising their discretion under Section 37 SCA (and vice versa). In a recent case,[18] the Court of Appeal held that if Section 44 of the Act applied, it would be wrong as a matter of principle to utilize Section 37 of the SCA to circumvent the restrictions of the Act. However, if no arbitration had been commenced or intended, but a party asked the court to protect its right to have its disputes settled in accordance with its arbitration agreement, then the court would be allowed, at its discretion, to protect the right to arbitrate by utilizing Section 37 of the SCA to grant an anti-suit injunction.

C.2.4 Foreign arbitrations

Under Section 25 of the Civil Jurisdiction and Judgments Act 1982 (as amended[19]) and Section 44 of the Arbitration Act, the courts may grant interim relief in support of arbitration proceedings anywhere in the world. However, Section 2(3) of the Arbitration Act confers a discretion on the court to refuse to exercise its powers in relation to foreign arbitration proceedings where it would be "inappropriate" to do so. Therefore, the courts

---

[16] *Cetelem SA v. Roust Holdings Limited* [2005] EWCA Civ 618, Clarke LJ at¶74.

[17] [2007] EWHC 1893 (Comm).

[18] *AES Ust-Kamenogorsk Hydropower Plant LLP v. Ust-Kamenogorsk Hydropower Plant JSC* [2011] EWCA Civ 647

[19] *Civil Jurisdiction and Judgments Act 1982 (Interim Relief) Order 1997* SI 1997/302.

generally adopt a restrictive approach, especially where the foreign arbitral proceedings are governed by a foreign law. For example, in *Commerce and Industry Insurance Co. of Canada v. Lloyd's Underwriters*,[20] the court refused to exercise its supportive powers because New York curial law was insufficiently similar to English arbitration law. More recently, in *Mobil Cerro Negro v. PDSVA*,[21] the Commercial Court set aside a freezing injunction in support of a New York arbitration, holding that the English court should not grant an injunction in support of foreign proceedings without a sufficiently strong link with the jurisdiction (such as assets within the jurisdiction or residence of a party) or some other factor of sufficient strength to justify such intervention. Therefore, when applying to the English courts to exercise their powers under Section 44 of the Act, it will be necessary to set out why it is appropriate for the court to intervene in the particular case despite the arbitration being based abroad.

C.3   Enforcement of Interim Measures

Under English law, a provisional award (including interim orders) made by an arbitral tribunal will, unless otherwise agreed between the parties, be binding on the parties. Therefore, after the court has granted permission to enforce an arbitral award or interim award pursuant to Section 66 of the Arbitration Act, the award may be enforced in the same manner as a court judgment. Section 101 of the Act also provides that awards subject to the New York Convention can, with the court's permission, be enforced in England in the same manner as a judgment or court order.

---

[20]   [2002] 1 Lloyd's Rep 219.

[21]   [2006] EWHC 1568.

Therefore, the English courts will, *prima facie*, enforce any interim award or order that appears valid on its face, regardless of whether the award was made in England or not, subject to the usual grounds for refusing recognition and enforcement of an award as set out in the New York Convention.

UNITED STATES

Donald J. Hayden,[1] Ethan A. Berghoff,[2] and
Joseph J. Mamounas[3]

A. LEGISLATION, TRENDS AND TENDENCIES

A.1 Legislation

The Federal Arbitration Act ("FAA"), implemented in 1925,
continues as the controlling and well-established foundation for a
strong national policy in favor of arbitration. In the last year,
there has been no legislation that has advanced in any significant
way to amend or alter the FAA or the broad acceptance of
arbitration as a viable and well-accepted vehicle for resolution of
both domestic and international disputes. At the state level, there
are also arbitration laws in place, particularly in jurisdictions
where commercial arbitration centers are located, that further
encourage and promote arbitration as an acceptable mechanism
for dispute resolution. In recent years, legislation to narrow the

---

[1] Donald J. Hayden is a Partner in Baker & McKenzie's Miami office. His practice
involves primarily cross border disputes being resolved through litigation and
arbitration. He leads Baker & McKenzie's Dispute Resolution Group in Miami and
is a member of the Steering Committee of the Firm's Global Arbitration Group.

[2] Ethan Berghoff is a Partner in Baker & McKenzie's Chicago office. He represents
clients in a broad range of international matters, including distributorship and
supply agreements, power, fuel supply and construction contracts as well as post-
acquisition disputes. He has also appeared before ICC, LCIA and ICDR
arbitration panels around the world.

[3] Joseph Mamounas is an Associate in Baker & McKenzie's Miami office. Mr.
Mamounas specializes in international arbitration and other cross-border
commercial disputes on behalf of multi-national U.S. and foreign clients.

scope of the FAA has never made it through the relevant legislative committee and efforts to limit the FAA's reach, often in the consumer context, have not had sufficient support. Commentators see no change in the present laws and the FAA's wide acceptance.

A.2 Trends and Tendencies

For the most part, the strong national policy in favor of arbitration has been reinforced through the court decisions at both the state and federal level. Some of the more significant cases of the last year are discussed in detail below in Section B. With some of the rules changes by the major arbitral institutions, there has been an attempt to better streamline arbitration, thereby making a more striking comparison to the costs and time delays experienced in litigation of disputes in U.S. courts, particularly those courts systems with large and congested dockets at the trial court level.

B. CASES

B.1 Second Circuit Dismisses Petition to Confirm an International Arbitral Award on Grounds of *Forum Non Conveniens*

Figueiredo Ferraz e Engenharia de Projeto Ltda v. Republic of Peru, 665 F.3d 384 (2d Cir. 2011)

An arbitration panel seated in Peru awarded Plaintiff Figueiredo Ferraz e Engenharia de Projeto Ltda over $21 million in January 2005. The award represented unpaid fees and interest due to Plaintiff under an engineering consulting agreement it entered into with the Programa Agua Para Todos, a Peruvian government agency (together with the Republic of Peru, "Defendants"). The Plaintiff did not attempt to enforce the award in Peru but instead filed a petition in the Southern District of New York to confirm the award pursuant to the Inter-American Convention on International Commercial Arbitration (the "Panama Convention") and, in the alternative, the Convention on the Recognition and Enforcement of Foreign Arbitral Awards (the "New York Convention").

Defendants admitted to having assets in New York against which the award could be enforced but moved to dismiss the U.S. petition on several grounds, including lack of subject matter jurisdiction based on sovereign immunity, *forum non conveniens* and international comity. The district court denied the motion on each of the grounds asserted but granted Defendants leave to file an interlocutory appeal on the non-jurisdictional questions only. On interlocutory appeal, a majority of the Second Circuit Court of Appeals reversed the district court's judgment and directed the district court to dismiss the petition on *forum non conveniens* grounds.

The Second Circuit determined that, although the Panama Convention established U.S. jurisdiction to enforce the arbitral award under consideration, it had the authority to reject that jurisdiction for reasons of convenience, judicial economy and justice. Although noting that enforcement of arbitral awards is normally a favored policy of the U.S. and is contemplated specifically by the Panama Convention, the Second Circuit found that the general policy had to give way to a significant public interest factor—a Peruvian statute implemented so as to cap the amount that Peruvian government entities pay as damages in civil suits. The Second Circuit found that Plaintiff also assumed the risk of having collection of an award subject to the cap statute when it entered into a contract with a Peruvian government entity.

In determining whether to dismiss a lawsuit on *forum non conveniens* grounds, U.S. courts are directed to consider the adequacy of the alternative forum as well as private and public interest factors. In this case, the Second Circuit held that the district court erred in concluding that confirmation of the award in a Peruvian forum would be inadequate because it would deprive Plaintiff of its ability to attach and execute against assets located in the U.S. The Second Circuit explained that, in the context of enforcement proceedings, an alternative forum is adequate so long as a defendant has *some* assets there. Thus, the fact that dismissal would deprive Plaintiff of its ability to reach a potentially larger amount of assets in its chosen forum (the U.S.) did not, by itself, make the alternative forum inadequate.

B.2 **Eleventh Circuit Upholds District Court's Grant of Discovery Applied for in Assistance of a Foreign Arbitration, Recognizing That an Arbitral Tribunal Is a Foreign Tribunal Qualifying for Assistance under Section 1782**

Consorcio Ecuatoriano de Telecomunicaciones S.A. v JAS Forwarding (USA), Inc., and JET Air Service Equador S.A., 685 F.3d 987 (11th Cir.)

This case concerned a dispute between Consorcio Ecuatoriano de Telecomunicaciones S.A. ("CONECEL") and Jet Air Service Equador S.A. ("JASE") relating to a sales contract. JASE initiated arbitration in Ecuador in accordance with the contract between the parties on the basis that CONECEL had failed to pay sums invoiced. CONECEL argued in defense that the invoices submitted by JASE were inflated.

JASE's U.S. counterpart, JAS Forwarding (USA), Inc., ("JASE USA"), operates in Miami and was involved in the invoicing operations at issue in the dispute. CONECEL brought an application under 28 U.S.C. § 1782 ("§ 1782") targeted at JASE

USA and requesting information concerning JASE's billing of CONECEL. CONECEL argued that this information was relevant to CONECEL's defense in the arbitration in Ecuador. CONECEL also argued that it was considering bringing civil and criminal actions in Ecuador against JASE and two CONECEL employees on the basis that they had colluded to increase the invoice amounts and that the evidence sought from JASE USA was relevant to those contemplated actions as well.

A district court has the authority to grant an application for judicial assistance under § 1782 if four statutory requirements are met: (1) the request must be made "by a foreign or international tribunal," or by "any interested person;" (2) the request must seek evidence, whether it be the "testimony or statement" of a person or the production of "a document or other thing;" (3) the evidence must be "for use in a proceeding in a foreign or international tribunal;" and (4) the person from whom discovery is sought must reside or be found in the district of the district court ruling on the application for assistance.

The Eleventh Circuit Court of Appeals addressed the issue of whether an arbitral tribunal fell within § 1782, eschewing the possibility of holding that the statute applied because of the contemplated court actions. The court noted that the Supreme Court, in *Intel Corp. v. Advanced Micro Devices, Inc.*, 542 U.S. 241 (2004), quoted from an article by Professor Hans Smit (the primary draftsperson of the statute) in which he said that the term "tribunal" included arbitral tribunals. Furthermore, taking its lead from the analysis used in *Intel*, the Eleventh Circuit looked at the issue as follows: "we examine the characteristics of the arbitral body at issue, in particular whether the arbitral panel acts as a first-instance adjudicative decision maker, whether it permits the gathering and submission of evidence, whether it has the authority to determine liability and impose penalties, and whether its decision is subject to judicial review."

The Eleventh Circuit noted that the arbitral panel had the authority to receive evidence, resolve the dispute, and award a binding decision. Furthermore the ultimate arbitral award would be subject to judicial review in the sense that a court could enforce the award or could upset it on the basis of defects in the arbitration proceeding or the grounds set forth in the New York Convention. The Eleventh Circuit thus held that the arbitral tribunal in this case qualified as a foreign tribunal for purposes of the statute.

The significance of this decision is that, ever since the Supreme Court's decision in *Intel*, the courts have been split on the issue of whether § 1782 discovery is available in aid of an international arbitration case. Here, the Eleventh Circuit confirmed explicitly that an arbitral tribunal may qualify as a foreign tribunal for the purposes of § 1782 so as to allow a district court to grant discovery in aid of foreign arbitral proceedings if the district court considers it appropriate in its discretion to do so.

The Eleventh Circuit noted that the Second and Fifth Circuits had declined previously to grant discovery in aid of foreign arbitral proceedings on the basis that an arbitral tribunal is not a foreign tribunal within the scope of § 1782. However, the Eleventh Circuit also noted that those decisions were rendered before the Supreme Court addressed the issue in *Intel*.

B.3   Sixth Circuit Upholds District Court's Judgment to Compel Arbitration in New Jersey in Face of Ambiguous Arbitration Clause

Control Screening LLC v. Technological Application and Production Co. (Tecapro), HCMC-Vietnam, 687 F.3d 163 (6th Cir.)

B. Cases

The parties had entered into a series of contracts for the sale of x-ray equipment from Control Screening to Tecapro, a Vietnamese state-owned company, for use in Vietnam. The parties had a dispute over one of the agreements, which contained language stating that such disputes "shall be settled at International Arbitration Center of European countries for claim in the suing party's country under the rule of the Center." In November 2010, Tecapro initiated arbitration proceedings in Belgium. In December 2010, Control Screening notified Tecapro that it would commence arbitration proceedings in New Jersey. In January 2011, Control Screening brought a motion to compel arbitration in New Jersey. The district court granted the motion, because "the only reasonable interpretation of the arbitration clause is that Tecapro could have sought to arbitrate in Vietnam and Control Screening in New Jersey." Tecapro appealed.

The Sixth Circuit first addressed Tecapro's argument that the district court did not have personal jurisdiction over it. The Sixth Circuit found that, although Tecapro had no physical presence in New Jersey, the series of sales contracts Tecapro concluded with Control Screening, which is located in New Jersey, along with emails, faxes and Skype communications related to these contracts, were sufficient to create specific jurisdiction over Tecapro.

The Sixth Circuit then turned to the arbitration agreement. It disagreed with the district court's interpretation of the forum selection clause, finding that the clause was a "mistake" because "the International Arbitration Center of European countries" named therein did not exist. The Sixth Circuit then explained that, under the New York Convention, as set forth in Chapter 2 of the FAA, an agreement to arbitrate, or any part thereof, can be null and void if it was the product of mistake. The Sixth Circuit found that, in this case, only the forum selection provision within the agreement was a "mistake," and therefore was null and void, but the remainder of the agreement to arbitrate continued to be binding.

Finally, the Sixth Circuit held that because under Chapter 1 of the FAA a district court may only compel an arbitration within its district, the lower court in this case had properly compelled arbitration in New Jersey—albeit for incorrect reasons. The Sixth Circuit therefore affirmed the judgment compelling arbitration.

C. THE GRANT AND ENFORCEMENT OF INTERIM MEASURES IN INTERNATIONAL ARBITRATION

C.1 Tribunal-Ordered Interim Measures

In the United States, neither the FAA nor the governing international treaties, specifically the New York and Panama Conventions, expressly authorizes an arbitral tribunal to issue interim relief. Thus, the predominant sources of interim relief are the parties' arbitration agreement, institutional arbitration rules, and state law (ordinarily of the state of the arbitration's situs).[4] The latter two are presented here.

Institutional Arbitration Rules

The availability of interim measures under institutional arbitration rules depends on the particular set of governing rules selected by the parties. Among the International Chamber of Commerce ("ICC"), American Arbitration Association ("AAA"), and United Nations Commission on International Trade Law ("UNCITRAL") rules, however, the respective interim-relief

---

[4] Casey Dwyer and Peter E. Greene, *Interim Measures in Antitrust Matters before Arbitrators*, in EU AND US ANTITRUST ARBITRATION: A HANDBOOK FOR PRACTITIONERS 1417, 1421 (Gordon Blanke & Phillip Landolt eds., Kluwer Law Int'l 2011).

provisions are quite similar and broadly allow a party to request interim relief where it is "appropriate" or "necessary."

Article 23(1) of the ICC rules states: "Unless the parties have otherwise agreed, as soon as the file has been transmitted to it, the arbitral tribunal may, at the request of a party, order any interim or conservatory measure it deems appropriate. The tribunal may make the granting of any such measure subject to appropriate security being furnished by the requesting party. Any such measure shall take the form of an order, giving reasons, or of an award, as the arbitral tribunal considers appropriate."[5]

Article 21(1) the AAA rules provides: "At the request of any party, the tribunal may take whatever interim measures it deems necessary, including injunctive relief and measures for the protection or conservation of property."[6]

Article 26 of the UNCITRAL Rules states: "(1) At the request of either party, the arbitral tribunal may take any interim measures it deems necessary in respect of the subject-matter of the dispute, including measures for the conservation of the goods forming the subject-matter in dispute, such as ordering their deposit with a third person or the sale of perishable goods. (2) Such interim measures may be established in the form of an interim award. The arbitral tribunal shall be entitled to require security for the costs of such measures."[7]

---

[5]   INT'L CHAMBER OF COMMERCE R. art. 23(1).

[6]   AM. ARBITRATION ASS'N R. art. 21(1).

[7]   UNITED NATIONALS COMM'N ON INT'L TRADE LAW R. art. 26.

Recent court decisions in the United States have also assumed that arbitrators have the inherent authority to issue interim relief, irrespective of the governing arbitral rules.[8]

State Legislation

Additionally, certain states have passed legislation explicitly conferring upon an arbitral tribunal the authority to issue interim relief. For example:

California Code of Civil Procedure section 1297.171 states: "Unless otherwise agreed by the parties, the arbitral tribunal may, at the request of a party, order a party to take any interim measure of protection as the arbitral tribunal may consider necessary in respect of the subject matter of the dispute."[9] In such instances, "[t]he arbitral tribunal may require a party to provide appropriate security in connection with a measure ordered under Section 1297.171."[10]

Florida Statutes section 684.0018 states: "Unless otherwise agreed by the parties, the arbitral tribunal may, at the request of a party, grant interim measures. An interim measure is any temporary measure, whether in the form of an award or in another form, by which, at any time before the issuance of the award by which the dispute is finally decided, the arbitral tribunal orders a party to: (1) Maintain or restore the status quo

---

[8] Alan Scott Rau, *Provisional Relief in Arbitration: How Things Stand in the United States*, 22 KLUWER LAW INT'L 1, 7 (2005); *see, e.g., Certain Underwriters at Lloyd's, London v. Argonaut Ins. Co.*, 264 F. Supp. 2d 926, 937 (N.D. Cal. 2003) ("There is no question that an arbitration panel has the authority to require escrow to serve as security for an ultimate award"; that authority "may be either derived explicitly from the arbitration agreement or implicitly from the panel's power to ensure the parties receive the benefit of their bargain").

[9] CAL. CODE CIV. PROC. 1297.171 (2012).

[10] CAL. CODE CIV. PROC. 1297.172 (2012).

pending determination of the dispute; (2) Take action to prevent, or refrain from taking action that is likely to cause, current or imminent harm or prejudice to the arbitral process; (3) Provide a means of preserving assets out of which a subsequent award may be satisfied; or (4) Preserve evidence that may be relevant and material to the resolution of the dispute."[11]

Texas Civil Practice and Remedies Code section 172.083 states: "(a) Except as agreed by the parties, the arbitration tribunal, at the request of a party, may order a party to take an interim measure of protection that the tribunal considers necessary concerning the subject matter of the dispute. (b) The arbitration tribunal may require a party to provide appropriate security in connection with the interim measure ordered."[12]

Types of Interim Measures

In the United States, the array of interim measures available to parties under the foregoing institutional arbitration rules and state law provisions can generally be grouped into three categories:

(1) measures to facilitate the administration of the arbitration, including orders to preserve evidence or to permit inspection of documents, goods, or property;

(2) measures to preserve the *status quo*, including preliminary injunctions; and

(3) measures to facilitate the enforcement of future award, including attachment of assets.[13]

---

[11] FLA. STAT. § 684.0018 (2012).

[12] TEX. CIV. PRAC. & REM. CODE § 172.083 (2012).

[13] *See,* e.g., Alan Redfern, et al., LAW AND PRACTICE OF INTERNATIONAL COMMERCIAL ARBITRATION 339 (Sweet & Maxwell, 4th ed. 2004).

"The case law, commentators, rules of arbitration organizations, and some state statutes are very clear that arbitrators have broad authority to order provisional remedies and interim relief, including interim awards, in order to make a fair determination of an arbitral matter. This authority has included the issuance of measures equivalent to civil remedies of attachment, replevin, and sequestration to preserve assets or to make preliminary rulings ordering parties to undertake certain acts that affect the subject matter of the arbitration proceeding."[14]

A party to a US-based arbitration must generally satisfy the traditional elements of a claim for preliminary injunction to be entitled to interim relief. These elements typically require the party to demonstrate that:

(1) he will suffer "irreparably injury" unless the injunction issues;

(2) the threatened injury to him outweighs whatever damages the proposed injunction may cause the opposing party;

(3) it is "substantially likely" that he will eventually prevail on the merits of the dispute, and

(4) the injunction, if issued, would not be adverse to the public interest.[15]

At least one state—Florida—has also adopted express standards for an arbitral tribunal to follow in awarding interim relief. In Florida:

(1) The party requesting an interim measure . . . must satisfy the arbitral tribunal that:

---

[14] Alan Scott Rau, *Provisional Relief in Arbitration: How Things Stand in the United States*, 22 KLUWER LAW INT'L 1, 2 (2005).

[15] *Id.* at 30.

C. The Grant and Enforcement of Interim Measures in International Arbitration

> (a) harm not adequately reparable by an award of damages is likely to result if the measure is not ordered, and such harm substantially outweighs the harm that is likely to result to the party against whom the measure is directed if the measure is granted; and
>
> (b) a reasonable possibility exists that the requesting party will succeed on the merits of the claim. The determination on this possibility does not affect the discretion of the arbitral tribunal in making any subsequent determination.
>
> (2) With regard to a request for an interim measure . . ., the requirements in subsection (1) apply only to the extent the arbitral tribunal considers appropriate.[16]

Arbitration institutions have attempted to develop procedures by which parties may obtain interim relief prior to the formation of the tribunal (although, as some commentators have observed, these efforts have not been very successful).[17]

In 2006, the AAA, for example, amended its International Arbitration Rules to address the scenario in which emergency relief is needed before the arbitral tribunal has been formed.[18] Under Article 37, if a party requires emergency relief prior to the constitution of the tribunal, it may apply to the case administrator, and the AAA will appoint a single emergency arbitrator within one business day of receipt of notice.[19] The emergency arbitrator "shall have the power to order or award any

---

[16] FLA. STAT. § 684.0019 (2012).

[17] Grant Hanessian & Jurgen Mark, *Provisional Relief*, INTERNATIONAL ARBITRATION CHECKLISTS 53, 62 (Grant Hanessian & Lawrence W. Newman eds., JurisNet, LLC 2009).

[18] *Id.* at 63.

[19] *See* ICDR Rules, art. 37.

interim or conservancy measure the arbitrator deems necessary, including injunctive relief and measures for the protection or conservation of property."[20]

Since 1990, the ICC has also had a mechanism to provide pre-tribunal interim relief. Specifically, the Pre-Arbitral Referee Procedure provides for the immediate appointment of a referee, who has the power "to order any conservatory measures or any measures of restoration that are urgently necessary to prevent either immediate damage or irreparable loss and so to safeguard any of the rights or property of one of the parties."[21] The referee also has the authority to order any party to make payments to another person, to order a party to take any step in accordance with the contract, and to order any measures necessary to preserve evidence.[22] Because this special procedure was an opt-in one that required written agreement of the parties to the arbitration, it never not gained widespread use.[23]

One of the most significant changes in the new ICC Rules that went into effect on January 1, 2012 was the addition of emergency arbitrator procedures allowing parties to seek interim relief before the arbitral tribunal has been formed.[24] This procedure applies unless the parties specifically "opt out." Pursuant to Article 29 and Appendix V of these rules, a party seeking urgent interim relief prior to the constitution of the tribunal may apply to the ICC Secretariat for relief.[25] After considering whether the emergency procedure applies, the

---

[20] *Id.*

[21] *See* ICC Rules For A Pre-Arbitral Referee Procedure, art. 2.1.

[22] *Id.*

[23] *Supra*, note 14.

[24] *See* ICC Arbitration Rules, art. 29, appendix V (2012).

[25] *Id.* at art. 29.

President of the ICC International Court of Arbitration must appoint an emergency arbitrator as quickly as possible to make an order resolving the issue.[26] Although the parties are bound by the emergency arbitrator's decision, once the tribunal is constituted, it has the power to modify, terminate or annul any order made by the emergency arbitrator. These new rules apply only to parties who have elected to arbitrate their dispute under the ICC Rules and where the arbitration agreement was made after January 1, 2012.[27] The rules also explicitly provide that a party may still seek interim relief from a competent judicial authority.[28]

The International Arbitration Rules of the International Institute for Conflict Prevention and Resolution, based in New York, also provide for interim measures of protection by a special arbitrator.[29] Pursuant to Rule 14, a party may request the appointment of a special arbitrator who may grant such interim measures as he or she deems necessary.[30] The parties may agree on a special arbitrator, failing which, within one business day of the request, the CPR will appoint one.[31] The CPR rules also provide that a request of a court for interim relief is not inconsistent with the agreement to arbitrate, nor does it constitute a waiver of that agreement.[32] These provisions authorizing interim measures of protection apply only to arbitrations agreed by the parties to proceed under the CPR Rules and where the

---

[26]   *Id.* at appendix V, art. 2.

[27]   *Id.* at art. 29, rule 6(a).

[28]   ICC Arbitration Rules, art. 29, rule 7 (2012).

[29]   *See* CPR International Arbitration Rules, rule 14 (2007).

[30]   *Id.*

[31]   *Id.* at rule 14.5.

[32]   *Id.* at rule 14.12.

arbitration agreement was made on or after November 1, 2007.[33] As is the case with the ICC Rules, parties may opt out and once the Tribunal has been constituted, the Tribunal may modify or vacate the award or order rendered by the special arbitrator.

C.2 Court-Ordered Interim Measures

Federal Law

The FAA provides procedures for the confirmation and enforcement of a domestic arbitration award, and, because the U.S. is a signatory to the New York Convention, U.S. courts must, under most circumstances, recognize and enforce foreign arbitral awards.[34] The New York Convention does not, however, expressly address the subject of court-ordered interim measures. As a result, a split has developed among the federal courts as to whether they possess jurisdiction to order interim measures in international arbitral disputes.

In *McCreary Tire and Rubber Co. v. CEAT*, the Third Circuit held that the mandatory language "shall . . . refer the parties to arbitration," appearing in Article II(3) of the New York Convention, prevented courts from taking any pre-final award action, apart from referring parties to arbitration, including granting interim relief.[35] There, McCreary Tire and Rubber Company, a Pennsylvania corporation, sued CEAT, an Italian corporation, for alleged breaches of a distributorship contract.[36] After McCreary was granted an attachment in Pennsylvania state court, CEAT removed the case to federal court seeking to

---

33   *Id.* at rule 14.1.

34   9 U.S.C. §§ 9, 207 (2012).

35   *McCreary Tire & Rubber Co. v. CEAT*, 501 F.2d 1032, 1037 (3d Cir. 1974).

36   *Id.* at 1033.

dissolve the attachment.[37] Reasoning that McCreary's request for provisional relief in the form of attachment violated the parties' arbitration agreement and frustrated the arbitral process, the court discharged the foreign attachment and held that Article II(3) divested courts of jurisdiction to issue interim relief in aid of international arbitrations.[38] Some federal courts, including the Fourth Circuit, have also adopted the reasoning in *McCreary*.[39]

Three years later, in *Carolina Power & Light Co. v. Uranex*, the Northern District of California explicitly rejected the *McCreary* court's reasoning, finding that prejudgment attachment is indeed available under the New York Convention:

> This court, however, does not find the reasoning of *McCreary* convincing [because] nothing in the text of the Convention itself suggests that it preludes prejudgment attachment. The [FAA], which operates much like the Convention for domestic agreements involving maritime or interstate commerce, does not prohibit maintenance of a prejudgment attachment during a stay pending arbitration. . . . There is no indication in either the text or the apparent policies of the Convention that resort to prejudgment attachment was to be precluded. . . .[40]

In *Borden Inc. v. Meiji Milk Products Co.*, the Second Circuit also rejected *McCreary*, holding that the issuance of an injunction in aid of arbitration is consistent with Article II(3) of

---

[37] *Id.* at 1033.

[38] *Id.* at 1038.

[39] *See, e.g., I.T.A.D. Assocs., Inc. v. Podar Brothers*, 636 F. 2d 75, 77 (4th Cir. 1981) (holding that an attachment of assets was contrary to the agreement to arbitrate and the New York Convention).

[40] *Carolina Power & Light Co. v. Uranex*, 451 F. Supp. 1044, 1051 (N.D. Ca. 1977).

the New York Convention.[41] More recently, the District of Connecticut in *Bahrain Telecommunications Co. v. DiscoveryTel, Inc.*, reaffirmed that it is the position of the Second Circuit that "federal courts have both the jurisdiction and authority to grant injunctions and provisional remedies in the context of pending arbitrations, including international arbitrations."[42] Moreover, the availability of similar interim relief from the arbitral tribunal does not foreclose the parties from seeking aid from the courts.[43]

Until this split in authority among the U.S. courts has been resolved, the availability under federal law of interim relief in aid of international arbitration from the courts is uncertain and will depend on the circuit in which the claim for such relief is brought.

State Law

Complementing this federal jurisprudence, some states have passed legislation addressing the availability of court-ordered interim measures in arbitration. For example:

Under Texas Civil Practice and Remedies Code section 172.175 "(a) A party to an arbitration agreement may request an interim measure of protection from a district court before or during an arbitration. . . . (c) In connection with a pending arbitration, the court may take appropriate action including: (1) ordering an attachment issued to assure that the award to which the applicant may be entitled is not rendered ineffectual by the dissipation of party assets; or (2) granting a preliminary injunction to protect a

---

[41]   *Borden, Inc. v. Meiji Milk Products Co., Ltd.*, 919 F.2d 822, 826 (2d Cir. 1990).

[42]   *Bahrain Telecomms. Co. v. DiscoveryTel, Inc.*, 476 F. Supp. 2d 176, 180 (D. Conn. 2007).

[43]   *Id.*

trade secret or to conserve goods that are the subject matter of the dispute."[44]

California Code of Civil Procedure section 1297.91 provides that "[i]t is not incompatible with an arbitration agreement for a party to request from a superior court, before or during arbitral proceedings, an interim measure of protection, or for the court to grant such a measure."[45] Florida law contains an identical provision and also explains that "[a] court has the same power of issuing an interim measure in relation to arbitration proceedings, irrespective of whether the arbitration proceedings are held in this state, as it has in relation to the proceedings in courts. The courts shall exercise such power in accordance with its own procedures and in consideration of the specific features of international arbitration."[46]

California Code of Civil Procedure section 1297.93 elaborates on the types of interim measures a court may grant, which "include, but are not limited to: (a) An order of attachment issued to assure that the award to which applicant may be entitled is not rendered ineffectual by the dissipation of party assets. (b) A preliminary injunction granted in order to protect trade secrets or to conserve goods which are the subject matter of the arbitral dispute."[47]

Finally, in New York, New York Civil Practice Law and Rules section 7502(c), confers on courts the power to grant interim relief in arbitration proceedings: "The supreme court in the county in which an arbitration is pending or in a county specified in subdivision (a) of this section, may entertain an application for

---

[44] TEX. CIV. PRAC. & REM. CODE § 172.175 (2012).

[45] CAL. CIV. PROC. CODE §§ 1297.91 (2012).

[46] FLA. STAT. §§ 684.0001, 684.0028 (2012).

[47] CAL. CIV. PROC. CODE §§ 1297.93 (2012)

an order of attachment or for a preliminary injunction in connection with an arbitration that is pending inside or outside this state . . . but only upon the ground that the award to which the applicant may be entitled may be rendered ineffectual without such provisional relief."[48]

The time needed to obtain interim relief from a court varies widely and would depend in large part on the volume of cases on the court's calendar and the complexity of the relief sought. That is, where an application would require extensive argument, for example, a busy judge would likely have fewer and less-immediate opportunities to schedule the hearing, even if the application were styled as an emergency matter. In our experience, however, a motion for preliminary injunction can generally be adjudicated in as few as three and perhaps as many as ten business days.

In the United States, a federal court's power to grant anti-suit injunctions enjoining persons subject to its jurisdiction from commencing or continuing litigation in a foreign forum is well-established.[49] Although there is no uniform standard employed across the federal circuits for granting anti-suit injunctions, generally the moving party must make two threshold showings. First, the domestic and foreign lawsuits must involve the same parties.[50] The first condition does not require that the parties in the domestic and foreign are identical. Rather, courts evaluate whether the parties involved are "sufficiently similar."[51] Parties

[48] N.Y. C.P.L.R. 7502(c) (2012).

[49] *Quaak v. Klynveld Peat Marwick Goerdeler Bedrijfsrevisoren*, 361 F.3d 11, 16 (1st Cir. 2004) (*citing China Trade and Dev. Corp. v. M.V. Choong Yong*, 837 F.2d 33, 35 (2d Cir. 1987)).

[50] *Id.*

[51] *Paramedics Electromedicina Commercial, LTDA. v. GE Med. Sys. Info. Tech., Inc.*, 369 F.3d 645, 652 (2d Cir. 2004).

are sufficiently similar when "the real parties in interest are the same in both matters."[52] Second, the resolution of the U.S. suit must be dispositive of the foreign proceeding.[53]

Beyond the two threshold requirements, U.S. Circuit Courts of Appeal consider certain discretionary factors, including protection of the enjoining court's jurisdiction, considerations of international comity, public policy, and other equitable factors, to evaluate whether their authority to grant an anti-suit injunction should be exercised.[54] A split exists as to which factors to apply. The First, Second, Third, Sixth, Eighth, and District of Columbia Circuits adhere to a "restrictive" or "conservative" standard. Emphasizing principles of international comity and respect for the actions of courts in other jurisdiction, these courts are the least likely to grant a petition for an anti-suit injunction.[55] The Fifth, Seventh, and Ninth Circuits apply a more "liberal" or "expansive" standard that emphasizes the potentially vexatious nature of foreign litigation. The Fifth Circuit's decision in *Kaepa, Inc. v. Achilles Corp.* exemplifies this approach.[56]

---

[52] *Motorola Credit Corp. v. Uzan*, No. 02 Civ. 666 (JSR), 2003 U.S. Dist. LEXIS 111, at *6 (S.D.N.Y. Jan. 7, 2003).

[53] *Canon Latin Am., Inc. v. Lantech (CR), S.A.*, 508 F.3d 597, 601 (11th Cir. 2007).

[54] Arif Ali, Katherine Nesbitt and Jane Wessel, *Anti-Suit Injunctions in Support of International Arbitration in the United States and the United Kingdom*, 11 INT'L ARB. L. REV. 12, 13 (2008).

[55] *See*, e.g., *Paramedics Electromedicina Commercial*, 369 F.3d 645; *Laif X Sprl v. Axtel, S.A. de C.V.*, 390 F.3d 194 (2d Cir. 2004) (affirming denial of anti-suit injunction).

[56] *Kaepa v. Achilles Corp.*, 76 F.3d 624 (5th Cir. 1996) (reaffirming the standard under which an anti-suit injunction may be granted: "when foreign litigation would (1) frustrate a policy of the forum issuing the injunction; (2) be vexatious or oppressive; (3) threaten the issuing court's *in rem* or *quasi in rem* jurisdiction; or (4) prejudice other equitable considerations." (*citing In Re Unterweser Reederei Gmbh*, 428 F.2d 888, 890 (5th Cir. 1970)).

Further, a majority of federal courts considering the issue have held that a federal court also possesses the authority to enjoin an arbitration, even though the FAA does not address a court's power to do so.[57] Federal courts have issued anti-arbitration injunctions in situations where, for example, the court found no valid, binding arbitration agreement or where the court determined that the party had waived its right to arbitrate.[58] In general, courts that have permitted anti-arbitration injunctions have done so based on an implied authority "concomitant" to their express authority to compel arbitration in Section 206 of the FAA.[59] For example, in *SATCOM International Group PLC v. ORBCOMM International Partners, LP*, the Southern District of New York reasoned that, because a court has unequivocal authority to order arbitration where appropriate, "the court should have a concomitant power to enjoin arbitration where arbitration is inappropriate."[60] Other federal courts have based their authority to enjoin an arbitration on sources outside the FAA, including the All Writs Act, which allows federal courts to issue "all writs necessary or appropriate in aid of their respective jurisdictions," and Federal Rule of Civil Procedure 65, which allows a federal court to issue a preliminary injunction.[61]

---

[57] Jennifer L. Gorskie, *US Courts and the Anti-Arbitration Injunction*, 28 KLUWER LAW INTERNAT'L 295, 296 (2012).

[58] Colm McInerney, *The Practice of United States Federal Courts Regarding Anti-Arbitration Injunctions*, 26-12 MEALEY'S INTERNATIONAL ARBITRATION REPORT 14 (2011).

[59] *See*, e.g., *Societe Generale de Surveillance, S.A. v. Raytheon European Mgmt. Sys. Co.*, 643 F.2d 863, 867-68 (1st Cir. 1981).

[60] *SATCOM Int'l Group PLC v. ORBCOMM Int'l Partners, L.P.*, 49 F. Supp. 2d 331, 342 (S.D.N.Y. 1999).

[61] Colm McInerney, *The Practice of United States Federal Courts Regarding Anti-Arbitration Injunctions*, 26-12 MEALEY'S INTERNATIONAL ARBITRATION REPORT 14 (2011).

Courts in jurisdictions that have embraced the authority to confer provisional relief, such as those in the Second Circuit, will ordinarily also provide such relief in aid of an arbitration outside the United States.[62]

For example, in *Tampimex Oil Limited v. Latina Trading Corp.*, the Southern District of New York denied the defendant's motion to vacate an *ex parte* order of attachment of more than $1,500,000 of the defendant's property held in a bank account in New York in aid of an arbitration in London.[63] Further, in a recent New York state court decision, *Sojitz Corp. v. Prithvi Information Solutions Ltd.*, the court, in the absence of personal jurisdiction over the defendant, granted a pre-award attachment of assets located within New York in aid of a Singapore arbitration between two non-U.S. parties.[64] The court noted the legislature had, in CPLR 7502(c), discussed above, "granted the courts of New York authority to issue preliminary injunctions and attachments in aid of all arbitrations including those involving foreign parties or in which the arbitration is conducted outside of New York."[65]

---

[62] *See, e.g., Tampimex Oil Ltd. v. Latina Trading Corp.*, 558 F. Supp. 1201, 1203 (S.D.N.Y. 1983); *Atlas Chartering Svcs. v. World Trade Group*, 453 F. Supp. 861, 863 (S.D.N.Y. 1978); *Carolina Power & Light Co. v. Uranex*, 451 F. Supp. 1044, 1051 (N.D. Cal. 1977).

[63] *Tampimex Oil Ltd.*, 558 F. Supp. at 1203 ("The fact that parties have agreed in the contract to arbitrate disputes in London does not preclude plaintiff from instituting an action or securing an attachment in New York.").

[64] *Sojitz Corp. v. Prithvi Info. Solutions Ltd.*, 921 N.Y.S.2d 14, 17 (N.Y. Sup. Ct. 2011).

[65] *Id.* at 93.

Courts in California, Florida, Texas, are similarly empowered under state law to order and enforce interim measures attendant to a foreign arbitration.[66]

C.3 Enforcement of Interim Measures

Where a U.S. jurisdiction's laws have recognized a tribunal's authority to issue interim measures and courts have been willing to enforce those measures, we are aware of no meaningful distinctions between the ways in which the interim measure and an award or court judgment would be enforced. The manner of enforcement—and the tools available to the enforcing party to ensure that the interim relief is executed—would, in both instances, be the same (as explained by the state statutes listed below, for example).

We are unaware of any particular categories of recognized interim relief that a U.S. court will not enforce. The laws of the United States and the states, however, delineate the grounds on which a court may refuse to enforce an interim measure order by an arbitral tribunal, as described in the following section.

U.S. courts have varying sources of authority for the enforcement of an arbitral tribunal's interim relief order. No source appears to make a distinction between the enforcement of an interim order made within or outside the jurisdiction, although all of the sources provide grounds for a court to refuse recognition and enforcement of the order, no matter its origin.

---

[66] CAL. CIV. PROC. CODE § 1297.12 (2012); FLA. STAT. § 684.0002(2) (2012) (providing that section 684.0028, "Court-ordered interim measures," is exempt from provision that "[t]his chapter . . . applies only if the place of arbitration is in this state."); TEX. CIV. PRAC. & REM. CODE § 172.001(b) (2012).

C. The Grant and Enforcement of Interim Measures in International Arbitration

Federal Law

The FAA requires that, in a domestic arbitration, "the court must grant [an order confirming the award] unless the award is vacated, modified, or corrected as prescribed in sections 10 and 11 of this title."[67] Under section 10(a)(4), a court may decline to confirm an award when "a mutual, final, and definite award upon the subject matter submitted was not made."[68]

Under the New York Convention, "[t]he court shall confirm the award unless it finds one of the grounds for refusal or deferral of recognition of the award specified in the said Convention."[69] Article V of the Convention enumerates seven grounds on which a court may refuse to recognize and enforce an award separate from those provided in section 10(a)(4) of the FAA.[70] Although the Article V grounds do not include express reference to the finality of an award, under the New York Convention, "the courts are agreed that the award in question must be 'final' in order to be eligible for judicial confirmation."[71]

A party attempting to avoid enforcement of an interim order issued by the arbitral tribunal in an international arbitration thus could assert that the order is not final and not confirmable. Courts have addressed the issue in a variety of ways, with some

---

[67] 9 U.S.C. § 9.

[68] 9 U.S.C. § 10(a)(4).

[69] 9 U.S.C. § 207.

[70] Convention on the Recognition and Enforcement of Foreign Arbitral Awards, June 10, 1958, 21 U.S.T. 2517, art. V.

[71] *Hall Steel Co. v. Metalloyd Ltd.*, 492 F. Supp.2d 715, 717-18 (E.D. Mich. 2007) (citing *Hart Surgical, Inc. v. Ultracision, Inc.*, 244 F.3d 231, 233 (1st Cir. 2001); *Publicis Comm. v. True North Comms., Inc.*, 206 F.3d 725, 728-29 (7th Cir. 2000); *Michales v. Mariforum Shipping, S.A.*, 625 F.2d 411, 414-15 (2d Cir. 1980)).

finding an interim order to be non-final and on that basis refusing to recognize it, others disagreeing and enforcing the interim order, and others still sidestepping the issue altogether and enforcing the award where the parties agreed to rules giving the tribunal the authority to issue interim relief.[72]

State Law

Various state statutes provide a basis for a court to recognize and enforce a tribunal's order of interim relief. In California, for example, Code of Civil Procedure section 1297.92 explains that "[a]ny party to an arbitration governed by this title may request from the superior court enforcement of an award of an arbitral tribunal to take any interim measure of protection of an arbitral tribunal pursuant to Article 2 (commencing with Section 1297.171) of Chapter 4. Enforcement shall be granted pursuant to the law applicable to granting the type of interim relief requested."[73]

Florida Statutes section 684.0026 provides that "[a]n interim measure issued by an arbitral tribunal shall be recognized as binding and, unless otherwise provided by the arbitral tribunal,

---

[72] *See* Peter J.W. Sherwin & Douglas C. Rennie, *Interim Relief Under International Arbitration Rules and Guidelines: A Comparative Analysis,* 20 THE AMERICAN REVIEW OF INT'L ARBITRATION 317, 324-326 (2009) (citing cases); *Hall Steel,* 492 F. Supp.2d at 718 ("[T]he courts have found that an arbitrator's award need not conclusively resolve all matters in dispute in order to qualify as 'final' and eligible for confirmation. The Sixth Circuit has explained, for example, that 'an interim award that finally and definitively disposes of a separate independent claim may be confirmed notwithstanding the absence of an award that finally disposes of all the claims that were submitted to arbitration. Similarly, an arbitrator's characterization of an award as 'interim' does not necessarily disqualify it from judicial confirmation, because '[t]he content of a decision – not its nomenclature – determines finality.'" (citing *Island Creek Coal Sales Co. v. City of Gainesville,* 729 F.2d 1046, 1049 (6th Cir. 1984)).

[73] CAL. CIV. PROC. CODE §§ 1297.92 (2012).

enforced upon application to the competent court, irrespective of the country in which it was issued."[74] "The court where recognition or enforcement is sought may, if it considers it proper, order the requesting party to provide appropriate security if the arbitral tribunal has not already made a determination with respect to security or if such a decision is necessary to protect the rights of third parties."[75]

In Florida, courts may refuse to recognize or enforce an interim measure "only (a) at the request of the party against whom it is invoked if the court is satisfied that: [s]uch refusal is warranted on the grounds set forth in s. 684.0048(1)(a)1., 2., 3., or 4.," which pertains to the recognition or enforcement of an arbitral award; "[t]he arbitral tribunal's decision with respect to the provision of security in connection with the interim measure issued by the arbitral tribunal has not been complied with; or . . . [t]he interim measure was terminated or suspended by the arbitral tribunal or, if so empowered, by the court of the state or country in which the arbitration takes place or under the laws of which that interim measure was granted."[76] Such recognition or enforcement may also be refused "(b) [i]f the court finds that . . . [t]he interim measure is incompatible with the powers conferred upon the court, unless the court decides to reformulate the interim measure to the extent necessary to adapt it to its own powers and procedures for the purpose of enforcing that interim measure and without modifying its substance; or "any of the grounds set forth in s. 684.0048(1)(b)1. or 2. apply to the recognition and enforcement of the interim measure." [77]

---

[74] FLA. STAT. § 684.0026(1) (2012).

[75] FLA. STAT. § 684.0026(3).

[76] FLA. STAT. 684.0027(1)(a) (2012).

[77] FLA. STAT. 684.0027(1)(b).

Finally, Texas Civil Practice and Remedies Code section 172.175(b) holds that "[a] party to an arbitration may request from the court enforcement of an order of an arbitration tribunal granting an interim measure of protection under Section 172.083. The court shall grant enforcement as provided by law applicable to the type of interim relief requested."[78]

---

[78] TEX. CIV. PRAC. & REM. CODE § 172.175(b).

UZBEKISTAN

Alexander Korobeinikov[1]

A. LEGISLATION, TRENDS AND TENDENCIES

A.1 Legislation

While the first arbitration court to be created in Uzbekistan was established in 2002, special legislation (the Law on Arbitration Courts) was adopted only in 2006. While the main provisions of the law are based on UNCITRAL Model Law principles, there are some significant features. For example, under this Law the arbitral tribunal has to apply only Uzbek legislation and violation of this rule is a ground for setting aside the award.

In addition to the Law on Arbitration Courts, arbitration is also regulated by the relevant provisions of the Commercial Procedural Code and the Civil Procedural Code. The Civil Procedural Code contains rules regarding arbitration procedure and the enforcement of arbitration awards relating to non-commercial disputes. The Commercial Procedural Code sets out the rules applicable to the enforcement of arbitral awards for commercial disputes.

A.2 International Treaties

Uzbekistan is a party to a number of international and regional treaties which relate to arbitration proceedings, including the New York Convention 1958[2] as well as several CIS treaties.

---

[1]   Alexander Korobeinikov is a Senior Associate in Baker & McKenzie's Almaty office and a member of Baker & McKenzie International Arbitration practice group.

[2]   Convention on the Recognition and Enforcement of Foreign Arbitral Awards. New York, 10 June 1958.

Additionally, it should be noted that Uzbekistan is a party to the ICSID Convention, therefore investors have a right to seek settlement of their dispute in the framework of this convention. In this regard, it should be mentioned that the laws of Uzbekistan do not contain an express agreement to arbitrate disputes with foreign investors. The only relevant provision is contained in Article 10 of Law of the Republic of Uzbekistan On Guarantees and Measures to Protect Foreign Investors' Rights, dated 30 April 1998 (N 611-I). Under this law:

A dispute associated with foreign investments (investment dispute) directly or indirectly, can be settled on agreement of the parties by consultation between them. If the parties are not able to achieve an agreed settlement, the dispute shall be solved either by an economic court of Uzbekistan or by arbitration in accordance with the rules and procedures of international agreements (conventions) on the settlement of investment disputes, which Uzbekistan has joined.

However, in accordance with the decision of the Uzbek Constitutional Court issued in November 2006, this provision cannot be treated as consent to arbitrate disputes with foreign investors. The reference to arbitration in the article is purely declaratory and does not add anything to the fact that the investor may have a right to resort to arbitration pursuant to an agreement or treaty. Investors wishing to launch arbitration against Uzbekistan must rely on a direct agreement with the state or invoke provisions of a treaty where Uzbekistan expressly consented to arbitration. Investors who cannot rely on such provisions may only bring their disputes against Uzbekistan to the local economic courts.

B. Cases

A.3 Trends and Tendencies

After adoption of the Law on Arbitration Courts, the Uzbek Chamber of Commerce, together with other professional associations, created more than 50 arbitration institutions and in 2011 arbitration courts reviewed more than 7,800 cases. Therefore arbitration has clearly become more popular as an alternative method of resolving disputes.

Additionally, it should be noted that there is not any special legislation which sets forth rules for international arbitration proceedings in Uzbekistan. Therefore, currently Uzbek authorities are considering adoption of a special law regulating the activity of international arbitrations and the enforcement of foreign awards.

B. CASES

Despite the recent development of a legal framework, foreign parties do not arbitrate much in Uzbekistan and opt instead for arbitrating abroad.

We are currently aware of only one pending investment arbitration filed by the UK gold mining company Oxus Gold Plc under the UNCITRAL Rules of Arbitration. As stated in the last press-release of Oxus Gold Plc, this arbitration was commenced by Oxus in 2011, accusing Uzbekistan of illegally expropriating the shares of the UK company in the Amantaytau Goldfields Project in the Kyzylkum desert. At the time of going to press, the arbitral tribunal had rejected Uzbekistan's preliminary challenge of its jurisdiction, stating that the UK—Uzbekistan BIT also provide protection for indirect investments.

C. THE GRANT AND ENFORCEMENT OF INTERIM MEASURES IN INTERNATIONAL ARBITRATION

As mentioned above, there are no special rules regulating international arbitration proceedings in Uzbekistan. Therefore, it is unclear whether the state courts will provide assistance to international arbitral tribunals in connection with the enforcement of interim measures.

However, under the local Law on Arbitration Courts, parties can seek an interim measures order from the state court only if the arbitral tribunal grants interim measures, and the decision of the arbitral tribunal has to be provided to the state court as an attachment to the party's application.

At the same time, there do not appear to be any precedents of the Uzbek courts using the above provisions of the Law on Arbitration Courts and so it is still unclear how they will be applied in practice.

VIETNAM

Chi Anh Tran,[1] Andrew Fitanides[2] and Quy Hoai Nguyen[3]

A. LEGISLATION, TRENDS AND TENDENCIES

A.1 Background and Overview of the Applicable Law

Vietnam has a growing economy and an improved investment regime. In 2007, Vietnam acceded to the WTO and the United States granted permanent normal trade relations. These developments have made Vietnam an attractive destination for foreign investment, and increased investment will lead to more disputes. Historically in Vietnam, arbitration has not been a popular choice for resolving disputes, particularly those involving foreign and foreign-invested enterprises. This year, however, reforms contained in Law No. 54/2010/QH12 on Commercial Arbitration (the "Law on Commercial Arbitration"),[4] which replaced the often-criticized 2003 ordinance on commercial arbitration (the "Ordinance"),[5] have greatly improved Vietnam's arbitration regime, suggesting arbitration will increase in popularity going forward.

---

[1] Chi Anh Tran is an Associate in Baker & McKenzie's office in Ho Chi Minh City and a member of the Dispute Resolution Practice Group. Her principal practice areas include dispute resolution, compliance and competition law.

[2] Andrew Fitanides is an Associate in Baker & McKenzie's Ho Chi Minh City office and a member of the Dispute Resolution Practice Group working primarily in commercial litigation.

[3] Quy Hoai Nguyen is an Associate in Baker & McKenzie's Ho Chi Minh City office and a member of the Dispute Resolution Practice Group.

[4] Law No. 54/2010/QH12 on Commercial Arbitration, adopted on 17 June 2010, effective on 1 January 2011 ("Law on Commercial Arbitration").

[5] Ordinance No. 08/2003/PL-UBTVQH11 on Commercial Arbitration, adopted on 25 February 2003, effective on 1 July 2003, superseded by the Law on Commercial Arbitration.

Vietnam is a signatory of the New York Convention.[6] However, Vietnam is not a party to the ICSID Convention. The Bilateral Trade Agreement between Vietnam and the United States allows for settlement by binding arbitration of certain disputes between natural and juridical persons of diverse nationality. However, Vietnam's arbitration law is still developing and is still some way from the UNCITRAL Model Law, the basis for the arbitration laws of other jurisdictions in the region.[7] Although court litigation remains the most common dispute resolution mechanism in Vietnam, commercial arbitration offers important advantages, including faster resolution due to simplified procedural and evidentiary requirements, greater flexibility regarding the confidentiality of proceedings and greater predictability.

Some uncertainty remains as to whether a given dispute may be subject to resolution by arbitration. Under the Law on Commercial Arbitration, arbitration may only be used to settle disputes: (1) arising out of commercial activities; (2) where one of the involved parties engages in commercial activities; or (3) other disputes stipulated by law.[8] Under Vietnamese law, commercial activity is broadly, but vaguely, defined, introducing the risk that an arbitration award may be set aside if a Vietnamese court holds the dispute to be non-commercial in nature.[9] The Law on Commercial Arbitration also limits the

---

[6] The status of the convention is available at: http://www.uncitral.org/uncitral/en/uncitral_texts/arbitration/NYConvention_status.html.

[7] Some provisions of the Law on Commercial Arbitration, such as Articles 47, 48 and 50, incorporate elements of the UNCITRAL Model Law.

[8] Article 2 of the Law on Commercial Arbitration. Notably, "other disputes stipulated by law" are not defined.

[9] Law No. 36/2005/QH11 on Commerce defines commercial activity as "activity for profit-making purposes, comprising purchase and sale of goods, provision of services, investment, commercial enhancement, and other activities for profit making purposes."

applicability of arbitration in disputes relating to consumers.[10] For example, customers of goods and services have the right to refer their disputes to the court, even if they have entered a valid arbitration agreement.

Additionally, significant obstacles remain to the efficient and equitable recognition and enforcement of foreign arbitral awards under Vietnamese law. These practical issues are discussed in detail below with reference to specific cases.

A.2 Arbitration in Vietnam

The Law on Commercial Arbitration introduces important improvements concerning the appointment of arbitrators, choice of law and language of proceedings, available interim relief measures and allows for the creation of foreign arbitral institutions in Vietnam. In order to appreciate the significance of these reforms, it is important to understand the overall framework of Vietnam's arbitration regime.

A.2.1 Disputes involving a "foreign element"

Vietnam employs a bifurcated arbitration regime that distinguishes between domestic disputes and those involving a foreign element. A dispute involving a foreign element is indirectly defined as a dispute that arises out of a civil relation involving a foreign element, as provided in the Civil Code of Vietnam.[11]

Under the Civil Code, a civil relation involves a foreign element if:[12]

---

[10]   Article 17 of the Law on Commercial Arbitration.

[11]   Civil Code No. 33/2005/QH11, adopted on 14 June 2005, effective on 1 January 2006 ("Civil Code").

[12]   Article 758 of the Civil Code.

- at least one of the parties is foreign; or

- at least one of the parties is a Vietnamese national residing overseas; or

- the basis for establishment, modification or termination of such relation was the law of a foreign country or such basis arose in a foreign country or the assets involved in the relation are located overseas.

As explained below in greater detail, parties generally have more options in disputes involving a foreign element in comparison to purely domestic disputes.

A.2.2 Arbitration centers

The Law on Commercial Arbitration provides for the establishment and operation of domestic arbitration centers. The Law also permits foreign arbitration centers to operate in Vietnam through branches or representative offices, although arbitral awards issued by these bodies remain foreign arbitral awards for the purpose of enforcement in Vietnam. There are currently no foreign arbitration centers in Vietnam.

Six well-known domestic arbitration centers are operating in Vietnam.[13] The best-known of these, VIAC, is a non-governmental body established by the Chamber of Commerce and Industry of Vietnam. Although the Law on Commercial Arbitration and VIAC's rules allow the center to employ the parties' choice of arbitration rules, in practice VIAC refuses to apply arbitration rules other than its own on the basis that such other rules would be viewed as contrary to Vietnamese law.

---

[13]   These are, the Vietnam International Arbitration Center ("VIAC"); the Hanoi Commercial Arbitration Center; the Ho Chi Minh City Commercial Arbitration Center ("TRACENT"); the Can Tho Commercial Arbitration Center; the Asian International Commercial Arbitration Center ("ACIAC"); and the Pacific International Arbitration Center ("PIAC").

A.2.3 Arbitration procedures

Appointment of arbitrators

Significantly, the Law on Commercial Arbitration now allows non-Vietnamese citizens to qualify as arbitrators. This is a promising improvement from the perspective of foreign or foreign-invested enterprises because of the perceived greater expertise and impartiality of foreign national arbitrators.

The appointment of arbitrators is conducted according to the arbitration center's rules. For example, unless the parties have agreed that their dispute will be heard by a single arbitrator, under VIAC rules a three-member arbitration panel will be created. Each party has the right to select an arbitrator from VIAC's list. The two members thus selected will then nominate a third arbitrator to serve as Chairman of the arbitration panel.

Although ad hoc arbitration was allowed under the Ordinance, it is not known to have ever been used. However, recent reforms make ad hoc arbitration a viable option. Under the Law on Commercial Arbitration ad hoc arbitration is conducted by a panel of three arbitrators, unless the parties have agreed otherwise. In cases where the parties are unable to agree on the appointment of arbitrators, a competent court may appoint arbitrators to hear the dispute.

Role of Vietnamese courts in domestic arbitration

Either party may petition a court of the first instance to set aside the award of a domestic arbitration center. This decision may be appealed. A domestic arbitration award may be set aside for a variety of substantive and procedural defects.[14]

---

14 Article 68 of the Law on Commercial Arbitration. The grounds for setting-aside a domestic arbitral award are: absence of a valid arbitration agreement; defects in the forming of the arbitral panel or in arbitral proceedings which run contrary to the agreement of the parties or the Law on Commercial Arbitration; lack of

A.2.4 Enforcement of an arbitral award

Award from domestic arbitration centers

A valid domestic arbitral award is equivalent to the final decision of a Vietnamese court. Where an award debtor refuses to honor an award, and has not sought to set it aside, the prevailing party may request the assistance of the civil judgment enforcement authorities.

Award from foreign arbitration centers

In principle, foreign arbitral awards are enforceable in Vietnam. The Civil Procedure Code[15] provides for the recognition and enforcement in Vietnam of any award from a nation that is a signatory of a relevant international convention (*e.g.*, the New York Convention) or, otherwise, on the basis of reciprocity. However, a foreign arbitral award must be recognized and approved for enforcement by a Vietnamese court before it becomes the equivalent to a legally effective decision of a Vietnamese court or domestic arbitration center. Court approval also allows assets derived from enforcement to be transferred abroad.

The three-judge panel hearing an application for the recognition and enforcement of a foreign arbitral award may not review substantive issues of the dispute, only the basis for the recognition and enforcement of the award in Vietnam. Recognition may be denied if the:

---

subject matter jurisdiction for the center to hear the dispute; forged evidence or material benefits to an arbitrator which produces a conflict of interest; or, the arbitral award is contrary to basic principles of Vietnamese law.

[15] Civil Procedure Code No. 24/2004/QH11, adopted on 15 June 2004, effective on 01 January 2005 amended by the Law No. 65/2011/QH12 adopted on 29 March 2011, effective on 1 January 2012 (the "CPC").

- parties lacked the capacity to sign the arbitration agreement or arbitration clause;
- arbitration agreement is invalid under applicable law;
- respondent did not receive sufficient notice of the appointment of arbitrators or the arbitration proceedings;
- award was validly set-aside, revoked or suspended;
- award was not binding on the parties;
- subject-matter of the dispute is not capable of settlement by arbitration under Vietnamese law; or
- court deems it as contrary to the basic principles of Vietnamese law to allow recognition and enforcement.

A.2.5 Other issues

Choice of law

In a dispute involving a foreign element, the arbitral tribunal will apply the law chosen by the parties without regard to its variance from the basic principles of Vietnamese law.[16] However, the parties should be mindful that any award may be set aside or rendered unenforceable at a later stage if Vietnamese courts hold that the application of foreign law was "contrary to the basic principles of Vietnamese law."

Language

Under the Law on Commercial Arbitration, where the parties have not agreed to the language to be used, the arbitral tribunal may, at its own discretion, choose the language to use for any arbitration involving a foreign element.[17] Where no foreign

---

[16] Article 14 of the Law on Commercial Arbitration.

[17] *Id.* at Article 10.

element is present, arbitral proceedings must be conducted in Vietnamese, except for disputes in which at least one party is a foreign invested enterprise.

Interim relief

The Law on Commercial Arbitration empowers arbitral tribunals to grant interim measures not previously available under the Ordinance.

A.3 Trends and Tendencies

The success of the new Law on Commercial Arbitration will depend on the willingness of the Vietnamese courts to recognize and give effect to the arbitral process. However, Vietnamese courts have a history of ambivalence towards arbitration. This ambivalence is made possible by the broad discretion of Vietnamese courts to set aside arbitral awards. As the following cases demonstrate, awards have been set aside for the invalidity of the arbitration agreement, procedural defects, ambiguity in the terms of the arbitration clause, and general public policy reasons.

B. CASES

The little that is known about (normally confidential) arbitral proceedings comes from the very few available decisions of Vietnamese courts on set-aside petitions. However, the following cases provide a glimpse of some of the more noteworthy issues raised by Vietnamese courts when considering the setting-aside of domestic arbitral awards, or the recognition of foreign arbitral awards.

B. Cases

B.1 Lack of Capacity to Enter Arbitration Agreement

Ben Thanh Corporation ("Sunimex") v. Recofi S.A. Company Limited ("Recofi")

On 25 October 1996, Sunimex and Recofi contracted for the sale and purchase of wheat flour from France. The contract's arbitration clause specified resolution of disputes by the International Chamber of Commerce ("ICC") in France.

Following Sunimex's breach, the dispute went to the ICC in France which held that the arbitration clause failed to indentify the ICC International Court of Arbitration ("ICC Arbitration") as the arbitral authority, and persuaded the parties to sign a new arbitration agreement based on the model ICC arbitration clause. ICC Arbitration heard the case, and, in March of 1999, an award was issued in favor of Recofi (the "Award").

Recofi petitioned for the recognition and enforcement of the Award in Vietnam. On 24 April 2001, the People's Court of Ho Chi Minh City refused recognition of the Award, holding that it was invalid because Mr. Vuong Cong Minh, who executed the arbitration agreement on behalf of the Sunimex, was not authorized to do so.[18]

Under Article 16.1(a) of the Ordinance on Recognition and Enforcement of Foreign Arbitral Awards in Vietnam, a foreign arbitral award shall not be recognized or enforced in Vietnam if the parties to the arbitration agreement lacked the capacity to sign the agreement in accordance with the law applicable to each party. For international contracts, this results in a significant risk of non-enforceability because it may be difficult for a foreign party to confirm whether the Vietnamese signatory is authorized under the entity's internal regulations to execute such

---

[18]   Decision No. 78/QD-XQQTT.

agreements. In *Sunimex v. Recofi*, the Vietnamese court interpreted the relevant statute narrowly to invalidate the arbitration agreement, without regard to the relationship of the parties or their commercial dealings.

Best practices, therefore, require that parties to an arbitration agreement obtain proof that the individuals executing the agreement are authorized to do so—regardless of whether the arbitration is conducted at a domestic or foreign arbitration center.[19] A domestic arbitral award may be set aside at the request of either party if the arbitration agreement is invalid.[20]

B.2 Violations of Arbitration Proceedings

PT Badega Agri Abadi Company ("PT") v. Soon Chi Co., Ltd ("Soon Chi")

A dispute between PT (Indonesia) and Soon Chi (Taiwan) was heard by the Indonesia National Board of Arbitration. On 1 November 2006, an award was made in favor of PT (the "Award"). PT petitioned the Ministry of Justice of Vietnam ("MOJ") for recognition and enforcement against Soon Chi's assets in Hung Yen Province. Recognition and enforcement was decided by the People's Court of Hung Yen Province ("Hung Yen Court").

PT was unable to satisfy the Hung Yen Court's request to provide original copies of certain legal documents[21] of PT and its legal representative, including the sale and purchase contract between PT and Soon Chi and the Award. Soon Chi

---

[19] Article 18.2 of the Law on Commercial Arbitration.

[20] *Id.* at Article 68.2(a).

[21] Publically available information on the case does not specify which documents were requested.

subsequently disclaimed that it had entered into any contract with PT, and requested that the court rule based on the non-original documents PT had previously provided to the Hung Yen Court. Soon Chi also introduced evidence that PT was never an established juridical entity.

On 10 August 2007, the Hung Yen Court issued a decision refusing to recognize the Award on the basis that there was insufficient evidence to prove that the signatory of the contract (and therefore the arbitration agreement) was the legal or authorized representative of Soon Chi at the time of execution, or that the representative of Soon Chi presenting at the arbitration hearing was the legal or authorized representative of Soon Chi.[22]

The Hung Yen Court also noted that the contract provided for disputes to be settled according to the rules of Badan Arbitrase Nasional Indonesia (BANI). Pursuant to BANI's Rules, the Award should have been forwarded to the relevant parties, and two copies sent to BANI for delivery to the relevant district courts for registration. This procedural defect, combined with PT's inability to provide original copies of the relevant documents to the court, resulted in the denial of recognition of the Award for failure to comply with arbitration rules.[23]

This case indicates that a foreign arbitral award may only be enforced in Vietnam where the arbitration proceedings complied with the arbitration rules and, to some extent, the laws of Vietnam in terms of arbitration procedures.[24]

---

[22] Decision No. 03/2007/ST-KDTM.

[23] Article 370.1(a), (c) and (dd) of the CPC.

[24] *Id.* at Article 370.1(dd).

B.3 Dispute Resolution Body Unspecified

Jackson Mechanical Industrial Co., Ltd ("JMIC") v. Dai Dung Metallic Manufacture Construction & Trade Co., Ltd ("Dai Dung")

The People's Court of Ho Chi Minh City ("HCMC Court") refused JMIC's petition to set aside the 17 June 2009 Arbitral Award of Ho Chi Minh City Commercial Arbitration Center in favor of Dai Dung (the "Award").[25] JMIC had argued the Award should be set aside because the Vietnamese and Chinese versions of the arbitration agreement identified different dispute resolution bodies—the Ho Chi Minh Commercial Arbitration Center and the HCMC Court, respectively. On 11 September 2009, the HCMC Court ruled that because JMIC had not objected to the authority of Ho Chi Minh Commercial Arbitration Center during arbitration, it had assented to resolution by the body.[26]

This case was decided under the Ordinance, which states that an "arbitration agreement shall be invalid if it fails to specify, or to specify clearly, the subjects of the dispute or the arbitration organization authorized to resolve disputes, and the parties have failed to enter into any supplementary agreement."[27] Nevertheless, the HCMC Court overlooked this defect in the arbitration agreement, finding JMIC assented to arbitration by the Ho Chi Minh Commercial Arbitration Center. Under the Law on Commercial Arbitration, the failure to specify an arbitration body no longer renders an arbitration agreement invalid. Furthermore, an agreement to arbitrate may be established

---

[25] Decision No. 04/2009/QD-TT.

[26] Decision No. 2637/2009/KDTM-QDST.

[27] Article 10.4 of the Ordinance.

between parties through a variety of communications including: telegrams, faxes, telexes, and electronic mail.[28]

B.4 Public Policy Objections

Tyco Services Singapore Pte. Ltd v. Leighton Contractors (VN) Ltd

On 17 October 1995, Tyco Services Singapore Pte. Ltd (Singapore)("Tyco") entered into a Joint Venture Contract ("JVC") with Leighton Contractors (VN) LTD (Vietnam) ("Leighton") to construct a hotel in Vietnam. The JVC dispute resolution clause stated:

> Any dispute between the parties shall be finally settled by an independent arbitrator according to a request of a party and this arbitrator is appointed by the Chairman of the Australian Institute of Engineers. The arbitration will take place in Queensland according to the law of Queensland.

Various disputes arose during the performance of the JVC which were submitted to an arbitration center in Queensland, Australia ("Queensland Arbitration"). The Queensland Arbitration resulted in awards in favor of Tyco for USD1,865,342 and AUD789,961. Leighton refused to pay and Tyco petitioned the MOJ of Vietnam to recognize and enforce the award in Vietnam.

Recognition and enforcement was heard by the HCMC Court at the first instance level. Leighton argued that the award should not be recognized because the JVC was itself invalid since it had not been approved by the Ministry of Planning and Investment, and since Tyco was not licensed as a foreign contractor when it formed the JVC with Leighton, as required by Vietnamese law. The HCMC Court rejected Leighton's argument on the invalidity

---

[28] Article 16.2 of Law on Commercial Arbitration.

of the JVC on the grounds that it was a substantive issue which could not be revisited, upholding the two arbitral awards issued in the Queensland Arbitration. Furthermore, the HCMC Court ruled that at most, the JVC only suffered a defect in formality which made it voidable, not void, under the Civil Code. The HCMC Court reasoned that Leighton should therefore have requested the Court to declare the JVC invalid within the period prescribed by law. Because it had not, the JVC remained valid.

Leighton appealed to the Supreme People's Court of Vietnam to overturn the decision of the HCMC Court. On 21 January 2003, the Supreme People's Court of Vietnam reversed the decision of the HCMC Court, refusing the recognition of the foreign arbitral award on the basis that to do so would run "contrary to the basic principles of Vietnamese law"[29] because Tyco had entered into the JVC in Vietnam without a license as a foreign contractor. The Supreme People's Court of Vietnam considered the contract a violation of Vietnamese law impacting the national interest and, therefore, that Tyco should not benefit from recognition or enforcement in Vietnam.

C. THE GRANT AND ENFORCEMENT OF INTERIM MEASURES IN INTERNATIONAL ARBITRATION

In principle, interim relief is only available after legal proceedings at a domestic court or a domestic arbitration have been initiated. It is practically impossible to seek injunctive relief before initiating a case. Vietnamese courts will not grant interim relief of any kind (including injunctive relief) in aid of foreign arbitration.

---

[29] The Supreme People's Court based its decision on Article 16.2(b) of the Ordinance on the Recognition and Enforcement of Foreign Arbitral Awards which was replaced by the CPC. However, the same provision has been restated under Article 370(2)(b) of the CPC.

C. The Grant and Enforcement of Interim Measures in International Arbitration

For domestic arbitration, both local courts and the arbitral tribunal have the authority to issue injunctive relief, including specific performance. The arbitral tribunal may, in its power, adopt one or a number of following interim measures against the parties to the dispute:[30]

- Prohibition of alteration of the conditions of the property under the dispute;

- Prohibition of a party from taking or coercion of a party to take one or a number of certain actions for the purpose of preventing actions that may cause adverse affect to the course of arbitral proceedings;

- Attachment of the property under the dispute;

- Request of preservation, storage, sale or disposition of any property of either party or of the parties to the dispute;

- Temporary request concerning the payment of money between the parties;

- Prohibition of transfer of the rights to properties with respect to the properties under the dispute.

The powers of the tribunal are narrower than that of a court in relation to commercial disputes. Courts may grant the following types of injunctive relief:[31]

- Attaching property in dispute;

- Prohibiting any transfer of property rights with respect to the property in dispute;

- Prohibiting any change in the status quo of the property in dispute;

---

[30]   Article 49.2 of Law on Commercial Arbitration.

[31]   Article 102 of the CPC.

- Permitting the harvest and sale of subsidiary food crops or of other products or commodities;

- Freezing accounts at banks, other credit institutions and the State Treasury, freezing property at places of bailment;

- Freezing property of the obligor;

- Prohibiting a concerned party from conducting, or compelling a concerned party to conduct certain acts.

- Other preliminary emergency measures as stipulated by law.[32]

In most cases, parties tend to apply to the arbitral tribunal for injunctive relief in arbitration cases. However, in situations when the tribunal has not yet been established, parties may request that local courts grant injunctive relief.

Certain measures such as freezing bank accounts and other assets can only be granted by courts. However, Vietnamese courts cannot grant interim relief in the form of specific performance in the context of an arbitration; they can only do so in the context of domestic litigation.

Although the procedure for applying for injunctive relief is provided in the laws, in practice judges are often conservative in making these decisions. The Vietnamese court that makes the wrong decision with respect to injunctive relief must pay compensation to the aggrieved party.

In the event that the court or arbitral tribunal issues an order granting an injunctive relief to a party, such order will be enforced on an urgent basis by the competent enforcement agency.

---

[32] There has been no guidance on such "other measures."